Perspectives on Indigenous Pedagogy in Education:

Learning From One Another

Sheila Cote-Meek
York University, Canada

Taima Moeke-Pickering
Laurentian University, Canada

A volume in the Advances in Educational Technologies and Instructional Design (AETID) Book Series

Published in the United States of America by
    IGI Global
    Information Science Reference (an imprint of IGI Global)
    701 E. Chocolate Avenue
    Hershey PA, USA 17033
    Tel: 717-533-8845
    Fax: 717-533-8661
    E-mail: cust@igi-global.com
    Web site: http://www.igi-global.com

Copyright © 2023 by IGI Global. All rights reserved. No part of this publication may be reproduced, stored or distributed in any form or by any means, electronic or mechanical, including photocopying, without written permission from the publisher.
Product or company names used in this set are for identification purposes only. Inclusion of the names of the products or companies does not indicate a claim of ownership by IGI Global of the trademark or registered trademark.

                Library of Congress Cataloging-in-Publication Data

Names: Cote-Meek, Sheila, DATE- editor. | Moeke-Pickering, Taima, DATE- editor.
Title: Perspectives on indigenous pedagogy in education: Learning from one
   another / Sheila Cote Meek, and Taima Moeke-Pickering, editors.
Description: Hershey, PA : Information Science Reference, 2023. | Includes
   bibliographical references and index. | Summary: "This edited book of
   contributed chapters presents culturally sustaining pedagogies to
   support Indigenous Americans in the classroom by providing a background
   for past relations with Indigenous groups to frame a context for
   educational experiences, a discussion on present day Indigenous
   education and a framework for the future of Indigenous educational
   experiences"-- Provided by publisher.
Identifiers: LCCN 2022007809 (print) | LCCN 2022007810 (ebook) | ISBN
   9781668434253 (hardcover) | ISBN 9781668434260 (paperback) | ISBN
   9781668434277 (ebook)
Subjects: LCSH: Indigenous peoples--Education. | Culturally relevant
   pedagogy.
Classification: LCC LC3715 .F56 2022 (print) | LCC LC3715 (ebook) | DDC
   370.117--dc23/eng/20220601
LC record available at https://lccn.loc.gov/2022007809
LC ebook record available at https://lccn.loc.gov/2022007810

This book is published in the IGI Global book series Advances in Educational Technologies and Instructional Design (AETID) (ISSN: 2326-8905; eISSN: 2326-8913)

British Cataloguing in Publication Data
A Cataloguing in Publication record for this book is available from the British Library.

All work contributed to this book is new, previously-unpublished material.
The views expressed in this book are those of the authors, but not necessarily of the publisher.

For electronic access to this publication, please contact: eresources@igi-global.com.

Advances in Educational Technologies and Instructional Design (AETID) Book Series

ISSN:2326-8905
EISSN:2326-8913

Editor-in-Chief: Lawrence A. Tomei, Robert Morris University, USA

MISSION

Education has undergone, and continues to undergo, immense changes in the way it is enacted and distributed to both child and adult learners. In modern education, the traditional classroom learning experience has evolved to include technological resources and to provide online classroom opportunities to students of all ages regardless of their geographical locations. From distance education, Massive-Open-Online-Courses (MOOCs), and electronic tablets in the classroom, technology is now an integral part of learning and is also affecting the way educators communicate information to students.

The **Advances in Educational Technologies & Instructional Design (AETID) Book Series** explores new research and theories for facilitating learning and improving educational performance utilizing technological processes and resources. The series examines technologies that can be integrated into K-12 classrooms to improve skills and learning abilities in all subjects including STEM education and language learning. Additionally, it studies the emergence of fully online classrooms for young and adult learners alike, and the communication and accountability challenges that can arise. Trending topics that are covered include adaptive learning, game-based learning, virtual school environments, and social media effects. School administrators, educators, academicians, researchers, and students will find this series to be an excellent resource for the effective design and implementation of learning technologies in their classes.

COVERAGE

- Hybrid Learning
- Adaptive Learning
- Digital Divide in Education
- Instructional Design Models
- Collaboration Tools
- Instructional Design
- Web 2.0 and Education
- Virtual School Environments
- Online Media in Classrooms
- Social Media Effects on Education

IGI Global is currently accepting manuscripts for publication within this series. To submit a proposal for a volume in this series, please contact our Acquisition Editors at Acquisitions@igi-global.com or visit: http://www.igi-global.com/publish/.

The Advances in Educational Technologies and Instructional Design (AETID) Book Series (ISSN 2326-8905) is published by IGI Global, 701 E. Chocolate Avenue, Hershey, PA 17033-1240, USA, www.igi-global.com. This series is composed of titles available for purchase individually; each title is edited to be contextually exclusive from any other title within the series. For pricing and ordering information please visit http://www.igi-global.com/book-series/advances-educational-technologies-instructional-design/73678. Postmaster: Send all address changes to above address. Copyright © 2023 IGI Global. All rights, including translation in other languages reserved by the publisher. No part of this series may be reproduced or used in any form or by any means – graphics, electronic, or mechanical, including photocopying, recording, taping, or information and retrieval systems – without written permission from the publisher, except for non commercial, educational use, including classroom teaching purposes. The views expressed in this series are those of the authors, but not necessarily of IGI Global.

Titles in this Series

For a list of additional titles in this series, please visit:
ttp://www.igi-global.com/book-series/advances-educational-technologies-instructional-design/73678

Fostering Science Teaching and Learning for the Fourth Industrial Revolution and Beyond
Garima Bansal (Australian Council for Educational Research, India) and Umesh Ramnarain (University of Johannesburg, South Africa)
Information Science Reference • copyright 2023 • 290pp • H/C (ISBN: 9781668469323) • US $215.00 (our price)

Phenomenological Studies in Education
Jason D. DeHart (University of Tennessee, Knoxville, USA)
Information Science Reference • copyright 2023 • 328pp • H/C (ISBN: 9781668482766) • US $215.00 (our price)

Implementing Rapid E-Learning Through Interactive Materials Development
Mohammad Issack Santally (University of Mauritius, Mauritius) Yousra Rajabalee (Mauritius Institute of Education, Mauritius) and Ravi Rajputh (University of Mauritius, Mauritius)
Information Science Reference • copyright 2023 • 300pp • H/C (ISBN: 9781668449400) • US $215.00 (our price)

Practices That Promote Innovation for Talented Students
Julia Nyberg (Purdue University Global, USA) and Jessica Manzone (University of Southern California, USA)
Information Science Reference • copyright 2023 • 300pp • H/C (ISBN: 9781668458068) • US $215.00 (our price)

Cases on Error Analysis in Foreign Language Technical Writing
Nadezhda Anatolievna Lebedeva (Kherson State Agrarian and Economic University, Ukraine)
Information Science Reference • copyright 2023 • 300pp • H/C (ISBN: 9781668462225) • US $215.00 (our price)

For an entire list of titles in this series, please visit:
ttp://www.igi-global.com/book-series/advances-educational-technologies-instructional-design/73678

701 East Chocolate Avenue, Hershey, PA 17033, USA
Tel: 717-533-8845 x100 • Fax: 717-533-8661
E-Mail: cust@igi-global.com • www.igi-global.com

Editorial Advisory Board

Vicki Bouvier, *Mount Royal University, Canada*
Keri Cheechoo, *Wilfred Laurier University, Canada*
Amanda Hardy, *Rainbow District School Board, Canada*
Sereana Naepi, *Auckland University, New Zealand*
Cheryle Partridge, *Laurentian University, Canada*
Michelle Pidgeon, *Simon Fraser University, Canada*
Brock Pitawanakwat, *York University, Canada*
Carolyn Roberts, *University of the Fraser Valley, Canada*
Robyn Rowe, *Queens University, Canada*
Amy Shawanda, *University of Toronto, Canada*
Moana Theodore, *Otago University, New Zealand*
Joey-Lynn Wabie, *Laurentian University, Canada*
Jeffrey Wood, *Laurentian University, Canada*
Sherri Vansickle, *Brock University, Canada*

Table of Contents

Preface xiii

Acknowledgment xxv

Chapter 1
Amplifying and Centering Indigenous Pedagogies in Post-Secondary Education 1
    Sheila L. Cote-Meek, Brock University, Canada
    Taima Moeke-Pickering, Laurentian University, Canada

Chapter 2
Embodying Knowledge and Pedagogy Through an Indigenous Oral System 16
    Vicki Bouvier, Mount Royal University, Canada

Chapter 3
Circle Work: Being Together as a Relation 40
    Carolyn Roberts, University of the Fraser Valley, Canada

Chapter 4
All Our Relations: Stories From the Classroom and the Land 56
    Joey-Lynn Wabie, Laurentian University, Canada
    Taylor Watkins, Laurentian University, Canada
    Simon Leslie, Laurentian University, Canada
    Marnie Anderson, Laurentian University, Canada
    Anastacia Chartrand, Laurentian University, Canada
    Arijana Haramincic, Laurentian University, Canada

Chapter 5
The Art of Teaching: Métis Beadwork and Indigenous Legal Pedagogy 95
    Danielle Lussier, Royal Military College of Canada, Canada & Queen's University, Canada

Chapter 6
Inside Out, or Storytelling Through Truths and Reclamation 127
    Keri Cheechoo, Wilfrid Laurier University, Canada

Chapter 7
The University as a Site for ₡ÁT̯: Storytelling as Pedagogy 136
    Jack Horne, Trent University, Canada

Chapter 8
An Indigenous Early Childhood Pedagogy 170
    Jeffrey Wood, Laurentian University, Canada

Chapter 9
Reconciliatory Pedagogies: Embodying Our Walk as Settler Teachers in
Canadian High Schools 193
    Erin Keith, St. Francis Xavier University, Canada
    Krista LaRue Keeley, Regina Public Schools, Canada

Chapter 10
Indigenous Pedagogies and the Implications of EdTech, Data, and AI in the
Classroom 215
    Robyn K. Rowe, Queen's University, Canada
    Amy Shawanda, University of Toronto, Canada

Compilation of References 248

About the Contributors 271

Index 277

Detailed Table of Contents

Preface xiii

Acknowledgment xxv

Chapter 1
Amplifying and Centering Indigenous Pedagogies in Post-Secondary Education 1
    Sheila L. Cote-Meek, Brock University, Canada
    Taima Moeke-Pickering, Laurentian University, Canada

Indigenous traditions and worldviews inform how we come to know, how we learn, and how we share. Relationships encompass all living entities, the land, the sacred, the knowledge, and the legacies of our ancestors. These are meaningful components in Indigenous teachings and pedagogies. The disruption of colonization and its impact is necessary for critical analyses. Therefore, indigenizing and decolonizing are mutually intertwined processes that inform a critical lens in education. It is the desire by generations of Indigenous peoples to retain their cultural values and knowledges in education, thus ensuring a continuity into the future. This educational envisioning "creates a shared and collective vision for not only sustainability but for resisting ongoing colonialism" (Cote-Meek & Moeke-Pickering, p. 31). It is in this resistance that clues can be found on how to transform educational institutes that better inform teaching and research practices, so they are conducive to Indigenous self-determination.

Chapter 2
Embodying Knowledge and Pedagogy Through an Indigenous Oral System 16
    Vicki Bouvier, Mount Royal University, Canada

Centering and embodying an oral knowledge system to guide learning and assessment challenges educational institution's cognitive imperialism. Through experiences as an educator, the author has witnessed the rush to amalgamate Indigenous content into classrooms without an awareness or knowing that Indigenous knowledge has its own systematic processes of ascertaining and validating knowing. Acknowledging that Indigenous knowledges have systems, just like that of written knowledge, is imperative if institutions are serious about honouring Indigenous knowing, being, and doing. This chapter will provide teachings, as learned from Elder Crowshoe, of an Indigenous oral knowledge system—theory, ontology, and axiology—that guide sharing and acquisition of knowledge. Thereafter, the concepts of truthing, circumambulation, and the third perspective will be detailed with hope to inform educators and students on how knowledge is conceptualized in an oral system and how educators and students alike might share, cultivate, and assess learning and knowledge acquisition.

Chapter 3
Circle Work: Being Together as a Relation 40
Carolyn Roberts, University of the Fraser Valley, Canada

Circle work has been used by Indigenous people since time out of mind. This pedagogical practice creates spaces of relationality and community building within our current day educational system. This space that Circle work creates allows for a learning community to understand our interconnectedness as humans and helps to develop empathy for others. Circle work brings people together in our humanity rather than dividing us in our differences, focusing on community building, with the hope of giving people the opportunity to actively decolonize how they educate within the classroom. This practice can be used by all educators willing to step into a wholistic teaching practice within their classroom.

Chapter 4
All Our Relations: Stories From the Classroom and the Land 56
Joey-Lynn Wabie, Laurentian University, Canada
Taylor Watkins, Laurentian University, Canada
Simon Leslie, Laurentian University, Canada
Marnie Anderson, Laurentian University, Canada
Anastacia Chartrand, Laurentian University, Canada
Arijana Haramincic, Laurentian University, Canada

The authors shared their reflections about a 12-week master-level course at a northern Ontario university revisioned by an Algonquin anicinabe ikwe scholar and a settler graduate teaching assistant using experiential arts, storytelling, and land-based pedagogical practices. Through the holistic nature of the course, learners explored topics through their own holistic health and well-being. Learners learned the importance of storytelling which culminated in a medicine storysharing session and roundtable discussion. The authors' reflections highlighted the interactive nature of the course fostering the ability for students to learn how teaching and knowledge can be delivered in a memorable and impactful way. There were also feelings of discomfort when it came to letting go of preconceived notions about education since the course went against the academic training commonly found in Westernized educational institutions. This chapter includes various materials, including the course outline and ideas for personal exploration using experiential arts and land-based creative modalities.

Chapter 5
The Art of Teaching: Métis Beadwork and Indigenous Legal Pedagogy 95
    Danielle Lussier, Royal Military College of Canada, Canada & Queen's
        University, Canada

In this chapter, the author discusses the art of teaching, situating the use of beadwork practice mobilized in a classroom setting as an Indigenous legal pedagogy grounded in theories of persuasive legal aesthetic. She situates the pedagogical practice as one to support learning in the four spheres of intellectual, emotional, physical, and spiritual learning, and unpacks how whole-learner approaches to education can support both Indigenous learners who continue to live with the fallout of decades of forced assimilative education in Canada, and non-Indigenous Learners who are often engaging with Indigenous practices, peoples, and teachings for the first time in university settings as a result of ongoing systemic curricula failure at elementary and high school levels across Canada.

Chapter 6
Inside Out, or Storytelling Through Truths and Reclamation 127
    Keri Cheechoo, Wilfrid Laurier University, Canada

This chapter will explore the ensuing trifecta of themes: "storytelling," "Indigenous education theory and practice," and "creating culturally sustaining pedagogies" by speaking to and through the intertextualities, potentialities, and complexities of mino-pimatiswin, to engage and embody best practices around student engagement and support. The chapter begins with a conversation about Indigenous education theory and practice by offering an opportunity to learn about the importance of engaging ethical space by enacting ethical relationality, and how these concepts extend into kinship theory and practice. This chapter then shifts an introspective storytelling lens towards the author to share how, as an Iskwew scholar and educator, she teaches mino-pimatisiwin through a trauma informed perspective. This chapter will also speak to culturally safe care by (re)conceptualizing the red road by introducing culturally sustaining pedagogies.

Chapter 7
The University as a Site for ȻÁȾ: Storytelling as Pedagogy............................ 136
    Jack Horne, Trent University, Canada

When the author began conducting this research in 2015, he was surprised by the lack of Indigenous writing critical of the academy. He conducted extensive research to identify peer-reviewed academic journals and book chapters written by Indigenous scholars in the years up to and including 2016. The author expected to find a wealth of information but was instead confronted with the limited content that only highlighted the lack of progress that has been made toward integrating true Indigenous knowledge into the academy. The research was intended to support the argument that Indigenous knowledge had already secured a place in the academy. Instead, the author discovered that additional Indigenous academic writing was needed on the subject. The author hopes this chapter will save current and future Indigenous scholars from repeating research the author has already done. In the W̱SÁNEĆ language dialect of SENĆOTEN, the word ȻÁȾ translates as "being difficult" or "a difficult situation." This chapter will explore the difficulties the author has experienced through his academic journey while employing the Indigenous practice of storytelling as pedagogy.

Chapter 8
An Indigenous Early Childhood Pedagogy 170
   Jeffrey Wood, Laurentian University, Canada

This chapter explores the principles necessary to implement an Indigenous early childhood pedagogy and the importance of the land, language, culture, and identity in learning for Indigenous children. This approach sees children in relation; sees them holistically, including the physical, emotional, mental, and spiritual; helps nurture the gift each child has for the community; focuses on the language, traditional teaching, ceremony, and storytelling; and finally decolonizes the curricula and the classroom. To effectively teach indigenous culture we need to teach the language and to teach the language we need to be on the land.

Chapter 9
Reconciliatory Pedagogies: Embodying Our Walk as Settler Teachers in
Canadian High Schools 193
   Erin Keith, St. Francis Xavier University, Canada
   Krista LaRue Keeley, Regina Public Schools, Canada

Two Canadian settler teachers explore the intention and iterative, enduring process of reconciliation in high school classrooms through storytelling of their own lived experiences. They respectfully 'call-in' other settler teachers who may feel paralyzed for fear of appropriation and the heaviness of this reconciliatory work. Weaving in how the 5Rs have guided the two teachers' journeys toward incorporating Indigenous pedagogies into their praxis and suggesting how these principles could support other settler educators who are beginning their decolonization journey, an Interwoven Living Framework that illuminates their learning 'from' is developed. The framework is grounded in actionizing the 5Rs through the critical work of listening to, learning from, working, and walking with First Peoples. Using narratives, the teachers story their "walk" inspired by the words of an Indigenous student from their class, Poppy. They share a place to begin towards truly understanding how to become an entrusted Indigenous ally-to-be and how to actionize this collective work in high school landscapes.

Chapter 10
Indigenous Pedagogies and the Implications of EdTech, Data, and AI in the Classroom 215
    Robyn K. Rowe, Queen's University, Canada
    Amy Shawanda, University of Toronto, Canada

The increased integration of educational technologies (EdTech) in recent history, combined with modern wireless connectivity and cloud potential, has led to a surge in data being extraction from the educators and learners who use them. Consequently, scientific innovations in artificial intelligence (AI) systems trained by large volumes of data are changing the educational landscape. Naturally, pedagogical approaches to education are evolving in line with philosophical, ideological, and theoretical understandings of technology, its uses, and its applications. This chapter explores the complex and evolving role of EdTech, its design, development, and deployment through Indigenous Pedagogies. In it, the authors weave through discussions that embrace Indigenous epistemologies, worldviews, cultures, and traditions. At the same time, they consider the transformative potential of embedding Indigenous Pedagogies into the ways we think about technology, beyond present understandings of EdTech. In doing so, the authors generate a discussion that aims to empower, educate, and lead to meaningful EdTech action.

Compilation of References 248

About the Contributors 271

Index 277

Preface

As editors of this remarkable collection, we are excited to present *Perspectives on Indigenous Pedagogy in Education: Learning from One Another*. This book brings together a diverse range of voices and experiences, illuminating the complexities of negotiating and integrating Indigenous pedagogies in education. It is a testament to the growing recognition of the importance of Indigenous knowledges and worldviews in transforming educational practices and systems.

In grappling with the ongoing impact of colonization, our exploration centers on Indigenous pedagogies and ways of knowing that have shaped Indigenous education on Turtle Island. We have sought to add to the growing literature and deepen our understanding of Indigenous pedagogy and its importance. In some chapters you will also note their pedagogies highlight that some students may be challenged and feel a degree of discomfort in the classroom as they learn and gain new understandings of Indigenous pedagogical practices and activities. Questions that are explored provide insight into What is Indigenous pedagogy? Why is it important? How do we bridge the gap between Indigenous theory and practice in the classroom? What can we learn from intergenerational Indigenous approaches to education? And how does Indigenous pedagogy intersect with Indigenous epistemology and ways of knowing?

Throughout this text, we present a rich tapestry of perspectives on Indigenous pedagogies in education. Our contributors examine various themes, such as oral systems, circle-work, land-based learning, beadwork, place-based learning, and storytelling, all of which form integral parts of Indigenous education. We also explore the intricate relationship between Indigenous education theory and practice, illuminating the ways in which they inform and shape each other from early childhood, high school and post-secondary perspectives.

Importantly, this book serves as a catalyst for ongoing collaboration and exchange among educators. It highlights the shared commitment to supporting Indigenous pedagogy, showcasing how educators are committed to ensuring that Indigenous knowledges and perspectives are incorporated into teaching practices.

Within these pages, you will find thought-provoking discussions on perception and pedagogy in the classroom, the role of authentic history in framing Indigenous perspectives, and the power of collaborative and supportive pedagogy. Moreover, we offer practical recommendations for educators, empowering them to create culturally sustaining pedagogies that respect and reflect Indigenous cultures and identities.

We extend our sincere gratitude to the contributors who have shared their knowledge and experiences in this collection. Their expertise and insights have enriched our understanding and have the potential to impact the field of education in profound ways.

We hope that *Perspectives on Indigenous Pedagogy in Education: Learning from One Another* serves as a source of inspiration, reflection, and action for educational preparation programs, practicing teachers, and professors of education and Indigenous studies courses. May it contribute to a greater appreciation and understanding of Indigenous pedagogies, paving the way for a more inclusive and transformative education system that truly honors and celebrates Indigenous knowledges and worldviews.

Amplifying and Centering Indigenous Pedagogies

In this chapter, Sheila Cote-Meek and Taima Moeke-Pickering delve into the significance of Indigenous traditions and worldviews in shaping knowledge acquisition, learning processes, and knowledge sharing. They emphasize the interconnectedness of relationships, encompassing all living entities, the land, the sacred, the knowledge, and the legacies of ancestors. These components form the foundation of Indigenous teachings and pedagogies.

The authors highlight the necessity of critically analyzing the disruption caused by ongoing colonization and its impact. Indigenizing and decolonizing education are viewed as intertwined processes that foster a critical lens in understanding and addressing the effects of ongoing colonization. By engaging in these processes, Indigenous communities strive to retain their cultural values and knowledge within the education system, ensuring the continuity of existence.

The chapter emphasizes the importance of creating a shared and collective vision that goes beyond mere sustainability but also actively resists ongoing colonialism. By resisting ongoing colonialism and its effects, insights can be gained on transforming educational institutions to better support Indigenous self-determination. The authors advocate for the inclusion of Indigenous perspectives and knowledge into teaching and research practices, thereby creating an environment that respects and promotes Indigenous self-determination.

Preface

Through this chapter, Cote-Meek and Taima Moeke-Pickering contribute to the broader conversation on Indigenizing education. They provide insights and perspectives that can assist educators, researchers, and policymakers in understanding the significance of centering Indigenous pedagogies. By amplifying Indigenous voices and knowledge systems, educational institutions can foster a more inclusive and equitable learning environment that supports Indigenous self-determination and empowers Indigenous communities.

Overall, the chapter serves as a call to action, urging individuals and institutions to critically examine their practices, transform their approaches to education, and actively contribute to decolonization efforts. By centering Indigenous pedagogies, education can become a catalyst for positive change, reconciliation, and the preservation of Indigenous cultures, values, and knowledges.

Embodying Knowledge and Pedagogy through an Indigenous Oral System

In this chapter, Vicki Bouvier explores the importance of centering and embodying an Indigenous oral knowledge system as a guide for learning and assessment. The author addresses the issue of cognitive imperialism within educational institutions and reflects on their experiences as an educator witnessing the rush to incorporate Indigenous content into classrooms without understanding the systemic processes of Indigenous knowledge.

The chapter emphasizes the need to recognize that Indigenous knowledge has its own systemic processes of ascertaining and validating knowing, similar to written knowledge systems. To truly honor Indigenous ways of knowing, being, and doing, it is imperative for institutions to acknowledge and understand these systems. By doing so, educators and institutions can authentically integrate Indigenous knowledge into teaching and learning practices.

The author draws on the teachings of Elder Reg Crowshoe to provide insights into an Indigenous oral knowledge system, including its theory, ontology, and axiology. These teachings offer a foundation for understanding how knowledge is shared and acquired within an oral system. The chapter explores concepts such as truthing, circumambulation, and the third perspective, which further enhance the understanding of how knowledge is conceptualized within an Indigenous oral system.

The chapter aims to inform educators and students on the intricacies of an oral knowledge system and how it can shape the sharing, cultivation, and assessment of learning and knowledge acquisition. By embracing an Indigenous oral system, educators can move beyond a surface-level inclusion of Indigenous content and engage in a deeper, more meaningful exploration of Indigenous knowledge.

The chapter encourages educators to approach teaching and learning with humility, openness, and respect for Indigenous ways of knowing. It serves as a resource for educators seeking to incorporate Indigenous oral knowledge systems into their pedagogical practices, fostering a more holistic and inclusive approach to education that recognizes and values diverse ways of knowing and learning.

Circle Work: Being Together as a Relation

In this chapter, Carolyn Roberts explores the pedagogical practice of Circle work, which has been utilized by Indigenous peoples for what the author refers as time out of mind. Circle work creates spaces within the current educational system that foster relationality and community building. It offers a powerful approach to learning that allows individuals within a learning community to recognize and embrace their interconnectedness as human beings. By engaging in Circle work, participants develop empathy for others and focus on building a sense of community rather than highlighting differences.

The practice of Circle work emphasizes the importance of inclusivity and respect for all participants. It encourages individuals to come together as equals, fostering an environment where every voice is heard and valued. Through the Circle, participants can actively engage in the process of decolonizing education within the classroom.

The chapter highlights the transformative potential of Circle work in creating a holistic teaching practice. It emphasizes that Circle work is not limited to Indigenous educators; rather, it can be embraced by all educators who are willing to adopt a holistic approach to teaching. By incorporating Circle work into the classroom, educators can create a space where students feel seen, heard, and respected.

Circle work offers a way to challenge traditional power dynamics and hierarchies within the educational system. It invites educators and students to engage in meaningful dialogue, reflective listening, and collective decision-making. Through this process, participants can deepen their understanding of themselves, others, and the world around them.

By embracing Circle work, educators have the opportunity to actively participate in decolonization efforts within education. It provides a framework for building inclusive and respectful learning communities that celebrate diversity, promote empathy, and nurture a sense of belonging. The chapter serves as a guide for educators who are interested in incorporating Circle work into their teaching practice and offers insights into the transformative potential of this pedagogical approach.

Preface

All Our Relations: Stories From the Classroom and the Land

In this chapter, the authors, Joey-Lynn Wabie, Taylor Watkins, Simon Leslie, Marnie Anderson, Anastacia Chartrand, and Arjana Karamincic, share their reflections on a 12-week master-level course at a northern Ontario university. The course was reconceptualized by an Algonquin anicinabe ikwe scholar and a settler graduate teaching assistant, incorporating experiential arts, storytelling, and land-based pedagogical practices. The course aimed to provide a holistic learning experience where students explored topics through the lens of their own holistic health and well-being.

The authors highlight the importance of storytelling as a central element of the course. Students engaged in storytelling, and participated in a medicine story sharing session and roundtable discussion. These experiences demonstrated the interactive and engaging nature of the course, allowing students to understand how teaching and knowledge can be delivered in a memorable and impactful way.

However, the authors also acknowledge that there were moments of discomfort for both students and instructors. The course challenged preconceived notions about education, as it diverged away from the traditional academic pedagogical approaches commonly found in Westernized educational institutions. This discomfort was a result of letting go of ingrained educational paradigms and embracing new approaches rooted in Indigenous ways of knowing and being.

The chapter includes various resource materials, such as the course outline wheel and ideas for personal exploration using experiential arts and land-based creative modalities. These materials provide practical examples and guidance for educators interested in incorporating similar approaches in their own classrooms.

Overall, this chapter highlights the transformative power of experiential arts, storytelling, and land-based pedagogies in creating meaningful and impactful learning experiences. By centering holistic well-being and embracing Indigenous ways of knowing, educators can foster a deeper connection between students, the land, and the content being taught. The authors' reflections serve as an inspiration and guide for educators who are interested in integrating Indigenous pedagogies including land-based practices and student feedback into their teaching.

The Art of Teaching: Métis Beadwork and Indigenous Legal Pedagogy

In this chapter, the author Danielle Lussier explores the Art of Teaching through the lens of Métis beadwork and Indigenous Legal Pedagogy. The use of beadwork practice in a classroom setting is situated as an Indigenous Legal Pedagogy that draws on theories of Persuasive Legal Aesthetic. The author demonstrates how this pedagogical approach supports learning in the intellectual, emotional, physical, and spiritual spheres, emphasizing a holistic and whole-learner approach to education.

The chapter addresses the specific context of Indigenous Learners who continue to be impacted by the historical legacy of Forced Assimilative Education in Canada. It also acknowledges non-Indigenous Learners who may be encountering Indigenous practices, Peoples, and teachings for the first time in university settings due to the systemic curricular exclusion at elementary and high school levels across the country.

By incorporating Métis beadwork into the classroom, the author illustrates how Indigenous Legal Pedagogy can engage students in a meaningful way. The practice of beadwork serves as a tangible and visual representation of legal concepts and principles, allowing students to connect with the material on intellectual, emotional, and sensory levels. This approach supports a deeper understanding and appreciation of Indigenous legal traditions and ways of knowing.

Furthermore, the author highlights the transformative potential of this pedagogical practice for both Indigenous and non-Indigenous learners. For Indigenous students, it offers an opportunity to reclaim and revitalize cultural practices that were historically suppressed. For non-Indigenous students, it fosters a respectful engagement with Indigenous knowledge and a greater understanding of the ongoing impact of colonial education.

The chapter underscores the importance of addressing systemic curricular failures and gaps in education, particularly in relation to Indigenous content and pedagogies. By integrating Indigenous Legal Pedagogy and incorporating Métis beadwork, educators can create inclusive and engaging learning environments that promote a more comprehensive understanding of Indigenous legal traditions and contribute to reconciliation efforts.

In summary, by centering Indigenous practices and incorporating holistic approaches, educators can create a more inclusive and transformative educational experience for both Indigenous and non-Indigenous learners.

Inside Out, or Storytelling Through Truths and Reclamation

In this chapter, Keri Cheechoo delves into the interconnected themes of storytelling, Indigenous education theory and practice, and the creation of culturally sustaining pedagogies. The chapter explores the concept of mino-pimatisiwin, delving into its intertextualities, potentialities, and complexities.

The chapter begins by examining Indigenous education theory and practice, providing insights into the importance of engaging ethical space and enacting ethical relationality. The author explores how these concepts extend into kinship theory and practice, emphasizing their significance in fostering meaningful and respectful educational experiences.

Shifting the focus inward, the author shares their personal experiences as an Iskwew scholar and educator, teaching mino-pimatisiwin through a trauma-informed perspective. This introspective storytelling lens offers valuable insights into how mino-pimatisiwin can be integrated into educational settings, taking into account the experiences and needs of students.

The chapter also delves into the concept of culturally safe care by (re) conceptualizing the red road, a metaphorical path that represents Indigenous ways of being and knowing. By introducing culturally sustaining pedagogies, the author explores the potentialities and complexities of reframing our thinking, embodying harm reduction, and recognizing and challenging our biases.

Through thought-provoking queries such as "What if we (re)frame the way we think?" and "What if we decide that our biases have no place on this road?", the author invites readers to critically reflect on their own practices and beliefs, encouraging transformative approaches to education that honor Indigenous perspectives and promote a sense of cultural safety.

This chapter offers valuable insights for educators seeking to create inclusive and empowering learning environments, grounded in the principles of mino-pimatisiwin and guided by the (re)conceptualization of the red road.

The University as a Site for Cát: Storytelling as Pedagogy

In this chapter, Jack Horne explores the concept of the university as a site for Cát, which means knowledge or understanding in the SENĆOTEN language. The author reflects on their research journey and the lack of critical Indigenous writing within the academy. The chapter aims to fill this gap by providing a resource for both Indigenous and non-Indigenous scholars, examining early Indigenous academic scholarship and drawing from the author's own experiences during their PhD program from 2014 to 2016.

The author approaches the chapter in a storytelling format, recognizing its ability to convey nuance and facilitate an informal literature review of early Indigenous scholars. By embracing storytelling as pedagogy, the author highlights the importance of oral traditions in Indigenous cultures and the power of narratives to convey knowledge, insight, and inspiration. The use of storytelling also reflects the author's intention to offer their research as a gift to Indigenous scholars, saving them from having to replicate the work already done.

Through the exploration of Indigenous academic scholarship, the chapter aims to demonstrate the presence and significance of Indigenous knowledge within the university setting. By examining the experiences and contributions of early Indigenous scholars, the author sheds light on the efforts and challenges faced in securing a space for Indigenous knowledge in academia. In summary, the chapter serves as a resource for both Indigenous and non-Indigenous scholars, providing insights and inspiration for those navigating the intersections of Indigenous perspectives and academic scholarship.

An Indigenous Early Childhood Pedagogy

In this chapter, Jeffery Wood explores the principles and foundations necessary for implementing an Indigenous early childhood pedagogy. The author emphasizes the significance of the land, language, culture, and identity in the learning journey of Indigenous children.

Wood advocates for a holistic approach that recognizes children in relation to their environment and considers their physical, emotional, mental, and spiritual well-being. The chapter highlights the importance of nurturing the unique gifts that each child brings to their community and fostering a deep connection to their Indigenous heritage.

Central to this pedagogical approach is the focus on language, traditional teaching, ceremony, and storytelling. The author emphasizes that teaching Indigenous culture effectively requires the teaching of language, and to teach the language, educators need to engage with the land. By actively incorporating these elements into the curriculum and classroom practices, educators can decolonize traditional educational structures and create spaces that celebrate and honor Indigenous knowledge and ways of being.

In summary, Wood provides valuable insights and guidance for early childhood educators interested in implementing an Indigenous pedagogy that is rooted in cultural authenticity, respect, and reciprocity.

Reconciliatory Pedagogies... Embodying Our Walk as Settler Teachers in Canadian High Schools

In this chapter, Erin Keith and Krista LaRue Keeley, both Canadian settler teachers, share their personal stories and experiences to explore the intention and ongoing process of reconciliation within high school classrooms. Through their experiences, they invite readers to join them on their journeys and address the concerns that settler teachers may have, including fears of appropriation and the weightiness of engaging in reconciliatory work.

The authors approach the topic with respect and offer a "call-in" to other settler teachers who may feel hesitant or overwhelmed by the task at hand. They aim to create a safe space for dialogue and learning, recognizing the complexities involved in decolonization and reconciliation within the educational context.

Preface

The chapter highlights the significance of the 5Rs framework in guiding the authors' journeys toward incorporating Indigenous pedagogies into their teaching practices. The 5Rs—respect, relevance, reciprocity, responsibility, and relationships—provide a foundation for understanding and action. The authors suggest that these principles can support other settler educators who are at the beginning stages of their decolonization journey.

To further illuminate their learning process, the authors develop an Interwoven Living Framework that emerges from their experiences. This framework emphasizes the critical work of listening to, learning from, working with, and walking alongside First Peoples. It provides a roadmap for settler educators to actively engage in the process of reconciliation and decolonization.

By openly sharing their own challenges, reflections, and growth, the authors inspire and empower settler teachers to embark on their own reconciliatory journeys. In summary, chapter serves as a valuable resource for educators seeking guidance and support in incorporating Indigenous perspectives and fostering meaningful relationships within their classrooms, ultimately working toward creating more inclusive and equitable educational spaces.

Indigenous Pedagogies and the Implications of EdTech, Data, and AI in the Classroom

In this chapter, the authors Robyn Rowe and Amy Shawanda explore the evolving role of Educational Technologies (EdTech) in education, particularly in the context of Indigenous Pedagogies. They highlight the integration of EdTech in recent years and the subsequent data extraction from educators and learners. The authors also discuss how advancements in Artificial Intelligence (AI) systems, fueled by vast amounts of data, are reshaping the educational landscape.

The chapter delves into the philosophical, ideological, and theoretical understandings of technology, its uses, and its applications in education. It emphasizes the importance of incorporating Indigenous epistemologies, worldviews, cultures, and traditions in the design, development, and deployment of EdTech. The authors seek to move beyond the current understanding of EdTech and explore the transformative potential of embedding Indigenous Pedagogies into technological approaches.

By weaving together discussions on Indigenous knowledge systems, the authors aim to empower and educate readers, encouraging them to take meaningful action in the realm of EdTech. In summary this chapter serves as a platform for generating a dialogue that embraces Indigenous perspectives and promotes inclusive and culturally responsive approaches to technology in education.

Preface

As editors of this edited book on Indigenous pedagogies in education, we are honored to present a collection of chapters that explore the rich and diverse landscape of Indigenous knowledge systems and their transformative potential within educational contexts. The chapters within this book represent a collective effort to amplify and center Indigenous voices, perspectives, and practices, shedding light on the invaluable contributions of Indigenous peoples to the field of education.

Indigenous pedagogies embody a holistic approach to teaching and learning, rooted in deep connections to land, culture, language, and community. They reflect the wisdom accumulated over generations and hold the key to nurturing well-rounded, empowered individuals who are in tune with their surroundings and committed to the betterment of their communities.

Through the lens of Indigenous pedagogies, the contributors to this collection offer critical insights, theoretical frameworks, and practical strategies that challenge dominant paradigms, disrupt oppressive systems, and foster cultural revitalization. They emphasize the importance of ethical relationships, community engagement, storytelling, language revitalization, and land-based practices in educational settings. These chapters invite educators, researchers, policymakers, and community members to engage with Indigenous pedagogies and envision a more inclusive and culturally responsive education system.

The authors within this book bring a wealth of knowledge and lived experiences to their respective chapters, offering diverse perspectives from various Indigenous communities across Canada. We commend their dedication, passion, and commitment to sharing their expertise and perspectives. Their contributions contribute to a growing body of literature that aims to decolonize education and pave the way for more equitable and inclusive learning environments.

We would like to express our gratitude and say Chi-miigwech (a big thank you) to all the authors for their thoughtful and thought-provoking contributions. Their work not only challenges the status quo but also provides a foundation for further dialogue and action in the field of Indigenous education. We also extend our appreciation to the reviewers, our research assistant and the team at IGI Global who provided valuable feedback and guidance throughout the publication process.

It is our hope that this book serves as a valuable resource for educators, researchers, students, and anyone interested in understanding and embracing Indigenous pedagogies. May it inspire transformative change within educational institutions, contribute to reconciliation efforts, and foster a deeper appreciation for the wisdom and resilience of Indigenous peoples.

Preface

In closing, we acknowledge that the journey towards a more just and inclusive education system is ongoing. This book represents a significant step forward in amplifying Indigenous voices and centering Indigenous pedagogies. We invite readers to join us on this collective path of learning, unlearning, and reimagining education guided by the principles of respect, reciprocity, and reconciliation.

Chi-miigwech. Kia Ora. Thank you.

Sheila Cote-Meek
York University, Canada

Taima Moeke-Pickering
Laurentian University, Canada

About the Cover Art

Artist: Sheldon Meek

Sheldon Meek is an Anishinaabe artist and is a member of the Kitigan Zibi Anishinabeg. His work is inspired by his culture and traditions. He has completed art pieces that are mounted in the Sacred Heart Church of the First Peoples in Edmonton, Alberta. He has also completed a number of commissioned art pieces.

Artwork: *The Messenger*

The Messenger is an interpretation of a teaching that was passed down from my grandfather, Samuel Cote to my mother, Lucienne Cote Meek who shared with me the spiritual understanding of the fox for our people. The fox is a messenger and through the imagery depicted in the book cover I am reminded that there are many messages we receive from Shkagamik-kwe (Mother earth) and how important these teachings are to understanding Indigenous knowledges and worldviews. The fox brings messages to the community and like those messages shared in this book, the authors are sharing their experiences and understandings in the hope that Indigenous education thrives.

Acknowledgment

To all the Indigenous academics that have come before us, thank you for laying a strong foundation for transforming Indigenous education. To current and future academics who continue to forge a pathway in Indigenous education, thank you. Miigwech, Kia Ora to Sheldon Meek for gifting us your artwork for the book cover, to all the chapter authors for your contributions, insights, and strategies for Indigenizing and decolonizing education, to the Editorial Advisory Board for your attention to the reviews, and to Kuan-Yun Wang for reviewing and assisting with ensuring conformity to APA.

We would like to acknowledge our own mothers, Lucienne Cote Meek (Teme-Augama Anishnabai) and Ngamihi Norma Crapp (Ngati Pukeko/Tuhoe), our first cultural intellectual influencers and teachers. Miigwech and Kia Ora for grounding us in our traditional cultural values and motivating us to be strong women who facilitate change.

To those working in education may you continue to advocate, amplify and support creating a better system for Indigenous peoples in education.

Chapter 1
Amplifying and Centering Indigenous Pedagogies in Post-Secondary Education

Sheila L. Cote-Meek
Brock University, Canada

Taima Moeke-Pickering
https://orcid.org/0000-0001-9524-9850
Laurentian University, Canada

ABSTRACT

Indigenous traditions and worldviews inform how we come to know, how we learn, and how we share. Relationships encompass all living entities, the land, the sacred, the knowledge, and the legacies of our ancestors. These are meaningful components in Indigenous teachings and pedagogies. The disruption of colonization and its impact is necessary for critical analyses. Therefore, indigenizing and decolonizing are mutually intertwined processes that inform a critical lens in education. It is the desire by generations of Indigenous peoples to retain their cultural values and knowledges in education, thus ensuring a continuity into the future. This educational envisioning "creates a shared and collective vision for not only sustainability but for resisting ongoing colonialism" (Cote-Meek & Moeke-Pickering, p. 31). It is in this resistance that clues can be found on how to transform educational institutes that better inform teaching and research practices, so they are conducive to Indigenous self-determination.

DOI: 10.4018/978-1-6684-3425-3.ch001

INTRODUCTION

We are grateful to the Creator, Sky Father, and Earth Mother, to all their children that look after the skies, the cosmos, the universe, the earth, animals and fishes from the forests, rivers, streams, mountains, and ocean. Thank you for the teachings to live a good life in harmony and for replenishing our bundles and kete (baskets).

We are grateful for the elders/kaumatua for their teachings and wisdom. We thank you for being respectful guardians of our traditional cultural teachings.

We are grateful for the learning that our educational journeys have taken us on and grateful to all who contributed their gifts and wisdom along this journey. We are reminded of the good work that many people contribute toward the struggle for Indigenous education and the healing work they do for their communities.

We are grateful for the educators that continue to inspire and create critical education.

We are grateful to our colleagues, students and the graduates who are doing great work in Indigenous education.

We are grateful to our families, our communities, and friends, who have been a source of nourishment and love.

We are grateful to non-Indigenous allies challenging racism, demanding space and resources for Indigenous education.

We are grateful for resilience despite the tough lessons that have come our way. We are grateful for the clarity and courage to be a part of transforming Indigenous education in academia.

The opening is a tribute to our ancestors, friendships and communities inspiring a legacy of our traditions for future generations. Traditional greetings seek to foster old and new connections and provide a healing pathway into our story.

Boozhoo, Kwe kwe, Semaa Kwe ndishnikaaz, Mukwa dodem, Teme-Augama Anishnabai. My spirit name is Tobacco Woman, I come from the Bear Clan and come from the Teme-Augama Anishnabai, the people of the deep water. I introduce myself in my own language so that, as a reader you know who I am and how I am connected to this land. It provides an understanding of my path and purpose in my life. I have a deep passion for transforming educational systems so that they are more inclusive, relevant, and sustaining for Indigenous peoples.

Ko Mataatua te Waka, Ko Kaputerangi te Maunga, Ko Ohinemataroa te Awa, Ko Ngāti Pukeko te Iwi, Ko Tamati Waaka te Rangatira, Ko Poroporo taku Marae, Ko Taima Moeke-Pickering toku ingoa. My name is Taima Moeke-Pickering and I am a Maori of the Ngati Pukeko and Tuhoe tribes from Aotearoa New Zealand. I am a full professor in the School of Indigenous Relations at Laurentian University, Sudbury, Ontario where I have lived and worked for 17 years on the traditional territory of the Atikameksheng Anishnawbek.

This chapter tells the story from the lens of two Indigenous intellectuals who frame Indigenous scholarship as a rightful place in post-secondary academia. Much of our scholarly views and activities contribute to giving voice and agency to Indigenous ways of being and knowing, the importance of traditions and ceremonies, championing Indigenous research methodologies and inspiring futuristic ideas for Indigenous education for the next generation. Creating spaces often on the academic margins means confronting and navigating racism and sexism, interrupting pay and tenure disparities, and engaging in tough conversations with colleagues, unions, and administrators to name a few. While these actions are necessary, they often incur a backlash: workplace harassment, compromised safety, delayed promotion, marked as non-scholarly academics or stigmatized as resistors. Despite this, we have continued to create direct actions to persuade a sustainable Indigenous resurgence movement in academia. This chapter provides insight into how Indigenous intellectualism actions can be carried out in academia and highlights the importance of Indigenous pedagogies in post-secondary education.

Setting the Context

Education for Indigenous peoples will always be central to self-determination strategies despite the colonized interference. Therefore, the co-intention to uphold Indigenous ways of being and knowing that disrupts Western academic strongholds remains a core component of advancing Indigenous education. Cote-Meek (2020) notes that disruption is important in the academy, especially in those places dedicated to a "a place where new ideas and ways of understanding the world are supposed to be valued" (p. xix). The hierarchy and privileging of Western knowledges as noted by Lavallee (2020) "implicate the academy as a colonial institution" (p. 123), because these institutions normalize Western ways as being primary thus rendering marginalized education as being the other or an appendage (Heffernan, 2022). We should not believe, that bringing Indigenous ideas and thoughts into academia is the be all and end all in transforming an institution. Rather, we should be aware that the structures and systems that hold the academy together require constant resistance and disruptions if we are to create and build sustainable places in academia, whereas disciplines like psychology, and the sciences, always seem to retain their place within the academy regardless of economic upheavals or changes of leadership. Therefore, as we envision a future, we must future proof Indigenous education to ensure that it is imbedded within the institution with its own Indigenous led academic and cultural rigours. It is therefore on us, as Indigenous educators to consistently challenge and critique academia. This pedagogy of cultural resistance and Indigenous self-determination remain ongoing. But should it be? Thinking about Indigenous futurism also means we imagine a time when we can just focus on our teaching, governance, and research, within a relevant model that supports Indigenous education that is sustainable, exciting, and empowering.

This chapter outlines three core components for Indigenous pedagogies to be robust. Firstly, situating the rightful place of indigenizing pedagogies; secondly laying out a foundation for decolonizing pedagogies and lastly, outlining a transforming pedagogy in Indigenous education, an ability to find all possible and appropriate interventions.

For this chapter, we reference those Indigenous knowledge experiences in a post-secondary academic institution. Accordingly, this chapter is centered on the experiences and aspirations for Indigenous education within academic institutions.

INDIGENIZING PEDAGOGIES

Indigenous pedagogies are more than a method or practice for teaching. Indigenous pedagogies incorporate both pre-colonization and self-determination strategies identified by Indigenous peoples (Battiste, 2013; Smith, 2021). The Indigenous world always sources the sacred, an intention that begins the process of learning (Weenie, 2020). The direct source of Indigenous knowledges and traditions are passed orally across generations from within one's own family, elders, community, events, or experiences. Indigenous knowledges span hundreds of years (way before the Treaties), and often these are accumulated and gathered into sources of wisdom, traditions, and worldviews (McGuire, 2020; Weenie, 2020). Lands and language are synonymous with Indigenous knowledges. The primary teachers of Indigenous cultures are from the community, where sources of land, history, culture, and language form the sacred bundles of traditional teachings (McGuire, 2020).

Remembering and thoughtfulness is an important part of Indigenous knowledges. Most cultures have traditional concepts where softness and kindness permeate their customs, memories, and actions such as Mino-bimaadiziwin (to live a good life) (McMillan, 2023; Nabigon, 2006). This is an important balance to remember when teaching the impacts of colonization on Indigenous peoples. Learning the truth about what happened to our ancestors especially in contexts of war, violence and subjugation is felt and transmitted intergenerationally.

An Indigenous pedagogy recognises the importance of reconnecting Indigenous people(s) to cultural sources for maintaining their wellbeing and ensuring that our educational journey and destiny is safe, respectful, and empowering. For example, the Indigenous Social Work program at Laurentian University, Ontario fosters balance and respect in their pedagogical approaches by drawing on the traditional teachings of the Anishnaabe Medicine Wheel and Seven Grandfather/Grandmothers as an Indigenous methodology for training social workers. This approach of applying Indigenous pedagogies make it possible for Indigenous practitioners to apply helping practices that are relevant to Indigenous communities. The root causes of social and health ills are traced to the impact of ongoing colonisation.

Indigenous knowledges influence how one understands the world as well as how one experiences the world around them. What constitutes our lived experiences as Indigenous peoples is thus informed by Indigenous knowledges. This is an important concept to grasp because it underpins why we, as Indigenous peoples, need to tell our own stories from our own stance and worldview. As Linda Tuhiwai Smith (2021) asserts, we should be rejecting stories, findings and analysis talked about us by the other:

It appalls us that the West can desire, extract and claim ownership of our ways of knowing, our imagery, the things we care about and produce, and then simultaneously reject the people who created and developed those ideas and seek to deny them further opportunities to be creators of their own culture and own nations. (p.1)

We are the first voice as Indigenous peoples, and it is critical that we amplify our own narratives, knowledges, and experiences. Most Indigenous faculty, bring a combined Indigenous experience and worldview into academia and in general "this analysis has been acquired organically and outside of the academy" (Smith, 2021, p. 5). Accordingly, there are a wide range of Indigenous worldviews and pedagogies that have emerged in the literature, many drawing from the depth of traditional teachings and worldviews (McGuire, 2020; Nabigon, 2006; Weenie, 2020) and, assisting Indigenous peoples to construct decolonizing and empowering pedagogies (Absolon & Herbert, 1997; Archibald, 2008; Cote-Meek, 2014; Durie, 1994; Lavallee, 2020; Smith, 2021; Tuck & Yang, 2012). A simple google search on Indigenous education will lead to a multitude of Indigenous-based theses, articles, webinars, and books, demonstrating the range of Indigenous cultural intellectualism that has been shaped by teachers, researchers, and leaders of Indigenous knowledge. Indigenous academics (same as our ancestors) put in a lot of love and labour to create and store Indigenous knowledge for the next generations. We often hear teachings in Indigenous circles on the concepts of "to become a good ancestor" or "standing on the shoulder of our ancestors". These teachings affirm the importance of an alignment of co-mutual intention pedagogy which includes indigenizing and decolonizing. They also affirm the intergenerational nature of resistance and resilience but importantly survivance (Vizenor, 1999), self-determination and sovereignty. Hence, we strongly advocate, that Indigenous educators (who are connected to their communities, or direct sources of Indigenous cultural knowledges) teach and pass on Indigenous knowledges to the generations now and coming.

A lot has changed in the space of "Indigenous" academia over the last 30 years, and this is exciting. However, while this is affirming news for Indigenous educators, we must always be vigilant in protecting our research and traditional knowledges. For example, in a recent case study by McMillan (2023) on *Anishinaabe Values and Servant Leadership, a Systemic Literature Review (SLR)* that was conducted between January and February 2021, the aim was to locate Indigenous sources relevant to the Anishinaabe Values of Mishomis (Grandfather) Teachings which also included references to the Seven Grandfather Teachings and Mino-bimaadiziwin (the good life). 740 sources were found on google (McMillan, 2023, p. 9). Perhaps the most revealing point of McMillan's (2023) study, was that although these cultural teachings that have been passed down orally over hundreds of years are used in the ordinary life of Anishinaabe peoples, that academic validity only counts for those times that traditional teachings appear in peer-reviewed legitimate sources. Case in point, of the 740 sources found by McMillan (2023), only 36 would be counted as valid. Subjugation of our knowledge remains omnipresent. An indigenizing lens would have afforded more value to Indigenous sources than just peer-reviewed sources. Imagine how vast our knowledge would be if we used as many sources as we can to understand the Indigenous world and their gifts!

We started this section with the notion that Indigenous pedagogies are much more than just a method or practice for teaching for the classroom or research findings, although the delivery, the curriculum, the content and the assessment does matter too. What we have highlighted, is in an Indigenous pedagogy, the social, cultural, and political community levels matter too when applying an Indigenous pedagogy. Indigenizing pedagogies amplifies our own traditions and cultural values, and we validate our own ways of knowing in and out of academia. In this regard, an indigenizing pedagogy is a co-mutual intention (between our ancestors and us), a deliberate self-determining pedagogy that upholds our values, customs, cultures, and traditions.

DECOLONIZING PEDAGOGIES

A decolonizing educational framework provides educators with a set of guidelines for working with groups who have been oppressed (Freire, 1970; Moeke-Pickering, 2010;

Tuck & Yang, 2012). Freire (1970) espoused the view that to surmount the situation of oppression, people must critically recognise its causes so they can create a new order. Decolonizing worldviews in education proposes to create a new order, one that amplifies strategies for change. Tuck and Yang (2010) emphasize that decolonization strategies for Indigenous and non-Indigenous persons "will take a different shape" given each have differing histories, contexts and responsibilities (p. 5). There will be areas where both Indigenous educators and non-Indigenous educators overlap in co-mutual areas such as resisting and fighting against systemic oppression and/or uplifting equitable potential in academia. We deliberately highlight this difference because Indigenous educators often do twice the work of both indigenizing and decolonizing and secondly, for this reason we encourage non-Indigenous educators to focus their efforts on decolonizing the institute and picking up their responsibilities of breaking down systems of oppression such as racism and sexism. Decolonizing strategies must create a new order therefore resources to achieve such must be equitable. At a meeting with international Indigenous scholars Distinguished Professor Graham Hingangaroa Smith (personal communication, 24 November 2022) reminded us, that Indigenous peoples get involved too much in the "politics of distraction". Indigenous educators, continually find themselves mitigating ongoing oppression and racism (Cote-Meek, 2014; Smith, 2023). Decolonizing should not be the sole journey of the oppressed yet sadly we acknowledge that a lot of Indigenous labor is doing the heavy lifting of calling out and addressing systemic racism and advocating/leading decolonization in academia. As Tuck and Yang (2012) espouse, decolonizing is not just a metaphor or a figure of speech, it is action! Undoubtedly, there is an advantage in engaging allies to share the load of decolonizing.

Over our combined 30 years, we have witnessed and been a part of co-intention decolonizing education, the deploy of strategies that uphold Indigenous ways of doing and being in academia. Freire (1970, p. 51) would name this as a "revolutionary leadership".

A revolutionary leadership must accordingly practice co-intention education. Teachers and students (leadership and people), co-intent on reality, are both Subjects, not only in the task of unveiling that reality, and thereby coming to know it critically, but in the task of re-creating that knowledge. As they attain this knowledge of reality through common reflection and action, they discover themselves as its permanent re- creators. In this way, the presence of the oppressed in the struggle for their liberation will be what it should be: not pseudo-participation, but committed involvement. (Freire, 1970, p. 51)

In this context, the co-intention between Indigenous educators and allies is to unveil a new reality though teaching, research and governance, thus creating an existence and place for Indigenous knowledge everywhere including Western academia.

A decolonizing framework in education is a critical analysis tool to understand the colonial impacts on Indigenous peoples (Tuck & Yang, 2012). Inherent in a decolonization framework are the discrimination duo – racism and sexism. Unless you follow the trajectory of colonization, racism and sexism, your decolonizing framework will mute the root causes of systemic violence against Indigenous peoples. Therefore, decolonization requires a deep understanding of colonization and its intersections with racism and sexism. This critical analysis helps students to mine the deeper layers of discrimination inflicted on Indigenous, racialized peoples, and how women herstories and gender diverse persons and their roles have been devalued and dismantled. An example is the Indian Act 1867-1951 in Canada, which denied generations of Indigenous women of their status and their rights to claim Indigeneity. This discrimination still permeates the social, cultural, and political standing of Indigenous women in Canada today.

Decolonizing analyses also draw attention to the exclusionary practices that have attempted to prevent Indigenous peoples from entering and succeeding in the academy. We have been both a witness and victim of colonized classrooms and being held back from important milestones in academic promotion processes. The root cause is attributed to the systemic racism that exists and is set up to guard a system exclusive for the privileged and so-called intelligent members of society (typically white males) (Cote-Meek, 2014; Moeke-Pickering, 2010). Systemic racism ensures that the "colonized" are excluded. Thus, ensuring, for example, that there will never be enough of us to be in key administrative academic positions to make sustainable change. A decolonizing lens suggests that a critical mass is necessary to make meaningful change. Since the Truth and Reconciliation Report (Truth and Reconciliation Commission of Canada [TRC], 2015) many institutes across Canada are recruiting and hiring Indigenous faculty and/or creating Indigenous Research Centres. This is great news. Although we see increases in Indigenous faculty hires and Indigenous administrative positions, this does come with challenges. As illuminated by Cote-Meek's (2014) research on *Colonized Classrooms*, dealing with ongoing racism within the academy and directly from colleagues impact the overall mental health and wellbeing of Indigenous faculty and students alike. A decolonizing pedagogy is a reminder to respectfully check on the wellbeing of Indigenous faculty, students, and Elders, to see how they are. Battling all forms of discrimination is energy depleting and exhausting. Many Indigenous faculty draw on their own cultures to pick themselves up and battle on, but this is not always sustainable. We must ask ourselves the question on whether the institute is also creating relevant access to resources and wellbeing that ensure the success and retention of Indigenous faculty members?

If our goal of decolonization is to create a new order (Freire, 1970) then our strategies must also be more than hiring more Indigenous faculty, having more allies, or bringing Indigenous knowledges and ceremonies into the academy. These all have their place in the academy, but it is not a replacement for institutional change and transforming the institute to a new order. Further, systemic racism against Indigenous peoples cannot be eradicated by sending anyone on a course or to one or two ceremonies -- It is much more than just a decolonizing of the mind. A true decolonizing pedagogy must alter/modify/change/transform an institution. It must have a sustainable and rightful place for Indigenous learning and should be resourced. The struggle to prove that Indigenous peoples have a rightful place in academia with sustainable transformative change is a constant. In the next section, we provide insights into key aspects that inform transforming pedagogies in academia.

TRANSFORMING PEDAGOGIES

Distinguished Professor Graham Hingangaroa Smith (personal communication, 24 November 2022) and leader in Indigenous transformational change, is concerned that there is not enough weight on the transforming elements of education and that we must identify more explicitly what the issues are and analyze what is going wrong. A transforming pedagogy in Indigenous education is an ability to find all possible and appropriate interventions.

Institutional transformative change includes changing the institutional culture at all levels (Duffy & Raigeluth, 2008), it should be fundamental and irreversible (Gass, 2010), it must be radical and sustainable (Eckel & Kezar, 2003), it must establish a clear and concrete vision for Indigenous education (Cote-Meek, 2022), and must ensure a critical seat at the leadership table (Smith, 2023). It follows that a transforming pedagogy must have Indigenous leaders and decision-makers at the governance level. In a paper by Kofi Campbell (2020) *Why don't Canadian universities hire more racialized and Indigenous senior administrators?* he states:

Perhaps that's because university administrators have done little to change their institutions beyond putting out the same carbon-copy EDI statements, and hiring EDI champions and then not properly supporting them. The solution? Hire more racialized and Indigenous administrators who can speak to these issues at the tables where decisions actually get made. (p. 1)

An imperative of a transforming pedagogy insists that we, as Indigenous peoples, have a right to access education anywhere, therefore a rightful place at the decision-making table is necessary.

In previous articles we have written about the principles of transformative change strategies in academia. Since our 2011 article entitled *Indigenous Pedagogies and Transformational Practices* (Cote-Meek and Moeke-Pickering, 2011) our comprehension for transforming academies has expanded from negotiating Indigenous spaces in academia, hiring more faculty, and creating more Indigenous content to focussing on transformation that thinks "big and boldly" (Cote-Meek, 2022, p. xvii). Cote-Meek (2022) suggests it is time for academia to come to terms with colonization and racism, this also includes "deconstructing existing racialized constructions of Indigenous peoples" (p. xxvii). Further, she recommends that at a minimum, a university should commit to the inclusion of Indigenous knowledges in the curriculum; representation on the board of governors and decision-making bodies; embed Indigenous councils into governance; negotiate retention strategies of Indigenous faculty; re-examine research ethics to be inclusive of Indigenous protocols; dedicate and name spaces; enhance student supports and incorporate land-based curriculum to name a few.

Perhaps at this juncture, you as the reader may wonder, why we are putting so much effort into transforming an unwilling institute and not building Indigenous-based education in our tribal and First Nations communities. This is an excellent point! In Canada, the ten provincial governments have exclusive responsibility for all levels of publicly funded education. The key word is "publicly funded". Through its educational policies, the Government of Ontario, Ministry of Education, for example, determines the funding, the types and validity of degrees, and governance, all in alignment with their strategic plans. On their recent website Indigenous education in Ontario (2023), it states:

We are committed to working with Indigenous partners and the education sector to improve access to education for Indigenous students in Ontario and support First Nation, Metis and Inuit student achievement and well-being. (p.1)

While the Government of Ontario, Ministry of Education lists several strategies and targeted funds useful for Indigenous education, "improving access" is a far cry from bold, economical sustainable changes that Indigenous educators envision. Targeted funding is not sustainable, it merely means that the target changes based on need as governed by those holding the public purse.

Institutions and educators have begun the work of responding to The Truth and Reconciliation Commission (TRC) Report and the 94 Calls to Action (TRC, 2015), a guiding document for healing Canada's relationships with First Peoples. The response by institutes can be viewed as riveting and dismal at the same time. We have witnessed the establishment of task forces to cluster hiring to new and improved protocols and policies for Indigenous education, to new Indigenous scholarships, recognition events of Orange Shirt Day and the National Day for Truth and Reconciliation, to new memberships at governance levels. These responses show a pathway to inclusive Indigenous education. We are excited for these pathways, however the protective wisdom and critical lens inside us, invokes us to seek deeper transformative analysis. Despite these efforts there is still much work to do in transforming the system.

Dr. Malinda Smith, Vice-Provost (Equity, Diversity and Inclusion, EDI) at the University of Calgary and a trusted Black ally, was one of five speakers on a panel talking about structural inequity in Canadian institutions. Smith warns "when institutions want something, they do it by dedicating leadership, resources to getting it done" (as cited in Monteiro, 2020). Further, Smith shares it is difficult to believe in institutions who, "don't have racial justice" or "a parallel framework for racial justice" (as cited in Monteiro, 2020). If you recall right from the outset of this chapter, we talked about the stubborn "isms" that uphold and maintain systemic power of institutes. Smith's caution is a good reminder to be vigilant, that resources for Indigenous equity should not just be additive but transforming. On this same panel was Ms. Jean Becker, Acting Associate Vice President of Human Rights, Equity, and Inclusion at the University of Waterloo, who has been working as an Indigenous leader in education for 30 years. For Jean Becker, "the most intractable barrier is the colonial mindset" (as cited in Monteiro, 2020). Becker's statement pairs with our own analysis, that transforming change is more than adding resources, it is also changing the racism that keeps the colonial mindset in power. For now, the TRC dedicated strategies are a welcome change, but we urge and encourage educators and institutes to translate these strategies into sustainable transformation.

Heffernan's (2022) study examined equity in inequitable settings by reviewing 40 years of social justice research literature. Regarding First Nations students in Australasia, he found that once they did enter the colonial landscape of the university, that the university had "not really changed; it facilitated passage-ways" such as bridging programs, scholarships and support services and targeted employment (p. 57). Further, Heffernan's (2022) review suggests that the university is "creating temporary access where social demands require" (p. 57). What is clear from Heffernan's study, is that equity or social justice pathways are temporary, that these gateways and passageways can be decreased or removed. This points to the tenuous nature of existing changes within the education system. When seeking longer term, sustainable and transforming changes we need to go far beyond creating these temporary access and success measures.

While this chapter has focussed on Indigenous education within mainstream institutes, it is important to acknowledge and support that Indigenous education also includes tribal and First Nation-based educational institutes. It is exciting to note, the transforming pedagogies that Indigenous Universities have developed. For example, in Aotearoa, New Zealand, Maori established their own Wananga (Maori Universities). Likewise, Kenjgewin Teg, is an Anishinabek educational institute based in Ontario, Canada. All, center their respective tribal-First Nation governance, create their own degrees (sometimes in collaboration with other institutes), developed, and implemented policies, plans and actions for their respective educational systems. We believe that Indigenous led institutes present an important transforming framework that aligns with Indigenous traditions and principles. This sends a positive message and affirmation to all educators that Indigenous peoples themselves are committed to designing their own Indigenous education systems. We assert that a transforming pedagogy must include genuine collaborations with Indigenous-based Universities and institutes not only as a resource for teaching and research, but for dedicated linkages to land-based and traditional teachings. We all have a duty and responsibility to ensuring Indigenous peoples, their knowledges, cultures and traditions thrive.

While we have discussed some of the major tenets of transformative pedagogies it is important to note that these are starting points. For Tuck and Yang (2012), they are not just expecting an institute to add more critical consciousness courses or more hires. Rather, a real transforming institute is one that gives up their land, power and privilege. As Cote-Meek (2014) notes one of the central tenets of colonization has been about the land and the extraction of resources of the land. In order to effect transformative change, the land must be a central tenet of decolonization. As noted, earlier Tuck and Yang's (2012) notion that decolonization is not a metaphor, it requires "Land Back". For Tuck and Yang (2012), the land is more than a site that locates and accumulates histories, underneath it is Mother Nature, which "has a culture, and it is a Native culture" (p. 30). We concur. Every mainstream academic institute is on stolen Indigenous lands across Canada. That is a lot of acreage and as landowners, they should surely do the right thing. Give it back to the traditional landowners and rent from them at a fair price. Would this not be a great end point to a truly transformative change.

CONCLUSION

The focus of this chapter is about transforming the academy and making it safe and robust for Indigenous students, leaders, faculty, and researchers. Why? In this current context, many Indigenous peoples choose Universities to complete their education. Our view is that Indigenous peoples should be able to access education and feel welcomed and importantly see themselves reflected within the institute.

They should be afforded every opportunity to be successful and complete their studies free from systemic barriers.

We must reiterate, that deconstructing colonization that is both violent and ongoing is an emotional journey, so requires kindness and respectfulness. We must be careful not to open wounds without the proper healing, support, and resources. It is incredibly difficult to challenge the oppressor, or those in power. So, it is necessary to create space for Indigenous peoples to define their authentic place and pace in transforming work.

Indigenizing and decolonizing pedagogies provide a solid foundation for supporting Indigenous education and promotes priorities that are relevant for Indigenous peoples. It lays the groundwork for disrupting colonization including racism, sexism, and discrimination in education. A transforming pedagogy centers Indigenous educational aspirations and practices, so that we have a rightful place and space in education anywhere.

In conclusion, we are passionate about leaving a robust legacy for Indigenous education in academia hence this paper was centered on pedagogies that make the most transforming changes. It is hoped that this chapter affirms the work that has been done so far for Indigenous education, but that it also leaves ideas for expanded possibilities such as 'Land Back' for continuing Indigenous education for many more years to come.

Chi Miigwech and Kia Ora.

REFERENCES

Absolon, K., & Herbert, E. (1997). Community action as practice of freedom: A first Nations perspective. In B. Wharf & M. Clague (Eds.), *Community organising: Canadian experiences* (pp. 205–227). Oxford University Press.

Archibald, J. (2008). *Indigenous storywork: Educating the heart, mind, body, and spirit*. UBC Press.

Battiste, M. (2013). *Decolonizing Education – Nourishing the Learning Spirit*. Purich.

Campbell, K. (2020, May 8). Why don't Canadian universities hire more racialized and Indigenous senior administrators? *University Affairs*. https://www.universityaffairs.ca/opinion/in-my-opinion/why-dont-canadian-universities-hire-more-racialized-and-indigenous-senior-administrators/

Cote-Meek, S. (2014). *Colonized Classrooms– Racism, Trauma and Resistance in Post-Secondary Education*. Fernwood Press.

Cote-Meek, S. (2020). From colonized classrooms to Transformative change in the Academy: We can and must do better! In S. Cote-Meek & T. Moeke-Pickering (Eds.), *Decolonizing and Indigenizing education in Canada* (pp. xi–xxiii). Canadian Scholars.

Cote-Meek, S., & Moeke-Pickering, T. (2011). Indigenous pedagogies and transformational practices. In G. Williams (Ed.), *Talking back, talking forward: Journeys in transforming Indigenous educational practice* (pp. 27–32). Charles Darwin University Press.

Cote-Meek, S., & Moeke-Pickering, T. (Eds.). (2022). *Decolonizing and Indigenizing education in Canada*. Canadian Scholars.

Duffy, F., & Raigeluth, C. (2008). The school system transformation (SST) protocol. *Educational Technology, 48*(4), 41–49.

Durie, M. (1994). *Whaiora: Maori health development*. Oxford University Press.

Eckel, P., & Kezar, A. (2003). Key strategies for making new institutional sense: Indgredients to higher education transformation. *Higher Education Policy, 16*(1), 39–53. doi:10.1057/palgrave.hep.8300001

Freire, P. (1970). *Pedagogy of the oppressed*. Penguin Books.

Gass, R. (2011). *What is transformation? And how it advances social change*. ST Project. http://stproject.org/wp-content/uploads/2012/03/What_is_Transformation.pdf

Government of Ontario, Ministry of Education. (2023). *Indigenous Education in Ontario*. MoE. https://www.ontario.ca/page/indigenous-education-ontario

Heffernan, T. (2022). Forty years of social justice research in Australasia: Examining equity in inequitable settings. *Higher Education Research & Development, 41*(1), 48–61. doi:10.1080/07294360.2021.2011152

Lavallee, L. (2022). Is Decolonization possible in the Academy. In S. Cote-Meek & T. Moeke-Pickering (Eds.), *Decolonizing and Indigenizing education in Canada* (pp. 117–134). Canadian Scholars.

McGuire, P. (2022). Gii Aanikoobijigan Mindimooyehn: Decolonizing views of Anishinaabekwe. In S. Cote-Meek & T. Moeke-Pickering (Eds.), *Decolonizing and Indigenizing education in Canada* (pp. 19–30). Canadian Scholars.

McMillan, T. (2023). Anishinaabe Values and Servant Leadership: A Two-Eyed Seeing Approach. *The Journal of Values Based Leadership*, *16*(1), 11. https://scholar.valpo.edu/cgi/viewcontent.cgi?article=1428&context=jvbl

Moeke-Pickering, T. M. (2010). *Decolonisation as a social change framework and its impact on the development of Indigenous-based curricula for Helping Professionals in mainstream Tertiary Education Organisations* [Doctoral thesis, The University of Waikato]. The University of Waikato Research Comms. https://hdl.handle.net/10289/4148

Monteiro, L. (2020, Sept 1). Structural inequity runs de ep in Canadian institutions, panel says. *The Record*. https://www.therecord.com/news/waterloo-region/2020/09/01/structural-inequity-runs-deep-in-canadian-institutions-panel-says.html

Nabigon, H. (2006). *The hollow tree: Fighting addiction with traditional Native healing*. McGill-Queens University Press. doi:10.1515/9780773576254

Smith, L. T. (2021). *Decolonizing methodologies: Research and Indigenous peoples* (3rd ed.). Zed Books. doi:10.5040/9781350225282

Truth and Reconciliation Commission of Canada. (2015). *Calls to action*. Government of Canada. https://www2.gov.bc.ca/assets/gov/british-columbians-our-governments/indigenous-people/aboriginal-peoples-documents/calls_to_action_english2.pdf

Tuck, E., & Yang, W. (2012). Decolonization is not a metaphor. *Decolonization*, *1*(1), 1–40.

Vizenor, G. (1999). *Manifest manners: Narratives on postindian survivance*. University of Nebraska Press.

Weenie, A. (2022). Askiy Kiskinwahamakewina: Reclaiming land-based pedagogies in the Academy. In S. Cote-Meek & T. Moeke-Pickering (Eds.), *Decolonizing and Indigenizing education in Canada* (pp. 3–18). Canadian Scholars.

Chapter 2
Embodying Knowledge and Pedagogy Through an Indigenous Oral System

Vicki Bouvier
Mount Royal University, Canada

ABSTRACT

Centering and embodying an oral knowledge system to guide learning and assessment challenges educational institution's cognitive imperialism. Through experiences as an educator, the author has witnessed the rush to amalgamate Indigenous content into classrooms without an awareness or knowing that Indigenous knowledge has its own systematic processes of ascertaining and validating knowing. Acknowledging that Indigenous knowledges have systems, just like that of written knowledge, is imperative if institutions are serious about honouring Indigenous knowing, being, and doing. This chapter will provide teachings, as learned from Elder Crowshoe, of an Indigenous oral knowledge system—theory, ontology, and axiology—that guide sharing and acquisition of knowledge. Thereafter, the concepts of truthing, circumambulation, and the third perspective will be detailed with hope to inform educators and students on how knowledge is conceptualized in an oral system and how educators and students alike might share, cultivate, and assess learning and knowledge acquisition.

INTRODUCTION

Taanishi, Victoria Bouvier, dishinikawshon Michif niyanaan ma kayash paarantii la rivyar roozh pi Boggy Creek d'oshcin ni kipischi didaan Calgary, Alberta. Hello, my name is Victoria Bouvier, I am Michif. My long-ago relatives are from the Red River and Boggy Creek, Manitoba, I live in Calgary, Alberta.

I walk in the world honoured to carry and live the name of my late grandmother Victoria Bouvier (nee Malaterre). Born in St. Lazare, Manitoba, she was among relatives who were part of the Buffalo Brigades. My grandfather Jean-Baptiste Bouvier, born in St. John, North Dakota, is a descendent of the Bouvier's from Grant Town (later renamed St. Francois Xavier). My father was born in Boggy Creek, Manitoba, into a long line of strong Michif people who fought for their rights and self-determination. This lineage is in the writing of this chapter.

I was born in the foothills adjacent to the Rocky Mountains, where the Elbow and Bow Rivers meet, in Calgary, Alberta. Growing up in this urban context, my formative years were spent within the political milieu of the Métis Nation of Alberta as well as spending cherished time with my maternal Scottish Grandmother, Myrtle May Wachtler. In Calgary, the knowledge, and practices of the Blackfoot, Tssu'Tina, and Stoney Nakoda peoples encircled my upbringing. These teachings are within me as are my connections with Boggy Creek. Bound to a different ecology than my ancestors, I see myself as a visitor on the lands where I grew up with responsibilities to strive for good relations. I have made relatives in this territory through learning and living out the practices and processes of this place.

In particular, Piikani (Blackfoot) Elders Dr. Reg Crowshoe and Rose Crowshoe have guided me through their Blackfoot understandings for several years. My relationship with Elder Reg Crowshoe began in 2012 when teaching an Indigenous Relations program. While we taught alongside each other, I can recognize now that there were distances between our knowledge systems. For example, I employed Western tools (such as icebreaker exercises to engage students and illustrate concepts) that Reg and Rose still tease me about. The teasing is appreciated as a sign of love, but also helps me see all I have learned and embodied since then. In my previous career as an early childhood educator, I was not taught in post-secondary about or from Indigenous perspectives so my understanding of holistic or relational pedagogies was limited; I merely taught the way I was taught.

Learning alongside Elder Reg Crowshoe, offered me the "education" that I had not previously received in any post-secondary courses, or earlier schooling for that matter. As our relationship blossomed, we first sat in circle on a classroom floor. I relied less on PowerPoint presentations and traditional classroom structures, to center circle teachings with smudge, then created a week-long Indigenous Studies course in a tipi. I can see now that these years taught me to listen, observe, and assess stories from an oral knowledge system. With continued guidance from him, these teachings and experiences subsequently led to crafting my own pedagogical processes and lifting up an oral knowledge system as my doctoral methodology.

This chapter[1] will share the teachings, as I have learned from Elder Reg Crowshoe[2], of an Indigenous oral knowledge system which describes natural, absolute, practical laws and ethics. Thereafter, I discuss the concept of *Aachimooshtowihk* - an individual truth sharing followed by circumambulation which builds upon *Aachimooshtowihk* and orientates storying as a collective enactment of coming to know and validation. Lastly, I will describe how I have applied these concepts and practices in my pedagogy as to provide educators and students an understanding of how knowledge is conceptualized in an oral system and how educators and students alike might share, cultivate, and assess learning and knowledge acquisition. As more institutions work to "Indigenize" their respective contexts, the Western education system that places written documentation and assessment at the helm of validating knowledge needs to be challenged while simultaneously offering practices for learning, documenting, and assessing that exist within oral knowledge systems. My hope for this chapter is to stress that it is not sufficient to just "bring" content into educational systems; we need to understand the systemic nature of knowledge governance. I argue that sharing in a circle, or merely storytelling does not go deep enough to reveal the complexities of Indigenous knowledge systems. We must understand the systemic nature of knowledge or risk recolonizing knowledge if we are to rely on the system to which knowledge is generated from.

UNDERSTANDING AN INDIGENOUS ORAL KNOWLEDGE SYSTEM

Coming Into an Oral System

Centering and embodying an oral knowledge system to guide learning and assessment challenges educational institution's cognitive imperialism (Battiste, 2013). Through my experiences as an educator, I have witnessed the rush to amalgamate Indigenous content into classrooms without an awareness or knowing that Indigenous knowledge has its own systematic processes of ascertaining and validating knowing. Acknowledging that Indigenous knowledges have systems, just like that of written knowledge is imperative if institutions are serious about honouring Indigenous knowing, being, and doing.

Learning in and with an oral knowledge system uses different practices to validate knowledge. As many institutions across Canada employ Indigenization strategies in their respective places, understanding Indigenous oral systems needs to be heavily considered and acknowledged in academic institutions. Tensions between the two knowledge systems, one written, the other oral, creates unnecessary dichotomies that only hinder the building of mutually beneficial respectful relationships.

While teaching alongside Elder Reg Crowshoe for the first few years, I did not realize at the onset that I would soon be changing the direction of my doctoral research plan to situate my inquiry within an oral system of knowledge generation and validation. Admittedly, like my master's thesis, I thought I would be using semi-structured interviews and transcribing data. However, like all great teachings, they are never actualized until much later.

My first interactions with the oral system did not happen in books, but rather with smudge, in a circle, often in a tipi; the first practices of orality. I knew I had felt an oral system before because it was familiar but the systemic nature of knowledge acquisition and validation in this way was new to me. As I became more and more assimilated in the oral system, I knew that this was becoming the methodology that would guide my doctoral inquiry. I remember sitting with Elder Reg Crowshoe and my doctoral supervisor discussing an oral system as methodology in the university and particularly if the process was one that we wanted to enact and advocate for. Elder Reg Crowshoe encouraged me to use the methodology as he believed that it was time for the academic institution to begin stepping out of the proverbial box and assess their own rules and policies to ensure they included and protected Indigenous knowledge systems.

Western academic institutions have strict guidelines and rules about what constitutes knowledge and its validation. As I prepared to have an oral knowledge system guide my inquiry, I knew I would be challenging the institution's cognitive imperialism (Battiste, 2013). Not only was I coming into a relationship with oral knowledge systems, but so was the Faculty of Graduate studies. My field of study[3] was comprised entirely of video chapters which warranted special permissions from the Faculty of Graduate Studies and the Education faculty to forgo a traditional written dissertation. Once ready for the candidacy defense, I paralleled ceremony and the oral exam to validate the candidacy in both systems. The candidacy paper *and* oral exam, as I offered, were outside the traditional parameters thus requiring the institution to rethink the ways in which they approach and tend to academic validity. As one of the first students to use ceremony for validation at my institution, the University was forced to understand what was required to have Indigenous knowledge systems in action and the resources needed to honour those processes. For example, a ceremony to validate knowledge relies on protocols that require additional funding for knowledge keepers to facilitate the process. At the time of my doctoral candidacy defense, there were no policies that stipulated how to parallel the system and furthermore, how to financially resource these processes. The written system of knowledge validation is so normalized that other systems are not even conceivable. Utilizing an Indigenous oral knowledge system requires creating new policies that allow and protect Indigenous knowledges. This is crucial to ensure that they flourish while at the same time disrupt and dismantle the supremacy of western academic traditions and the written word.

My process of coming into and learning about an oral system started with searching for an understanding of oral systems of knowledge generation and validation. To deepen my understanding, I sought literary brilliance to further inform my inquiry. Unfortunately, there is little research that has been conducted that provides direction and guidance for engaging with and through an oral knowledge system for learning, knowing *and* validation in classrooms and more specifically, post-secondary. I highlight three writings that I found helpful in my coming into an oral system.

First, Jo-ann Archibald's (2008) seminal book, *Indigenous Storywork: Educating the Heart, Mind, Body, and Spirit* was the first book I engaged with that brought me into the realm of storytelling from an Indigenous perspective. Her research set the foundation to conceptualize how to have a respectful relationship with stories but also with Elders and storytellers. Archibald (2008) guides educators on a beautiful exploration on the importance of stories, Elders' knowledge, and understanding story frameworks from within an Indigenous paradigm. Her teachings are undoubtedly crucial for educators honouring Indigenous stories however, we also need to understand how to protect the stories and Elders in the academic institutions. Moreover, a further exploration of the cultural protocols that are required to protect storywork is increasingly important.

The second was a text I quickly became old friends with, Lee Maracle's (2015) prolific text, *Memory Serves Oratories*. This enduringly provocative book provides guidance in theorizing orality and outlines an ontology that points to assessing oratory. Her beautiful articulation of memory, truthing, and oratory are indeed a map however, within those teachings she leaves space for individuals to find their own local-specific processes of knowledge and assessment.

Lastly, an article by Sharla Peltier (2014) titled "Assessing Anishinaabe Children's Narratives: An Ethnographic Exploration of Elders' Perspectives" provided further guidance in understanding orality. This article provides promising insights into assessing children's stories from Elder's knowledge and understanding of storytelling. The research identified that non-Indigenous formulas to assess stories and deciphering what makes a good story is often unequivocal to the ways in which Indigenous worldviews determine good stories. As a result, Sharla Peltier (2014), conducted a research study to have Anishinnabemowin speaking Elders listen to stories of children subsequently creating "elder codes" (p. 181) that would demarcate a good story from their cultural perspective. This project allowed educators to view storytelling from a culturally relevant perspective which is different from a western academic assessment of literature and narratives. This is helpful for storytelling; however, the validation of stories and information is still left without academic scholarship.

Responsibilities to an Oral System

Responsibility is a core ligature when acquiring knowledge. Aligning systems together with careful attention as to not impose or suppress is difficult; however, it is possible to shorten the distance between Indigenous and Western knowledge systems so they can work together in parallel. In my respective contexts, I see individuals and institutions trying to bring Indigenous knowledge content into courses or processes without understanding that Indigenous knowledge is a system, not just information to be consumed. It is the responsibility of educators and administrators to acknowledge the systematic nature of orality and understand it alongside any curriculum brought into academia or they run the risk of recolonizing knowledge. Not only do we, as educators, need to deconstruct how we teach, but we also have a responsibility to deconstruct how we assess knowledge and information which ultimately helps protect knowledge.

Venue, Action, Language, Song (VALS)

Academic institutions are relying on Elders to provide them with guidance and knowledge in their pursuits to Indigenize and decolonize. In doing so, educators and administrators need to know how to identify the right information and who has the privilege to share it. When Elder Reg Crowshoe shares his teachings, he always situates himself within his knowledge, through his perspective and with the proper references. Beginning his stories in this way provides the listeners with his credentials which signal his right to teach and share the specific knowledge. Much like how I shared at the beginning and throughout this chapter, I am providing you my credentials in how I came to this knowledge and what I was permitted to share. In Indigenous Oral Systems, one cannot share knowledge if they do not have the right.

Figure 1. Video of VALS

The ethics of an oral system require individuals to follow a process for navigating and obtaining rights and privileges; Elder Reg Crowshoe describes this as venue, action, language, and song (VALS). In an interview (see QR code), Elder Reg Crowshoe describes the process of VALS for obtaining rights and privileges through an oral knowledge system (Napier, 2013). The venue is the story told about how one obtained knowledge and understanding. For example, what was the reason, who was there, where did it take place. Actions are what transpired to create the story. For example, what practices and protocols were involved. Language are the discourses relied on to tell the story. For example, what are the theories, teachings, and language utilized to conduct the process. The song is the final physical enactment that is sung for an individual or group indicating they now have a right or privilege.

Pedagogical approaches that honour oral systems to navigate rights and privileges experience challenges within Western academia because they adhere to ethics that may differ from current traditional approaches. VALS is akin to a parchment paper showing completion of some level of education. Institutions must parallel western credentials with the oral system credentials Elders and knowledge keepers have. Paralleling knowledge systems and the accumulation and achievements in each respective knowledge system, is one important step in releasing the tension between to the systems. By doing so, institutions lessen the risk of recolonizing by protecting Indigenous knowledge.

AN INDIGENOUS ORAL SYSTEM

Indigenous knowledge systems exist all over the world and many have the same structure with differing stories, languages, processes, and practices. It is important to note that in sharing Elder Reg Crowshoe's teachings, I am articulating specific teachings and practices belonging to a certain territory. Moreover, in sharing his teachings, I also share my interpretations and how they apply or have been applied in my respective contexts. Wherever one is situated when reading this, that is the place to which the knowledge will come from and will dictate the protocols needed to access and validate knowledge. The following laws, as shared by Elder Reg Crowshoe, formulate an Indigenous knowledge system.

Natural Laws

Within any system of knowledge there are laws that govern worldviews, relationships, and interactions. Within an oral system, natural laws are the foundation of worldviews.

Elder Reg Crowshoe (2020) articulates, "everything that was created was natural laws, the air, the vacuum in space, the plants, the animals, all humans, anything that was created was natural law" (personal communication, September 5). Natural laws are defined through creation stories and understandings are elicited from the teachings in the story. Through smudge, Elder Reg Crowshoe has shared tenets of the Blackfoot creation story with me to prompt an understanding of natural laws.

The earth was created when Creator felt lonesome and through this feeling, he wanted to conceive of something that would ease his loneliness; this feeling is the "original emotion". Out of original emotion, came "original thought" as he contemplated what to create to help him with his loneliness. After thinking, Creator collected stardust and rolled it into a ball blew on it as it spiralled out becoming suspended in the sky; this became known as earth. When Creator, made earth, he began thinking of what else to create within earth; everything he created is deemed as "original creation". Once entities were created on earth, Creator projected sound into all of creation; the earth, the animals, the wind all received sound — they received language, this is described as "original sound". (Elder Reg Crowshoe, Piikani, personal communication, September 5, 2020)

This sharing, which captures only minute details of a very complex story, teaches the four elements of creation — emotion, thought, creation, and sound — as the beginnings of our world, and the initial tenets that teach us about humanity. Creation stories teach us how all aspects of creation came to be while also depicting the positioning of humans in the schema of creation. There are many creation stories, for example, the creation of day and night or the creation of constellations; these will all be dependent on who is telling the stories and the land they speak from. Natural laws explain natural order and the interconnectedness and interdependence of our universe.

Absolute Laws

Through observing and witnessing interactions between all of creation, phenomenon can be explained and understood as absolute laws.

Absolute laws are things like, theories, medicine theories, or laws that govern us, and the way those absolute laws came about was as all the natural things that were created as natural law, [started to] interact, they create a story, and as they create a story, that story becomes an absolute law. (Elder Reg Crowshoe, Piikani, personal communication, September 5, 2020)

Observing the interconnectedness and interactions of the natural world provide storied maps for humans to understand how we are to engage with all life (Cajete,

2019). The interplay of relationships provides knowledge to humans; when validated as a story, they become absolute laws that govern human behaviour. We follow the laws to honour the continuance of life. One of these stories that guide humans is how smudge was brought to people, the niitsitapi (Blackfoot, real people). Elder Reg Crowshoe has shared the story of smudge with me many times, it is the story of Scarface, here is an excerpt of his teachings:

[Creator] took that feather and wiped off the scar on his face, the scar represented all the hardships in the tribe you came from, now you can go back and help them because I'm taking off these hardships....the smoke represents the feather that creator used on Scarface, and you purify all that hardship all the bad stuff, purify yourself, that's why we use the smudge to start, call to order, and purify those away. That's why we smudge, through stories like that, we talk about as knowledge and official ways to do things because we didn't have books back in those days it was just stories like that that we used. (Elder Reg Crowshoe, Piikani, personal communication, January 6, 2019).

The experience of Scarface informs me of the importance of starting processes with smudge to begin with a clear mind and heart. In lighting the smudge, I acknowledge smudge as a being signaling the spiritual dimension as inherently part of the learning, knowing, and validating. The word, spiritual, does not insinuate a sacredness, yet a recognition that all beings have a spirit and are part of creation (Elder Reg Crowshoe, Piikani, personal communication, February 20, 2020). Depending on the ceremony or purpose of a gathering, spirit-beings could be plants, animals, thunder, healing, or in the context of this chapter — knowledge. Interacting with knowledge spirit is guided by certain protocol as to have an ethical engagement and to ensure that the relationship does not cause harm to oneself or others (Ermine, 2007). Using proper protocol to acknowledge and respect the spirit promotes an equilibrium which causes the least resistance in achieving the purpose of the ceremony or gathering, or teaching (Deloria, 1998; Ermine, 2007). Elder's teachings say that when someone enacts the proper protocols, things will happen smoothly, not without challenges of course, but the path will be easier.

Absolute laws come in a multitude of interactions. Watching the connection between plants, sun and water is a perfect example of absolute laws. Through observations, I can deduce that a plant needs water and sun to thrive, without sun they will die. Smudge is an absolute law; I have learned through Elder Reg Crowshoe and other Elders that smudge is the connector between us and Creator, or if in a group, the connector between all of us and each of us with Creator.

Practical Laws: Cultural Protocol

In our learning when we have gifted tobacco, we have made our commitment, we are acknowledging that knowledge has spirit, we are acknowledging that there is spiritual beings and entities that guide our learning process, that guide us in coming to know.... (Bouvier, 2022)

Practical laws are human actions that keep relationships in balance and renewal. The laws are contrived from both natural and absolute laws. Practices are influenced by the ethic of natural consequence, meaning, that if humans do not follow practical laws natural consequences can befall the individual, family, community, and/or natural environment. Practical laws come to fruition when observing our natural environments and noticing actions and behaviours that harm or solidify good relations. These laws are practices and/or protocols that establish and maintain ethical relationality. Cree scholar, Willie Ermine (2007), speaks to ethics as knowing what harms or enhances the life of sentient beings. Ethical relationality is using the knowledge of what is harmful or life enduring to guide actions with relatives (Donald, 2016; Kimmerer, 2013). For example, when I harvest sage, I follow protocol, so I have permission to take sage from the earth and use it for health and well-being. Knowing that I am taking the life of the plant, my offering is the acknowledgement that I am taking and honouring the life being given. Taking sage without protocol is ignoring practical laws and will invoke natural consequences. Practical laws exist to keep relationships in balance and with the least amount of conflict and harm between beings. Practical laws are invoked not only between humans-more-than-humans but humans-humans, and humans-self. Human beings are to interfere minimally with creation. If we are to interfere with life forces beyond ourselves, then we enact protocols to signal we are aware of what we are doing and honour the being that will allow us to receive their gifts for survival. Non-interference is a principle of all the laws (Deloria, 1998). As all beings have a spirit thus agency, they invoke their inherent right to decision making. To interfere with this goes against all the laws.

Smudge is a practical law and invokes the teachings of *ikkimmapiiyipitsiin* which Elder Reg Crowshoe translates to sanctified kindness. The essence of this phrase acknowledges that all life forms are equal and deserve the same respect. *ikkimmapiiyipitsiin*, translated through morphemes becomes *ikkimma* (pity) and *piiyipitsiin* (compassion). Elder Reg Crowshoe, explaining pity in the context of the phrase means that we are asking others to take pity on us as we try to be humble and know we will make mistakes. *piiyipitsiin*, means compassion to which we are taught that compassion informs our relationships with all of creation. *ikkimmapiiyipitsiin* acknowledges that we are fallible creatures all deserving of compassion — sanctified kindness.

Ethics and Axiology

Ethics are imperative to Indigenous knowledge systems; they keep individuals accountable to the ways in which we access, protect, analyze, and share information. Ethics are informed by the theory and ontology that mobilize knowledge. Cree scholar Margaret Kovach (2021) frames axiology with this question, "what is the plan for accessing…knowledge" (p. 92). Moreover, our chosen axiology is determined by what knowledge we are accessing (Kovach, 2021). The ethics of respect and disrespect come from an oral system of knowledge, specific to Elder Reg Crowshoe's Piikani perspective (citation). If one acknowledges an emotion, such as anger, and acts respectfully with the protocols needed, the anger will eventually subside. However, if we act with disrespect, it will linger and continue to exhibit itself in our mind, bodies, and relationships. As mentioned in the previous section, protocols are employed to maintain relational balance and harmony therefore, to stay in balance with our emotions, there are protocols to control whatever we are feeling.

Sioux scholar Vine Deloria Jr. (1998) describes respect as being pivotal in the maintenance of good relations. For Deloria (1998), respect encompasses two arteries; embodying self-discipline to act responsibly and establishing communication and agreements with all life forms. Self-discipline is repetitious; protocol is a sustained process, not a one-time transaction. We experience life-forces consistently; we need protocol embedded in the way we engage with others. Self-policing is a term Elder Reg Crowshoe has stressed when learning in an oral knowledge system. Like self-discipline, self-policing inscribes us to be our own source of accountability and internal gauge of ethical conduct. There is a level of awareness we develop as we employ the protocols of engaging with others while simultaneously taking responsibility to learn from our mistakes and incorporate new knowledge into our life.

Communicating with all life forms and constructing agreements is the protocol, or in other words, the gift that we offer life forms to communicate our intentions and act in accordance with ethical priorities. Above, I mentioned the act harvesting sage which I offered tobacco as the ethical binding of the harvest. I communicated my intentions with sage and formed an accord with her on my use of her medicine. Offering her a gift just once does not form and renew our relationship; when I return to harvest, I need to exercise protocol each time. In this example, I am referring to my relationship with sage, but human relationships also need the repetition of offering protocol and forming agreements; this creates trust which is essential in healthy relationships.

SHARING THROUGH AN ORAL KNOWLEDGE SYSTEM: TRUTHING AND CIRCUMAMBULATION

Aachimooshtowihk

aachimooshtowihk — sharing one's declaration, or truth, with others. aachimooshtowihk signals a process of coming together to share one's truth as to inform or direct others; this is truthing. (Graham Andrews, Michif, personal communication, March 2021)

Oral knowledge systems are paralleled to written knowledge, both have theories, processes, practices, assessments, and ethics to understand, generate, renew, and validate knowledge. The differentiation between the two systems is the worldview that governs the processes, practices, and validation of knowledge. Oral systems are governed by processes which are enlivened and protected by smudge; smudge as both the call to convene and connection to all of creation.

Smudge is our first acknowledgement of ourselves in relationship. Through smudge we are signifying "ikkimmapiiyipitsiin (sanctified kindness)…[our obligation] to honour the life of all beings" (Bouvier, 2018, p. 41). Being led by smudge in a learning process, for example a circle, we are obliged to be ethical with our words and actions. Being ethical with our words is the responsibility to be truthful, to say things straight and not mislead or change stories or meanings. Elder Reg Crowshoe translated, "omanii – meaning 'real spirit talk' which invokes a sense of responsibility to be truthful" (Bouvier, 2018, p. 41). The Michif phrase akin to *omanii* is *aachimooshtowihk* meaning sharing one's declaration, or truth, with others.

Aachimooshtowihk is governed by smudge. When you are with smudge, telling your story, there is an individual obligation to be truthful with your word. Additionally, with the smudge, because we are speaking to all of creation, we are responsible to the words we speak, they indeed are powerful. It is important to understand that the truthing process is a shared experience, inherently collective and relational (Little Bear 2009; Maracle 2015; Simpson, 2017, Styres, 2017). Smudge and collective sharing are embedded in the validation of stories, the collective retelling of stories, and the validation of that knowledge; that is a practice of oral recording keeping (Reg Crowshoe, Piikani, personal communication, n.d). Learning together in shared places, we become part of one another's stories through sharing. The layers of perspectives that collective sharing and truthing offer enriches the possibilities of understanding our own story through relating to others.

Storying up Through Circumambulation

Oral knowledge systems perceive the universe as participatory and co-creative thus we are perpetually in experience. Foundational to Indigenous knowledge is understanding that we are co-creative beings consistently engaging with life forces that are inherently always in relationship. Our participation with all of creation is always circular and cyclical.

Figure 2. Beaded medallion

The circle, which is a key element within oral knowledge systems, is both symbolic and processual. Circle, as symbol, is imbued with philosophical associations such as: unity, wholeness, and interconnection while circle, as process, denotes practical ways to conduct gatherings or events in which we assemble, relate, discuss, learn, understand, and make decisions. As seen in Figure 2., beaded medallion, the spiral represents the cyclicality of the circular processes with the cosmological scenery in the background signifying the importance of understanding and enacting the theory and ontology of oral knowledge systems as enlivening the circle. On a general level, circles are a process for validating knowledge and stories which are guided through various protocols and enactments. Each circle, based on who is guiding the circle and for what purpose, may have different ways in which the circle is facilitated.

When practicing circles as informed by Indigenous knowledge systems, Elders' participation and/or guidance is crucial. Elders hold the stories and knowledge of ensuring the circle is facilitated in the proper way. Moreover, they too are part of the truthing process and are looked to when validating knowledge. Often, in an oral system, there are generations of knowledge present. The individuals present have varying degrees of information and thus relied on when needed. This reinforces the oral system of transferring knowledge.

Circle as practice relies on cyclical iterations for knowledge generation and truthing (Maracle, 2015; Simpson, 2017; Styres, 2017). Circularity reveals patterns and consistencies by way of observing stories, experiences, and situations that describe the interactions of us and environments. Through keen observations, understandings, and wisdoms of oneself, relationships are kindled and reaffirmed. Iterative narrative and kinetic processes activate a framework that can broaden understandings of ourselves in our relationships. Maracle (2015) deems ambulating through narratives as storying up; "the story calls upon listeners to lend their imagination and voice to it, contribute to its unfolding, and reshape their conduct based on their personal understanding of the relationship or the absence of relationships" (p. 246). Symbolized through the beaded medallion, storying-up suggests circular iterations guided by a specific epistemological understanding. Circularity is intentional and guided by the purpose or mandate of the gathering.

Maracle's (2015) storying up, aligns fittingly with the term circumambulation — "a ritual term meaning literally 'to walk a circle around' a holy place, person, or object…. One walks around what is set apart, circumscribed as charged or sacred; one might even say that circumambulation sets something apart by circumscribing it with one's own body" (Eck, 2005, p. 1795). Circumambulation is a time old practice in Indigenous cultures all around the world. I have experienced circumambulation; for example, certain ceremonies rely on the number four to guide the amount of rounds the process will be performed in a circle. The reason behind the circumambulated rounds is deemed by the natural and absolute laws and will differ based on the worldview enacted from. Engaging in a collective dialogical and kinetic process by capturing moments in our lived experiences and then narrating them in a collective exemplifies circumambulation. By this, I understand storying up as a process that is reliant on circumambulation through dialogue and engagement to expand and generate understandings that were previously unknown, hidden, and/ or unconscious. Circumambulation is undoubtedly kinetic therefore as should be our learning. Indigenous oral systems require students to perform the teachings, to learn through doing, doing leads to knowing. Moreover, the learning and knowing must be connected to cultural sustainability and relevant to direct lived realities.

Circumambulation is iterative and induces "searching for what lies beneath the obvious" (Maracle, 2015, p. 232) to "transform the way we see, to broaden the field of vision, [and] to inspire us to 'turn around'" (Maracle, 2015, p. 250). Others in the learning include humans and our more-than-human relatives. There is an understanding that beings are present in the circle, either tangibly or intangibly and are considered part of the learning in an oral system. Styres, (2017) reinforces this,

Indigenous rationality considers self to be in-relationship – we exist together here in this place and therefore I do not consider the individual distinct and separate from connected and interdependent relationships to the Land and to the energies that exist within all of creation (human/non-human, animate/inanimate. (p. 112)

Knowledge expansion and generation rely on observing others to mirror beliefs, values, practices that assist in allowing one to understand themselves, as relational beings, in reaffirmed or new ways. Iteration requires time and attention, something that our educational agendas do not often allow. Contemplations need time to grow into understandings, and understandings need time to grow into wisdoms. Affording students time to live out their learning is essential in an oral system.

PEDAGOGICAL APPLICATIONS: ASSESSING STORIES

Through my dissertation, I strived to establish a process by way of an oral knowledge system as how to assess stories for information and understanding. I sought to actively challenge the western education system that places written documentation and assessment at the helm of validating knowing while offering ways that we can learn, document, and assess differently. The process that I articulate for assessing stories below is not mine however, it was taught to me by Elder Reg Crowshoe to which I created my own interpretation of the teachings. Working with Elders to learn about the systematic process of sharing and validating knowledge is essential if we are serious about honouring Indigenous knowledge in institutions. Educational institutions need to consider how we are bringing students into relationship with knowledge and how we are teaching them to assess and carry that knowledge into their everyday lives. I am responsible for bringing what I have learned into places where I teach and to propose processes that can align western and Indigenous knowledge systems beside one another[4]. As I rely on the third perspective (Figure 3.) to inform my own pedagogy, refining it in my own practice exposes students to possibilities and broadens their understanding of learning and assessment.

The assessment framework came from the ground up – literally. As I sat with Elder Reg Crowshoe, repeatedly, in circle, first on a classroom floor, then on a blanket in a tipi, and then while dancing – feet on the ground – in ceremony I did not realize, at the time, I was learning how to see and assess stories and experiences from an oral knowledge system. I am still a learner and will be for the rest of my life and perhaps, with repetition, I will become more refined in the gift of seeing the teachings that stories enwrap. The assessment process I offer below, did not come from books but through my relationship with Elder Reg Crowshoe, with language, and with land. Learning through the oral system invokes a specific kind of listening, one that requires the interaction between my head, heart, body, and spirit (Archibald, 2008; Ermine, 1995; Ghostkeeper, 2007; Holmes, 2000; Meyer, 2013). Listening to stories to discern messages is not only an intellectual act, but it also requires the acknowledgement of your whole being in a symbiotic relationship with other beings, inclusive of the story itself, and the language that the story sits within.

Language

When I talk about a worldview, when I talk about creation, when I talk about who you are, where's your creation, you have the makings of that creation, you know who you are, the language is proof of that creation, so there isn't any difference, that's where I wanted to say from the worldview perspective, you speak from that worldview, than you are who you are. (Reg Crowshoe, Piikani, personal communication, September 5, 2020)

In February 2020, as Elder Reg Crowshoe and I packed up from a day of teaching together, I brought out a piece of paper to show him; I was hoping I had captured his teachings of the third perspective properly (Figure 3.). As someone who makes sense of concepts through visual images, I designed the diagram based on my understandings of the teachings received from him in many circles with smudge. Looking upon the image and hearing my explanation, he replied, "the third perspective is also the language". With an extremely perplexed facial expression, I responded "yes of course!". I walked away from that exchange feeling as if I knew nothing and questioned myself on why I did not catch that. More importantly, as I walked away, I was feeling discouraged, not by what Elder Reg Crowshoe had said, but by knowing that I could not use my Michif language as a third perspective because I can only speak and understand English. I felt hindered by my own limitation of not being able to speak Michif. My inability to speak my language is an enduring trauma and this interaction pointed to that in a very direct way. I am limited by speaking English and expressing myself fully as a Michif woman. Over the years, I have tried to acquire the language of my people little by little. As a researcher and educator, I acknowledge this limitation as I cannot fully "think" through stories as Michif.

Language reflects to the knowledge packages, which are stories, and those knowledge packages, I would say, are how you recognize the world and the environment. (Elder Reg Crowshoe, Piikani, personal communication, September 5, 2019)

Language has its own perspective and worldview. I have heard stories and concepts through Blackfoot and Michif languages, both before and during the research gatherings. I am not a fluent Michif speaker, nor a reliable conversationalist, but I am a learner trying to decolonize my brain and body into thinking from my Michif worldview, a worldview that English cannot offer me. Not being a fluent speaker, I knew I had to depend on those older ones who can speak the language and allow me to experience the worldview through them. Being taught concepts through Blackfoot and Michif, I came into relationship with those ideas differently.

Third Perspective

I feel your story. (Edmee Comstock, Michif, personal communication, January 6, 2020)

That question of what you struggled with, is how we would evaluate, as you move along, because the struggles come from here (points to chest) if we just gave you a test on a piece of paper about the photo, then it will all come from here (points to head) which that happens in school all the time, comes from here, but when we do the smudge and the question, then you're testing from how you connect from the head and heart, then the evaluation is really evaluating from an oral context. (Elder Reg Crowshoe, Piikani, personal communication, January 6, 2020)

One can hear what is being said, but it does not necessarily mean they are listening. We can listen to stories or narratives for entertainment purposes, or we can listen for answers to a lingering question or to receive help with a particular challenge. Storytelling involves a listener and teller, each integral to generating significance from the story. The storyteller's responsibility is communicating the details and to share important nuances of the story. Most often, the teller is skilled in narrating and can paint a vivid picture so the listener can feel part of the story. Like the storyteller, the listener has responsibilities to endure; "Listening is an emotional, spiritual, and physical act. It takes a huge emotional commitment to listen, to sort, to imagine the intent, to evaluate, to process and to seek the connection to the words offered so that remembering can be fair and just" (Maracle, 2015, p. 21). Both entities in the storytelling process have ethical obligations. The teller shares the story as it is known ensuring nothing has been altered or deleted. Moreover, the teller is responsible for stating personal lineage and their connection to the story. Obliged is the listener to listen intentionally, to care for the stories that are offered and to ascertain information that will respect the story and the teller (Archibald, 2008).

Assessing stories is always in action; it is a life skill because to know oneself and our responsibilities we must discern stories. In an oral knowledge system, certain questions are exercised to assess the happenings of classes and when evaluating student assignments. The questions that guide assessment include, how am I/they relating to the story? how is this informing who I/they are becoming and what I/they know? What are the struggles of both the listener and teller and in the story? How will I/they be a good relative and responsible to the story and the source of

Figure 3. The third perspective

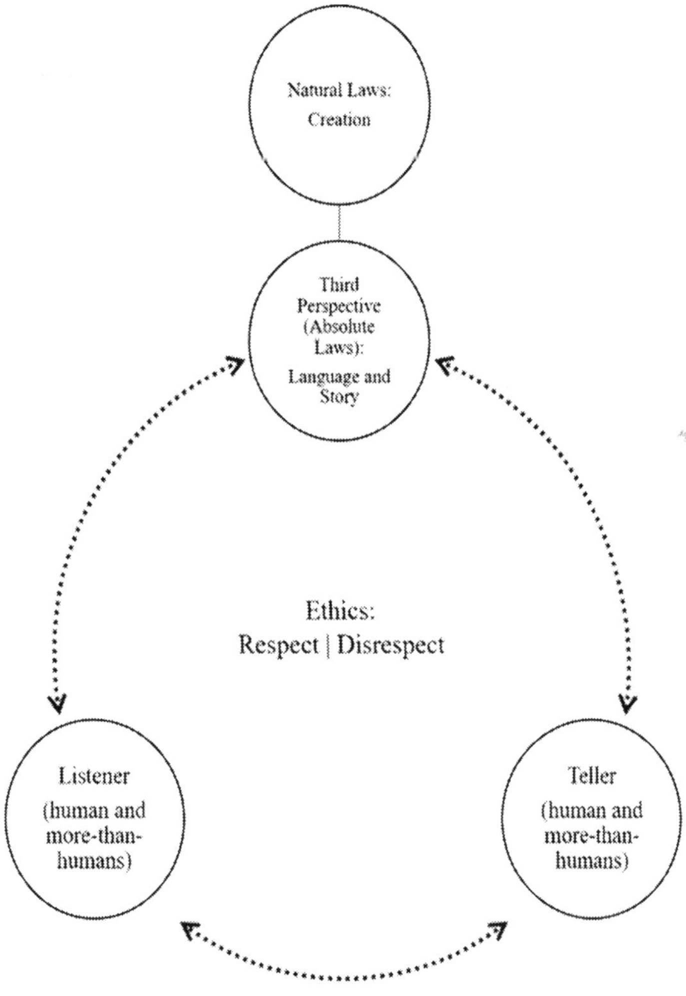

Note: Authors design

the story? In another way, we can see these questions as they relate to the creation that I shared earlier in the chapter. Original emotion, thought, creation, and sound formulate these questions. The struggle Creator was having with his emotion of lonesomeness, encouraged him to think about how to relate to his feelings thus deciding to act and create the Earth. *Thereafter, infusing sound into the earth giving all of creation their own languages.*

The third perspective (Figure 3.) induces a process that is derived from an oral systematic approach to knowledge acquisition. The third perspective is a relational enactment and a knowledge spirit. As a concept, the perspective asserts the listener and teller are engaging with other beings that are within story. Further, the language is also a perspective as it houses a worldview that informs how we perceive ourselves and our relationships. Moreover, the perspective, as a being, has its own agency and autonomy within the context of the interaction with the listener and the teller. The three do not collapse into one another yet inform each other and create knowledge that is then used for life purposes. In relying on this process, the listener engages with the teller while "seeing" their story as its own entity that holds knowledge. The listener is tending to the story with the intention of garnering what is meant for the listener to discern. Because the story itself is a being, the listener is to pay closer attention to the feelings, thoughts, acting, and saying within the story rather than the teller themselves. Elder Reg Crowshoe affirmed the role of telling and listening is to address the story, not the teller – to not make it personal.

Having a relationship with the third perspective, with the knowledge spirit, the listener has the opportunity to peel back layers of the stories to see what is beneath and how they are mirrored to the listener (Maracle, 2015). The power of stories is they can show us ourselves in such a way that we may not have considered before. The third perspective is also generative in that through the stories that are created, the teller and listener become a separate third perspective thus the third perspective is always being generated. The process of the third perspective is generative as each time we enter the triadic relationship, more stories will be created. Collective truthing occurs when we engage individually with the story then by hearing the interpretations and insights of others. Through this, narratives culminate and form patterns thus becoming central in meaning making.

Relying on the third perspective to provide a lens to "see" stories as their own beings with knowledge, over time listening and assessing skills are refined. "Observe looking for relationships between various things in it. That is to say, everything in the natural world has relationships with every other thing and the total set of relationships makes up the natural world as we experience it" (Deloria, 1998, p.34). As our listening and discerning skills sharpen, we can see patterns and relationships within a large network of stories and relationships.

The common adage associated with Indigenous worldviews is, all my relations, or we are all related. The Michif phrase, wahkootowin, reflects "all my relations in creation". Métis scholar, Brenda MacDougall (2010), expresses wahkootowin, "[i]n short, this world-view, wahkootowin, is predicated upon a specific Aboriginal notion and definition of family as a broadly conceived sense of relatedness with all beings, human and non-human, living and dead, physical and spiritual" (p. 3). Once we assess stories for meaning and understanding, we transpose of our learning onto our relationships to discern our responsibilities and how to live and enact goodness and make connections between ourselves and larger systems that we are a part of.

CONCLUSION

There is an existing tension between Western academic and Indigenous knowledge systems because they validate knowledge differently and have differing views of what constitutes knowledge. Having an oral knowledge system inform my pedagogical approaches and how I am defining knowledge and knowing has not been without challenges. The bureaucracy alone is a deterrent for many who want to engage with this work in their institutions. The lack of resources to support this work as well as the recurring cognitive imperialism (Battiste, 2013) makes it difficult to gain momentum and/or sustainability. Venue, action, language, and song, as well as the practices embedded in an Indigenous oral system have the capacity to guide us to a place wherein, we can imagine a different way of learning, knowing, and assessing Knowledge. Imaging, however, cannot be without the guidance and expertise of Elders and knowledge keepers. Their knowledge is equivalent to master's and doctoral degrees and therefore should be acknowledged and treated as such. To be serious about Indigenization, means to be serious about Indigenous knowledge and their systems that protect it. There are brilliant Indigenous scholars and educators who are already doing the work and challenging the Western academic institutions to do better in the face of reconciliation and decolonization. We need, however, all faculties, departments, and disciplines to make the necessary changes to re-centre the knowledge that comes from the land and the people to whose territories we reside.

REFERENCES

Battiste. (2013). *Decolonizing education : nourishing the learning spirit*. Purich Publishing Limited.

Bouvier, V. (2018). Truthing: An ontology of living an ethic of shakihi (love) and ikkimmapiipitsin (santified kindness). *Canadian Social Studies*, *50*(2), 39–44. doi:10.29173/css17

Bouvier, V. (2022). *Kaa-waakohtoochik (The ones who are related to each other): An inquiry of Métis understandings with/in/through the city* [Doctoral thesis, University of Calgary]. University of Calgary. https://prism.ucalgary.ca

Bouvier, V., & MacDonald, J. (2019). Spiritual Exchange: A Methodology for a Living Inquiry With All Our Relations. *International Journal of Qualitative Methods*, *18*. doi:10.1177/1609406919851636

Cajete, G. (2017). Children, myth and storytelling: An Indigenous perspective. *Global Studies of Childhood*, *7*(2), 113–130. doi:10.1177/2043610617703832

Deloria, V., Deloria, B., Foehner, K., & Scinta, S. (1998). *Spirit & reason the Vine Deloria Jr., reader*. Fulcrum.

Donald, D. (2016). Homo economicus and forgetful curriculum: Remembering other ways to be a human being. In J. Seidel, & D. W. Jardine (Eds.), Indigenous Education: New Direction in Theory and Practice (pp. 10-17). New Your: Peter Lang.

Donald, D. (2019). Homo economicus and forgetful curriculum. In J. Seidel, & D. W. Jardine (Eds.), Indigenous education: New directions in theory and practice (pp.103-125). New Your: Peter Lang.

Eck, D. L. (2005). Circumambulation. In L. Jones (Ed.), Encyclopedia of Religion (2nd ed., Vol. 3, pp. 1795–1798). World Catalogue.

Ermine, W. (2007). Ethical space of engagement. *Indigenous Law Journal at the University of Toronto Faculty of Law*, *6*(1), 193–203.

Kimmerer, R. W. (2013). *Braiding sweetgrass: Indigenous wisdom, scientific knowledge and the teachings of plants*. Milkweed Editions.

Kovach, M. (2021). *Indigenous methodologies: characteristics, conversations and contexts* (2nd ed.). University of Toronto Press.

Little Bear, L. (2009). Jagged worlds colliding. In M. Battiste (Ed.), *Reclaiming Indigenous voice and vision* (pp. 77–85). UBC Press.

Macdougall, B. (2010). *One of the family: Metis culture in nineteenth- century northwestern Saskatchewan*. UBC Press.

Maracle, L. (2015). *Memory serves oratories*. NeWest.

Meyer, M. A. (2013). Holographic epistemology: Native common sense. *China Media Research*, *9*(2), 94–101.

Napier, K. (2013, November 28). *Reg Crowshoe - Venue, Action, Language and Song* [Video]. Youtube. https://www.youtube.com/watch?v=HDOrB6RvdlU

Peltier, S. (2014). Assessing Anishinaabe children's narratives: An ethnographic exploration of Elders' perspectives. *Canadian Journal of Speech-language Pathology and Audiology : CJSLPA = Revue Canadienne d'Orthophonie et d'Audiologie : RCOA*, *38*(2), 174–193.

Simpson, L. B. (2017). *As we have always done: Indigenous freedom through radical resistance*. University of Minnesota Press. doi:10.5749/j.ctt1pwt77c

Styres, S. (2017). *Pathways for remembering and recognizing Indigenous thought in education: philosophies of Iethi'nihsténha Ohwentsia'kékha (land)*. University of Toronto Press.

KEY TERMS AND DEFINITIONS

Oral Knowledge System: An oral knowledge system is a systematic process informed by Indigenous knowledge, specific to a certain locale, that guides how information is accessed, assessed, and validated.

Aachimooshtowihk: (Michif phrase) Sharing one's declaration, or truth, with others. aachimooshtowihk signals a process of coming together to share one's truth as to inform or direct others; this is truthing.

Storying Up: A process that is reliant on iterative dialogue and engagement to expand and generate understandings that were previously unknown, hidden, and/or unconscious.

Circumambulation: This is referred to as performing rituals or ceremonies is a circular manner repeatedly over time and in a certain place.

The Third Perspective: The third perspective is a relational enactment and a knowledge spirit. As a relational enactment, the third perspective asserts that listeners and tellers of stories are engaging with other beings that are within story and to see the story for meaning and understanding through these relationships.

Ikkimmapiiyipitsiin: (Blackfoot phrase) Sanctified kindness. The essence of this phrase acknowledges that all life forms are equal and deserve the same respect.

Michif: The language spoken by Métis people in certain areas of Canada. This term is also used a cultural identifier.

ENDNOTES

[1] This chapter is derived from my doctoral dissertation, see citation in the references list.

[2] Because the teachings of Elder Reg Crowshoe, from the Blackfoot Piikani nation, were provided in a specific venue with specific actions to validate knowledge, he has provided guidance to me as to how to properly reference his teachings. The teachings I share in this chapter have been shared with me through proper protocol and with smudge. By articulating this, I am stating that Elder Reg Crowshoe has given me permission to share this knowledge.

[3] Research proposal as deemed in the Education faculty.

[4] For example, see Bouvier and MacDonald, 2019, and Bouvier and MacDonald, forthcoming.

Embodying Knowledge and Pedagogy Through an Indigenous Oral System

Chapter 3
Circle Work:
Being Together as a Relation

Carolyn Roberts
University of the Fraser Valley, Canada

ABSTRACT

Circle work has been used by Indigenous people since time out of mind. This pedagogical practice creates spaces of relationality and community building within our current day educational system. This space that Circle work creates allows for a learning community to understand our interconnectedness as humans and helps to develop empathy for others. Circle work brings people together in our humanity rather than dividing us in our differences, focusing on community building, with the hope of giving people the opportunity to actively decolonize how they educate within the classroom. This practice can be used by all educators willing to step into a wholistic teaching practice within their classroom.

INTRODUCTION

ha7lh skwáyel ta néwyap, Carolyn Roberts kwi en sna, men Janet Baker and Ed Kelly. Tiná7 chen t'la skwxwú7mesh úxwumixw, N'quat'qua úxwumixw, Tzeachten úxwumixw

(Introducing myself in my ancestral language of Skwxwú7mesh sníchim).

    I write this chapter with humility and respect for my connection to my relatives, my ancestors, and the Indigenous voices that I have learned from as both a student and educator. This sharing of knowledge is from my own personal lived experiences in the BC education system. My hope is that those who step into the work of bringing

DOI: 10.4018/978-1-6684-3425-3.ch003

Indigenous pedagogies into their classrooms will choose to build their own personal knowledge of Indigenous pedagogies, and engage in the work in a way that will not only support their personal learning, but benefit their classroom and students.

My name is Carolyn Roberts, and I come from a long line of ancestors that have been living with and on this land for thousands of years. My ancestors from my mother's side (Janet Baker) are from the Thevarge family from N'Quatqua Nation. My father's side (Ed Kelly) are from the Kelly Family from the Tzeachten Nation. Under the governmental policy of the Indian Act, I am a member of the Squamish Nation, because my mother married a Squamish man.

Circle work has been a practice in Indigenous communities since time out of mind. The practice of working in Circle helps support learning and community building, and offers a space for healing. In this chapter, I discuss Circle work as a pedagogical tool to use within the classroom or other educational spaces. The Circle work framework that I will present is a pedagogical tool and not a ceremonial or spiritual practice. It is a tool that can be used within any classroom, by all educators, to help build community and decolonize teaching practice.

There are five concepts found in Circle work: relationality, decolonization, witnessing, anti-racism, and time. Relationality is a foundational concept within Circle work, as it is built upon the understanding that everything we do in education is based on relationships. Decolonized teacher practice is a way that all educators can start to dismantle the educational system from within. Witnessing is a practice that is found within some Indigenous communities as a way to engage with the oral traditions of sharing Indigenous knowledges. It is a participatory practice that goes beyond just listening to someone share their knowledge with you, and asks you to be an active participant in the process of creating knowledge. Anti-racist education is critical in the work of education today. A crucial step in anti-racism work is when educational spaces are allowed to be a place where Indigenous students, Black students, and students who are people of colour are welcomed and shown that their voice has a place within the classroom. The colonial concept of time within the education system is something that educators find themselves fighting against the moment they arrive in their classroom. Time is dictated by the bell system, report cards, recess, lunch, learning deadlines, and the list goes on. Circle work is an invitation to create a different concept of time in the classroom.

While there are many educational benefits to using Circle work in the classroom, some key values are building community, allowing time for students and educators to create relationships, and enhancing communication skills. Circle work provides students and educators the opportunity to hear each other's voices in the classroom. Bringing in student voice, worldviews, and life experiences opens up the classroom as a space for learning about how to be anti-racist with each other.

As an educator, I have found the practice of Circle work to be transformative for my students within my many classrooms. It can bring humanity to the education process by building relationships and creating the space for a learning community to grow. Relationships are the foundation of all the work we do in education. Without the foundation of relationships, it is challenging to learn from each other, and to grow. I have used Circle work in my current post-secondary classrooms, with my school teams as a principal and vice principal, and in my classrooms as a K-12 educator in the public school system. I invite all educators into this work of supporting your classrooms and pedagogical practice through Circles: whether you come to this practice as an Indigenous person or a non-Indigenous person, please keep in mind that it is important to always acknowledge, in the opening of the Circle, that the origin of Circle work comes from Indigenous knowledge systems.

Canada's Truth and Reconciliation Report (Truth and Reconciliation Commission of Canada [TRC], 2015) reported the stories of the Indigenous peoples' of Canada experiences in the Indian Residential School System that was in place for more than one hundred years. Through these stories, the report created the 94 Calls to Action for the government to address the harm that was done within these places they called schools. The hope of the report was to build a road map to reconcile the relationship between the Canadian government and the Indigenous peoples of this land. Within the 94 Calls to Action is the call for the government to make mandatory the inclusion of Indigenous education courses, Indigenous pedagogies, and knowledges within the education system across Canada. This was intended to address all that has been left out of the Canadian education system to date, as it relates to the history of Indigenous peoples and their land. The educational Calls to Action in the TRC report have had an impact on teacher practice and curriculum in British Columbia's (BC's) education system. The BC Ministry of Education and Child Care has now made it mandatory to teach Indigenous histories, Indigenous pedagogies, and Indigenous knowledges in all BC classrooms. Introducing these practices to colonized classrooms comes with its own challenges; research shows that there has been a long history of misrepresentation and appropriation of Indigenous knowledges and pedagogies in the colonized classroom (Battiste, 2013a; Brayboy, 2005; Cote-Meek, 2014; Dion, 2022; Johnston-Goodstar, & VeLure Roholt, 2017). With this in mind, I encourage you to walk gently into this work. Take the time needed to learn about Circle work and how to approach it with an open heart and mind in the classroom. With this intention, the work will happen in a good way in your classrooms.

PREPARING YOURSELF

Indigenous and non-Indigenous educators are all welcome and encouraged to use this pedagogical tool. As you prepare for this work, know that it will take practice to get comfortable using Circle work in your classroom. Comfort might not come right away, so be gentle and kind to yourself as you practice, and make sure you plan for the time needed for the work. In my personal practice, I prepare easy opening questions about favourite foods, music, or movies that will help the group get to know each other. This light work and easy conversation helps people within the group make connections as the community starts to grow.

If it is our very first Circle together, I always open with who I am and who my ancestors are, as I did at the opening of this chapter. I let the Circle know whose shoulders I stand upon, because within my voice they will hear those voices who have come before me. I let them know who my mother and father are, and the communities I am connected to. I then offer the group an opportunity to introduce themselves in a similar way. This first introduction, where the group shares who they are and where they come from, helps them get to know each other on a deeper level and is the kind of introduction that is traditionally done within many Indigenous communities. Be mindful when setting this up, as some people may be uncomfortable with sharing. Some people may not know their family information, or may feel that they don't want to share those close details, so always allow them the space and grace to say that they are unsure, or that they would like to pass. It may take some people more time to feel comfortable or safe before they start to share personal information within the group. Again, walk with care into this work.

Relationality

For me, relationality is kinship, and kinship is a reminder that we are all connected. When working in the K-12 system, I was aware that administrators have the ability to build a culture of care in their schools, in the same way that educators have the ability to create a culture of care in their classrooms. I know from personal experience, that when I have students in a Circle with each other, the energy in the room always shifts, from the wild hum of buzzing in every corner of the room, to the eventual synergy of buzzing together. I found that Circles helped students to remember that we are all connected.

Circle work allows for relationality, a shift from being alone in the classroom to walking with and beside each other as a community. Martha Brown and Sherri Di Lallo (2020) discuss this concept as of walking together as a relationality-based method of teaching. They argue that the connection of walking together is what centers and grounds the relationship we have with each other, it and gives us a deeper understanding of what it means to care for each other. I concur with their thinking of grounding teaching practice as a relational based practice. Daniel Heath Justice (2018) opens his book, *Why Indigenous Literatures Matter*, with questions about how we can care for each other, and how we behave as good relatives, ancestors, and humans. Justice is asking us how we can honour and treat each other as family or kin. I believe this is needed in our world today, as we come out of the global pandemic and two years of separation.

When we build this community of relationship in Circle work, we are inviting people to see each other as whole human beings, and as relatives. This relational concept is shown within Indigenous languages that are rooted in a relationship-based context (Rosborough et al., 2017). For example, some Indigenous languages do not use names to speak about people in your family, and instead use terms that show the relationship you have with that person, like aunty, uncle, or brother. The kinship-like relationship fostered in Circle work supports a positive learning environment.

Nel Nodding (2012) argues that the goal for all teachers and educational policymakers should be a climate where caring relationships can flourish. Circle work supports a flourishing environment of care with those in the circle by building relationships with students and educators. The environment of care and relationality begins with how the Circle is set up. While you are in Circle, whether sitting or standing, you are facing each other. No one is in front, and no one is behind, creating a space that honours everyone, and where you can physically see each other when talking and sharing. Circle work is facilitated not from a hierarchical position, but from a position as a member of the Circle's learning community, moving beyond the colonial hierarchy of power and control. The Circle facilitates a discussion that equalizes and respects each member (Kanu, 2011). Having people in a Circle with no tables in front of them means that you are removing the opportunity for people to be separated by an object, and to be disconnected behind the technology and cellphones that students and participants usually bring. Eliminating the distraction of these devices, and the millions of things that are happening in the outside world, allows people in the Circle to be present with each other in the work, to focus on what is happening in the room, and to be fully engaged in the moment.

When opening the Circle, it is respectful to remind people that they are encouraged to share, but that they have a choice to speak or not to speak. Creating the space and grace for people to be open with each other and to share their experiences through their own stories takes time and consistency: this is how we create a community of care. Getting to know each other and listening to each other takes time, so this needs to be approached as a practice. Practising Circles each time you do work together creates and builds a community of relations and kin.

Preparing the Space

In education, we do not always have control over the spaces in which we teach, and this can make it challenging to create your ideal space for Circle work. We do have some control over making the space we are given as inviting as possible for this work. Circle work can happen in many different spaces: you are welcome to go outside and make a Circle, you can sit in Circle, you can stand in Circle. The key factor is to be in a Circle formation that, if possible, is free of any objects in the middle of the Circle, such as tables or bags. This open space connects to the relational accountability of being present in the Circle. If you are in a classroom setting, using chairs, it is important to prepare the space in advance by setting the Circle up with a chair for each person expected, it helps to show you as the facilitator when everyone is there. In my teaching, I have been told that if there are empty chairs, this means it is our ancestors joining us, so do not worry if there are more chairs then people in the space. If you have tables in the classroom space, move them to the side and do not leave them in the center of the circle. This allows for students and participants a place to put their belongings, away from them and the circle.

As the facilitator, make a point of welcoming people into the space in a kind and authentic way. Try as best you can to say hello and welcome everyone entering the room. This will help support how people are feeling as they are stepping into the work together, keeping in mind that you as the facilitator are a guide for the Circle work and a participant as well.

Decolonization

The current education system is built on the western colonial education model (Battiste, 2013a; Brayboy, 2005; Cote-Meek, 2014; Dion, 2022; Johnston-Goodstar, & VeLure Roholt, 2017). This model is top down, and is what Marie Battiste (2013b) says is, "marinated in [Eurocentrism]" (p.6). What is needed in decolonizing the classroom is a move away from what Paulo Freire (1970) calls the "banking concept" of education. This concept speaks to the way in which students are sitting passively within the classroom, acquiring knowledge not fully engaged in the learning process. Students in this environment are consumers of information, rather than active participants in the learning process.

Circle work decolonizes and changes the power relations that are steeped in colonial hierarchy and marinated in eurocentrism by changing the structure of the classroom and allowing for all members of the circle to have a voice and actively participate in the learning. In the colonized classroom, there is usually only one voice heard, one story told, and one way of teaching and being taught (Brayboy & Maughan, 2009). Circle work creates connections and shifts the learning from individual learning from the educator to the whole group learning from each other. It takes away the "banking concept" (Freire, 1970) where only the teacher knows everything, and the students are just empty vessels to fill up with knowledge. Circle work allows for all members of the Circle to be knowledge holders of their own lived experiences, and to be honoured, heard, and active together as participants in the learning process.

Jean-Paul Restoule (2018) outlines in his work that Indigenous pedagogies are based on interactions with each other and a response to the needs of the group to support learning. Circle work connects to Restoule's (2018) work by allowing for an interactive learning environment in the classroom that is responsive to students' needs by bringing in their voices and their lived experiences as knowledge holders into the classroom. Circle work uses the approach where the participant is the expert (Brown & Di Lallo, 2020). Honouring students, and hearing student voice in the classroom, is part of a decolonizing teaching process of moving the learning to a shared endeavour where the educator and students work together in the knowledge making process.

Witnessing

Witnessing in Circle work is foundational. Witnessing asks people to show up and to be fully present with each other in the moment, which is a skill that can be developed over time in classroom environments. Witnessing is defined from an Indigenous lens in *You Are Asked to Witness* (Carlson, 1997), which shares with readers the importance of being a witness within the ceremonial work of the Stò:lō people do within community and is a practice that has been done since time out of mind. A practice in oral traditions that is the foundational piece of passing on cultural knowledge to the next generation.

Within ceremonial work, it is a great responsibility to be asked to be a witness. You are accepting the honour to be the knowledge holder and truth teller of what is shared at that moment within the ceremony in that Indigenous community. It is then your responsibility to pass on the knowledge you have witnessed to your own Indigenous community, and to the next generation of Indigenous people in your community. If people have questions about the ceremony that you witnessed, it is your responsibility to be the truth teller and to relate what has happened. This responsibility to the work puts the listener/observer in a different relationship to what is happening around them, it requires you to be fully present and fully aware of all that is going on, so that they can be the truth teller of the story. Within oral communities, there are no books or written forms that are keepers of the stories. This makes witnessing very important in passing knowledge down to the next generation.

Circle Work

In Circle work, witnessing is also crucial. When you are in Circle together, you are required to be fully present with each other, listening to those around you share their stories and knowledge. This skill of being silent can be developed, and is an essential tool in Circle work. Circle work engages students with the opportunity to understand the importance of silence as part of the work done together as a community. Being able to center yourself and pause, and being able to listen without having to think about how you will respond or how you will try to help solve problems, is a practiced skill that serves people well when working through challenging situtations. When you are silent and listening to others – listening to listen, and not listening to respond – you are taking the responsibility to be fully engaged with what you are hearing. You are showing up as your full self, being present, listening respectfully, setting aside all other things, and committing to being together in the moment. This is also known as active listening, which helps us to avoid projecting our own thinking, feelings, and opinions onto others, and to instead really listen to people's stories. This skill gives us the opportunity to better understand people from the perspective of their own personal lived experience. This is a pedagogical approach that Fyre Graveline (1998) helps us to understand:

When we see silence only as produced through an exercise in domination, we are missing the significance of silence to voice. Aboriginal people are taught to respect silence as a pedagogical tool. In circle, we listen "as witnesses", respectfully, to the experience of others. (p. 145)

Graveline (1998) argues that being a witness to others honours our lived experiences and allows us to see each other as whole human beings. Witnessing then allows for Circle work to build bonds with people and supports a community of safety and trust. Witnessing is important as we build communities in educational classrooms as a way to dismantle colonial practices that have historically silenced voices in the classroom.

Anti-Racism

Circle work is a practice in decolonization as well as anti-racism. Erica Buchanan-Rivera's (2022) work in racial justice and identity affirming classrooms argues that creating liberatory spaces for students is not created by chance, but through intentional actions and equitable practices that are rooted in justice, collectivism, and accountability. I agree with Rivera's work, and believe that Circle work as a practice supports racial justice as a way of including all voices within the classroom, and building connections with students to support collectivism and accountability within the classroom. Circle work provides opportunities for students and communities to remove the hierarchy of power where the educator holds the knowledge and directs the class in a "banking concept" (Freire, 1970) style, and to instead allow the classroom to become a space of powerful opportunities for all voices to be heard within the conversations that happen within the Circle (Graveline, 1998).

Decades of scholarship in anti-racist education have acknowledged the power imbalance found within the classroom for Indigenous and non-white students. For instance, Lomawaima, (2000) explains, and I agree, that, "[t]he history of American Indian education can be summarized in three simple words: battle for power" (p.2). Lomawaima (2000) argues that Indigenous students have had generations of education within the western colonial system without having a voice within the curriculum or classroom. Circle work shifts this narrative to create space for Indigenous students to engage in a dialogue within the classroom, have a voice, and share their stories. This equalization of power happens because Circle work is facilitated and not directed by the teacher, thus encouraging those who have been historically silenced or marginalized to share their voice. The Circle is a space for contributions from all voices, and witnessing creates opportunities to share without being interrupted, spoken over, or spoken for. This empowers those in the Circle to find their voice, and affords listeners the opportunity to increase their empathy and understanding of lived experiences that may differ from their own.

Students that have been historically silenced in classrooms tend to use silence as a shield to protect their well-being (Pedro, 2014). Pedro's (2014) research addresses how Indigenous students make a conscious choice to stay silent within a western colonial classroom, instead of engaging with knowledge that does not acknowledge their existence. Indigenous students are continuously being told that they and their ancestors do not have a voice in the curriculum. This speaks to how the curriculum being taught was not created for Indigenous students, and builds upon the concept that people who have been historically silenced in the classroom and in the curriculum find it difficult to speak up within colonial classrooms. Circle work in the classroom changes this narrative and gives students who have been silenced in education the space and grace to speak and to be heard, allows for listeners to listen, and listeners to witness what happens in the Circle. This is an entry point for people to find their voice, and allows them the opportunity to take up space and speak up rather than sitting in silence.

With deep listening and human connections comes a transformative classroom of deep conversations that might not have happened within the colonial classrooms. Creating a strong community, and the room for brave and safe spaces, opens up opportunities to unpack difficult topics and collaborate on ways to work together. Circle work can be a place where social justice can manifest through open dialogue, and where the development of communication skills creates opportunities for students to learn about their own privilege and their own personal bias (Graveline, 1998).

Circle Work

When you have the opportunity for critical dialogue in the classroom, opportunities for learning about harmful social norms and racism can be a part of the learning process and allow for conversations with those who deal with racism and oppression on a daily basis to share how they are impacted.

Knowing and understanding that Circle work is a practice, when you first start doing Circles in a new group, you may find that people are uncomfortable with being open and vulnerable in a new space. This can stem from people wanting to avoid situations that make them feel discomfort or uneasiness, as research from Brown and Di Lallo (2020) has stated. Understanding that this work can make people feel uncomfortable makes it important to step in to this work gently and remind people about what Circle work is and why you are doing it in your classroom. To help support people who are not feeling ready to be open in the circle, you can also remind them that they do not have to share and they are always welcome to pass. If you continue to practice Circles with the same group, this discomfort may dissipate with time. Building the community and safe environment for people to be comfortable in, will support that safe and open space for people to share. This does not happen overnight; it is a practice. Circle work does not remove racism, prejudice, or implicit bias that people may bring into the Circle, but the Circle does allow the opportunity for people to see other people, and hear directly about their lived experiences, and there is hope that this introduces a connection and empathy with each other. When in Circle, it is important to be reflective about our own assumptions and biases. We must be critically aware of our own worldview and privilege, and how our thoughts and circumstances may not align with others in the Circle. Most importantly, we must be humble in a |Circle and demonstrate an open heart and open mind to the experiences of others. When you step into the Circle, stay curious and be open.

Circle work is a tool that contributes to anti-racism work in the classroom and school communities. Graveline's (1998) research shows this through reflections from her research participants:

Not until last week have I come to total grips with the fact that the incident two years ago was not a personal attack on me, but indeed a direct product of oppression. I only fully realised this after hearing a class full of students sharing their experiences of oppression last week. It hit me, if I experienced the oppression on a daily basis even half as strong as some of the students said they did, then I would most likely express anger and frustration in not so appropriate ways. (Ken, Jan 29, as cited in Graveline, 1998, p.145.)

Through Ken's reflection, he really listened to and heard the lived experience of oppression from his students. By actively listening to and witnessing stories of the harm, he was able to see the devastating impacts of racism and oppression.

Using Circle work in your community, and encouraging people to honestly speak about their lived experiences, will create an opening to address the daily racism that happens in the education system. As an Indigenous person, I don't always have the opportunity to speak up about – and speak back to – the harms that I endure on a daily basis. In higher education, I often find myself in unwelcoming spaces that do not allow me to share my voice and ideas, because there is no space for Indigenous voices. Having the opportunity and space to speak in Circles helps me to survive the harm I endure daily within educational spaces. This underlines the importance of giving everyone in the Circle the opportunity to speak.

Brown and Di Lallo (2020) discuss the importance of allowing the time and space for the "magic" to happen within Circles, as they are the space for social justice and an equalization of the playing field for all voices. Jo Ann Archibald (2019) calls this the "synergy" of the work. When you take the time to practice Circles and build community, the synergy of the Circle connects all those who participate, and it becomes transformative. The synergy changes the energy of the group by shifting from separate people, to a group collective.

As we move into new ways of educating, it is critical for educators to listen to and hear the voices of the students in our classrooms. This is key learning in shifting our lens to a decolonial and anti-racist view. It is also important for the facilitator of the Circle to have a knowledge and understanding of how racism occurs and unfolds in the colonial education system, so that they do not perpetuate racism within the Circle. For example, if a racist comment is said within the Circle, it must be addressed at the time it is said. By not immediately addressing the incident, both the comment and the lack of action become acts of aggression and racism (Cote-Meek, 2014). The facilitator is then compounding the act of racism by letting unaddressed words and comments continue to harm those who have heard them. No one in the Circle can feel safe and heard.

Harm can also be experienced when people are asked and expected to speak on behalf of their community or nationality. This practice functions as a form of "racial spotlighting". Dorinda Carter Andrew (Carter Andrews et al., 2019) defines racial spotlighting as placing students in the position of being a token spokesperson for their entire race; often, the student will be brought to the front of a classroom to be the point person on everything related to their race or ethnicity. As Carter Andrews et al (2019) go on to explain, this practice – whether well-meaning or not – functions as a racial microaggression as it contributes to highlighting a student's minority race status, making them uncomfortable, silent, and even worried that they will be called upon to answer things they may not know anything about. This is unsettling for students, and could make them either avoid attending class, avoid participation, or even withdraw from the class.

Circle Work

Both of these examples show how racism and harm can happen within the Circle space. It prioritizes the importance for facilitators of Circle work to have a background knowledge in anti-racist practices, race, and racism in the classroom, so that they do not continue to expose students to harm within this work.

Time

When I share Circle work with leadership teams and educational teams, one of the biggest reasons for a reluctance to do this work is that it is time consuming and just not feasible in the fast-paced, time-centered world of education. Noel Gough (2002) uses the term "clockwork curriculum", meaning that everything within the school system is driven by time, and where it can feel like there is never enough time for anything meaningful. This is modeled in the education system with bells guiding the day, recess, lunch, prep time, report card periods, class times, assemblies, holidays, Pro-D Days, and the list goes on. My personal experience with Circle work has proven that the transformation of relationships and connections that happen within a Circle far outweigh the consumption of time.

Time as we know it in the school system is a colonial, linear, western concept that controls all of the spaces in education. It is something that is commodified and consumed, like almost everything else in society. The concept of time within many Indigenous communities is very different from the colonial concept of time. In many Indigenous communities, and from my personal experience of being in my home Indigenous community, things take the time they need. For me, this means that once you step into the work, you are there until the work is done. There is no compartment of time where you start at a prescribed hour and end at a prescribed hour. The way it works is when things start, then the work begins, it doesn't matter if it is ceremonial or educational. Then when the work is done, then you are done, but there is no set time for this to happen. You learn at the pace you learn at, you are supported through out the process, and once you have completed the work or mastered the work, then you are done.

The pressure of colonial time puts demands on the learning process, and the space needed for learners to authentically engage in learning. Colonial time is one of the most stressful challenges in the education system. Circle work takes time because there is no quick fix, quick method, or fast tracking to building community. Meaningful interactions with other students in the learning community builds the foundation of the space needed for relationships to grow.

Facilitating and leading groups through Circle work will take practice, but the outcome will be priceless. I use the term practice intentionally, as it will take practice and time to commit to this work as part of your teacher or administrator practice, in the same way you need to practice an instrument or train for a sport. As you get to know your team or students, you will be able to feel their energy, and know how they are doing and if they need support. This kind of connection and relationality is essential as we come out of a worldwide pandemic and isolation. Knowing your group as kin will allow relationality so that your group can come to this work with a different and deeper understanding of care for each other. This comes from actively listening, witnessing, and honouring each other, rather than actively talking, trying to fix problems, or come up with solutions to the issues of the day.

FACILITATING CIRCLE WORK

These are some steps that I use to bring Circle work into my classroom:

When possible, I have students in chairs in the formation of a Circle with tables off to the side. If people are missing that day and there are more chairs than people, then I know that our ancestors are with us.

If we are in an outdoor space, or if we have been sitting for a long time, I encourage the Circle to be a standing Circle.

I start the Circle by letting people know who I am and whose shoulders I stand upon. I do this out of respect for the ancestors that have come before me, and speak through me in the work that I do as an educator.

I offer the Circle as a space for us to grow and build our learning community.

I open up the Circle by inviting people to step in with an open heart and open mind. If there are late arrivals, I invite them to join us.

I speak to the importance of being a witness within the Circle. This means that when it is time for people to speak, everyone else is asked to be a respectful witness to their words, listening with an open heart and mind, and not talking. This shows that everyone's contribution to the Circle is important and of equal value.

I make sure that everyone in the group has a chance to share, if they would like to, by inviting them to share or speak within all conversations. So that this is not an oppressive structure for those who are not comfortable in the space, II allow for people to speak or not to speak, if that is their choice. Silence is an acceptable response for when people choose not to speak. I honour and support people's choices by nodding and moving on to the next speaker.

It is important for all voices to be honoured and heard within the Circle; it is important that once a Circle is opened, everyone who is in the Circle stays there until the Circle is complete.

At the end of the Circle, I welcome people to share whatever they are feeling, or whatever they would like to put into the Circle before we close for the day. This gives people the opportunity to close the Circle in a way that feels best for them.

When doing this work as a facilitator, you may encounter strong emotions within the Circle, and it is the role of the facilitator to remain aware and honour those feelings. Understanding that these emotions could contribute to experiences of harm and oppression for others in the Circle, the facilitator needs to have a solid understanding of how microaggressions and racism harm people, so that they can address any harm that could happen in Circle, and so that they have approaches for addressing strong emotions. Circle work is cultivated as a safe space where people can be fully who they are as humans; this means that the facilitator needs the ability to see everyone in their fullness, as well as understand their own personal privilege and biases.

I have described the steps that I use to bring the pedagogical tool of Circle work to my classrooms. These steps may not be the same for all people who do Circle work; if you choose to do Circle work in your classroom, take some time to discover the steps that are best for you as an educator within the work. In sharing the ways that I engage in Circle work, I am offering a starting point for your own exploration of using this tool within your classroom.

CONCLUSION

I believe that being together in Circle work creates a deeper understanding of each other at our human core. It moves us away from the colonial mindset that we are all individual and divided, and brings us together as a community of kin. The focus is on our interconnectedness, rather than our separation by nationality, gender, class, age and more. This wholistic and Indigenous approach to the classroom will ultimately support the group, and actively transform people's lives and lived experiences in the classroom when they can learn, make knowledge, and grow together as a community of care. This provides an opportunity for the learning community to build each other up, create a space for confidence building, hone communication skills, and develop empathy for others. Circle work is a practice in decolonizing the classroom, with a focus on anti-racism and relationality. The hope with this work is for people to leave the work better than when they stepped into the Circle. It moves us away from the colonial educational practices that prioritise time efficiency, hierarchy, and quick fixes. This brings us back to where we started in this chapter, in a beautiful Circle; everything that we do in education begins and ends with relationships.

I raise my hands in deep gratitude to all those who step into the work of decolonizing educational spaces. The work is not easy, and it takes a daily toll on those who continue to push back against how things have always been done. I appreciate you. I see you. And I know that with you, we have hope for a better education system for the generations to come.

With my deep respect, Carolyn

REFERENCES

Andrews, D. J. C., Brown, T., Castillo, B. M., Jackson, D., & Vellanki, V. (2019). Beyond damage-centered teacher education: Humanizing pedagogy for teacher educators and preservice teachers. *Teachers College Record, 121*(6), 1–28. doi:10.1177/016146811912100605

Archibald, J. A. (2019). Raven's Story About Indigenous Teacher Education. In E. McKinley & L. Smith (Eds.), *Handbook of Indigenous Education*. Springer. doi:10.1007/978-981-10-1839-8_1-2

Battiste, M. (2013a). *Decolonizing education: nourishing the learning spirit*. Purich Publishing.

Battiste, M. (2013b). You can't be the doctor if you're the disease: Eurocentrism and Indigenous renaissance. *CAUT Distinguished Academic Lecture*, 1-19.

Brayboy, B. M. J. (2005). Toward a Tribal Critical Race Theory in Education. *The Urban Review, 37*(5), 425–446. doi:10.100711256-005-0018-y

Brayboy, B. M. J., & Maughan, E. (2009). Indigenous Knowledges and the Story of the Bean. *Harvard Educational Review, 79*(1), 1–21. doi:10.17763/haer.79.1.l0u6435086352229

Brown, M. A., & Di Lallo, S. (2020). Talking Circles: A Culturally Responsive Evaluation Practice. *The American Journal of Evaluation, 41*(3), 367–383. doi:10.1177/1098214019899164

Buchanan-Rivera, E. (2022). *Identity affirming classrooms: spaces that center humanity*. Routledge, Taylor & Francis Group.

Carlson, K. T. (Ed.). (1997). You are asked to witness: the Stó:lō in Canada's Pacific Coast history. Stó:lō Heritage Trust.

Cote-Meek, S. (2014). *Colonized classrooms: racism, trauma and resistance in post-secondary education*. Fernwood Publishing.

Dei, G. J. S. (1993). The challenges of anti-racist education in Canada. *Canadian Ethnic Studies, 25*(2), 36.

Dion, S. (2022). *Braided learning: illuminating Indigenous presence through art and story*. Purich Books.

Freire, P. (1970). *Pedagogy of the Oppressed*. Seabury Press.

Gough, N. (2002). *Voicing curriculum visions* (Vol. 151). Counterpoints.

Graveline, F. J. (1998). *Circle works: transforming Eurocentric consciousness.* Fernwood Publishing.

Johnston-Goodstar, K., & VeLure Roholt, R. (2017). "Our Kids Aren't Dropping Out; They're Being Pushed Out": Native American Students and Racial Microaggressions in Schools. *Journal of Ethnic & Cultural Diversity in Social Work, 26*(1-2), 30–47. doi:10.1080/15313204.2016.1263818

Justice, D. H. (2018). *Why Indigenous Literatures Matter.* Wilfrid Laurier University Press.

Kanu, Y. (2011). *Integrating Aboriginal perspectives into the school curriculum: Purposes, possibilities, and challenges.* University of Toronto Press.

Lomawaima, K. T. (2000). Tribal sovereigns. *Harvard Educational Review, 70*(1), 1–21. doi:10.17763/haer.70.1.b133t0976714n73r

Noddings, N. (2012). The caring relation in teaching. *Oxford Review of Education, 38*(6), 771–781. doi:10.1080/03054985.2012.745047

Restoule, J. P. (2018). Where Indigenous Knowledge Lives: Bringing Indigenous Perspectives to Online Learning Environments. In E. McKinley & L. Smith (Eds.), *Handbook of Indigenous Education.* Springer., doi:10.1007/978-981-10-1839-8_62-1

Rosborough, T., Rorick, C. L., & Urbanczyk, S. (2017). Beautiful words: Enriching and Indigenizing Kwak'wala revitalization through understandings of linguistic structure. *Canadian Modern Language Review, 73*(4), 425–437. doi:10.3138/cmlr.4059

San Pedro, T. J. (2015). Silence as Shields: Agency and Resistances among Native American Students in the Urban Southwest. *Research in the Teaching of English, 50*(2), 132–153.

Truth and Reconciliation Commission of Canada. (2015). *Canada's Residential Schools: The Final Report of the Truth and Reconciliation Commission of Canada* (Vol. 1). McGill-Queen's Press-MQUP.

Chapter 4
All Our Relations:
Stories From the Classroom and the Land

Joey-Lynn Wabie
Laurentian University, Canada

Marnie Anderson
Laurentian University, Canada

Taylor Watkins
Laurentian University, Canada

Anastacia Chartrand
Laurentian University, Canada

Simon Leslie
Laurentian University, Canada

Arijana Haramincic
Laurentian University, Canada

ABSTRACT

The authors shared their reflections about a 12-week master-level course at a northern Ontario university revisioned by an Algonquin anicinabe ikwe scholar and a settler graduate teaching assistant using experiential arts, storytelling, and land-based pedagogical practices. Through the holistic nature of the course, learners explored topics through their own holistic health and well-being. Learners learned the importance of storytelling which culminated in a medicine storysharing session and roundtable discussion. The authors' reflections highlighted the interactive nature of the course fostering the ability for students to learn how teaching and knowledge can be delivered in a memorable and impactful way. There were also feelings of discomfort when it came to letting go of preconceived notions about education since the course went against the academic training commonly found in Westernized educational institutions. This chapter includes various materials, including the course outline and ideas for personal exploration using experiential arts and land-based creative modalities.

DOI: 10.4018/978-1-6684-3425-3.ch004

Copyright © 2023, IGI Global. Copying or distributing in print or electronic forms without written permission of IGI Global is prohibited.

"What happens to one, what happens to all; thus, all flourishing is mutual" (Kimmerer, 2013).

INTRODUCTION: SITUATING SELF

kwe kwe, ziigwankwe n'dizhnaakaaz, atik dodem. mahingan sagahigan first nation n'doonjibaa. Algonquin anicinabe ikwe n'daaw. Hello, my name is spring woman, caribou clan. I am from Wolf Lake First Nation. I am an Algonquin woman. My English name is Joey-Lynn Wabie. I am an uninvited guest living in Atikameksheng Anishnawbek territory. My passion is sharing traditional Algonquin spiritual health through our culture and traditions as a learner myself. I see the importance in community building at work and in my personal life, which often overlap. I have been teaching full time at Laurentian University as an associate professor, and sessionally since 2011. I also volunteer in the community with grassroots organizations who bring culture, language, and traditions to urban Indigenous peoples. My heart is first and foremost with my family and in the community.

My name is Taylor Watkins, and I was the graduate teaching assistant for this course. I am a non-Indigenous settler currently residing on the traditional territory of the Atikameksheng Anishinabek and neighboring reserve: Wahnapitae First Nation. As a settler, I understand I have privilege on these lands. I am working through how I can best be a contributing treaty relative, and know I have and will continue to make mistakes but promise to keep learning.

With lattes in hand, Taylor and I sat in my office thinking about how we can approach this course after receiving the go ahead to change the course delivery. How can we learn with others and balance the power structure commonly found within university graduate level courses? We used a whiteboard to sketch the framework, and added in the existing course description, objectives, and elements of the earth's natural resources. Recognizing that the Medicine Wheel is integral to Indigenous cultures, we divided the course into four sections with the sacred elements as quadrant headings: Earth, Fire, Air, and Water. According to Manitowabi (2018), the Medicine Wheel teachings contain the values and principles for how Indigenous people are to conduct themselves in order to reach mino bimaadiziwin – the good life. There are many versions of the Medicine Wheel teachings depending where one resides, yet the foundation concepts are similar. The Medicine Wheel reminds us that everything comes in fours – the four seasons, the four stages of life, the four races of humanity, four cardinal directions, and so forth. Interestingly, there are really seven directions associated with the Medicine Wheel – the four cardinal directions (north, south, east and west) as well as the sky, the earth and the centre which we believe we were able to honour and incorporate within our course.

Underneath each quadrant, we chose readings, guest speakers, and activities. Once completed, we brainstormed on how to include comprehensive and reflective assignments and inserted them evenly throughout the 12 week course. The books we chose as required readings were Kimmerer's (2015) book, *Braiding Sweetgrass: Indigenous Wisdom, Scientific Knowledge and the Teachings of Plants*, and Benton-Banai's (2010) book, *Mishomis Book: The Voice of the Ojibway*. Our course began in the winter session taking place in the classroom and wiigwam with graduate students at the master's level.

About Accessibility

We usually find a discussion about accessibility near the end of writings, as an afterthought. We would like to add it as part of the conversation from the beginning. We all come earthside to Shkagamik-Kwe (Mother Earth) as gifts from the Creator. There are teachings all around us; in our daily lives, relationships with others and ourselves through our years which can impact our accessibility to a variety of locations and experiences. We believe that every person has the right to a relationship with the four elements of Earth, Fire, Air, and Water in a way that best suits them.

As an instructor and graduate teaching assistant within this course, we took for granted that there were no accessibility issues, other than the technological one that came with students attending via video conferencing. We now realize the naiveté of this and offer suggestions moving forward that can assist others who are interested in incorporating connection with the land into their pedagogy.

Review the accessibility policies within the institution. Are there physical changes that can be made to the land to ensure equitable access? Within our university we are in the process of paving the walkway to the wiigwam and working with the facilities department to ensure proper drainage to the ground within the wiigwam so it remains level and relatively easy to access.

Ensure that learners are asked ahead of time if accommodations are needed. This can be done by the instructor on an individual basis keeping confidentiality at the forefront. Although placing full responsibility on the person to explain what they need for accessibility is not ideal, it can reduce the need to guess their accommodations. An email prior to the beginning of the course or announcement during the first class can help the instructor adjust their teaching to ensure equity within the classroom.

Adjusting the environment to ensure everyone's participation is equitable. If a person uses a wheelchair for mobility, the instructor and university have an obligation to ensure they have access. If not, then we adjust the way we teach, not the learner. If a person uses assistive listening devices, it is the instructor and university's obligation to ensure that assistive devices for vision and hearing can operate successfully within the wiigwam.

We understand that individualized education is highly contextualized. It is based on the environment, season, location, who is teaching etc. so these suggestions are not meant to fit all possible accessibility situations. It does create an open conversation of caring and ensuring that everyone is involved.

INTRODUCTION

The mutual flourishing in educational settings begins with the recognition that the integration of Indigenous cultural values and ways of knowing are often neglected in western educational institutions, which is imperative for all learners to understand Indigenous ways as being here since time immemorial. Valuing and centering Indigenous values in educational areas can foster a learning environment relevant to Indigenous learners, while providing non-Indigenous learners the opportunity to become informed regarding Indigenous history and culture through an Indigenous perspective (Huguenin, 2020). Education utilizing Indigenous pedagogies supports a holistic learning environment for all learners through ancestral teachings, storytelling, and land-based learning. Indigenous ways of knowing and epidemiological underpinnings are deeply linked to Indigenous pedagogies that are experiential and emphasize the concepts of learning by doing and learning from one another (Restoule & Chaw-win-is, 2017).

In this chapter, we will share our stories about a 12 week master-level course at a northern Ontario university that was revisioned by an Algonquin anicinabe ikwe scholar and a settler graduate teaching assistant using experiential arts, storytelling, and land-based pedagogical practices. This course examined how Indigenous and non-Indigenous people interact with Shkagamik-Kwe (Mother Earth) through the four sacred elements: earth, fire, air, and water. Using a medicine wheel framework (Bopp et al., 2012), we will share how the course commenced in the East with earth, transitioned to the South with fire, West with air, and concluded in the North with water.

Using reflective arts-based modalities, storytelling, and time with the land, various topics regarding natural resources, climate change, forest sustainability, management of protected areas and parks, mining exploitation, and environmental health and healing were explored. Through the holistic nature of the reflective arts-based exercise, learners explored the course learnings through their physical, mental, emotional, and spiritual health and well-being. Learners also learned the importance of storytelling which culminated in a medicine story sharing session and roundtable discussion open to the community.

This course went against the mainstream academic training commonly found in westernized educational institutions, allowing learners to creatively articulate the interconnectedness between the health of the land and oneself. There is a direct connection between holistic health and the land which was discussed throughout the course incorporating the concept of 'all our relations' which included principles of reciprocity, respect, and balance. Shawanda (2020), uses the Anishinaabe phrase nii'kinaaganaa (nee-kuh-naw-guh-naw) in her scholarly work, which can be translated to "all my relations". Therefore, this chapter will include various materials, involving the course outline and application ideas for personal exploration using experiential arts and land-based creative modalities.

Course Outline

Our course outline wheel in Figure 1 frames the weeks, elements, topics, and guest speaker types that were integral to the learners' experiential learning.

Figure 1. Course outline wheel

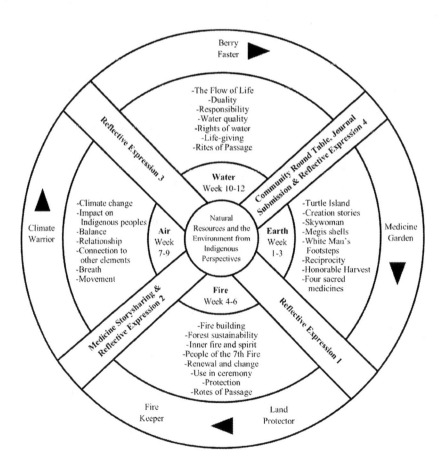

As we look to the centre of the wheel, that is where we placed the heart of the course. As we move outwards, we see the elements with the corresponding weeks they were explored in starting in the East and moving around clockwise. After each quadrant is complete, there is a reflective expression activity, which will be explained further in the chapter. You will also see halfway through the course, there is a Medicine Storysharing assignment, and the culminating assignment at the end: Community Round Table.

Commencing in the East, learners were oriented to the structure of the course in relation to the Medicine Wheel. Students were provided with the opportunity to explore how Indigenous and non-Indigenous peoples interact with Shkagamik-Kwe (Mother Earth), evaluate the concept of natural resources from the Anishnaabe and Indigenous understanding, explore various issues regarding natural resources utilizing Anishinaabe teachings, and foster an understanding of the concept of reciprocity in relation to the land. According to Kimmerer (2013), the concept of reciprocity can be understood through the recognition that our relationship to the land is one often of taking. However, considering how one might reciprocate the gifts of Shkagamik-Kwe was a primary theme that emerged throughout this quadrant. A critical focal point for the introduction to the course content was developing an understanding that Shkagamik-Kwe serves as both the physical manifestation and embodiment of creation.

Remaining in the East quadrant, the sacred element of Earth was explored more in-depth through the concept of mining exploitation from Indigenous perspectives. Students were introduced to a prominent barrier between westernized science and Indigenous traditional practices in that there are different ways of knowing, communicating, and connecting with the land. Through the concepts of the honorable and dishonourable harvest (Kimmerer, 2013), which are deeply rooted in gratitude and reciprocity, learners reflected on whether mining exploitation upholds the principle of reciprocity. Additionally, learners explored the sacredness of the four medicines: tobacco, cedar, sweet grass, and sage by establishing a narrative from the perspective of one of the four sacred medicines, and engaged in a self-reflective expression emphasizing the concept of environmental health and well-being through the use of art-based creative modalities.

Proceeding into the South quadrant, the sacredness of fire and the concept of fire building were vital focal points. The sacred fire is viewed as a symbol of life and spirit, which firekeepers are appointed to care for. Learners were acclimated to the South quadrant by exploring the symbolic meaning of fire in the Indigenous culture, the concept of duality, and gender-diverse rites of passage. Students were oriented to the significance of the dual nature of the creative and destructive sides of fire and the importance of respecting and understanding the opposing sides of this powerful element. Learners adopted an understanding of the people of the seventh fire, emphasizing that in the Indigenous culture, it is assumed that the people of the seventh fire walk among us, and subsequently the eighth fire will serve as an eternal fire of peace, love, brotherhood, and sisterhood (Benton-Banai, 2010).

In relation to the sacredness of fire, concepts revolving around forest sustainability and management of protected areas and parks were explored. Students evaluated the importance of forests for subsistence, economic, and ceremonial practices while exploring the importance of reciprocity in relation to forest sustainability. Indigenous land-based learning was a critical aspect integrated into this quadrant, which incorporated ways of knowing, learning, and being, while honouring the ancestral and physical aspects of land (Wabie et al., 2021). The wiigwam was used by the students to engage in land-based activities, including: (1) fire teachings; and (2) sharing circles. Learners were immersed in a self-reflective expression exercise using art-based creative modalities to reflect on the importance of tending to their inner fire.

Continuing in a clockwise direction, students transitioned into the West quadrant, where they explored the sacred element of air. The concept of climate change was the first to be explored in the West quadrant. Learners embarked on a journey to review the cultural relationship Indigenous people have with the environment, investigate how climate change is impacting Indigenous ways of life while exploring the effects of climate change in relation to the land and water. Indigenous peoples' relationship with the land is based on a profound spiritual connection to Shkagamik-Kwe which is adversely impacted by the changing climate (Turner, 2013). Additionally, learners explored the significance of air by adopting an understanding that air is the vital spirit passing through all things and is the manifestation of movement, freshness, and communication (Assembly of First Nations, 2012). From an Indigenous perspective, air is understood as the force that brings all people into existence from their first breath (Assembly of First Nations, 2012).

Remaining in the West quadrant, the last concept to be explored was the sacredness of the four winds and directions. Students were provided with the opportunity to adopt a greater understanding of the significance and meaning underlying the four sacred winds and directions. Additionally, learners evaluated the symbolic representation of the Medicine Wheel and the various interconnected relationships of one's physical, mental, emotional, and spiritual self. As self-exploration was a critical component of the West quadrant, learners were encouraged to participate in a meditation session and a watercolour activity to explore the creative significance of air. Learners were lastly immersed in a self-reflective expression exercise using art-based creative modalities to reflect on how the creative nature of air serves as a tool for their own sustainability in the physical world.

Concluding with the North quadrant, students were provided with the opportunity to evaluate the interconnectedness of water and all living beings, explore the connection water has to Shkagamik-Kwe, and gender-diverse rites of passage. According to Clarke and Yellowbird (2021), water serves as the blood of Shkagamik-Kwe and cleanses herself and all living beings. Despite water being a life-giving force, water can give life, take life, and remake life (Clarke & Yellowbird, 2021). Beyond exploring the duality of this sacred element, learners explored the impacts climate change has imposed on Shkagamik-Kwe's water systems. For instance, students explored how climate change has and continues to adversely impact the water systems, such as the rapid deterioration of water quality and overall supply. Further, learners analyzed how this deterioration and interference directly affects Indigenous peoples' relationship with Shkagamik-Kwe's water systems.

Lastly, learners concluded the course by exploring the concepts of water rights and allocations, understanding Indigenous peoples' water rights, and exploring the challenges of water governance. According to the Water Policy and Governance Group (2010), conflicts often arise from water policy and management decisions that are dominated by westernized perspectives; thus, excluding other ways of knowing. Students adopted an understanding that there is a lack of cultural reference in legislation pertaining to water, and there is a severe lack of Indigenous perspectives on proposed federal water strategies (Walkem, 2004). Ultimately, learners explored the interconnectedness of water through the creation of resin keychains and engaged in a self-reflective expression emphasizing the significance of water using art-based creative modalities. Here is the description of the course outline (a more detailed description of the course outline can be found in the Appendix).

Assignments

Reflective Expressions. Learners engaged in a reflective expression activity including creation of art, after the completion of each quadrant (i.e., East, South, West, North). They recorded their reactions to topics and significant or internal conflicts as they moved through the course. At the end of each quadrant, they shared their reflective expression in class. These reflective expressions were designed to foster introspection or self-reflection. Reflective practice is a very important tool to pick up in our own self-growth and development as human beings on Shkagamik-Kwe. It helps us to look twice. In this way, we develop respect – necessary to being good relatives to everyone and everything. Learners reflected on the information learned in each quadrant and expressed them through art, poetry, creative dance, journal entry, or any other avenue discussed with the instructor. Our guidelines:

- Explain your Reflective Expression and how it connects to your learning.
- Explain the effect this learning has on your Body, Mind, and Spirit.

- Answer: What is your key take away? How will you use what you have learned to continue being a good relative?

At the end of the course, the learners had four reflective expression pieces which was needed for the last assignment: Journal submission.

Medicine Storymaking. In line with the course objectives, learners were asked to establish a narrative from the perspective of one of the four sacred medicines: tobacco, cedar, sweetgrass or sage in a creative manner. Learners needed to gather information on the medicine, and reflect on how they would write from that perspective. Plant medicines are animate beings with spirits. We posed the questions:

- Which medicine are you? What are your characteristics? *Need to research this and add at least 2 sources.*
- What do you look like? Incorporate a sketch, trace, or add a picture of you (as a sacred medicine).
- Who are your relations? What do you see and feel around, above, and below you? Who or what are you most connected to?
- What are your goals as a sacred medicine? What are your fears?
- What do you wish people knew about you and the environment you live in?

Their Medicine Story was three pages and in the form of storytelling. Stories present deep insights into the affective dimension of human learning, socialization in community, and is a vehicle for the transfer of cultural knowledge and values bringing us toward a decolonizing storied participatory approach. We informed the learners this form of writing will go against the mainstream academic training that they are used to, but to sit in the discomfort it may bring as it will also bring about growth.

Medicine Storysharing. Learners were asked to share their stories to the community. There is a responsibility to ensure that as graduate learners, they are expected to be accountable to the community by sharing their knowledge. We invited learners to share with their family and friends, while the instructor posted the figure below on social media for any interested person to attend.

Journal Submission. Learners were asked to submit their completed coursework for journal submission. This provided students with the experience of submitting to a peer reviewed academic journal. They were given two choices:

- Submit your Medicine Story with an introductory and concluding page.
- Submit your four reflective pieces with an introductory and concluding page.

All Our Relations

Figure 2. Invitation to attend medicine storysharing event

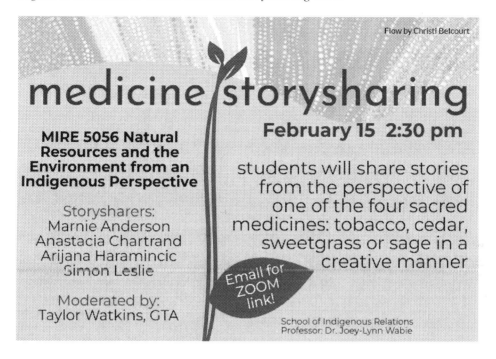

Figure 3. Community round table invite

The learners submitted their work to an undergraduate Indigenous student journal. They were asked to forward the confirmation email that their work was submitted in order for them to receive full marks.

Community Round Table. Learners sat in a circle with each other at a community round table with an audience and shared what they have learned in this course. Figure 3 was distributed to their family and friends, and also shared by the instructor on social media. The course's graduate teaching assistant acted as moderator and guided them with questions that were given to them two weeks in advance. Questions revolved around the content learned throughout the semester (e.g., four sacred elements/directions, climate change, the concept of reciprocity, etc.). We also let them know that the audience questions would be unscripted so they must be prepared!

Course Objectives

Upon the completion of the 12-week master-level course, learners were able to: (1) identify natural resources from an Anishnaabe/Indigenous understanding and explain them easily to others; (2) identify Anishinaabe/Indigenous understandings of natural resources and how they connect to the environment; (3) articulate how the earth's natural resources are interconnected to self and their research; (4) articulate concepts of environmental health and healing from an Anishinaabe/Indigenous understanding; (5) illustrate how certain sacred medicines are integral to the health and well-being of the environment and self through storymaking and sharing; and (6) demonstrate how natural resources can be used sustainably in the management of the environment.

Course Delivery Rationale

The rationale for our course delivery was for it to be Anishinabe-led (with an Algonquin Anicinabe scholar) using pedagogies based on our own epistemology, centering our knowledge, stories, and truths in order to learn. This was further supported through the use of books by authors whose words centered on similar epistemological approaches, with Kimmerer being an enrolled member of the Citizen Potawatomi Nation, and Benton-Banai being Ojibwe. Our pedagogical approach included storytelling, arts and land-based experiential learning. Storytelling provides information about circumstances, places, people, and events that are intended to ensure that Indigenous people remember who they are, how they should behave, what they should know and value, and about their people (Cajete, 2007; Caxaj, 2015; Yellow Bird, 1995). Our ways hold strength and encompass the whole self, not only one aspect; it holds our physical, mental, emotional, and spiritual aspects within our own contexts while interrelating with others. Our ways are not created in a vacuum. They have been created since before there were formal schools of learning.

Our next pedagogical approach we used was arts-based learning and sharing. Arts-based methods have been used effectively to advance agendas for healing, decolonizing, transforming, and mobilizing communities (Hammond et al., 2018). Coholic, Cote-Meek and Recollet (2012) have pointed out Anishinaabe peoples have been using art as an expression of themselves since time immemorial and link traditional Indigenous cultural practices with the relevance and importance of art when using arts-based methods with Indigenous peoples. Throughout our reflective expressions which were arts-based, learners were able to implement decolonizing and transformative methods which honoured long standing Indigenous cultural practices that continue to be relevant within the academy.

We also incorporated the land through discussion of its importance to our health and also physical connection to it within our course. Our time in the wiigwam sharing our reflective expressions, and answering discussion questions was intentional. Tuck, McCoy and McKenzie (2014) endorse land education as it puts Indigenous epistemological and ontological accounts of land at the center, including Indigenous understandings of land, Indigenous language in relation to land, and Indigenous critiques of settler colonialism. It attends to constructions and storying of land and repatriation by Indigenous peoples, documenting and advancing Indigenous agency and land rights. Furthermore, Indigenous land-based pedagogy offers a way of fostering individual and collective empowerment for learners by re-embedding them in the land-connected social relationships that settler-colonialism, through education and otherwise, sought to destroy (Henderson, 2000; Wildcat et al., 2014). This individual and collective empowerment which Wildcat et al. (2014) and Henderson (2000) discuss is imperative as part of the continued Indigenizing taking place within educational institutional settings. The connection to land and distance away from the curated rooms within schools benefit learners as it allows them to return to self and find their own personal rhythm of learning and connecting.

The wiigwam was built in 2018 at our university with the Indigenous Student Affairs department, Atikamkesheng Anishnawbek, the School of Indigenous Relations, and the McEwen School of Architecture. Wabie, London, and Pegahmagabow (2021) share the creation and reasoning behind its structure:

The planning of the location took place over fifteen years ago when a tipi was built in the same space. This tipi, although not regional, was symbolically a place to hold space that would be unique and identifiable as Indigenous. This preparation was significant, and we want to honour the hard work that went into the original mapping and building of the tipi and its meaning. In 2017, the tipi poles blew down in a storm and there was discussion amongst the Indigenous department, faculty, and staff that this was our opportunity to create a space that was more regional and aligned to the culture and traditions of this area. It is this trailblazing work that was completed prior to the building of the wiigwam that allows the current space to be held. (p.51)

It is worthy to note that this particular wiigwam is regional to the area and Indigenous faculty et al. decided this was their opportunity to build something that was culturally accurate and representative of the territory. It would be constructive to reach out to the local Indigenous population in your area and partner with them to ensure it aligns to the culture and traditions in your area. It may be a longhouse, tipi, or other structure, depending on the location you are in.

As Indigenous scholars, if we do not see ourselves reflected in the academy, then we have an obligation to create that space for Indigenous learners so they feel they belong. There have been many Indigenous senior scholars who have created a path for junior Indigenous peoples who are newly minted PhD holders or are in academia at the undergraduate or graduate level. It is the junior Indigenous scholars' turn now to take on that responsibility: not to reinforce the archaic system of mainstream education but bring Indigenous ways of knowing, being, and doing forward as the legitimate systems of learning they have always been.

Within the next section, we will read from the perspective of the learners who took this course and their reflections on it.

IN THE LEARNERS' WORDS

In this section, learners who completed the course will each share one quadrant, what they experienced, and their reflections on how it impacted their learning. They will introduce themselves, share the background of the quadrant, tell us about the guest speakers, and then reflect on the content.

East Quadrant: Earth (Week 1-3)

Look at the legacy of poor Eve's exile from Eden: the land shows the bruises of an abusive relationship. It's not just land that is broken, but more importantly, our relationship to land. As Gary Nabhan has written, we can't meaningfully proceed with healing, with restoration, without "re-story-ation." In other words, our relationship with land cannot heal until we hear its stories. But who will tell them. (Kimmerer, 2013, p. 9)

Situating Self

Boozhoo, my name is Simon Leslie, and I am a settler originally from Treaty 3 territory. I am currently residing in the N'swakamok/Sudbury area as I complete a Master's of Indigenous Relations, and have arrived to the area after a decade of teaching in remote First Nation communities in Quebec and Labrador. This journey has been part of a continued effort to better understand my role as an ally with Indigenous peoples nationally and internationally through educational practice.

Background of the Quadrant (East)

To start our journey, just as with Nanabozho's first expedition around the earth (Benton-Banai, 2010; Kimmerer, 2013), we set out to discover how we should interact with the natural world in the east. The east provided us with the opportunity to learn from one of the wisest teachers, Shkagamik-Kwe, by following one of the many paths lined with megis shells and the footsteps of the Anishinaabeg who have made this place home for generations (Benton-Banai, 2010; Kimmerer, 2013). The quadrant began with Kimmerer's (2013) portrayal of Skywoman and her creation of Turtle Island, and Benton-Banai's (2010) retelling of the creation of man from the breath of Gitchie Manito. The introduction to Anishinaabeg creation stories highlighted the importance of land to Indigenous nations, and provided a model of how immigrants might become naturalized. Following the lead of Skywoman and *Plantago major* also known as White Man's Footsteps; each story reminded us of the reciprocity that is required for immigrants to become Indigenous to place, and requires individuals to be true to their gifts and honour the gifts of others (Kimmerer, 2013). The discussions we had in class wove like braids of sweetgrass, helping to purify our interaction with the content and each other, bringing a positive energy to the conversations.

Our discussions deviated dramatically when we were faced with the topic of resource extraction. With Canada's prominence on the international stage for mineral resource extraction, questions arose regarding the environmental, social, and economic benefit of maintaining such activities as a nation. Although extractive activities such as mining had emerged in North America well before the arrival of European settlers (Manitowabi et al., 2018, p. 39), class discussions became critical of any socioeconomic or ecological benefit when political initiatives would likely not follow "the precepts of the Honorable Harvest—to take only what is given, to use it well, to be grateful for the gift, and to reciprocate the gift [it in turn]" (Kimmerer, 2013, pp. 20-21). The concern of not following the Honorable Harvest principle was accentuated by the history of resource extraction, marred by reclamation mismanagement and detriment to surrounding wildlife, ecological habitats, and

Indigenous and non-Indigenous communities internationally. This mismanagement extended to the social realm, with challenges emanating from "man camps" that bring drugs and violence to remote areas, that in turn, "deeply affecting Indigenous women and gender-diverse individuals" (Knott, 2018, p. 148).

Guest Speaker

To finish our discussions in the earth quadrant, our guest speaker joined us from the university's Indigenous student centre to present on the four sacred medicines and her experiences with creating their medicine garden. She has been the lead on the university's medicine garden (in collaboration with others) since 2016 when it began to be a part of their programming for students. With sweetgrass, tobacco, and juniper to start, all but the sweetgrass fell to the wayside, with sweetgrass remaining true to its nature of being the first to prosper on the earth (Kimmerer, 2013, p. 5). Gradually, the other three sacred medicines (tobacco, sage and cedar) were added to the garden, along with the three sisters (corn, beans, and squash) and other relations to keep the sacred medicines company. Our guest spoke of the need for some plants like tobacco to be smothered with love in order for them to flourish, and the need to procure each of the sacred medicines from individuals who are following the respectful ways of planting, picking, and gifting. She presented on the importance of each plant, the medicinal properties, the attention they need to thrive, and the practices that will keep our relationship with them alive.

Reflections

Although content and curriculum are often the core focus of many academic courses, it can be easy to forget that the instructors' approach to education can be invaluable to our comprehension as learners. For me, as I am sure is true for others, the Anishinaabe-oriented pedagogy of the course provided insight into a Anishinaabeg frame of reference that would otherwise be inaccessible when content is prioritized over the process. Lessons situated with Anishinaabeg values and styles of pedagogy helped to shift the learning of curricular outcomes closer to Leanne Simpson's (2014) retelling of Kwezens' educational immersion on the land, with story, culturally informed discourse, and the centering lived-experience further augment how we as learners processed the information.

One of the most significant sources of learning came from the instructors' implementation of story and allegory. My appreciation of storytelling as pedagogy has become more pronounced as I have progressed through my master's program. Through this course, allegory has helped me to gain a deeper insight into the themes that connect Anishinaabe worldviews to the natural world. Every quadrant introduced narratives from Indigenous authors who shared the use of metaphor and symbolism that "help[ed] to reveal, and make visible, Indigenous ideas, thinking, and thought" (Kovach, 2021, p. 48). As Simpson (2013) conveys:

...storytelling within the Nishnaabeg traditions is a wonderful way of teaching and inspiring not only children but also people of all ages. ... This is the brilliance of our traditions - our stories are seeds, encoding multiple meanings that grow and change with the passage of time. They are a dynamic, engaging conversation that requires personal engagement and reflection and that our people embody and carry with them throughout their lives. (p. 3)

This sentiment was true for this course, where we were able to find unique interpretations of course content while also constructively helping to inform each other's perspectives. With narratives present in the formal readings, informal conversations, and assignments: allegory and symbolism provided students with the opportunity to freely reflect on their own ways of knowing while vicariously viewing the lesson through an Indigenous lens. Furthermore, the process of storytelling gave students a chance to form a relationship with the material that utilized lived-experience to contextualize the wisdom presented throughout the course.

The benefits of allegory extended to assessment, providing students with the opportunity to create a reflective expression of their learning through any artistic endeavour. The natural benefit of non-interference, or prioritizing an individual's freedom to choose how to express their knowledge, is that the freedom to find one's own calling fits well with Anishinaabeg tenets and also encourages each student to authentically and comprehensively engage with the material. While everyone leaped at the opportunity to follow what came naturally, the use of literary and allegorical devices throughout the reflective expressions provided everyone with the opportunity to find meaning in light of others' insights and narratives.

The final contribution was from each of the guest speakers. Each were knowledge holders in their own right, who were carrying culture amidst the content they shared. Each possessed expertise beyond the academy and conveyed their understanding of culture, ways of knowing, and tradition through process and presence. A turn of phrase, the use of humour, tone of voice, timing, and posture all held lessons for those who knew how to listen. Each presentation became more relevant when presenters remained true to themselves, their culture, and traditions, revealing their knowledge of the natural world through relational thinking.

South Quadrant: Fire (Week 4-6)

Situating Self

Aanii, my name is Marnie Anderson, and I am Anishinabe and a mixed European kwe/woman. I currently live in Wahnapitae First Nation and grew up in the N'swakamok/Sudbury region. I began my Master's part-time in September 2019 and started this course in 2022 after a tremendous loss in my life. I am providing a preface to ensure readers understand my emotional perspective on this course.

Background

Proceeding in a clockwise direction, we transitioned into the south quadrant of the Medicine Wheel. The South is the direction that represents strength and fullness and symbolizes the sacred element – fire. Benton-Banai (2010) shared that fire is a gift from the Creator. If you respect the fire, it will bring warmth; however, if you neglect it or don't respect it, it may be destructive. Through this quadrant, we learned about the concepts; of the sacredness of fire, forest sustainability, parks, and protected areas. Lastly, using the Seven Grandfather teachings, we embarked on a journey attempting to balance the destructive and creative forces of one's inner fire and spirit.

We reviewed the sustainable use of forests and their importance to subsistence, economic and ceremonial practices. Additionally, we learned the importance of reciprocity concerning forest sustainability and the history of dispossession by the Indigenous people. Discussions about the interwoven operation of trees working collectively, communicating with one another through an underground network showing the intelligence of the plant and fungi network were prominent in the south quadrant. Additionally, forest fires are viewed as a destructive force; however, they also are a vital part of nature that plays a crucial role in the ecosystem for renewal and change—cleaning the forest floor of extra debris and opening it up to sunlight. Following the knowledge sharing, learners went outside to the wiigwam, located on campus, and utilized the space for their reflection and sharing on the fire quadrant. The location provided a new physical space that positioned us in a circle and allowed for storytelling and knowledge sharing.

Guest Speakers

To learn the significance and symbolic meaning of fire in Anishnabe culture, we listened to our guest speaker who shared the significance and symbolic meaning of fire in Anishnabe culture. Following his presentation where he actively made a fire, we were provided an opportunity to reflect on various discussion questions that revolved around the sacredness of four different fires: camp fire, forest fire, sacred fire, and inner fire.

"The Creator gave the people a fire stick- to bring good things to the land" (Kimmerer, 2013, p. 363). For many First Nations, fire can open a spiritual doorway, allow spiritual communication, and carry the prayers that are sent for healing. This concept was reflected in the guest speaker's discussion and highlighted that the fire which must be attended to is our inner fire, and according to Kimmer (2013), "the hardest fire to take care of is your own fire and your own spirit" (p.363). This section bridged into the subsequent discussion on the Seven Grandfather teachings and Inuit Qaujimajatuqangit (Inuit Knowledge). After reviewing the seven teachings, learners were asked to reflect on which Grandfather teaching resonated with them most in a self-reflexive discussion. The Seven grandfathers are Humility, Bravery, Love, Honesty, Wisdom, Truth, and Respect (Benton-Banai, 2010, p. 64). In reference to Benton-Banai (2010), these were given as 7 gifts out of the vessel of the grandfathers and each should be used in a good way. To cherish knowledge is to know **Wisdom**, to know **Love** is to know peace, To honour all creation is to have **Respect**, **Bravery** is to face foe with integrity, **Honesty** in facing a situation is to be brave, **Humility** is to know yourself as a sacred part of creation, and **Truth** is to know all these things.

Our second guest speaker shared her knowledge of protected lands of the logging occurring in her territory and spoke to the repercussions of resource extraction and the harm inflicted on the communities, land, and wildlife. She discussed her advocacy work with the moose in her territory as a responsibility. She showed us her love for the moose and the habitat they need to thrive. Throughout her presentation, she showed respect for the animals and land of her ancestors and explained how her family always roamed. These examples of current advocacy broadened my understanding of the significant efforts being made advocating for an animal's health and, in turn, improving our health and access to animals as sustenance.

The guest speakers were thoughtfully chosen to represent the quadrant of fire and brought a clearer understanding of the sacredness of fire and its importance to land. Watching the firekeeper demonstrate how to make fire with shkitaagin and discuss its importance within ceremony and culture resonated with me. Fire (for my family) has incredible importance within the family sugarbush; not only to make the syrup but also to warm my inner fire when helping.

Reflections

The pedagogy in which this course was delivered gave me ongoing comfort and outlook on life, for which I am forever grateful. The reflexivity woven through the fire quadrant increased my insight into different perspectives and my own. The reflection and discussion questions were vital because they provided new knowledge that others thoughtfully shared throughout the course. Storytelling was the underlying part I enjoyed as I shared my reflection, and listening to others' stories provoked something that felt reciprocal and even spiritual. Everyone's creativity was seen heavily through the Medicine assessment, and for me, it brought new ways to share information and the courage to try something new.

Learning within the fire quadrant was timely. It allowed me to reflect on the sacredness of fire and my inner fire. I felt motivated to learn more about advocacy, which sparked a passion for the territory around me and the animals that reside on it. Learning that starting something small, like advocating for moose, can have a big impact and is so important for the renewal of relationships and taking care of our animal and plant relations. Finally, the interactive nature of the course along with the access to the wiigwam space really allowed me to learn how teaching and knowledge can be delivered in a way that is memorable and impactful. Walking out onto the land throughout the course brought more meaning as I learned about the intrinsic web of tree life.

West Quadrant: Air (Week 7-9)

Situating Self

My name is Anastacia Chartrand. I am non-Indigenous, currently living on the traditional territory of the Anishnaabeg, specifically the shared territory of Atikameksheng and Wahnapitae First Nations. I work towards being an ally through continual learning. Still, I do not have the experiences and knowledge of the Indigenous people.

Background

Our exploration of the West quadrant began with discussions on climate change, including the cultural relationships Indigenous peoples have with the environment, how the changing climate affects the Indigenous ways of life, and the effects that are particular to land and water. We discussed the most prevalent impacts of climate change on the normal balance of the natural world and societal elements impacting health. We also discussed how the Earth's temperature is influenced by natural processes like solar and volcanic activity. However, many scientists agreed that human activity is the primary cause of global warming (Government of Canada, 2019).

The lessons the instructor covered were on how and why Indigenous People already face challenges exacerbated by climate change, including the loss of land and resources, human rights violations, and economic marginalization. Indigenous

People are among the first to face the consequences of climate change (United Nations, n.d.). As much as we explored climate change's cause and impact, we equally discussed Indigenous ways of life. Indigenous peoples' spiritual ties to Shkagamik-Kwe, leading them to practice respect, humility, and reciprocity, have shaped their relationships with the land (Turner, 2013). Indigenous innovation, leadership, and knowledge have been crucial for defending threatened animals and opposing environmental harm (Stefani, 2021). It is important to protect the land because it is connected with traditional knowledge and teachings and sustains our present and future generations.

We spent valuable time evaluating how air symbolizes the mental and spiritual processes, bringing understanding and inspiration through thought and form. We explored the connection between air pollution and human health, the damage to community and livelihood, and specifically, the intrinsic link between the violation of land and women (Knott, 2018). After talking about the numerous effects of climate change, we moved on to the effects of taking action. Addressing poverty, halting climate change, and averting mass extinction are all possible by restoring our devastated ecosystems (United Nations, 2022).

We reviewed how air pollution impacts human health and what steps may be taken to improve air quality. We also spoke about how the atmosphere acts as a "superhighway" in the sky for water to travel everywhere on Earth and how air pollution may negatively affect the quality of the planet's water supplies. We looked at the connection between fire and air. We investigated the breath of life through the creation story, the history of the Midewiwin, the Megis shell, and the water drum. We came away from the second lecture knowing that humans depend on the environment and natural resources to survive and that Indigenous Peoples recognize and embrace their interconnectedness with nature.

The final lecture from the west reviewed the significance and meaning behind the four directions and evaluated the symbolic representation of the Medicine Wheel. We acknowledged that the Medicine Wheel's circle represents how everything in life is interconnected, as well as the ongoing cycle and connection between the visible and invisible, the material and the spiritual, life and death, and the daily rising and setting of the sun (Beaulieu, 2018). The quadrant concluded with learnings of the four sacred directions, with discussions of the four directions and their various meanings.

Guest Speaker

We heard from a guest lecturer whose presentation was titled "Striving for Mno Bmaadiziwin (the good life) in a climate crisis Ezhiwebak maa kiing (climate change)" (personal communication). Her stories motivated excitement for taking climate action with examples of how she has done this in her own life. She shared related anecdotes about the ways in which she has taken responsibility to defend Mother Nature. Some of these stories included the strengths of having a neighbourhood program for children and helping youth fill their bundles through activities towards preserving food, protecting water, letter-writing campaigns, and taking climate action. She emphasized the need to create and uphold an economy based on abundance and sharing and the need to keep raising awareness and seeking education on climate change. Her stories were woven with gratitude and acknowledgment for the land, medicines, Elders, knowledge keepers, and ancestors. "We do not inherit the Earth from our Ancestors, we borrow it from our children" (personal communication), is a memorable quote from the lecture, reminding us that we need to be committed to taking climate action for future generations.

Transitioning to the air quadrant began with introspective contemplation about what significance this element holds in our lives and what we can do to help lessen the impacts of climate change on Shkagamik-Kwe. A student-guided meditation invited learners to attune to the influence and power of air and appreciate our effortless yet essential relationship with this pure element. During the air quadrant, we engaged in a watercolour activity using our breath through a straw to move paint around and create our own unique artwork that signified the element of air. At the end of the quadrant, we were asked to increase our awareness of the power of a single breath. We were invited to take a moment, go for a walk, sit out in nature, watch the clouds' continuous movement, and reflect on learning from the west.

Reflection

During the course, I was in my final undergraduate year of Environmental Studies, and I found the methodological approach to learning extraordinarily refreshing and inspiring to incorporate into my studies and everyday life. Before this course, I studied many classes that dealt with the science of climate change. I have already encountered lectures regarding air pollution and its impact on water quality among different evaluations of climate change. My previous academic experiences contributed to a deeper awareness of the warming climate but failed to elicit pathos and a human narrative. The lectures, story sharing, and reflexive practices, particularly those centered on the air quadrant and climate change, were critical in shaping my understanding of my role in the environmental crises. In particular, the story-sharing of our guest speaker was highly inspiring. I became inspired to start acting vehemently against climate change, which prompted me to take action towards the twin crises of climate change and biodiversity loss.

Air is always there around us, but because the human eye cannot perceive it, we commonly ignore it. Similar to the importance of air, efforts that feel small towards climate action are nevertheless significantly impactful even if they are not immediately apparent in relation to the larger objectives of climate change. We need to continuously remind ourselves that even while our small actions may not have a direct impact on the world's well-being, they do have an indirect impact by inspiring others to take action. We must never forget to express our gratitude to the natural elements, such as air, which have sustained us from our first breath, and keep doing all we can to protect them.

The use of reflection as a learning tool was helpful in refining my understanding and application of the material, lending to a better long-term understanding over time. Oftentimes in other classes, I would find myself in a lecture agreeing with the materials but later having difficulty sharing the content with others. Through the reflexive practices, I was able to easily and confidently share knowledge with friends and family. By having an opportunity to participate verbally and be asked thought-provoking questions throughout the learning process, I was better able to make connections between new knowledge and my existing experiences. The round table discussions allowed for creative and open dialogue between classmates to develop contributed ideas that enhanced our overall comprehension. Talking through the content and hearing from others helped me to build and refine new understandings that were, and still are, rewarding. There's a real value that comes with being able to actively listen to others. Hearing stories from the other students in the class helped widen my understanding of the significance of air and how my interpretation and experiences are not necessarily always the same as others.

Being invited into nature to breathe and watch the clouds as a reflection on our learning was not only refreshing but impactful. Being able to connect with nature in this way is something I hope to make more time for. This kind of practice can help me become more conscientious about interacting with nature and a better relative.

North Quadrant: Water (Week 10-12)

"Water gives life, takes life, and remakes life." (Clarke & Bird, 2021, p.92)

Situating Self

Ullukkut. My name is Arijana Haramincic. I am non-Indigenous, a settler, living in the city of Iqaluit, and working throughout the Inuit territory of Nunavut in the Canadian Arctic. I am a social worker, a master's student, a mother, an immigrant, a friend and a spouse. I strive to better understand my role as an ally to and with Indigenous people in decolonizing and Indigenizing social work spaces.

Background

The fourth and final quadrant was water, signifying the flow of life, simultaneously the end and the beginning. Water is essential for all living things. "Water gives life, takes life, and remakes life" (Clarke & Bird, 2021, p.92). The flow of water mimics the flow of life, and the never ending energy of the Creator connects all living things. This was the final quadrant of the Medicine Wheel, signifying the end of one cycle and the beginning of the new journey in the East. As we entered the Northern quadrant, we watched The Water Walker, a documentary with Autumn Pelletier, that reflected on how the water rights and allocations impact Indigenous communities across Turtle Island.

Water was presented as an element of duality, capable of creation and destruction, cleansing, rejuvenation, and regeneration. We explored the impact of climate change on water and water quality. When water interacts with earth, it creates life, but also takes life. There is a fundamental difference between the worldviews of Indigenous and non-Indigenous peoples. Non-Indigenous peoples believe their knowledge empowers them to control water, while the scientific knowledge, in the view of the Indigenous peoples, in the absence of understanding the sacred nature of water has harmed the health and quality of water. Indigenous people who remain tied to the waters are impacted by water scarcity, poor water quality, and contamination of marine resources. The impacts of water degradation and scarcity have been felt first by Indigenous Peoples who live closest to and rely heavily upon water. Canada's dispossession and denial of Indigenous Peoples water rights have damaged both Indigenous peoples and the environment.

Our course readings included the denial of Indigenous water rights which has been ongoing since colonization, and there is no secure protection of Indigenous Peoples' water rights in Canada (Walkem, 2004). In non-Treaty areas (most of British Columbia, parts of Quebec and Ontario), reserve lands carry small water allotments. The Canadian governments have unilateral authority to enter into agreements regarding water. Walkem (2004) argues that Canada is in no position to make agreements pledging interests in water resources. We learned how Indigenous communities are voicing their concerns that there is a severe lack of Indigenous input into proposed federal water strategies, and complete absence of any cultural references in legislation pertaining to water. Problems often arise from water policy and management decision making that are dominated by non-Indigenous perspectives, excluding other ways of knowing.

In addition, we learned that water flows its natural course and is dictated by the shape of the land, while recognizing the natural cycles and rhythms of its own force. Water is required to sustain all life, and acknowledgement of this truth forms the foundation of Indigenous laws and responsibilities.

Guest Speaker

We listened to a young Algonquin woman's story of how she transitioned into womanhood. Through storytelling, she shared her experience of when she experienced her first moontime and what she was feeling at the time. She shared the teachings that were given to her by the Elder who put her through her rites of passage: the Berry Fast. These teachings were connected to water and the sacrifice she made for one full year to honour herself, family, community, and nation.

Reflection

As a non-Indigenous student, familiar with the mainstream pedagogy and its expectations, the approach utilized at the beginning of the course was a surprise. My lack of familiarity with Indigenous styles of teaching caused me some discomfort with our divergence from expectations. There was a worry about not knowing what to expect and what was expected of me, and it took 'letting go' of preconceived ideas about education. Reflecting on the course, I became aware how the Indigenous pedagogy used, facilitated the ease of learning and integrating knowledge in a spontaneous way. The attention was given to development of the learner as a whole person, rather than subject matter knowledge, that is separate from who the student is as an individual.

The way the learning materials were presented, as well as evaluation of the concepts learned facilitated more holistic integration of the knowledge and smoother knowledge transfer from the instructor, guest speakers, Elders and each other through mutual sharing. We learned through being immersed in the experiences of Indigenous ceremonies, and experiences of the water, how it is being seen, used, and relates to other elements and all beings. We created the unique experience through our own circle of sharing through creative art, and experienced within and from each other.

The teaching was non-intrusive, non-anxiety producing and supportive of individual growth in an individually diverse way. We created our own expressions, and jointly we created a ceremony of honouring the four elements of life, life itself, acknowledging the intergenerational role our relatives have in passing knowledge and wisdom, by sharing with each other.

We have been touched, and impacted, because of the pedagogy used and the gentle facilitation by the professor, not only on the cognitive level but, emotional and spiritual levels too, thus integrating the knowledge presented through and within body, mind and spirit. We were inspired by the materials and challenged to go beyond the cognitive understanding and simply memorizing and/or repeating the knowledge learned but use the knowledge to express it in a unique way, by creating forms of art that reflect materials presented as well as our own social location and relationship to each other, within the subject matter. No other mainstream pedagogy can achieve these goals in such a cohesive and equitable way, allowing the students to be the followers, facilitators, listeners and knowledge sharers, intermittently and simultaneously. It presented the ebb and flow of knowledge transfer and sharing thus mimicking the flow of water and confirming the basic value and belief that we are all one, as is the water, and what happens to one, happens to all of us.

Summary of Learners' Reflections

Self-reflection was a critical focal point and readily integrated throughout the entirety of the course content. As lessons were primarily situated within Indigenous values and pedagogy, this helped learners find unique perspectives on the course content. In summary, a substantial source of learning stemmed from the instructors' implementation of allegory and the importance of storytelling and sharing. Allegory helped one learner gain insight into the themes that connect Anishinaabe worldviews to the natural world. For another learner, storytelling was vital to understand the importance of listening to others, which upheld the principle of reciprocity as previously defined by Kimmerer (2013). Additionally, the interactive nature of the course and the integration of land-based learning fostered the ability for learners to learn how teaching and knowledge can be delivered in a memorable and impactful way.

Another learner described the methodological approach to learning as refreshing and inspiring to incorporate further into one's everyday life. The discussions, story sharing, and self-reflective expressions were critical in helping to foster an understanding of the environmental crises from differing perspectives. It is essential to continuously remind oneself that small actions may not impose a direct impact; however, they may indirectly help inspire others to act. Lastly, as some students expressed being more familiar with westernized pedagogical practices, feelings of discomfort arose when it came to letting go of preconceived notions about education. The evaluation of concepts was conducted through a more holistic knowledge transfer through one's mind, body, and spirit and mutual sharing from others. The course content and evaluations were supportive of individual growth. Learners were challenged to go beyond westernized pedagogical approaches (e.g., simply memorizing and/or repeating the knowledge learned), enabling them to be the followers, facilitators, listeners, and knowledge sharers.

CONCLUSION

In summary, as we moved through the Medicine Wheel framework over 12 weeks, experiential, land, and arts-based activities were embedded within each quadrant where learners had the chance to consider what they had discovered, how it had affected their bodies, minds, and spirits, and how they could apply what they had learned to continue being good relatives. There was a rhythm and flow to the course creation, implementation, and evaluation of learners' art creation and storytelling. We started with the Medicine Wheel, included the four elements, ensured there were sharing circles within the classes, spent time in the wiigwam on campus, worked with natural elements, and ensured our rubrics followed the body, mind, spirit framework with a focus on community and relational accountability. We ensured we were including the land in our class by spending time with her. Land-based teaching is part of transformative education and innovative solutions to address the general well-being of students on campus by taking students out of the classroom and on to the land, who is our first teacher (Wabie et al., 2021). Learners shared their reflections about being in this revisioned master level course from a holistic perspective.

REFERENCES

Assembly of First Nations. (2012). *Honouring air*. https://www.afn.ca/honoring-air/

Benton-Banai, E. (2010). *The Mishomis Book the Voice of the Ojibway*. University of Minnesota Press Beaulieu, K. (2018, August 24). The seven lessons of the medicine wheel. *SAY Magazine*. https://saymag.com/the-seven-lessons-of-the-medicine-wheel/#:~:text=The%20circle%20acknowledges%20the%20connectedness,the%20daily%20sunrise%20and%20sunset

Bopp, J., Bopp, M., & Lane, P. (2012). *The sacred tree: Reflections on Native American spirituality*. Four Worlds Development Institute.

Cajete, G. A. (2007). Children, myth and storytelling: An Indigenous perspective. *Global Studies of Childhood*, 7(2), 113–130. doi:10.1177/2043610617703832

Caxaj, C. S. (2015). Indigenous storytelling and participatory action research: Allies toward decolonization? Reflections from the Peoples' International Health Tribunal. *Global Qualitative Nursing Research*, 2, 1–12. doi:10.1177/2333393615580764 PMID:28462305

Clarke, K., & Yellow Bird, M. (2021). *Decolonizing Pathways Towards Integrative Healing in Social Work*. Routledge.

Coholic, D., Cote-Meek, S., & Recollet, D. (2012). Exploring the acceptability and perceived benefits of arts-based group methods for Aboriginal women living in an urban community within northeastern Ontario. *Canadian Social Work Review*, *29*(2), 149–168.

Government of Canada. (2019). *Causes of climate change*. Government of Canada. https://www.canada.ca/en/environment-climate-change/services/climate-change/causes.html

Hammond, C., Gifford, W., Thomas, R., Rabaa, S., Thomas, O., & Domecq, M. C. (2018). Arts-based research methods with indigenous peoples: An international scoping review. *Alternative*, *14*(3), 260–276. doi:10.1177/1177180118796870

Hart, M. (2004). *Seeking mino-pimatisiwin: An Aboriginal Approach to Helping*. Fernwood Publishing Company.

Henderson, J. Y. (2000). Ayukpachi: empowering Aboriginal thought. In M. Battiste (Ed.), *Reclaiming Indigenous voice and vision* (pp. 248–278). University of British Columbia Press.

Huguenin, M. (2020). *Integrating Indigenous Pedagogy in Remote Courses*. Trent University. https://www.trentu.ca/teaching/integrating-indigenous-pedagogy-remote-courses

Kimmerer, R. W. (2013). *Braiding sweetgrass: Indigenous wisdom, scientific knowledge and the teachings of plants*. Milkweed Editions.

Knott, H. (2018). Violence and extraction stories from the oil fields. In K. Anderson, M. Campbell, & C. Belcourt (Eds.), Keetsahnak: Our missing and murdered Indigenous sisters (pp. 147-159). University of Alberta Press.

Kovach, M. (2021). *Indigenous methodologies: Characteristics, conversations, and contexts*. University of Toronto Press.

Lavallee, L. (2009). Practical application of an Indigenous research framework and two qualitative Indigenous research methods: Sharing circles and Anishnaabe symbol-based reflection. *International Journal of Qualitative Methods*, *8*(1), 21–40. https://journals.sagepub.com/doi/10.1177/160940690900800103. doi:10.1177/160940690900800103

Manitowabi, S. (2018). *Historical and contemporary realities: Movement towards reconciliation*. Pressbooks. https://ecampusontario.pressbooks.pub/movementtowardsreconciliation

Restoule, J.P., & Chaw-win-is. (2017). *Old ways are the new way forward: How Indigenous pedagogy can benefit everyone.* The Canadian Commission for UNESCO's IdeaLab. http://lss.yukonschools.ca/uploads/4/5/5/0/45508033/20171026_old_ ways_are_the_new_way_forward_how_indigenous_pedagogy_can_benefit_ everyone_final.pdf

Shawanda, A. (2020). Baawaajige: Exploring dreams as academic references. *Turtle Island Journal of Indigenous Health*, *1*(1), 37–47. doi:10.33137/tijih.v1i1.34020

Simpson, L. (2013). *The Gift is in The Making Anishinaabeg Stories.* High Water Press. https://www.portageandmainpress.com/content/download/17792/220444/ version/1/file/9781553793762_TheGiftisintheMaking_excerpt.pdf

Simpson, L. B. (2014). Land as pedagogy: Nishnaabeg intelligence and rebellious transformation. *Decolonization*, *3*(4), 1–25. https://doi.org/http://whereareyouquetzalcoatl.com/mesofigurineproject/ EthnicAndIndigenousStudiesArticles/Simpson2014.pdf

Stefani, G. (2021). *Indigenous Leaders at the Frontlines of Environmental Injustice and Solutions.* NRDC. https://www.nrdc.org/experts/giulia-cs-good-stefani/indigenous-leaders-frontlines-environmental-injustice-and-solutions

Tuck, E., McCoy, K., & McKenzie, M. (2014). Land education: Indigenous, post-colonial, and decolonizing perspectives on place and environmental education research. *Environmental Education Research*, *20*(1), 1–23. doi:10.1080/1350462 2.2013.877708

Turner, A. (2013). *Honouring Earth.* Assembly of First Nations. https://www.afn.ca/honoring-earth/

United Nations. (2022). *When Mother Earth sends us a message.* UN. https://www.un.org/en/observances/earth-day

United Nations. (n.d.). *Climate Change.* Department of Economic and Social Affairs. https://www.un.org/development/desa/indigenouspeoples/climate-change.html

Wabie, J., London, T., & Pegahmagabow, J. (2021). Land-based learning journey. *Journal of Indigenous Social Development*, *10*(1), 50–80. https://journalhosting.ucalgary.ca/index.php/jisd/issue/view/5258

Walkem, A. (2004). *Indigenous Peoples Water Rights: Challenges and Opportunities in an Era of Increased North American Integration.* University of Victoria. https://www.uvic.ca/research/centres/globalstudies/assets/docs/publications/ IndigenousPeoplesWaterRights.pdf

Water Policy and Governance Group. (2010). *Water Challenges and Solutions in First Nations Communities*. Social Sciences and Humanities Research Council of Canada. https://uwaterloo.ca/water-policy-and-governance-group/sites/ca.water-policy-

Wildcat, M., McDonald, M., Irlbacher-Fox, S., & Coulthard, G. (2014). Learning from the land: Indigenous land based pedagogy and decolonization. *Decolonization*, *3*(3), i–xv.

Yellow Bird, M. J. (1995). Spirituality in First Nations story telling: A Sahnish-Hidatsa approach to narrative. *Reflections: Narratives of Professional Helping*, *1*(4), 65–72.

ADDITIONAL READINGS

Assembly of First Nations. (2008). *Climate Change and Water: Impacts and Adaptations for First Nations Communities*. AFN. https://www.afn.ca/uploads/files/env/08-03-27_climate_change_and_water_research_paper_final.pdf

Gauer, V. H., Schaepe, D. M., & Welch, J. R. (2021). Supporting Indigenous adaptation in a changing climate: Insights from the Sto':lo- Research and resource management centre (British Columbia) and the Fort Apache Heritage Foundation (Arizona). *Elementa*, *9*(1), 00164. doi:10.1525/elementa.2020.00164

Jackson, S., MacDonald, D. H., & Bark, R. H. (2019). Public attitudes to inequality in water distribution: Insights from preferences for water reallocation from irrigators to Aboriginal Australians. *Water Resources Research*, *55*(7), 6033–6048. doi:10.1029/2019WR025011

Knott, H. (2018). Violence and extraction stories from the oil fields. In K. Anderson, M. Campbell, & C. Belcourt (Eds.), Keetsahnak: Our missing and murdered Indigenous sisters (pp.147-159). University of Alberta Press.

Manitowabi, S. (2018). *Mining: The Historical and Current Context in Canada*. E-campus Ontario. https://ecampusontario.pressbooks.pub/movementtowardsreconciliation/chapter/mining-the-historical-and-current-context-in-canada/

Parks Canada. (2021). *The life-giving forest*. Parks Canada. https://www.pc.gc.ca/en/nature/science/aires-areas/pimachiowin-aki

Walkem, A. (2004). *Indigenous Peoples Water Rights: Challenges and Opportunities in an Era of Increased North American Integration*. University of Victoria. https://www.uvic.ca/research/centres/globalstudies/assets/docs/publications/IndigenousPeoplesWaterRights.pdf

Water Policy and Governance Group. (2010). *Water Challenges and Solutions in First Nations Communities*. Social Sciences and Humanities Research Council of Canada. https://uwaterloo.ca/water-policy-and-governance-group/sites/ca.water-policy-and-governance-group/files/uploads/files/vonderporten_and_deloe_2010_0.pdf

KEY TERMS AND DEFINITIONS

All Our Relations: The connection between everything on the earth, sky, and beyond. Includes animate and inanimate beings naturally found in these places.

Anishinaabe: A specific term used in the Ojibwe language meaning: person.

Berry Fast: Rites of passage that young Algonquin and Ojibwe girls go through when they experience their first moontime. These specific rites of passage last thirteen moons.

Land Based: Learning that occurred on the land, including all our relations.

Community: A term used to describe a specific group of individuals sharing common values, culture, and views.

Holistic: A term used to describe the interconnectedness of one's physical, spiritual, mental, and emotional being.

Indigenous: A term commonly used to include First Nations, Métis, and Inuit

Medicine Wheel: A symbol used to describe concepts and terms focusing on balance.

Moontime: A term used to describe a woman's menstruation cycle referred to in this manner due to its connection to the moon cycles.

Natural Resources: Term to describe the earth, fire, air, and water elements

Reflective Expressions: A practice of self-introspection to help grow and develop the mind, body, and spirit.

Reciprocity: A term used to describe the concept of sharing for mutual benefit.

Rites of Passage: A tradition that marks the journey from childhood to adolescence, includes the family and community, usually facilitated by an Elder or older family member.

APPENDIX

LAURENTIAN UNIVERSITY

SCHOOL OF INDIGENOUS RELATIONS

MASTER OF INDIGENOUS RELATIONS

MIRE 5056 Natural Resources and the Environment from Indigenous Perspectives

Academic Year:
Class time: Tuesdays (1:00pm-3:50pm)
Location:
Professor: Dr. Joey-Lynn Wabie (she/her)
Graduate Teaching Assistant: Taylor Watkins (she/her)
Student Hours: By Appointment
Tel:
Fax:
Office Room:
E-mail:

This course was revisioned by Dr. Joey-Lynn Wabie & Taylor Watkins.

CALENDAR DESCRIPTION

This course examines how Indigenous and non-Indigenous people interact with Mother Earth (Shkagamik-Kwe). The concept of natural resources is analyzed from the Anishnaabe/Indigenous understanding. Anishinaabe teachings are used to examine various issues regarding natural resources, climate change, forest sustainability, management of protected areas and parks, and mining exploitation and environmental healing. An understanding of sharing will be analyzed and understood from the Medicine Wheel, Seven Grandfather and Ancestral teachings.

COURSE OBJECTIVES

When you have successfully completed this course, you will be able to do the following:

1. Identify natural resources from an Anishnaabe/Indigenous understanding and be able to explain them easily to others
2. Identify Anishinaabe/Indigenous understandings of natural resources and how they connect to the environment
3. Articulate how the earth's natural resources are interconnected to self and your research
4. Articulate concepts of environmental health and healing from an Anishinaabe/Indigenous understanding
5. Illustrate how certain sacred medicines are integral to the health and well-being of the environment and self through storymaking & sharing
6. Demonstrate how natural resources can be used sustainably in the management of the environment

COURSE VISUAL

Refer to figure 1 within the chapter.

TEXTBOOKS

Benton-Banai, E. (2010). *The Mishomis Book the Voice of the Ojibway*. University of Minnesota Press.

Kimmerer, R. W. (2013). *Braiding sweetgrass: Indigenous wisdom, scientific knowledge, and the teachings of plants.* Milkweed Editions.

ASSIGNMENTS

- All assignments must be received & completed on the assigned due date
- Extensions will be granted only in extenuating circumstances.
- Once you have completed an assignment, please make a copy for your records
- Do not copy material directly from your text or reference materials. You should express your ideas in your own words. When using reference materials

ensure that you use a consistent APA approach to your citations, footnotes, endnotes, etc. Either purchase or download the latest APA Manual, 7th Edition to assist you.
- Familiarize yourself with the use of Webadvisor and D2L particularly uploading files.

Medicine Storymaking 20%

Émilie Bourgeault-Tassé will be attending our class on February 1 to speak about the Medicine Garden at LU. She will share its story: who was involved in its creation, what was needed for it to happen, when it began, where it is located, and why it was needed. Each person will be required to ask her a question. Think about what goes into the role of a Medicine Garden caretaker. What does she need to know? What elements is she working with to ensure the medicines grow? What about seasonal care? When are the harvest times? Which medicines can be planted together or have to be separate? What environmental elements will have an impact on the medicines (+ or).

In line with the course objectives, students will be responsible to establish a narrative from the perspective of one of the four sacred medicines: tobacco, cedar, sweetgrass or sage in a creative manner. Students will need to gather information on the medicine, and reflect on how you will write from their perspective. Plant medicines are animate beings with spirits. How will you ensure this is embodied in your writing? The reader must gain the following from your story:

- Which medicine are you? What are your characteristics? *Need to research this and add at least 2 sources.*
- What do you look like? Incorporate a sketch, trace, or add a picture of you (as a sacred medicine). *Appropriate size here →*
- Who are your relations? What do you see and feel around, above, and below you? Who or what are you most connected to?
- What are your goals as a sacred medicine? What are your fears?
- Tell the reader at the end what you wish they know about you and the environment you live in and with.

Your Medicine Story must be 3 pages and in the form of storytelling. This will go against the mainstream academic training that you are used to. You can gear the story to any audience you would like: children, adolescents, adults, older adults. Think about who this story is for and who you are telling a story to.

Medicine Storysharing 10%

You will share your story with the class on February 15 in an 'open mic' setting open to the LU community and interested members of the public. Invite your friends and family!

Reflective Expressions 20%

You will engage in a reflective expression activity including creation of art, which will occur after the completing of every quadrant (i.e., East, South, West, North).

You will record your reactions to topics and significant or internal conflicts as you move through the course. You will then have the opportunity at the end of each direction to share your reflective expression in class. These reflective expressions are designed to foster introspection or self-reflection. Reflective practice is a very important tool to pick up in our own self-growth and development as human beings on Mother Earth. It helps us to look twice. In this way, we can develop respect – necessary to being good relatives to everyone and everything. You are to reflect on the information learned through each quadrant and express them in a way that you would like (e.g., art, poetry, creative dance, journal entry, etc.)

- Explain your Reflective Expression and how it connects to your learning.
- Explain the effect this learning has on your Body, Mind, and Spirit.

- Answer: What is your key take away? How will you use what you have learned to continue being a good relative?

Students are to keep all reflective expression pieces for the next assignment.

Journal Submission 10%

You have two choices for journal submission:

1. Submit your Medicine Story with an introductory and concluding page.
2. Submit your reflective pieces with an introductory and concluding page.

Journal submissions will be opening soon: https://jps.library.utoronto.ca/index.php/tijih

In order to get marks for this assignment you must forward me the confirmation email from TIJIH that your work was submitted.

Community Round Table 40%

Students will all be asked to sit with each other at a community round table with an audience and share what they have learned in this course. A moderator will guide you with questions that will be given to 2 weeks in advance. Questions will revolve around the content learned throughout the semester (e.g., four sacred elements/directions, climate change, the concept of reciprocity, etc.). Audience questions will be unscripted so you must be prepared!

METHOD OF DETERMINING FINAL GRADE

This course follows the grading scheme described in the university calendar.

Determination of final grade

ASSIGNMENT	% of FINAL GRADE	DUE DATE
Medicine Storymaking	20%	
& Sharing	10%	
Reflective Expressions x4	20%	
Community Round Table	40%	
Journal Submission	10%	

All Our Relations

Grading scheme

Percentile Numerical	Letter Grade	Value
90%-100%	A+	10
85%-89%	A	9
80%-84%	A-	8
75%-79%	B+	7
70%-74%	B	6
65%-69%	C+	5
60%-64%	C	4
55%-59%	D+	3
50%-54%	D	2
40%-49%	E	1
0%-39%	F	0

A – Exceptional Performance (80-100%): comprehensive in-depth knowledge of the principles and materials treated in the course; fluency in communicating that knowledge and originality and independence in applying material and principles.

B – Good Performance (70-79%): thorough understanding of the breadth of materials and principles treated in the course and ability to apply and communicate that understanding effectively.

C – Satisfactory Performance (60-69%): basic understanding of the breadth of principles and material treated in the course and ability to apply and communicate that understanding competently.

D - Minimally Competent Performance (50-59%): adequate understanding of most principles and material treated in the course, but significant weakness in some areas and in the ability to apply and communicate that understanding.

F – Failure (0-49%): inadequate or fragmentary knowledge of the principles and materials treated in the course of failure to complete the work required in the course. Disrespectful behavior in class also may lead to a failure.

CLASS SCHEDULE

Detailed schedule

EAST	EARTH
Class 1	**Introduction to MIRE-5056** • Review course outline framed through Anishinaabe teachings which will be supported by western paradigms, if needed. • Review course expectations, assignments, and primary resources • Review the structure of the course in relation to the Medicine Wheel **Read: Braiding Sweetgrass** (Chapter 1 - Section 1: Skywoman Falling) Pg. 3-10, (Chapter 1 - Section 4: An Offering) Pg. 33-38, (Chapter 4 - Section 1: In the Footsteps of Nanabozho) Pg. 205-215 **Read: The Mishomis Book** (Chapter 1: Ojibway Creation Story) Pg. 1- 4

Class 2	**Mining Exploitation** • Review the concept of Mining Exploitation • Analyze the connectedness of the land **Read: Braiding Sweetgrass** (Chapter 3 - Section 4: Miskos Kenomagwen) Pg. 156-166 & (Chapter 3 - Section 6: The Honorable Harvest) Pg. 173-201 **Read: Selected Reading** Knott, H. (2018). Violence and extraction stories from the oil fields. In K. Anderson, M. Campbell, & C. Belcourt (Eds.), *Keetsahnak: Our missing and murdered Indigenous sisters* (147-159). University of Alberta Press. **Read: Selected Reading** Manitowabi, S. (2018). Mining: The Historical and Current Context in Canada. In *Historical and contemporary realities: Movement towards reconciliation*. E-campus Ontario.
Class 3	**Medicine Garden** • History and creation of the ISA's Medicine Garden at Laurentian University • Sacredness of the four medicines • Evaluate the concept of environmental health & healing • Lessons learned from tending the garden **Read: Braiding Sweetgrass** (Chapter 2 - Section 2: Witch Hazel) Pg. 72-81 & (Chapter 3 - Section 6: The Honorable Harvest) Pg. 173-201 **Read: The Mishomis Book** (Chapter 10: The Clan System) Pg. 74-78 **Reflection Expression 1** (Earth Quadrant) due at the end of class at 3:50pm. **GUEST PRESENTER (1:00pm-1:45pm)**: Émilie Bourgeault-Tassé, Medicine Garden, Indigenous Student Affairs
SOUTH	FIRE
Class 4	**Fire Teaching** • The significance and symbolic meaning of fire in the Indigenous culture • Sacredness of fire • Men and Gender Diverse People and Rites of Passage **Read: Braiding Sweetgrass** (Chapter 5 - Section 5: People of the Seventh Fire) Pg. 360-373 **Read: The Mishomis Book** (Chapter 3: The Original Man and his Grandmother Nokómis) Pg. 11-20 & (Chapter 13: The Seven Fires) Pg. 89-93 **GUEST PRESENTER (1:00pm-1:45pm)**: Darren McGregor, Fire Teachings
Class 5	**Forest Sustainability** • Review the sustainable use of forests • Evaluate its importance for subsistence, economic, and ceremonial practices • Analyze the importance of reciprocity in relation to forest sustainability **Read: Braiding Sweetgrass** (Chapter 1 - Section 2: The Council of Pecans) Pg. 11-2 & (Chapter 3 - Section 2: The Three Sisters) Pg. 128-140 & (Chapter 4 - Section 7: Old-Growth Children) Pg. 275-292 **Open Mic Class from 2:30-4:00 pm** **Assignment 1** (Medicine Stories) due at <u>beginning of class</u>. Please be prepared to share with others. It must also be uploaded to D2L dropbox.
	READING WEEK
Class 6	**Parks and Protected Areas** **Read**: Protecting lands and water/The life-giving forest, Parks Canada: https://www.pc.gc.ca/en/nature/science/aires-areas/pimachiow in-aki Layering of responsibilities **Reflection Expression 2** (Fire Quadrant) due at the end of class at 3:50pm. **GUEST PRESENTER (1:00pm-1:45pm)**: Shannon Chief, Protecting Algonquin territories & moose
WEST	AIR

All Our Relations

Class 7	**Climate Change** • Review the cultural relationship Indigenous peoples have with the environment • Evaluate how climate change is impacting Indigenous ways of life • Climate change in relation to land and water **Read: Braiding Sweetgrass** (Chapter 3 - Section 4: Mishkos Kenomagwen: The Teachings of Grass) Pg. 156-166 **Read: The Mishomis Book** (Chapter 6: Waynaboozhoo and the Search for His Father) Pg. 35-51 & (Chapter 7: Waynaboozhoo and His Return to the People) Pg. 52-59 **GUEST PRESENTER (1:00pm-1:45pm):** Shelley Essaunce, Climate Warrior
Class 8	**The Breath of Life** • Review the concept of air being a life-giving force that is necessary for survival • Evaluate how air symbolizes the mental and spiritual processes which brings understanding and inspiration through thought and form **Read: The Mishomis Book** (Chapter 9: The Old Man and the First Midewiwin Ceremony) Pg. 67-73 **Watch:** https://youtu.be/YRs5_sYAi-k
Class 9	**Sacredness of the Four Winds/Directions** • Review the significance and meaning behind the four directions • Evaluate the symbolic representation of the Medicine Wheel and the series of interconnected relationships between the mind, spirit, body, and heart **Read: The Mishomis Book** (Chapter 4: The Earth's First People) Pg. 21-28 **Read: The Sacred Tree** (Chapter 5: The Gift of the Four Directions) Pg. 32-62 **Reflection Expression 3 (Air Quadrant) due at the end of class at 3:50pm.**
NORTH	WATER
Class 10	**Water: The Interconnection of all Living Beings** • Women and Gender Diverse People and the Rites of Passage **Read: Braiding Sweetgrass** (Chapter 2 - Section 4: The Consolation of Water Lilies) Pg. 98-104 & (Chapter 3 - Section 8: Witness to the Rain) Pg. 293-300 **Read: The Mishomis Book** (Chapter 2: Original Man Walks the Earth) Pg. 5-10 & (Chapter 5: The Great Flood) Pg. 29-34 & (Chapter 10: The Clan System) **GUEST PRESENTER (1:00pm-1:45pm):** Julia Coleman, Berry Fast experience
Class 11 You will be given the questions for the Community Round Table.	**Climate Change Impacts to Water Systems** • Evaluate how climate change has and continues to impact the water system • Analyze how this interference impacts the relationship Indigenous peoples have with Mother Earth's water systems **Read: Selected Reading** Climate Change and Water: Impacts and Adaptations for First Nation Communities (Assembly of First Nations, 2008) PDF **Read: Selected Reading** Supporting Indigenous Adaptations in a Changing Climate (Gauer et al., 2021) PDF **Read: Selected Reading** Decolonizing Pathways Towards Integrative Healing in Social Work (Chapter 4 - Water) Pg. 88-92
Class 12	**Water Rights & Allocations** **Read: Braiding Sweetgrass** (Chapter 5 - Section 2: The Sacred and the Superfund) Pg. 310-340 **Read: Selected Reading** Indigenous Peoples Water Rights: Challenges and Opportunities in an Era of Increased North American Integration (Walkem, 2004) PDF **Read: Selected Reading** Water Challenges and Solutions in First Nations Communities (Water Policy and Governance Group, 2010) PDF **Reflection Expression 4 (Water Quadrant) due at the end of class at 3:50pm.**
HOLISTIC	EARTH, FIRE, AIR, WATER
Class 13	**Community Round Table scheduled at 1:00pm-3:50pm.** **Journal Submission due by 11:59 pm. Please forward email to me at email address**

*Please note: all selected readings are on d2l, some of your classes might be land-based, and you will have various guest speakers.

Selected Readings

Assembly of First Nations. (2008). *Climate Change and Water: Impacts and Adaptations for First Nations Communities*. https://www.afn.ca/uploads/files/env/08-03-27_climate_change_and_water_research_paper_final.pdf

Gauer, V. H., Schaepe, D. M., & Welch, J. R. (2021). Supporting Indigenous adaptation in a changing climate: Insights from the Sto`:lo- Research and resource management centre (British Columbia) and the Fort Apache Heritage Foundation (Arizona). *Elementa Science of the Anthropocene*, 9(1). https://doi.org/10.1525/elementa.2020.00164

Jackson, S., MacDonald, D. H., & Bark, R. H. (2019). Public attitudes to inequality in water distribution: Insights from preferences for water reallocation from irrigators to Aboriginal Australians. *Water Resources Research*, 55, 6033–6048. https://doi.org/10.1029/2019WR025011

Knott, H. (2018). Violence and extraction stories from the oil fields. In K. Anderson, M. Campbell, & C. Belcourt (Eds.), *Keetsahnak: Our missing and murdered Indigenous sisters* (147-159). University of Alberta Press.

Manitowabi, S. (2018). Mining: The Historical and Current Context in Canada. In *Historical and contemporary realities: Movement towards reconciliation*. E-campus Ontario. https://ecampusontario.pressbooks.pub/movementtowardsreconciliation/chapter/mining-the-historical-and-current-context-in-canada/

Parks Canada. (2021). The life-giving forest. https://www.pc.gc.ca/en/nature/science/aires-areas/pimachiowin-aki

Walkem, A. (2004). *Indigenous Peoples Water Rights: Challenges and Opportunities in an Era of Increased North American Integration*. University of Victoria. https://www.uvic.ca/research/centres/globalstudies/assets/docs/publications/IndigenousPeoplesWaterRights.pdf

Water Policy and Governance Group. (2010). *Water Challenges and Solutions in First Nations Communities*. Social Sciences and Humanities Research Council of Canada. https://uwaterloo.ca/water-policy-and-governance-group/sites/ca.water-policy-and-governance-group/files/uploads/files/vonderporten_and_deloe_2010_0.pdf

Chapter 5
The Art of Teaching:
Métis Beadwork and Indigenous Legal Pedagogy

Danielle Lussier
https://orcid.org/0000-0002-2330-4109
Royal Military College of Canada, Canada & Queen's University, Canada

ABSTRACT

In this chapter, the author discusses the art of teaching, situating the use of beadwork practice mobilized in a classroom setting as an Indigenous legal pedagogy grounded in theories of persuasive legal aesthetic. She situates the pedagogical practice as one to support learning in the four spheres of intellectual, emotional, physical, and spiritual learning, and unpacks how whole-learner approaches to education can support both Indigenous learners who continue to live with the fallout of decades of forced assimilative education in Canada, and non-Indigenous Learners who are often engaging with Indigenous practices, peoples, and teachings for the first time in university settings as a result of ongoing systemic curricula failure at elementary and high school levels across Canada.

INTRODUCTION: WAYFINDING

I am Dr. Danielle Lussier, and I am Red River Métis and Citizen of the Manitoba Métis Federation born and raised in the homeland of the Métis Nation on Treaty 1 Territory. I am a beadworker, a legal scholar, a textile artist and, most importantly, mum to three tiny Métis growing up as visitors on the shores of Lake Ontario.

DOI: 10.4018/978-1-6684-3425-3.ch005

In this chapter, I will discuss the Art of Teaching, situating the use of beadwork practice mobilized in a classroom setting as an Indigenous Legal Pedagogy grounded in theories of Persuasive Legal Aesthetic (Lindberg, 2018). I will discuss how this pedagogical practice can support learning in the four spheres of intellectual, emotional, physical, and spiritual learning. I will also unpack how whole-learner approaches to education can support both Indigenous Learners who continue to live with the fallout of decades of Forced Assimilative Education (Battiste, 2013) in Canada, and non-Indigenous Learners who are often engaging with Indigenous practices, Peoples, and teachings for the first time in university settings as a result of ongoing systemic curricula failure at elementary and high school levels across Canada (Pete, 2017).

THE ART OF TEACHING

A common vocabulary is critical to moving forward in a good way, especially in contexts of cross-cultural communication where we might understand concepts in different ways (Wilson, 2017). While this may seem simplistic, it is worth taking a moment to define the core concept explored in this chapter: pedagogy. For the purposes of this discussion, I will use the term "pedagogy" in its most basic sense, as defined by the Merriam-Webster dictionary (2020), referring simply to "[t]he art, science, or profession of teaching".

As with other artistic practices, I do not understand pedagogy to be a static concept, but rather one that evolves over time. In the same way that not all art forms are appropriate for all spaces, pedagogical practices can and should vary depending on audience, context, and location. Further, I agree with Paulo Freire's (1992) position that "teaching is not the pure mechanical transfer of the contour of a content from the teacher to passive, docile students" (pp. 59-60). To teach, and to learn, requires active engagement of mind, and heart.

In 1995, Gloria Ladson-Billings argued in favour of the development of *Culturally Relevant Pedagogies* that would support not only academic success and the development or maintenance of cultural competence, but also the development of "critical consciousness through which [students] challenge the status quo of the current social order" (pp.160-62). This could be achieved, she suggested, through a variety of means, ranging from valuing and incorporating knowledge from community experts into the classroom experience through to engaging in cultural practice or using music as a bridge between "school learning" and other ways of knowing (p. 161).

Building on Ladson-Billings' theory of *Culturally Relevant Pedagogy* (1995), Sina J. Fakoyede and Femi S. Otulaja (2020) explored the mobilization of beads and beadwork as "cultural artifacts" (p.194) to support learning in a science classroom setting in South Africa. In this study that explored the impact of incorporating these cultural tools into the classroom on learning, the researchers conceptualized beads and beadwork through Bourdieu's (1978) lens of "embodied cultural capital" (as cited in Fakoyede and Otulaja, 2020, p. 197) as beadwork was understood to hold cultural significance for the Learners.

Fakoyede and Otulaja (2020) found that employing beads as a pedagogical tool had multiple positive outcomes for both Learners and the educator engaged in the classroom setting. For example, despite limited experience with the pedagogical practice grounded in principles of "learning by doing," the classroom instructor saw their classroom "transformed" (Fakoyede & Otulaja, 2020, pp. 203-207). The two researchers noted that partway through the experience of engaging with the beads, "learners' demeanor changed… and they began the process of expressing self-efficacy" (p. 204). Learners began to engage with the curriculum content posing questions and, at times, embodying the role of teacher within their work groups. In short, empowered by the use of culturally relevant materials, Learners demonstrated and exercised agency in the classroom in ways in which they had not before (Fakoyede and Otulaja, 2020)

Fakoyede and Otulaja's (2020) research findings are an encouraging example of how incorporating culturally relevant materials and pedagogical practices into the classroom environment holds tremendous transformative possibilities. Even in the context of this study, where the "embodied cultural capital" mobilized in the classroom was largely divorced from the curriculum content, remarkable changes in Learner and educator behaviours and engagement were observed. Though this study could be distinguished in a dozen ways from the use of Beadwork Practice as a pedagogical approach in legal education that I will propose in this chapter, I share it here as a marker of hope. If beads can empower science Learners and inspire passion for learning about molecular structures, just imagine what transformative power they might hold for legal education – a discipline where beads already carry law.[1]

Ladson-Billings' (1995) conceptualization of pedagogy as a bridge between worlds, as mobilized in the research of Fakoyede and Otulaja (2020) echoes the work of Indigenous scholars and their allies such as Marie Battiste (2013), and Val Napoleon et al., (2016). While not grounded in Indigenous worldview, much of Ladson-Billings' (1995) research speaks back to, and sometimes expressly informs, the work of Indigenous scholars who engage with questions of pedagogy as a tool for challenging Eurocentric constructs in the classroom.

In considering the work of Ladson-Billings (1995), Métis scholar Bryanna Rae Scott (2020) agreed that acknowledgement and validation of Indigenous Learners' knowledge systems and their lived experience of education is essential before educators can "authentically engage students in their learning" (p. 42). I personally understand this as building trust-based relationships in the classroom, a process which should be grounded in reciprocity. As bell hooks (2003) posits, "[c]reating trust usually means finding out what we have in common as well as what separates us and makes us different" (p. 109).

In her research, Ladson-Billings (1995) confirmed that the nature of the relationships between educators who employed culturally relevant pedagogies and their students were grounded in equity, with an understanding that the educators would sometimes take on the role of Learner, and Learners could act as teachers (p. 163). Further, she found that these relationships were not limited to school hours, with educators insisting on the creation of a "community of learners" beyond the four walls of the classroom and in the broader community (p. 163).

The idea of fluid, trust-based, and reciprocal relationships that exist beyond the classroom is one that resonates with me as both an Indigenous educator and lifelong Learner. I concur with Shawn Wilson (2008) when he reminds readers that "It is not possible for [Indigenous people] to compartmentalize the relationships that we are building apart from the other relations that make us who we are" (p. 91). This borderless fluidity, when considered in the context of teaching, stands in direct opposition to most Eurocentric conceptualizations that continue to prevail in post-secondary education, where knowledge is generally shared in a top-down way and hierarchies abound (Kennedy, 2017, p. 20).

Decolonizing the legal academy will take time, and the process will be imperfect; however, we must try. This is the duty owed to the generations who follow (Lindberg, 1997). Citing Elder Brenda Ireland and Elder Stan Wilson, Sylvia Moore (2017) reminds us that, when considering the decolonization of education, all we can do at any given time is our best. Given our starting point, the act of setting out down a good road of learning together can, in and of itself, be a remarkable achievement (Moore, 2017, pp. 89-90). Developing and implementing innovative pedagogical practices can, I believe, help smoothen the path.

Marie Battiste (2003) suggests that it is not only possible but also necessary for educators to engage in reflection on how pedagogical practice might occupy the spaces in between Indigenous and Western worldviews (p. 103). She advocates for educators to work to "respectfully blend Indigenous epistemology and pedagogy with Euro-Canadian epistemology and pedagogy to create an innovative ethical, trans-systemic Canadian educational system" (p. 168). The pedagogical hurdle educators must clear when engaging in trans-systemic methods, Battiste (2003) argues, is "not just reducing the distance between Eurocentric thinking and Aboriginal ways of knowing but engaging decolonized minds and hearts" (p. 168).

For me, espousing or developing Indigenous (legal) pedagogy is an act of decolonial resistance and love wherein we move beyond the simple transfer of knowledge and work to foster "a sense of collective agency, both to curb the excess of dominant power and to revitalize Indigenous communities" (Cote-Meek, 2014, p. 31). While

I do not believe that any one particular pedagogical practice can be a magic elixir that will instantly repair the hearts and minds of individuals and communities devastated by centuries of colonial interactions, I do understand pedagogy as a powerful decolonial tool that can serve to support the development of relationships necessary to move forward in a good way.

Discussions surrounding the use and development of Indigenous pedagogies usually begin with, or eventually return to, *Red Pedagogy* (Grande, 2010). Originally articulated and refined by Quechua scholar Sandy Grande (2010), *Red Pedagogy* is situated in a "space of engagement" at "the crossroads of Western theory and Indigenous knowledge" (p. 203). *Red Pedagogy* is effectively a "counter-hegemonic effort to occupy the space in between Western and Indigenous knowledge while centring Indigenous worldview in learning and teaching" (Cote-Meek, 2014, p.158). The interrelatedness of all things – including politics, culture, spirit, intellect, and place – is a core tenant of *Red Pedagogy* (Grande, 2010), as is an understanding that Indigenous scholars generally consider sovereignty and self-determination to be critical conversations in spheres of education (Cote-Meek, 2014; Grande, 2000).

One might describe *Red Pedagogy* as walking in two worlds, encouraging all community members, through the use of "community-based power," to engage deeply with questions of both colonialism and decolonization (Grande, 2010, pp. 204-205). We meet, Grande (2010) suggests, in the "liminal and intellectual borderlands... working to remember, redefine, and reverse the devastation of the original colonist encounter" (p. 203).

Sheila Cote-Meek (2014) meanwhile, suggests that a "sense of collectivity" (p.160) is born from this act of engaging parties from all positions within the colonial encounter. The idea of working in solidarity towards a common goal of resisting colonization is one Grande (2010) herself describes as replacing "to each his own" with "we are all related" (p. 206).

Like other scholars before me, I find Grande's (2010) *Red Pedagogy* to be both a source of hope (Cote-Meek, 2014) and a source of encouragement (Purton et al., 2020, p. 187). For the sake of clarity, however, it is worth expressly stating that my own work in the development of Indigenous Legal Pedagogies, while grounded in many of the same understandings of knowledge and interrelatedness of all things, differs from Grande's (2010) work in a significant way. Specifically, Grande (2010) situates her pedagogy in the sphere of intellectualism and foundational theory (thinking) rather than practical pedagogies for teaching, learning, and knowledge mobilization (doing). Grande (2010) states:

Red Pedagogy is not a methodology but rather a consciousness and way of being in/reading the world. As such, it is not something that can be "done" by teachers or "to" students, nor is it a technique that can be lifted, decontextualized, and applied.

It is rather a way of thinking about knowledge and the processes of teaching and learning as it emerges within and through relationships - between students, teachers, communities, and places. (pp. 204-205)

In other words, if we return to the dictionary definition of "pedagogy" offered at the beginning of this chapter, Grande (2010) appears to position *Red Pedagogy* in the sphere of the "science of teaching," whereas I conceptualize my own work in the category of the "art of teaching." In this way, Grande's (2010) theory of *Red Pedagogy* serves as a framework to ground and inform some of the theoretical and intellectual elements of my own practice-based pedagogical approaches. The two approaches are not in opposition, but rather at two different points on the (circular) continuum of theory/practice.

In the years that followed the emergence of *Red Pedagogy* (2010), many scholars working in spheres of Indigenous education advocated for pedagogical approaches that support learning in each of the four spheres of understanding: cognitive/intellectual, emotional, physical, and spiritual (Prete, 2019; Saysewahum, 2015; Tanaka, 2016). This holistic (Battiste, 2013, p. 66; Cote-Meek, 2014, p.162) conceptualization of teaching aims to normalize the incorporation of Indigenous knowledge systems and promote "intellectual self-determination" (Ray & Cormier, 2012, p. 168), maintain balance (Saysewahum, 2015, p.29) and promote healing (Cote-Meek, 2014, pp.32-34).

Centring Indigenous knowledge systems and asserting intellectual self-determination are, in my view, inherently decolonial acts, as is insisting on healing as a foundational tenant of my own teaching practice. I concur with bell hooks (2003), citing Parker Palmer: "[e]ducation is about healing and wholeness. It is about empowerment, liberation, transcendence, about renewing the vitality of life. It is about finding and claiming ourselves and our place in the world" (p. 43).

Unfortunately, under colonial education frameworks, Indigenous Learners are encouraged, if not required, to bifurcate their understandings and knowledge systems in the name of objectivity (Wilson, 2008, p. 56), and through the use of Western pedagogies (Cote-Meek, 2014, p. 40). Emotion and heart-knowledge is not only excluded from the classroom setting but, in cases where it finds entry through the side door, professors are encouraged to restore the Eurocentric status quo of exclusion by referring students to supports, such as counselling, outside the classroom (Cote-Meek, 2014, pp. 39-41).

Rapidly referring Learners to resources outside the classroom has a multi-layered impact[2] on the classroom experience and learning process. First, it allows educators to avoid having to address ongoing colonialism and racism in the classroom (Cote-Meek, 2014, pp. 39-41). Further, by prioritizing intellectual knowledge transfer to the exclusion of emotion and other ways of knowing, the experience of Indigenous Learners is rendered invisible. The specific exclusion of emotion from the classroom problematizes the individual Learner and absolves the collective from any responsibility of addressing underlying and systemic discrimination (Battiste, 2013, p. 33; Cote-Meek, 2014, p. 39; hooks, 2003, p. 87).

A second related consequence of this silencing and erasure is that non-Indigenous students are denied the opportunity to confront their own positions of privilege and examine their pre-established, colonial constructions of law.[3] The impact of this twofold failure to support non-Indigenous and Indigenous Learners should not be underestimated. By denying the collective, the opportunity to learn together, the ability of the community to move beyond colonial understandings of law is thus limited, and the focus on cognitive learning to the exclusion of emotion and other ways of knowing propagates colonial understandings of knowledge and serves to exclude and devalue Indigenous knowledge systems in the classroom.

Shawn Wilson's (2008) work, while focused primarily on academic research and not necessarily the classroom experience, supports a vision of holistic approaches to learning when he argues that the more ways in which we can build relationships to ideas, the more profound our understandings of those ideas will be (p.78). To properly build relationships to ideas requires an examination of relational context which, generally speaking, is not a primary focus of Eurocentric pedagogies (Ray & Cormier, 2012, p. 169). A front-of-mind example in the context of legal education is when the focus centres on learning legal principles, the *ratios* and the *obiters* and the *stare decisis*, with lesser emphasis on the facts underlying the court case. While the facts of the case may be surveyed, often for the purposes of allowing one to distinguish cases and avoid or encourage the application of legal principles to their own "fact patterns," in my experience the after-effects of decisions on individual parties were very rarely considered in a systemic way as part of the classroom learning experience.

The real-world outcomes for the parties involved in precedent-setting cases are often divorced from the learning and practice of law. This can cause cognitive dissonance for Indigenous Learners, who often understand knowledge sharing as a relational process. As Lana Ray and Paul Cormier (2012), Wolf Clan from Lake Helen First Nation, remind us, "while knowledge is accessed through the mind, body, heart, and spirit, mental knowledge is better understood not just through the mind, but instead through active partnership with the heart" (p. 169). It can be challenging to engage the heart when learning is distilled to rules and divorced from context. In short, "[n]on-relational knowledge is problematic because it does not allow for a holistic understanding of the knowledge to emerge" (Ray & Cormier, 2012, p. 167).

Alternatively put, pedagogies that centre non-relational knowledge, that teach from western spaces focused on a cognitive understanding unconnected from other ways of knowing, do not serve as culturally relevant mechanisms of knowledge transfer for some Indigenous Learners (Cote-Meek, 2014, p. 40). Returning to the work of

Ladson-Billings (1995) then, one might consider her argument that, in mobilizing Learners' own cultures to facilitate knowledge transfer, culturally relevant pedagogy could support not only individual learning, but also collective empowerment (p. 160).

This conceptualization of learning as a tool for collective empowerment is arguably all the more critical in the context of learning and unlearning as a decolonizing practice in law schools, given the long history of the law in supporting the colonial project and the reality of post-secondary institutions as sites of racism and ongoing colonialism. Angelina Weenie (2020) reminds us that "[l]iving in a racist society creates woundedness. Therefore, we do need to find ways to counter the racism and colonial practices we are subjected to" (p. 11). In my opinion, to begin to address anti-Indigenous racism and ongoing colonialism in the classroom will require empowering the collective through the use of culturally appropriate pedagogies that make space for the four spheres of knowing – cognitive, emotional, physical, and spiritual. Decolonization of spaces should not, and cannot, be the responsibility of Indigenous people alone. As bell hooks (2003) reminds us, "the process of ending racism in thought and action is always a mutual enterprise. All our power lies in understanding when we should teach and when we should learn" (p. 78). She further argues that "[p]rogressive education, education as the practice of freedom, enables us to confront feelings of loss and restore our sense of connection. It teaches us how to create community" (p. xv).

INDIGENOUS LEGAL PEDAGOGIES

Gathering the threads of the forgoing discussion, if we understand "pedagogy" as the art of teaching, I would suggest that "Indigenous pedagogy" is the art of Whole Learner teaching (body, mind, heart, and spirit) for community empowerment. Further, I would submit that the development and use of holistic Indigenous pedagogies should serve not only Indigenous Learners in the classroom but the full cohort of students who form part of the law school community.

Albeit in very different ways, colonial disruption is experienced by all who engage with educational systems in Canada. The process of (un)learning and healing must engage the entire community. Healing is, after all, a lifelong journey that "is not…confined to particular spaces" (Cote-Meek, 2014, p. 40). While many would prefer to exclude it from classroom spaces under Eurocentric models of education (Cote-Meek, 2014), I believe that making space for healing is critical to the larger project of decolonizing the legal academy as all of our community members must heal from the damage done.

Community empowerment and collective learning is an aspect that underpins most Indigenous Legal Pedagogies, established, emergent, and currently in use in law schools across Canada. A concrete and common example is land-based learning. This pedagogical approach to teaching and learning Indigenous laws and legal orders is often spoken of as something of a "gold standard" of Indigenous Legal Pedagogy, and is a process that engages all four spheres required for balance in learning: students are physically engaged in hands-on practices while bodily situated on the land (physical), learning and teaching law (intellectual/cognitive) in a group setting that allows for the exploration of one's own relationships to law, people, and land (emotion), while engaging with community members in ceremony and learning throughout the process (spiritual).

The land-based programs that have been developed at various law schools are incredible examples of efforts to decolonize the teaching of law and incorporate Indigenous laws, legal orders, and ways of knowing into legal education. Further, scholars such as Tracey Lindberg (1997) are thinking aloud about land-based learning in urban settings, and how established and tested pedagogical practices might be mobilized in different spaces to support learning while empowering communities (p.127). Gaudry and Lorenz (2018) would almost most certainly categorize the development of land-based learning programs as efforts towards "decolonial indigenization [which] envisions the wholesale overhaul of the academy to fundamentally reorient knowledge production based on balancing power relations between Indigenous peoples and Canadians, transforming the academy into something dynamic and new" (pp. 218-219).

Educators are also working to integrate Indigenous Legal Pedagogies in a spirit of decolonial indigenization in a panoply of other ways at law schools across Canada. Building relationships is a key element to most, if not all, of these teaching practices. For example, many Indigenous legal scholars engage in pedagogical practice that valorizes the "transformative capacity of intergenerational relationships, mediated by Elders, for the restoration, renewal, and resurgence of Indigenous languages, knowledges, and practice" (Kaleimamoowahinekapu Galla & Holmes, 2020, p. 53). This emphasis on building community and valorizing Indigenous knowledge keepers and systems can, and frequently does, emerge in several contexts within the legal academy including classrooms, lectures, and community events.

Further, individual educators are developing targeted Indigenous Legal Pedagogies to support specific lines of inquiry in their research. Jeffery Hewitt (2017), for example, integrates the study of art and extra-intellectual Indigenous knowledge into his teaching and research practice. An illustration of this practice appears in a study he co-authored with Ruth Buchanan (2017), wherein they explore the law carried in both a handwritten treaty document and on a painted drum, analyzing soundscapes alongside the western law of contracts, modern international law, and Indigenous legal orders – to name but a few elements canvassed in their study (p. 294).

As Buchanan and Hewitt (2017) explain, "[r]eading the treaty and drum together points us in the direction of a different kind of relationality. They demonstrate that there is more than one way to perform and derive meaning from law" (p. 302). Heart knowledge is engaged in the research through the juxtaposition of the Treaty and the drum, which requires a recentering of knowledge systems and prompts reflection on how the reader understands their relationship to colonial legal objects (p. 295).

Beyond engaging Learners at cognitive and emotional levels, a workshop delivered in the context of the research also included physical elements– visiting the drum in a museum environment and developing new objects participants could take away from the workshop that reflected "the essence" of the object (Buchanan & Hewitt, 2017, p. 295). Buchanan and Hewitt (2017) explain:

As the drum was originally a British military drum painted with Anishinaabe cosmological representations – an intersocietal object – we opted to represent it with British-sourced glass jam jars with tin lids, in which a handful of wild rice grown in Anishinaabe territory was contained. Though the drum was on display behind glass and therefore unable to be sounded, when our trace was shaken, the rice against the tin lid sounded like the snare of the drum, thus allowing participants to collectively imagine (and reproduce) the soundscape of the drum itself. (p. 295)

In my understanding of the world, this act of physically carrying the trace of the learning home following an arm's length encounter with objects held in a colonial institution engages one's spirit. I can personally attest to spiritual considerations when engaging with the research, even in absence of participation in the workshop. For me, discussions of Anishnaabe worldview as they relate to law-scapes and the silencing of the drum as a legal object held in a museum collection behind glass in Britain (Buchanan & Hewitt, 2017, p. 298), for example, spoke to a level of learning and understanding beyond both mind and heart knowledge. This holistic practice and unpacking of law, both Indigenous and colonial, embedded in art viewed as "legal objects" (Buchanan & Hewitt, 2017, p. 299), is a critical example of the language of possibility offered through the use of Indigenous Legal Pedagogies.

For his part, Darcy Lindberg (2018) explores academic and professional processes, including a focus on "technical efficiency," that have resulted in a simultaneous elevation of black letter law within hierarchies of legal knowledge and delegitimization of Indigenous laws and legal orders in *Miyo Nêhiyâwiwin (Beautiful Creeness): Ceremonial Aesthetics and Nêhiyaw Legal Pedagogy* (p. 53). Proposing an Indigenous Legal Pedagogy grounded in Cree worldview, Darcy Lindberg (2018) argues for the integration of Indigenous knowledge systems and making space for holistic learning process that engage "aesthetics" – "the spectrum of sensory experience, ranging from the limited sensuality of black letter law to full sensory experiences like the sweat lodge ceremony" – in legal education (p. 55).

Darcy Lindberg (2018) argues that persuasive aesthetics, learning and practicing Indigenous law in a beautiful way, can serve multiple purposes. First, he reminds us that "Nêhiyaw law is often meant to be practiced beautifully in order to convey its persuasive authority" (p. 55). The use of holistic pedagogies can therefore serve to honour the spirit and authority of Indigenous legal orders while also challenging the status quo of the prioritization of the written word over other legal knowledge in legal education (Lindberg, 2018, p. 54).

Second, he argues that beautiful aesthetic experiences can assist students in engaging with Indigenous law as they can "draw individuals towards the sensory experience (Lindberg, 2018, p. 55). Drawing on his own experiences as an undergraduate law Learner at the University of Victoria's Faculty of Law, Darcy Lindberg (2018) describes a moment when he witnessed active resistance to engaging with Indigenous laws and legal orders on the part of his peers (p. 52). He suggests that such pushback can emerge as a defense mechanism when students' pre-established, colonial understandings of law are challenged in the classroom (Lindberg, 2018, p. 52). He argues that the use of Indigenous legal epistemologies in education, such as facilitating aesthetic interactions with Indigenous laws, can encourage students to move beyond a defensive intellectual space where engaging with Indigenous laws is limited to a process of questioning their legitimacy (Lindberg, 2018, p. 58).

While the manifestation of the art of teaching described in *Miyo Nêhiyâwiwin* carries significant possibilities for legal education, Darcy Lindberg (2018) cautions that to engage with Indigenous laws through aesthetic experiences in a meaningful way requires clear structures of reciprocity and accountability (pp. 62-64). Without thoughtful consideration and mutual investment in the learning process, there is a risk of pedagogy grounded in aesthetic experience being valued for its surface beauty alone, and not for its transformative learning potential (Lindberg, 2018, p. 64). I understand this risk to be one of "window dressing" (Lindberg, 2018, p. 64), wherein the beautiful processes are only valued, and are sometimes fetishized, for their output while the underlying law and pedagogy are dismissed or diminished through what are ultimately "racist tactics" (Cote-Meek, 2014, p. 156). A concrete example Darcy Lindberg (2018) offers is that of inviting Indigenous guests to give words of welcome at events without thoughtful engagement before, after, or during the event, which effectively turns the exercise into a performative aesthetic practice (p. 64). In my experience, this risks prompting further colonial interactions wherein Indigenous knowledge systems are diminished and further subjugated.

These risks, however, can be mitigated. Building community and investing in reciprocal relationships is but one way in which these risks can be managed. In my view, it is worth the effort. As Darcy Lindberg (2018) reminds us, the integration of innovative Indigenous practices in legal education that serve to "propel our legal pedagogies towards a greater understanding that celebrative gratitude, in all its playfulness and colour, is serious. If we let it be in all its many forms, law can be beautiful" (p. 65).

BEADWORK PRACTICE AS AN EMBODIED INDIGENOUS LEGAL PEDAGOGY

If we are being completely honest, for altogether too many years, I was blind to the beautiful potential of law. Through a Eurocentric lens, my vision was clouded, and I was unable to see past the colonialism collision (Lussier, 2021, p. 148). It was only when I made peace with the reality that legal education was not designed by Indigenous people or with Indigenous Learners and communities in mind that I was able to catch glimpses of celebrative gratitude, playfulness, community, and joy through the fog. Interacting with the work of Indigenous scholars who refuse to succumb to pressure to perpetually justify our laws and legal orders in relation to colonial law but who choose, rather, to recentre conversations through the use of Indigenous voice, worldview, and pedagogy, transformed my vision of what legal education could be.

The transformative potential for Métis beadwork to act as a vehicle for legal knowledge mobilization on par with the written word in legitimacy and power is core to my understanding of reimagined legal research and was where I began to think about beadwork in relation to the academy. I would invite readers who are interested in this parallel proposition to visit with my body of written and stitched work.[4] Almost simultaneously, the possibilities of Beadwork Practice employed in legal education as a holistic Indigenous Legal Pedagogy emerged in my peripheral vision.

We will spend the rest of this chapter exploring the practicalities of beadwork as an embodied pedagogy in the context of all four spheres required for a balanced lived experience – intellectual, emotional, physical, and spiritual (Lavelle, 2009)– and discussing the therapeutic aspects of the practice and the potential for community healing within the legal academy.

To guide our conversation, I will be explicit and state that I consider any pedagogical practice that serves to counteract ongoing colonialism and racism in the classroom to hold therapeutic and/or healing potential. Put another way, "anti-therapeutic" can be understood as actions supporting the status quo, reinforcing colonial structures and understandings of law, and failing to confront ongoing colonialism and racism in the academy. Further, I will add that I believe that love and care set the stage for effective learning. bell hooks (2003) reminds us, "[w]hen as teachers we teach with love, combining care, commitment, knowledge, responsibility, respect and trust, we are often able to enter the classroom and go straight to the heart of the matter" (p. 134). Providing opportunities for learning grounded in a practice of building reciprocal, trust-based relationships to ideas, people, and communities is thus critical to supporting learning and healing in these spaces.

Through the pedagogical practice described herein, beadwork operates in a few different ways beyond the most basic level of knowledge mobilization where beadwork functions as both artistic expression and as a mnemonic device. In the "learning by doing" aspects of the pedagogy, Beadwork Practice is used to encourage students to engage with course content in different ways and build intellectual, emotional, physical, and spiritual bridges between themselves and colonial and Indigenous laws. Integrated into the law school classroom as part of a holistic teaching practice involving reading, writing, and artistic expression, in this participatory, inclusive, and circle-based practice (Wilson, 2008), Learners and the lead educator learn together and are empowered to build both relationships and cognitive bridges between knowledge systems.

Before We Begin: Reflecting on Relationships to and with this Pedagogical Practice

A few general comments before we proceed, for the sake of clarity. First, as I am sure is clear by now, I am writing for multiple audiences. I write for my family, for my Learners and students, for my colleagues, for the generations that follow. I also write for the Western academy.

The following sections may read, to some, as a "how to" guide for my personal pedagogical practice, however nothing in this chapter should be read by non-Indigenous scholars as an invitation to adopt, adapt, or employ Beadwork Practice as a pedagogy in their own classrooms as their core teaching practice. While I personally believe it could be appropriate for non-Indigenous scholars to engage with Indigenous artists and knowledge keepers to incorporate beadwork practice into their learning plans as defined and guided learning experiences, it would be both inappropriate and appropriative for non-Indigenous scholars to read what I have written here and employ it into their own classrooms as their foundational pedagogy. What I describe below is not a checklist for how to engage in persuasive legal aesthetics as articulated through beadwork. It is a peek behind the curtain to a layered process of supporting Indigenous and non-Indigenous Learners intellectual and emotional development and building relationships and community around law learning. At the risk of repeating myself: I have written this so that you may begin to understand the depth of the academic and extra-intellectual work this embodied pedagogical practice entails. It is not for you to appropriate.

Speaking now to my Indigenous colleagues and Learners: the following sections should not be read as prescriptive or limiting. I do not intend for this work to be understood as a definitive guide or a set of requirements for incorporation of my/our cultural practice(s) into learning environments. There is no one-size-fits all approach to the mobilization of beadwork as a tool for learning and sharing in legal education. I humbly offer some suggestions below based on years of thinking and learning by doing. My hope is that you may hold this work up as a shield against colonial visions of what is appropriate, legitimate, and possible in legal education. More importantly, I hope it might inspire you to imagine possibilities for educating in full, joyful, and loving colour.

Circles and Spaces

This pedagogy is best employed through a circle format, which positions all participants as equal in the learning process and encourages sharing of both intellectual and extra-intellectual knowledge.

Citing Lewis Cardinal, Shawn Wilson (2008) reminds us "[t]he circle is found throughout Indigenous societies and their architecture and how they make governmental decisions. The circle is like a foundational platform… It's egalitarian, it's relational, it's a structure that supports inclusion, a wholeness" (p. 92). In other words, circles articulate an Indigenous understanding of relationality.

Discussing the use of sharing circles in the context of academic research, Lynn Lavallée (2009) positions circles as a culturally appropriate method for sharing knowledge:

Sharing circles are used to capture people's experiences. They are comparable to focus groups in qualitative research where researchers gather information on a particular topic through group discussion (Berg, 1995, as cited in, Lavallée, 2009, pp. 28-29). How they differ from focus groups is the sacred meaning they have in many Indigenous cultures and in the growth and transformation bases for the participants. Sharing circles use a healing method in which all participants (including the facilitator) are viewed as equal and information, spirituality, and emotionality are shared, a method that is familiar and comforting for some Aboriginal participants… (pp. 28-29)

Describing sharing circles used at the close of land-based learning experiences, John Borrows (2017) notes that the breadth and depth that participants shared and the manners in which they did so exceeded the sharing that takes place in classroom settings (p. 21). Other educators, such as Sylvia Moore (2017), have observed similar phenomena, remarking on the development of relationships between participants "at a depth uncommon in the Western educational context" (p. 35).

As participants build relationships to one another and to ideas, the collective is transformed. (Steinhauer et al., 2020, p. 84). I believe this is attributable to the energy generated in circle through the development of trust-based relationships and the process of active listening that participants engage in while learning from each other (Lavallée, 2009, pp. 28-29). Further, circle-based classroom practice makes space for all community members to find their voice, not only who are "loudest, most persuasive or most charismatic" (Ray, 2015, p. 237). In requiring Learners to "[put] down the notepad," circle-based learning disrupts colonial learning structures (Tanaka, 2016, p.62), and makes space for other ways of knowing. This fundamentally alters the classroom experience (Tanaka, 2016, p.67).

It is clear from the research cited above that circle-based pedagogy serves to support each of the spheres of learning: physical spaces are reconfigured, bringing all Learners and educators into equal and supported physical spaces. Within the circle, Learners and educators engage in respectful sharing through exchange of spiritual, emotional, and intellectual ideas. Echoing Lewis Cardinal and Shawn Wilson (2008), Sylvia Moore (2017) states the heart of the matter quite plainly: "[i]n the learning circles we were connected through our relationships and we were whole" (p. 35).

Beyond the academy, beadworkers also remark on the sense of wholeness born in beading circles:

I have always left the beading circle feeling centered and balanced, much, much better, on many different levels—physically, emotionally and psychologically... I always feel leaving the same way. I feel calm, I feel relaxed, I feel balanced, I feel somewhat fulfilled because I have sat with women. Always does that for me. It fills me up. It's a part of my wellness... I leave here feeling whole and healthier and balanced and, in more harmony, which is what I seek, and is probably what we all seek. (Edge, 2011, pp. 108-109)

Espousing a circle-based framework for this Indigenous Legal Pedagogy makes sense on several levels. At the most basic level, in addition to the reasons set out above, beadwork has traditionally been done in the home and around tables in shared spaces (Gray, 2017, p. 35).

This format, however, has implications on the physical spaces required to best engage with the pedagogical practice. To mobilize the pedagogy described herein, the ideal classroom space would see Learners and the lead educator seated around a round table in a space with natural light and adequate task lighting, with a common supply of materials in the centre of the table. For those educators who choose to offer smudging opportunities as part of their teaching, discussed further below, the ideal classroom will have windows that open or adequate ventilation.

As we learn through "spirit bead" teachings, however, nothing in life is perfect.[5] That is okay. As educators and lifelong Learners, we have all had the experience of teaching and learning in less-than-ideal physical spaces from time to time. A prime example experienced by many with the emergence of Covid-19 was the unanticipated and urgent shift to online learning.

Physical spaces should not serve as a barrier to mobilizing this pedagogy. Less than perfect temporary solutions are okay: desks and tables can be rearranged so that Learners can face each other. While we shelter at home and live and learn in online spaces, tools such as the "boardroom" function on the Microsoft Teams platform, which allows the host to "seat" participants around a virtual conference table and help ease the visual strain and disconnect of "gallery" view. When all is said and done, the critical piece is the feeling generated in the room when all participants are actively listening and engaged in learning and sharing in a supportive space. The pedagogy can most certainly be used in auditoriums and classrooms with fixed seating while we support the institutions that we operate within to build physical spaces that properly support Indigenous Legal Pedagogies.

Supplies

Learning begins, and relationships are born, through the creation of each Learner's beading box. There are a few ways in which to approach this phase of the work, the choice of which will depend on several factors including the timing of the course during the academic year, the geographic location of the law school, the availability of funding, the number of students in the course, the relationship of the faculty to the bookstore and law library, and the specific pedagogical objectives of the lead educator.

It is, for example, possible that educators themselves choose to assemble entry-level beading kits with the necessary materials for distribution to Learners. Others might prefer to build relationships with Indigenous suppliers, in person or online, to create course packs available for purchase by Learners in lieu, or in supplement, of textbooks. Some might choose to provide Learners a list of required items and suggested suppliers and ask them to engage in their own research before purchasing their supplies.

While slightly more onerous for the lead educator, my personal preference is a combination of all of the above. First, the creation of some preassembled supply kits is a non-negotiable, as lead educators should ensure that kits are put on reserve in the law library for use by Learners who prefer to access their course materials through the library. This serves a few different pedagogical objectives, including

ensuring accessibility of the course materials to those who find textbooks and supplies cost-prohibitive, and institutionally valorizing the materials on the same level as legal textbooks.

Working with Indigenous suppliers' fosters building relationships with local community members and, if there is a brick-and-mortar store in the community, encouraging Learners to begin developing their own relationships with Indigenous suppliers. Offering the option of premade course packs can support hesitant Learners by taking the guesswork out of their initial engagement with beadwork supplies, mitigating the initial barrier of fear of making mistakes that many law students face when engaging with Indigenous peoples and laws. Finally, engaging with the cultural economic enterprise of beadwork and supporting Indigenous entrepreneurs honours the multi-layered value of beadwork practice in Indigenous communities and reinvests dollars into communities.

Providing a suggested materials list and empowering Learners to build their own beading box can offer some agency and freedom to those Learners who may already engage in beadwork practice, or who have artistic, brand, or supplier preferences. This option requires the highest level of engagement for Learners, but, in my view, it also offers the best opportunity for Learners to begin building their community circle of practice.

Technique

Transferring knowledge of physical beadwork practice and anchoring artistic techniques for each Learner represents a significant opportunity for engaging with members of the broader community. This meets several community needs and pedagogical objectives.

Lead educators who have already established their own practices might wish to personally facilitate knowledge transfer in the classroom in collaboration with local beadwork artists and knowledge keepers. In-person learning and hands-on support, or curated online spaces focused on the development of artistic technique, afford opportunities for relationship building between educators and their students and is non-negotiable in this pedagogical practice. Speaking of legal principles shared during ceremony in a sweat lodge, Darcy Lindberg (2018) reminds us that legal knowledge transferred through writing alone would hold knowledge keepers to a lesser standard of knowledge. Legal knowledge transferred through physical ceremonial experiences, however, requires knowledge seekers to take responsibility for the embodiment process (Lindberg, 2018, pp. 60-61). The same principles apply to beadwork practice: the embodiment process carries weight in each of the spheres of learning and is foundational to the mobilization of the pedagogy.

As some of us continue to live and learn in online environments due to the global public health crisis, this knowledge sharing process becomes more complex, but is certainly not impossible. In online learning environments, for example, through the use of multiple cameras, educators can focus on the details of handwork techniques. The use of "screen sharing" functions can be employed to share teachings pre-recorded by educators or publicly available technique-oriented videos. Narrated slide decks can incorporate still images and infographics. The whole can be supplemented by oral teachings, and so on.[6]

In a decolonized academy this would go without saying, but today I will state it explicitly: when community members, artists, and knowledge keepers are invited into classroom spaces to support learning and contribute to knowledge transfer, there must be an element of reciprocity in the relationship. It is critical that lead educators ask what this means for each individual knowledge holder. In some cases, it might mean an opportunity to sit with Learners and share a meal following the knowledge exchange. Other times, these educators may prefer the exchange of medicines, cloth, or beading supplies. Sometimes an honorarium is preferred. When payment is made in cash, it is critical that knowledge holders are compensated commensurate with their knowledge and experience, and that their expertise is valued in the same ways that the legal academy values other invited guest lecturers and speakers. Indigenous knowledge systems have been subjugated through Eurocentric understandings of knowledge, and those individuals who carry knowledge and law on behalf of the community have been undervalued for too long. This is ongoing, and often emerges in situations where an expectation that Indigenous knowledge keepers will share their expertise for free or for insultingly inadequate stipends, demonstrating that the academy still does not consider Indigenous knowledge on par with western academic knowledge.

In-person circle work can be supplemented by the use of written technique guides[7] and online videos and tutorials to ensure that the process is as inclusive as possible. Offering a variety of formats of support for the development of technique is important when considering questions of Universal Design – we shall return to this discussion below.

As educators develop communities of practice within their law schools, there will eventually be a cohort of alumni who may wish to return to engage with current Learners. Offering opportunities for relationship building with former Learners supports wellbeing while also serving to support the development of critical professional connections. A significant barrier to academic and professional success in law is a severe lack of mentorship for Indigenous Learners and lawyers, facilitating connections between Learners, alumni, and practitioners can begin to bridge gaps and better support Learners as they transition into professional roles.

Inclusivity and Universal Design in Learning

I am preoccupied, especially following humbling learning experiences early in my career as an educator, by the question of inclusivity in the learning environments I am responsible for curating. I have been learning by doing and, full transparency: learning the art of teaching has a steep curve.

Article 2 of the United Nations Convention on the Rights of Persons with Disabilities (CRPD) (2006) defines "Universal Design" as "the design of products, environments, programmes and services to be usable by all people, to the greatest extent possible, without the need for adaptation or specialized design. While principles of Universal Design were initially conceptualized in the context of accessibility and design of physical spaces (National Disability Authority, 2017). *Universal Design in Learning* (UDL) has emerged as a specialized subdiscipline focused on accessibility and inclusion in education (Gordon et al., 2016). At the most basic level, principles of Universal Design in Learning call on educators to provide "multiple, flexible methods" of presentation, expression, apprenticeship, and engagement in the classroom, with a view to providing a "richer cognitive learning environment for all students" (Rose, 2001, pp. 66-67).

The deeper I dove into readings on *Universal Design in Learning* (Bracken & Novak, 2019), the more I began to feel an intellectual kinship to the theory and its accompanying practices. To use the language of Indigenist research, I came to understand *Universal Design in Learning* as seeking to support all Learners by offering multiple opportunities to build relationships to ideas. My own efforts to develop Indigenous Legal Pedagogy for use in legal education are, of course, also grounded in similar attempts to encourage holistic approaches to education and better support multiple ways of knowing and doing.

While the incorporation of Beadwork Practice into the classroom environment offers what I believe to be a significant language of possibility for reshaping and decolonizing legal education, when considering the pedagogy through the lens of Universal Design in Learning some barriers to full participation are immediately obvious. For example, to cut and sew hide requires a certain level of manual dexterity. To manipulate small beads and thread needles requires visual acuity. To sit long hours developing one's practice requires a certain level of physical health and stamina.

Undeterred, I continued to reflect on how Beadwork Practice could be mobilized in a classroom setting through the lens of Universal Design in Learning, turning my mind to questions of how the pedagogy might be employed in a more inclusive way. One pedagogical objective of the use of Beadwork Practice in the classroom is to recentre and value Indigenous knowledge systems while building bridges between Western and Indigenous understandings of law. The overall nature of the pedagogy is one of curated community-oriented learning. It would, therefore, be a natural extension of circle-based classroom learning to encourage collaboration and mutual support for the physical component of the beadwork practice. The use of group assignments requiring collaboration to complete the physical beadwork component could engage groups of students as a variation of the pedagogical practice that would support an inclusive learning environment.

While I originally conceptualized a circle-based pedagogy where each Learner engages in both collective learning and sharing and an individual beadwork practice, there is nothing to prevent a teams-based approach to learning under this pedagogical framework. Working in groups, Learners could collaborate to design and execute a single piece of beadwork, with members working on different elements of the practice. From research and pattern making to sewing, weaving, and drafting written work that supports the physical expression and interprets the mnemonic device, group members could select elements of the process that allow them to participate in the most comfortable way for them. This echoes the approaches often employed in community beading circles I lead, where various community members engage in different moments of the creation process, in the ways they feel most comfortable.

This idea of comfort, physical and emotional, is the final consideration I will discuss here. As previously discussed, many beaders note the meditative and calming aspects of beadwork practice. I am aware, however, of challenges that might arise for some Learners should they attempt to bring their beadwork practice into their home or dorm environments; resistance to practices that disrupt the status quo can emerge in spaces beyond the classroom. To ensure inclusivity in the learning experience, it is important that adequate classroom time is devoted to the practice to allow Learners to bring their projects to completion, should they not wish to bead outside the classroom. This can be accomplished a few different ways, depending on course scheduling – for example by devoting one of two weekly lectures to physical art in parallel to discussion circles, by allowing or encouraging Learners to bead throughout lectures, or by structuring weekly office hours in such a way that Learners have additional time to gather in circle should they desire or require it.

In the end, "[e]ducation is about healing and wholeness. It is about empowerment, liberation, transcendence, about renewing the vitality of life. It is about finding and claiming ourselves and our place in the world" (hooks, 2003, p. 43). With a little creative thinking and collaboration, the healing benefits of this pedagogical practice can be accessible to all.

Spheres of Learning

We will now unpack this holistic Indigenous Legal Pedagogy through the lens of each of the four spheres of learning – cognitive, emotional, physical, and spiritual – as attention to each of these elements is critical to ensure that the learning experience is balanced. This exercise in deconstructing the pedagogy and attempting to present the component parts in a linear fashion is, in fact, in direct opposition to the Indigenist research paradigms I espouse; however, my attempt to do so here is, once again, an exercise of hopeful resistance. In engaging with teaching practice that supports the whole Learner, I resist Western education frameworks that exclude layered Indigenous knowledge systems. The act is grounded in the hope that those who engage with my work will begin their journeys to understanding the complexity and depth of culturally informed pedagogies employed by Indigenous scholars.

Intellectual

Any act of learning is an intellectual event; the mind is engaged as students are exposed to new ideas. As we have previously discussed, in the legal academy learning is generally reserved exclusively to this sphere. Incorporated into the classroom, Beadwork Practice compliments the examination of all forms of academic materials relevant to the course being taught. As with readings on any syllabus, these materials could range from legal doctrine and jurisprudence to Treaties, legislation, through to interdisciplinary works in other disciplines. Depending on the course on offer, extra-intellectual works such as works of literature, written or recorded stories and narrative accounts, or videos may be included. The incorporation of Beadwork Practice into the classroom experience facilitates interactions with the law in new ways, allowing Learners to forge deeper relationships to ideas.

A Learner in a constitutional law course, for example, may choose to engage in Beadwork Practice to bead a sparrow when studying the 1990 case *R v Sparrow*. Throughout the meditative practice, the Learner sits with the ideas of s.35 (Canadian Constitution Act, 1982) case law and produces a mnemonic device that can serve to deepen their own understandings of the law and also transfer knowledge to others. In sharing knowledge through their beadwork, the Learner is held to a higher standard of learning – that of being able to explain – aurally, orally, or both – and unpack the teachings carried in their work.

The therapeutic aspect of the integration of Beadwork Practice into this sphere of learning is found in deconstructing Eurocentric understandings of learning. Recentring Indigenous perspectives in the classroom, the use of this pedagogy encourages Learners to reframe how to read the world and understand law. Considering extra-intellectual knowledge through an academic lens as Buchanan and Hewitt (2017) did in reading the painted drum alongside the handwritten treaty (p. 294), Learners are required to confront the historic and ongoing erasure of Indigenous voices and understandings in the classroom. They must ultimately grapple with how the subjugation of that knowledge has altered their own comprehension and learning of law in society.

Emotional

Considering law at the intellectual level through this broadened decolonial lens quickly engages emotion as students begin to contemplate their own role in the broader colonial project and how they may be contributing to the ongoing colonization of Indigenous peoples. We have already engaged in significant discussions about the damage resulting from the exclusion of emotion from the classroom experience. Without revisiting the conversation on the whole, we can take a moment now to gather the threads already loosely woven.

Keri Cheechoo (2020) suggests that "[e]thical relationality, or the act of being responsible for what we bring into any space with us, is critical [to the classroom experience]. It is also critical to remember that as educators we have agency to leave life's stressors at the school doors, but our students cannot help but carry their traumas into classrooms with them" (p. 263). In her understanding, ethical relationality "means recognizing that you are in a space with people who are unlike you and respecting those dissimilarities enough to meet halfway and learn from each other in the space where you meet" (Cheechoo, 2020, p. 258).

The idea of ethical relationality as articulated by Cheechoo (2020) is a core tenet of my pedagogical practice. In integrating Beadwork Practice, specifically circle-based beadwork practice, into the classroom experience, we are attempting to generate spaces of community and shared learning in between two worldviews and grounded in an act of persuasive legal aesthetics. Further, the circle framework serves to support students and Learners as they experience the shifts in understanding that come with the integration of Indigenous ways of knowing into the classroom setting. In a learning circle, all participants are encouraged to unpack their thoughts and understandings in a holistic way that remains cognizant of relationships between heart and mind knowledge. As Sylvia Moore (2017) shares, "[i]n the reciprocity of telling and listening, there is an acknowledgement that begins the healing or the repairing and strengthening of relationship threads" (p. 145).

In honouring and making space for emotion in the classroom, Indigenous ways of knowing are centred in the learning process, counteracting the ongoing colonial understandings of knowledge that continue to function within post-secondary education. In creating opportunities for Learners and students to learn from each other and build relationships, we begin to redefine and redistribute power that has long been unbalanced within the academy. The therapeutic elements of the emotional sphere of the practice are, in fact, innumerable.

Physical

Beyond the physical arrangement of the classroom space and the use of the circle-based learning strategies that underpin this pedagogy as discussed earlier in this chapter, the practice of beadwork itself also serves to engage the physical sphere of learning. For example, many beadworkers report physical changes when engaging in the artistic practice, including a slowing of the heart rate and breathing and a calming of the physical manifestations of anxiety (Lussier, 2021, p. 328). Further, interacting with beads and beadwork as legal objects, Learners engage all their physical senses in a multisensory experience that shatters the norm for a western classroom experience.

Touch and sight should require no further elaboration, and listening is also likely readily understood. Beyond auditory learning in the context of circle, however, there are other soundscapes associated with Beadwork Practice. As Lisa Shepherd (2016), Métis artisan, explains: "[t]here's life and there's a breath in the work that you are doing… I love the sound of the thread being pulled up through the fabric, through the hide. There's just something so alive about it." In my classroom, music contributes to the soundscape. Learners contribute to playlists that serve as a soundtrack for the community to use in moments reserved for practicing technique. My own contributions to the playlist feature contemporary Indigenous artists alongside traditional Métis jigs and reels, which serve as an entry point for conversations about lived Indigenous experience in Canada. In working collaboratively to develop the soundscape, students and Learners can each integrate audible touchstones that bring them comfort, inspire them, or keep them grounded in their practices. Playlists are also accessible online for Learners to use during the impromptu beading circles that inevitably emerge beyond the walls of the classroom, or to surround them with the soundtrack of their new community as they work on their projects alone.

Encouraging Learners to engage their sense of smell, meanwhile, flows naturally from engaging sight, touch, and hearing. Lois Edge (2011) describes not only the soundscape from the moments when she held moccasins sewn by her grandmother in the researcher room of a museum in Britain (p. 73), but also her instinct to lean over and smell the beadwork, seeking the scent of comfort that she recalled from her childhood (p. 72) spent sitting at her grandmother's kitchen table while she beaded (p. 3). In fact, artists will often smell supplies as part of the beadwork process to determine what elements to use (Farrell Racette, 2004, p. 250), a fact unsurprising to anyone who has ever had the privilege of inhaling the scent of home-tanned smoked moose hide.

Integrating the final physical sense, taste, via nourishment in the circle is a part of my own classroom practice. Were you to ask them, my Learners would probably report that I am quite militant about keeping food away from the beadwork, and yet there is always food and drink on offer in the spaces I curate. Morning sessions may include breakfast at the outset, soup and bannock emerges mid-day. While offering full meals will not be feasible for all educators or in all learning contexts, it is undeniable that the act of eating together strengthens community bonds.

As in the sphere of emotional learning, the therapeutic possibilities in this sphere are many. Making space for a multisensory circle-based classroom experience that supports all of the physical senses readily disrupts the status quo of Eurocentric classroom models. Engaging in Beadwork Practice can offer a calming physical effect for those struggling with stress (Farrell Racette, 2004), something often experienced by Indigenous Learners as they maneuver through post-secondary education (Battiste, 2013; Cote-Meek, 2014). These meditative side effects of the mobilization of this Indigenous Legal Pedagogy are also relevant to our exploration of the final sphere, spirituality.

Spiritual

Marie Battiste (2013) maintains that engaging with the spiritual can be understood as a "pedagogical challenge" (p. 184). I believe this is particularly true when teaching and learning happens in the context of secular western educational institutions. The conversation is further complicated by difficulties in distinguishing the idea of spiritual care from religion, as the two are often conflated. Given the long and fraught relationship between Indigenous education and various Churches who were engaged in the Forced Assimilative Education of Indigenous children through their leadership roles in the genocidal project of Residential Schools, it is not difficult to understand why some might shy away from conversations about care of the spirit integrated into pedagogical practice. While these conversations can be challenging, they are critical to fully understanding the transformative potential of Beadwork Practice as an Indigenous Legal Pedagogy.

Throughout this chapter I have frequently returned to the work of Shawn Wilson (2008) in *Research Is Ceremony: Indigenous Research Methods*, a monograph that represented an intellectual turning point in the context of my own research. Focusing on the decolonization of approaches to knowledge production, Wilson (2008) draws parallels between ceremonial practices and academic research. He sets the stage with general discussions of Indigenous understandings of ceremony, reminding readers that the "purpose of any ceremony is to build stronger relationships or bridge the distance between aspects of our cosmos and ourselves" (p. 11) before ultimately concluding that the act of research is, in and of itself, a ceremonial practice (p. 69).

The importance of consistently working to build healthy relationships, with an emphasis on the process and preparation required to be in a position to hear and understand what is being shared, is a theme woven into the fabric of Wilson's research

(2008, p. 60). The culmination of the research ceremony, he suggests, is the moment when the researcher, having dedicated themselves to building relationships to people and ideas, gathers the threads and makes connections between them (p. 89).

This understanding of academic research as ceremony is grounded in understandings of the interconnectedness of all things: "[i]f we take this way of looking at spirituality as connection to the cosmos, then any exercise that increases connection or builds relations is spiritual or ceremonial in nature" (Wilson, 2008, p. 91). Beadwork, for many, is one such opportunity to build relationships, and thus engages the sacred and the spiritual. For example, some beadworkers choose to engage in ceremonial practices such as smudging before beading to ensure that their hearts and minds are clear before engaging with their work (Gray, 2017, p. 24). This echoes the use of ceremonial practices such as smudging to open and/or close sharing and learning circles, an act that brings an additional element of spirituality into the learning process (Steinhauer et al., 2020).

Some beadwork artists consider beadwork itself to be a form of prayer (Belcourt, 2017, as cited in Gray, 2017, p. 5) and many understand beadwork practice as an act of meditation and spiritual care (Prete, 2019). Others still consider beadwork to be a form of medicine, a practice that grounds us in our spirituality and culture as Indigenous people and holds the potential for healing (Robertson & Navarro, 2020).

Many have argued, and I agree, that Indigenous pedagogies should seek to support the whole Learner, including the spirit (Lavallée, 2009; Saysewahumm 2015; Tanaka, 2016). Beadwork Practice, employed as an Indigenous Legal Pedagogy, presents an opportunity to honour the need to attend to the spirit and encourage whole learning experiences in the classroom. For the sake of absolute clarity, I firmly believe in freedom of religion, expression, and fundamental human rights. When I speak here of spirituality in learning, I am speaking not of religion, but of care of the spirit. Creating space for care of the spirit is element of the pedagogical practice that is made available for those who need or want it but would never be imposed as a mandatory element in the learning space.

That said, the role of spiritual care in the Beadwork Practice of those who wish to engage in it fills a significant need for some Indigenous Learners. Offering opportunities to those who wish to incorporate ceremonial elements into their learning is an act of decolonial love that changes the lived experience of law school for Indigenous peoples. Opening up these opportunities and spaces for discussion of holistic approaches to learning and understanding law also arguably holds the potential to change the ways in which all within the school of law understand Indigenous knowledge systems and conceptualize legal education.

If we understand all things to be interconnected, offering opportunities for care for the spiritual sphere is critical for an Indigenous Legal Pedagogy to be balanced and complete. In its potential to act as a ceremonial or spiritual practice, Beadwork

Practice as an Indigenous Legal Pedagogy can assist in creating a therapeutic community of care for those who wish or require it within law school.

PARTING THOUGHTS

In the executive summary of Final Report of the Truth and Reconciliation Commission of Canada (2015), the commissioners stated:

To the Commission, reconciliation is about establishing and maintaining a mutually respectful relationship between Aboriginal and non-Aboriginal peoples in this country. In order for that to happen, there has to be awareness of the past, acknowledgement of the harm that has been inflicted, atonement for the causes, and action to change behaviour. We are not there yet. The relationship between Aboriginal and non-Aboriginal peoples is not a mutually respectful one. But we believe we can get there, and we believe we can maintain it. Our ambition is to show how we can do that. (pp. 6-7)

At the outset of this chapter, I was clear that I do not believe that the use of any one particular pedagogical practice will somehow instantly repair the hearts and minds of individuals and communities devastated by centuries of colonial interactions. Rather, I understand pedagogy as a powerful decolonial tool that can serve to support the development of relationships necessary to move forward in a good way. If the goal of reconciliation, as the Commissioners suggest above, is developing mutually respectful relationships grounded in a common understanding of truth, I humbly propose that integrating Beadwork Practice, grounded in theories of Persuasive Legal Aesthetics, into the legal classroom experience offers a language of possibility. Supporting the four spheres of learning and encouraging all learners to gather together in a multisensory learning experience grounded in Indigenous ways of knowing offers a concrete opportunity to change behaviour and challenge the status quo of a strictly intellectual learning experience, while also facilitating the (re)building of community connections.

REFERENCES

Battiste, M. (2013). *Decolonizing Education: Nourishing the Learning Spirit*. UBC Press.

Bedard, R. (2014, July 8). *Beading 101 Technique Series, Beading Needle Style #2* [Video]. Youtube. www.youtube.com/watch?v=q9lhLRBs3Xw

Borrows, J. (2017). Outsider Education: Indigenous Law and Land-Based Learning. *Windsor Yearbook of Access to Justice, 33*(1), 1–27. doi:10.22329/wyaj.v33i1.4807

Bourdieu, P. (1978). Sport and social class. *Social Sciences Information. Information Sur les Sciences Sociales, 17*(6), 819–840. doi:10.1177/053901847801700603

Bracken, S., & Novak, K. (Eds.). (2019). *Transforming Higher Education Through Universal Design for Learning: An International Perspective.* Routledge. doi:10.4324/9781351132077

Buchanan, R., & Hewitt, J. G. (2017). Encountering Settler Colonialism Through Legal Objects: A Painted Drum and Handwritten Treaty from Manitoulin Island. *The Northern Ireland Legal Quarterly, 68*(3), 291–304. doi:10.53386/nilq.v68i3.41

Cheechoo, K. (2020). Reframing Reconciliation: Turning Our Back or Turning Back? In S. Cote-Meek & T. Moeke-Pickering (Eds.), *Decolonizing and Indigenizing Education in Canada* (pp. 247–266). Canadian Scholars.

Constitution Act. (1982). s 35, being Schedule B to the Canada Act 1982 (UK), c 11.

Cote-Meek, S. (2014). *Colonized Classrooms: Racism, Trauma and Resistance in Post-Secondary Education.* Fernwood Publishing.

Edge, L. E. (2011). *My Grandmother's Moccasins: Indigenous Women, Ways of Knowing and Indigenous Aesthetic of Beadwork.* [Doctoral Dissertation, University of Alberta]. ProQuest Dissertation and Theses Database. https://www.collectionscanada.gc.ca/obj/thesescanada/vol2/002/NR80952.PDF,

Fakoyede, S. J., & Otulaja, F. S. (2020). Beads and Beadwork as Cultural Artifacts Used in Mediating Learners' Agentic Constructs in Science Classrooms: A Case for Place-Based Learning. *Cultural Studies of Science Education, 15*(2), 197–207.

Farrell Racette, S. (2004). *Sewing Ourselves Together: Clothing, Decorative Arts and the Expression of Metis and Half-Breed Identity.* [Doctoral Dissertation, University of Manitoba]. University of Manitoba. https://mspace.lib.umanitoba.ca/handle/1993/3304

Freire, P. (1992). *Pedagogy of Hope: Reliving Pedagogy of the Oppressed.* Bloomsbury Academic.

Friedland, H., Napoleon, V., Fraser, H., & Laurent, L. (2016). An Inside Job: Engaging with Indigenous Legal Traditions Through Stories. *McGill Law Journal. Revue de Droit de McGill*, *61*(4), 725–754. doi:10.7202/1038487ar

Gaudry, A., & Lorenz, D. (2018). Indigenization as Inclusion, Reconciliation, and Decolonization: Navigating the Different Visions for Indigenizing the Canadian Academy, *AlterNative: an international journal of indigenous peoples, 14*(3), 218–227.

Gordon, D., Meyer, A., & Rose, D. (2016). *Universal Design for Learning*. CAST Professional Publishing.

Grande, S. (2000). American Indian Identity and Intellectualism: The Quest for a New Red Pedagogy. *International Journal of Qualitative Studies in Education : QSE*, *13*(4), 343–359. doi:10.1080/095183900413296

Grande, S. (2010). *Red Pedagogy: Native American Social and Political Thought*. Rowman & Littlefield Publishers.

Gray, M. (2017). *Beads: Symbols of Indigenous Cultural Resilience and Value* [Master's Thesis, University of Toronto]. TSpace. https://tspace.library.utoronto.ca/handle/1807/82564

Hooks, b. (2003). *Teaching Community: A Pedagogy of Hope*. Routledge.

Kaleimamoowahinekapu Galla, C. (Kanaka Hawai'i) & Holmes, A. (Kanien'keha:ka). (2020). Indigenous Thinkers: Decolonizing and Transforming the Academy Through Indigenous Relationality. In S. Cote-Meek & T. Moeke-Pickering, (Eds.), Decolonizing and Indigenizing Education in Canada (pp. 51-72). Canadian Scholars.

Kennedy, D. (2017). *Legal Education and the Reproduction of Hierarchy: A Critical Edition*. New York University Press.

Ladson-Billings, G. (1995). But That's Just Good Teaching! The Case for Culturally Relevant Pedagogy. *Theory into Practice*, *34*(3), 159–165. doi:10.1080/00405849509543675

Lavallée, L. F. (2009). Practical Application of an Indigenous Research Framework and Two Qualitative Indigenous Research Methods: Sharing Circles and Anishinaabe Symbol-Based Reflection. *International Journal of Qualitative Methods*, *8*(1), 21–40. doi:10.1177/160940690900800103

Lindberg, D. (2018). Miyo Nêhiyâwiwin (Beautiful Creeness): Ceremonial Aesthetics and Nêhiyaw Legal Pedagogy. *Indigenous Law Journal at the University of Toronto Faculty of Law*, *16*(1), 51–65.

Lindberg, T. (1997). What Do You Call an Indian Woman with a Law Degree? Nine Aboriginal Women at the University of Saskatchewan College of Law Speak Out. *Canadian Journal of Women and the Law*, 9(2), 301–355.

Lussier, D. (2021). A Legal Love Letter to My Children: If These Beads Could Talk. *Indigenous Law Journal at the University of Toronto Faculty of Law*, 18(1), 1–26.

Lussier, D. (2021). *Law with Heart and Beadwork: Decolonizing Legal Education, Developing Indigenous Legal Pedagogy, and Hearing Community* [Unpublished Doctoral Dissertation]. University of Ottawa.

Mona, C. (2017, September 19). *1 needle & 2 needle flat stitch beading techniques*. [Video]. Youtube. https://www.youtube.com/watch?v=smrfuN-fBT4

Moore, S. (2017). *Trickster Chases the Tale of Education*. McGill-Queen's University Press.

National Disability Authority. (2017). *History of UD*. Centre for Excellence in Universal Design. https://universaldesign.ie/what-is-universal-design/history-of-ud/

Pedagogy. (2020). Merriam-Webster. https://www.merriam-webster.com/dictionary/pedagogy

Pete, S. (2017, October 15). *Think Indigenous*. [Audio podcast]. Podtail. https://podtail.com/en/podcast/think-indigenous/think-indigenous-shauneen-pete/

Prete, T. (2019). Beadworking as an Indigenous Research Paradigm. *Art/Research International* 4(1), 28-57.

Purton, F., Styres, S., & Kempf, A. (2020). Speaking Back to the Institution: Teacher Education Programs as Sites of Possibility. In S. Cote-Meek & T. Moeke-Pickering (Eds.), *Decolonizing and Indigenizing Education in Canada* (pp. 175–192). Canadian Scholars.

R v. Sparrow, 1 Canadian Supreme Court Ruling 1075, 70 DLR (4th) 385 (1990).

Ray, L. (2015). *Mshkikenh Ikwe Niin (I am Turtle Woman): The Transformative Role of Anishinaabe Women's Knowledge in Graduate Research* [Doctoral Dissertation, Trent University]. Trent University Library and Archives. https://digitalcollections.trentu.ca/objects/etd-513

Ray, L., & Cormier, P. (2012). Killing the Weendigo with Maple Syrup: Anishinaabe Pedagogy and Post-Secondary Research. *Canadian Journal of Native Education*, 35(1), 163–176.

Robertson, K., & Navarro, J. (2020). *Beading as Medicine (Volume 1)*. Kimberley Dawn Robertson. https://www.kimberlydawnrobertson.com/product-page/beading-as-medicine-vol-1-zine

Robertson, K., & Navarro, J. (2020). *Beading as Medicine (Volume 2)*. Kimberley Dawn Robertson. https://www.kimberlydawnrobertson.com/product-page/beading-as-medicine-vol-2-zine

Rose, D. (2001). Universal Design for Learning. *Journal of Special Education Technology*, *16*(2), 66–67. doi:10.1177/016264340101600208

Saysewahum (McAdam S.). (2015). *Nationhood Interrupted: Revitalizing Nêhiyaw Legal Systems*. Purich Publishing.

Scofield, G. A., Briley, A., & Farrell Racette, S. (2011). *Wapikwaniy: A Beginner's Guide to Metis Floral Beadwork*. Gabriel Dumont Institute.

Scott, B. R. (2020). Reconciliation Through Métissage. In S. Cote-Meek & T. Moeke-Pickering (Eds.), *Decolonizing and Indigenizing Education in Canada* (pp. 31–50). Canadian Scholars.

Shepherd, L. (2016, May 25). The Flower Beadwork People. *Parks Canada*. [Video]. Youtube. www.youtube.com/watch?v= 54ipBLZJ6L4

Steinhauer, E., Cardinal, T., Higgins, M., Steinhauer, N., Steinhauer, P., Underwood, M., Wolfe, A., & Cardinal, B. (2020). Thinking with Kihkipiw: Exploring an Indigenous Theory of Assessment and Evaluation for Teacher Education. In S. Cote-Meek & T. Moeke-Pickering (Eds.), *Decolonizing and Indigenizing Education in Canada* (pp. 73–90). Canadian Scholars.

Tanaka, M. T. D. (2016). *Learning and Teaching Together: Weaving Indigenous Ways of Knowing into Education*. UBC Press.

Truth and Reconciliation Commission. (2015). *Honouring the Truth, Reconciling for the Future: Summary of the Final Report of the Truth and Reconciliation Commission of Canada*. UBC. https://irsi.ubc.ca/sites/default/files/inline-files/Executive_Summary_English_Web.pdf

Two Row Wampum– Guswenta. (2020 June 14). *Onondaga Nation: People of the Hills*. Onondaga Nation. https://www.onondaganation.org/culture

United Nations Convention on the Rights of Persons with Disabilities. (2006). *Convention on the Rights of Persons with Disabilities*. UN. https://www.un.org/development/desa/disabilities/convention-on-the-rights-of-persons-with-disabilities.html

Weenie, A. (2020). Askiy Kiskinwahama-ke-wina: Reclaiming Land-Based Pedagogies in the Academy. In S. Cote-Meek & T. Moeke-Pickering (Eds.), *Decolonizing and Indigenizing Education in Canada* (pp. 3–18). Canadian Scholars.

Wilson, S. (2008). *Research is Ceremony: Indigenous Research Methods*. Fernwood Publishing.

Woodward, S. (2017). *Universal Design 101*. Rick Hansen Foundation. https://www.rickhansen.com/news-stories/blog/universal-design-101

KEY TERMS AND DEFINITIONS

Beadwork: A traditional artistic practice that takes many different forms around the world. In the case of the Métis, who sometimes carry the moniker of "The Flower Beadwork People," beadworking is generally understood as a textile-based practice wherein beads are worked with needle and thread to enhance the visual aesthetic of clothing, household, and other items. Historically, Métis beadwork often included floral elements, though modern beadworkers continue to evolve their practices beading all manner of works that can, and do, serve as mnemonic devices and visual languages.

Indigenous Pedagogy: the art of Whole-Learner teaching (body, mind, heart, and spirit) for community empowerment.

Pedagogy: The art, or science, of teaching.

Persuasive Legal Aesthetics: Learning and practicing Indigenous laws, and legal orders, in a beautiful way. A (beautiful) theory of law learning advanced by Darcy Lindberg (2018).

Whole-Learner Teaching: Teaching that engages the four spheres of learning - cognition/intellectual, emotional, physical, and spiritual (understood in the sense of care of the spirit).

ENDNOTES

[1] While it is beyond the scope of this chapter to explore the longstanding place of beadwork in law on Turtle Island, I would invite readers to begin their exploration with this resource from the Onondaga Nation, which offers an introduction to the Two Row Wampum – one of the oldest treaties between Indigenous Nations and Settlers that was enshrined in beadwork. For for information, see Two Row Wampum– Guswenta. (2020 June 14). *Onondaga Nation: People of*

the Hills. https://www.onondaganation.org/culture/wampum/two-row-wampum-belt-guswenta/

2 I purposely insert this grammatical error, inserting "impact" where "effect" would be a more appropriate use of English, to underline the crater left behind by the devastating impact of excluding holistic pedagogical practice from classrooms.

3 Dr. Darcy Lindberg (2018) suggests that non-Indigenous student resistance to the incorporation of Indigenous laws in the law school environment is grounded in discomfort that emerges when teachings challenge these pre-held conceptualizations of law.

4 See, for example, Lussier, D. (2021). A Legal Love Letter to My Children: If These Beads Could Talk. *Indigenous Law Journal*, *18*(1), 1.

5 Spirit beads are mistakes, either inserted into or found naturally occurring, in beadwork. There are many spirit bead teachings, many of which relate to the idea that nothing in life can, or should, be perfect. To learn more, please seek out a knowledge holder in a community near you.

6 The paralysis I faced when tasked with reimagining my pedagogical practice for online learning environments was tremendous. I owe a debt of gratitude to Dr. Florian Martin-Bariteau for his encouragement and for "meeting" me on various platforms to test drive PowerPoints and features in the wee small hours after panicked phone calls that, on reflection, were probably not about the PowerPoints at all. Also, for his constant reminders that I am used to doing things that are challenging, and his reassurance that anything is possible… with the right tech.

7 See, for example, Scofield, G. A., Briley, A., & Farrell Racette, S. (2011). *Wapikwaniy: A Beginner's Guide to Metis Floral Beadwork*. Gabriel Dumont Institute, Saskatoon.

Chapter 6
Inside Out, or Storytelling Through Truths and Reclamation

Keri Cheechoo
Wilfrid Laurier University, Canada

ABSTRACT

This chapter will explore the ensuing trifecta of themes: "storytelling," "Indigenous education theory and practice," and "creating culturally sustaining pedagogies" by speaking to and through the intertextualities, potentialities, and complexities of mino-pimatisiwin, to engage and embody best practices around student engagement and support. The chapter begins with a conversation about Indigenous education theory and practice by offering an opportunity to learn about the importance of engaging ethical space by enacting ethical relationality, and how these concepts extend into kinship theory and practice. This chapter then shifts an introspective storytelling lens towards the author to share how, as an Iskwew scholar and educator, she teaches mino-pimatisiwin through a trauma informed perspective. This chapter will also speak to culturally safe care by (re)conceptualizing the red road by introducing culturally sustaining pedagogies.

INSIDE OUT, OR *STORYING THROUGH TRUTHS AND RECLAMATION*

Wachiye. Welcome to this space, I have been looking forward to this conversation. As always, I will begin our conversation by situating, or positioning myself. My name is Keri Cheechoo (she/her), and I am an Iskwew, a Cree woman. My community is

DOI: 10.4018/978-1-6684-3425-3.ch006

Long Lake #58 First Nation, which is in Northwestern Ontario, in the nation-state referred to as Canada. I am daughter, mother, sister, grandmother, wife, auntie, cousin, and niece. These are my relations, they hold my history and are my memory anchors (Gadgil, Berkes, & Folke, 1993; Mitchell, 2013). I am also a published poet. I use poetic inquiry (an arts-based methodology) in my work in a way that connects my spiritual aptitude for writing with educational research. As an Indigenous scholar, I use my poetry to make space for Indigenous voice by interrupting and subverting Western constructs of academic writing. I also frequently share narratives that conversationally speak to my lived experiences. I situate my pedagogy through both a praxis of ethical relationality, and my Nisgaa methodological framework which is framed by protocol, mamatowisin, or engaging inner mindfulness, and reciprocity.

This chapter will explore the ensuing trifecta of themes: "Storytelling," "Indigenous Education Theory and Practice," and "Creating Culturally Sustaining Pedagogies" by speaking to and through the intertextualities, potentialities, and complexities of mino-pimatiswin, to engage and embody best practices around student engagement and support. The chapter will begin with a conversation about Indigenous education theory and practice by offering an opportunity to learn about the importance of engaging an ethical space by enacting ethical relationality, and how these concepts extend into kinship theory and practice. These concepts will be unpacked and will explore how to respectfully support the space/s of Indigenous and non-Indigenous worldviews and perspectives while acknowledging truths about our shared histories and relationships (Donald, 2009). This is significant because this may create a space that offers an opportunity to guide how we think, how we relate to one another, and how to take care of ourselves and others.

This chapter will shift an introspective storytelling lens to share how, as an Iskwew scholar and educator, I teach mino-pimatisiwin through a trauma-informed perspective. Trauma-informed care should be delivered on the premise that a student's past and current experiences of trauma impacts their lived experiences. For further context, trauma-informed care can be considered kinship care; to hold space for individual regeneration and resurgence through kinship while working towards healing creates a good life, or mino-pimatisiwin. We can and should engage relationality and meet students where they are, without hesitation, without stigma. It is good medicine.

This chapter will also speak to culturally safe care by (re)conceptualizing the red road by introducing culturally sustaining pedagogies. It is my experience that the red road is a concept that signifies that an individual makes a decision every day to commit to Creator, to use medicines in a good way and to abstain from substances. *But, what if we (re)conceptualize the red road?* These pedagogies could mean that the engagement and care that a student is receiving is competent, safe, and equitable. The author will engage the potentialities, and complexities of the following queries: "What if we (re)frame the way we think?"; "What if we embody harm reduction?"

and "What if we decide that our biases have no place on this road?" When educators embody kinship and engage relationality, they make and hold space to reflect on their own biases, their cultural identity and how these ideologies influence their best practices.

As I was preparing to craft this chapter, I was reading through many different pieces written by Indigenous scholars such as Battiste (2002), Donald (2009), and Hart (2002), and I was struck by the fact that while we may have differences in pedagogies, the foundation remains the same: we all desire to shift the education our kin receive into a reflexively relational space. We want new generations to reach for the stars, because that is where all our relations, their ancestors, are. We want our children, nieces, nephews, grandchildren and all of their children to be (re)rooted, learn from the land, their land. We are working collectively to shift the periphery and the boundaries and dismantle the barriers upheld by anti-Indigenous racisms, assimilationist attempts, and ongoing colonialism.

There is no singular Indigenous education theory and practice discourse. As mentioned, there is a large collective of Indigenous scholars collaborating in a good way through their own epistemological spaces that include Worldviews, Ways of Knowing, and Ways of Being. Knowing this, I will share from my own positionality as a Cree scholar-educator who specializes in Indigenous education but will also incorporate teachings from those whose scholarship resonates with my own pedagogy such as Bell (2013), Carlson-Manathara (2021), and Vowel (2015). It is rewarding to note that even distinguished scholars such as Linda Tuhiwai Smith (2019) ruminate similarly about a collective educational movement, as thoughtfully noted in the Introduction in *Indigenous Education*:

I know that I gain new insights about my context when I read what others have said about their context and their experiences ... is it serendipitous that scholars write about matters that are shared by other Indigenous Peoples across jurisdictions, or do we indeed have a shared experience and a shared struggle in Indigenous Education. (p. x)

It makes good sense though—the very process of sharing experiences and sharing struggles generates community through a common goal— we want the children, youths and young adults in our lives to thrive.

To engage storytelling, I will share my lived experiences as a literacy resource teacher. To preface this narrative, I count the entire experience as one of the absolute best of my life: I am an Ontario-certified teacher, and remain in good standing, renewing my membership annually. I have been certified since 2014 and I am glad to see that seismic shifts in Indigenous education have occurred since then. Before teaching in a post-secondary setting, I was provided an amazing opportunity to be the literacy resource teacher/librarian at a First Nation school in a First Nation community. It was there that I became (re)acquainted with epistemological violence that encouraged a "me versus them" mentality during my time at the school. Maybe it was because I was new to the profession, new to the community or because I am a Cree woman with children of her own that I felt pushed to resist the ignorance and violence of settler teachers who also worked in the school. I do know now that I was unprepared to work alongside teachers who were hired because of lack— lack of certified teachers, lack of funding dollars, lack of being able to draw educators to a semi-remote place. I was literally unprepared. We were in different places, professionally. I could envision a larger picture, and I was ready to embody best practices to shift the literacy needs of the school over the next few years. Yet it was not easy. That epistemological violence I spoke of? The me versus them belief continued to flourish as I became more experienced with my new roles. I was met with pushback as I tried to facilitate as a literacy resource teacher whose pedagogy aligned with the community's school board's educational plan. My role specified that I was to visit each class and monitor student engagement, and unfortunately my presence created tension. Try as I might, I could not shift these teachers away from a literal teaching-from-a-box-format that they had been using. There was no real evidence of teaching during the literacy blocks, students worked on photocopied pages from a box, usually colouring during that time. Strategy after strategy crafted to improve student literacy were ignored and I began to realize that it was because I was an Indigenous educator that I was disregarded. The fact that I was a legitimate educator specializing in literacy was irrelevant. I walked into several anti-Indigenous conversations about me creating more work, especially after I pushed to create and uphold strategies and policies about student safety and wellness as being our number one priority as educators within that space. I encountered derision with everything from classroom literacy work-plans to outright anger when I provided fresh fruit to the students I interacted with daily, and honestly? It still boggles my mind.

I would like to share this next narrative, it is one that I have shared elsewhere to illustrate the absolute inequity Indigenous students face all over this nation-state referred to as Canada. One of the mandates for my position was that I prepare students for an Education Quality and Accountability Office (EQAO) test that is administered province-wide yearly to assess student success with literacy and mathematics. After researching previous EQAO scores, and realizing the scope of previous unsuccessful attempts of the school overall, I was both shocked and became determined to shift statistics. As I was preparing students by helping them become familiar with the process (no coaching or teacher input permitted, no chatting with peers, strategies on how to use our time efficiently), I realized that we were already in deficit. These sample questions being used for preparation were not crafted with First Nation children in mind especially First Nation children who live in a mostly remote community. A remote space where even seeing something like a plane is a rarity. Questions like "What are the white birds that we see all over called?" (Seagulls) or "What rumbles underground, and gets us from Point A to Point B?" (Subway) had the students stumped. White birds? Rumbling underground? With zero teacher or facilitator input during the weeks of intensive EQAO testing, and despite the amount of prep, those questions remained incomprehensible. There is no way to "teach to the test." The content in the questions continue to be just as much a surprise to students as they are to facilitators. Unsurprisingly, the school scored extremely low (again) and morale around student success remained low. Unfortunately, the government tactically uses information from accumulated scores to determine and underscore where successes and failures lay. I respectfully engaged data sovereignty while I was in consultation with other Indigenous literacy experts, and armed with an array of aggregated data, we determined that First Nation schools continue to be chronically underfunded, and that the evidence of the continuance with underfunding programming for First Nation schools was embedded within this aggregated data. Time and time again, funding continues to be reduced, literacy programming is cancelled, and First Nation children are left in deficit (Campbell, 2021). The inquiries we grappled with were, *how could we, a small core of determined Indigenous educators, promote mino-pimatisiwin, let alone flourish in that space*? The truth is that Colonialism is ugly and damn, is it ever persistent.

As mentioned earlier I strive to teach mino-pimatisiwin through relationality and trauma-informed principles. Trauma is "when we have encountered an out of control, frightening experience that has disconnected us from all sense of resourcefulness or safety or coping or love" (Brach, 2011). Trauma-informed principles inform relationality by "building trust [because it] is foundational to being trauma-informed. Operations and decisions are conducted with transparency thus allowing for the building of trust through respectful, compassionate, genuine and authentic relationships" (The Trauma-Informed Toolkit, 2013). Trauma-informed care should be delivered on the premise that a student's past and current experiences of trauma impacts their lived experiences. For additional context, my understanding of trauma-informed care can be considered kinship care, which is a space where we introduce and teach "Western ways as skills, not as identity replacement" (Brokenleg, 2008) so that students are grounded in intergenerational strength. If we can make and hold space for individual regeneration and resurgence through kinship while working towards healing, we can create a good life, or mino-pimatisiwin. We can and should engage relationality and meet students where they are, without hesitation, without stigma. It is good medicine.

Because I interacted with students from kindergarten to Grade 12 daily, I became heartbreakingly aware of ongoing effects of intergenerational trauma. Frequently, I set aside who I was as a literacy resource teacher, and just sat and listened. I listened to narratives from students in Grade 2 who spoke about their overwhelming sadness and confusion after learning about a familial suicide. I listened to students in Grade 7 who worried about having no food at home because their parents or guardians were absent or had spent money on negative coping strategies instead. I have let students nap during our time together because sometimes they felt safer at school, and their bodies could not stay awake any longer.

I have learned that compassion and empathy go a long way in helping students heal or feel validated. And that these experiences shared with me did not in any way *invalidate* them from living a good life. That their journey towards mino-pimatisiwin was still genuinely theirs. That they are already on it, and that nobody is keeping score. That some of the choices they made did not disqualify them from experiencing good things in the future. As a mom, a kookum, an educator, a scholar, it is so critical to me that young people know that mino-pimatisiwin is inclusive. Mino-pimatisiwin is not a space that only "perfect people" can access. Because of the accumulated traumas that can impact a young person— ranging anywhere from parental or guardian estrangement and abandonment, to addiction issues to violence in their homes—I learned early on that young people internalize these traumas as failings, that they are somehow accountable or responsible. I have also learned that when we view these young people through a trauma-informed lens, when we engage mamatowisin, we remind them that they continue to be worthy of every good thing in this world. That all their relations are rooting for their success. *This is kinship.*

My pedagogical praxis combines educational theory and practice with ethical relationality, and from there I engage mamatowisin, or inner mindfulness. My praxis creates and holds space for me in a way that I can continue to learn and grow and even thrive through this framework. Before I go much further, I would like to circle back to the concept of ethical space and ethical relationality. From my understanding, Dwayne Donald (2009) says that ethical space is a space of possibility that can only be created when we are dealing with two different worldviews, or knowledge systems. In other words, engaging in ethical relationality means recognizing that you are in a space with people who are unlike you, and respecting those dissimilarities enough to meet halfway, and learn from each other in the space where you meet.

I strive to embody ethical relationality in every instance of my life. This includes my relationships with my partner, children, and extended family, to my relationships with colleagues and friends, and even extend this concept into kinship theory and practice this *modality of being* to my relationships with my pet and plant friends. It is a way of life for me. And it has been life-alteringly authentic, offering opportunities for mino-pimatisiwin to progress naturally.

I think we should circle back, and make some integral connections. I want to speak to the spaces that are critical to me as an Iskwew. I had to first conceptualize the "red road" as I was taught it and then (re)conceptualize that very same road. I

Inside Out, or Storytelling Through Truths and Reclamation

am going to make and hold space to share about my upbringing, or childhood. My father subsisted through his childhood in the Indian Residential School System (IRS), and my mother is daughter to survivors of the Indian Residential School System. They both live what they know. My brother and I (myself) have been adopted from different places. We are both Cree from different Treaty areas and the family we had been adopted into are Anishnawbe, or Ojibway. Try as we might, we just could not become Anishnawbe because we are just ancestrally, inherently different, and unfortunately, we became Othered. Because of adopter-adoptee familial dynamics and discord, I frequently sat on the side lines as I watched the majority of my family embrace and embody their/our culture. I was taken to pow wows but was never invited to craft regalia or to learn to dance. I witnessed ceremony but was not included into that space, despite my interest and requests. I was told that the family followed the red road, and that they engaged everything that this might encompass, from creating a dance troupe, to engaging in ceremony, to travelling for pow wows, all of it. I was taught that living the red road is analogous with mino-pimatisiwin, living the good life. The only way forward. That partaking in things like alcohol or drug consumption, or smoking were a complete antithesis to the concept of the red road. That if you chose to do these things you were essentially "out" or ostracized and your presence could be considered problematic. The space felt palpably unforgiving, as I watched people turn their backs on one another and essentially abandon relatives. It always felt odd but because I lived my life on the periphery I did not have an opportunity to speak to anyone about it.

Fast forward to my adult life, and away from my adopted family, I realized just how harmful the concept of the red road could be. That grace was not extended to those whose choices had chased them into harmful or violent spaces was unbelievable. That evidence-based facts like the impacts of cultural genocide, inter/generational trauma, the sixties scoop, and more could just be ... ignored. That we are negatively overrepresented *everywhere*–from being incarcerated to the ongoing apprehension of our children to an increase in medical racisms and health disparities— and that these palpable impacts reverberate for generations. The red road was impractical to me. I did not want to sit in judgment of people, to criticize their choices, none of it.

And so, I sat with it. For years. I wanted mino-pimatisiwin but I did not want to be hypocritical. Then I was introduced to the concept of harm reduction. It had been around since the 1980s but it was new to me. Harm reduction as a public health strategy works to reduce the harms associated with certain behaviours, and after some intensive contemplation, I pondered an extension of considering harm reduction as a philosophy. And thus, my (re)conceptualization of the red road began. I began to (re)imagine opportunities for intertextualities, potentialities, and the complexities of embodying mino-pimatiswin— and then engaging and embodying best practices around student engagement and support—through this new lens. And boom. I realized that if I did the work to live and work in an ethically relational way through (un)learning my biases, was reflexive and respectful, and reciprocated along the way, I was making space. I was making and holding space for those with imperfect pasts and offering opportunities to see mino-pimatisiwin is not a space that only "perfect people" can access. There are no perfect people. We are all medicine.

And here we are, we have come full circle. Meegwetch for journeying with me—but before we part ways, I invite you to engage with the following inquiries: Will you consider (un)learning and (re)framing your thinking? Are you ready to engage and embody best practices around student engagement and support through trauma-informed principles and a harm reduction lens?

REFERENCES

Battiste, M. (2002). Indigenous knowledge and pedagogy in First Nations education: A literature review with recommendations. Report prepared for the National Working Group on Education, Indian and Northern Affairs Canada, Ottawa, ON.

Bell, N. (2013). Just do it: Anishinaabe culture-based education. *Canadian Journal of Native Education*, *36*(1).

Brokenleg, M. (2008). Culture and Helping. Presented in Winnipeg, Canada.

Campbell, C. (2021). Educational equity in Canada: The case of Ontario's strategies and actions to advance excellence and equity for students. *School Leadership & Management*, *41*(4-5), 409–428. doi:10.1080/13632434.2019.1709165

Carlson-Manathara, E. (2021). *Living in Indigenous Sovereignty*. Fernwood Publishing.

Donald, D. (2009). Forts, curriculum, and Indigenous Métissage: Imagining decolonization of Aboriginal-Canadian relations in educational contexts. *First Nations Perspectives*, *2*(1), 1–24.

Hart, M. A. (2002). *Seeking mino-pimatisiwin: An Aboriginal approach to healing*. Fernwood Publishing.

Manitoba Trauma Information and Education Centre. (2013). *The Trauma-Informed Toolkit*. Manitoba Trauma Information and Education Centre. https://trauma-informed.ca/wp-content/uploads/2023/04/trauma-informed_toolkit_v07-1.pdf

Royal Commission on Aboriginal Peoples. (1993). *Ethical Guidelines for Research*. The Commission.

Smith, L. T. (2019). Expanding the Indigneous Education Agenda: A Forward. In H. Tomlins-Jahnke, S. Styres, S. Lilley, & D. Zinga (Eds.), *Indigenous Education: New Directions in Theory and Practice* (pp. ix–xi). University of Alberta Press.

Truth and Reconciliation Commission of Canada. (2012). *An interim report*. Library and Archives Canada.

Vowel, C. (2015). *Indigenous Writes: A Guide to First Nations, Métis & Inuit Issues in Canada*. Portage & Main Press.

Chapter 7
The University as a Site for ĆÁŦ:
Storytelling as Pedagogy

Jack Horne
Trent University, Canada

ABSTRACT

When the author began conducting this research in 2015, he was surprised by the lack of Indigenous writing critical of the academy. He conducted extensive research to identify peer-reviewed academic journals and book chapters written by Indigenous scholars in the years up to and including 2016. The author expected to find a wealth of information but was instead confronted with the limited content that only highlighted the lack of progress that has been made toward integrating true Indigenous knowledge into the academy. The research was intended to support the argument that Indigenous knowledge had already secured a place in the academy. Instead, the author discovered that additional Indigenous academic writing was needed on the subject. The author hopes this chapter will save current and future Indigenous scholars from repeating research the author has already done. In the W̱SÁNEĆ language dialect of SENĆOTEN, the word ĆÁŦ translates as "being difficult" or "a difficult situation." This chapter will explore the difficulties the author has experienced through his academic journey while employing the Indigenous practice of storytelling as pedagogy.

DOI: 10.4018/978-1-6684-3425-3.ch007

The University as a Site for ĆÁȽ

INTRODUCTION

The author is from the W̱SÁNEĆ Nation, located at the southern end of Vancouver Island. He is a 57-year-old man, a second-generation residential school survivor, and a first-generation university student. The author retired from a career in the performing arts at the age of 42, and over the past 14 years, he has attended Camosun College, the University of Victoria (BA), and York University (MA). He is now a PhD candidate in the Indigenous Studies PhD program at Trent University. Attending four different educational institutions has given the author a unique perspective on teaching and learning practices in contemporary Canadian institutions of learning. In the W̱SÁNEĆ language dialect of SENĆOTEN, the word ĆÁȽ translates as "being difficult" or "a difficult situation". This chapter will explore the difficulties the author has experienced through his academic journey while employing the Indigenous practice of storytelling as pedagogy.

In June of 2015, Universities Canada released "Universities Canada Principles on Indigenous education" (Universities Canada, 2015). Ninety-seven universities put forth 13 recommendations for improving the recruitment and retention of Indigenous students and suggestions for fostering a university environment that is safer and more accepting for Indigenous students. While it is laudable for these universities to have put forth these recommendations, it is obvious that this short announcement represents the perspectives and goals of the universities, and not the voices of the Indigenous students. Despite the statement that these principles have been "developed in close consultation with Indigenous communities" (Universities Canada, 2015, para. 5), there are no citations, or any other indications of just which Indigenous communities or Indigenous people were consulted. Research the author conducted in April of 2016 for a final seminar paper in the Indigenous Studies PhD program at Trent University revealed that every one of the 13 proposed recommendations put forth by the Universities Canada announcement had already been addressed by numerous Indigenous scholars in academic work that dated back decades.

While taking a first-year course in the Indigenous Studies PhD program at Trent University, the author discovered a fundamental difference in the conception of research between themselves and a white professor. The course was titled INDG 6601 – Indigenous Studies Theory and Research Methods. The white professor assigned an exercise in which the author and his cohort were asked to draw a picture of what a literature review looked like. It was a simple exercise meant to offer a way of conceptualizing a literature review other than in the standard written format. The white professor's drawing was typical of a western approach to a literature review. She described it as an introductory paragraph, followed by major ideas surrounded by the corresponding literature references. In her rendering, the major ideas formed one or more paragraphs as needed, and the whole literature review ended with a concluding paragraph. It was very indicative of a standard, eurocentric literature review. The author's drawing depicted a winding path that represented both his life and his education journey. Along the journey, major ideas were formed, and new materials were added over time. Ultimately, the whole path became circular and returned to where it began—the W̱SÁNEĆ Nation.

The author chose to employ storytelling as methodology, and in fact he began the written assignment with "[s]torytelling remains an essential part of all Indigenous nations, and for this reason I would like to employ it as method in the first section [of this paper]" (personal communication, seminar assignment, 2015). The author intuited the potential problems as soon as he saw the two contrasting drawings, and so, prior to writing this assignment, he asked if the members of the cohort were expected to draft their papers based on the white professor's example. The white professor's exact words were: "We don't prescribe how you write your assignments," and so the author wrote from an Indigenous storytelling perspective. Section One of the author's paper was written in the storytelling format, and Section Two detailed why the white professor's approach did not work for the author's research. The white professor did not prescribe how the cohort were expected to write the assignment, and yet the author received an extremely low grade for not following her format.

Indigenous people who stand up for themselves and speak their minds are often labelled as difficult or unprofessional by those in charge. In the author's education journey, he has often heard Indigenous scholars he admires described as angry by various professors, instructors, and seminar cohorts. For example, Eve Tuck and Wayne Yang, authors of *Decolonization is Not a Metaphor* (2012), and Sheila Cote-Meek, author of *Colonized Classrooms* (2014), are a few of the scholars that the author has heard described as angry for simply articulating the truth. Neither of these works are angry enough, in the author's opinion, and do not even scratch the surface when it comes to the trauma inflicted upon Indigenous scholars in the academy. When Indigenous students enter these ivory towers, the expectation is for them to conform to the academy. The expectation is for Indigenous students to do all the work of reconciling an extremely specific kind of Indigenous Knowledge within the academy. It must be filtered and shaped to fit pre-existing moulds, and there are strict rules put in place to make sure that happens.

When the author began conducting this research in 2015, he was surprised by the lack of Indigenous writing critical of the academy. In response to the previously mentioned first-year storytelling assignment and the subsequent tensions with the white professor, the author wrote a final paper that featured Indigenous scholars in the academy. He conducted extensive research to identify peer-reviewed academic journals and book chapters written by Indigenous scholars in the years up to and including 2016. This research would eventually become a chapter in his PhD dissertation. The author expected to find a wealth of information but was instead confronted with the limited content that only highlighted the lack of progress that has been made toward integrating true Indigenous knowledge into the academy. The research was intended to support the argument that Indigenous knowledge had already secured a place in the academy. Instead, the author discovered that additional Indigenous academic writing was needed on the subject. The author hopes this chapter will offer insight and inspiration while saving current and future Indigenous scholars from having to repeat the research the author has already done. The author chose to use a storytelling format to allow for a nuanced flow and facilitate an informal literature review of early scholars.

THE AUTHOR'S EDUCATION JOURNEY

After the Douglas Treaty of 1852, the W̱SÁNEĆ Nation was divided into four reserve areas that corresponded to ancient W̱SÁNEĆ village areas. Currently, the four W̱SÁNEĆ reserve areas are W̱JOŁEŁP (Tsartlip), SȾÁUTW̱ (Tsawout), BOḰEĆEN (Pauquachin), and W̱SIḴEM (Tseycum). Education after colonization has been a delicate balancing act for the W̱SÁNEĆ Peoples. Soon after colonization, W̱SÁNEĆ children were either taken away to one of five residential schools located on or near to Vancouver Island, or they attended the Tsartlip day school. The Tsartlip day school was run by one priest and a few nuns. George Horne (GH) and Elsie Smith (ES) are the author's parents, and they are both from the W̱SÁNEĆ Nation. GH is from the SȾÁUTW̱ reserve and ES is from the W̱JOŁEŁP reserve. GH and ES each had different educational experiences, and it is important to examine these experiences because they have a direct bearing on the author's life and relationship to education. In keeping with the storytelling methodology, their stories are included next.

ES never attended residential school, and neither did any of her siblings. Family legend indicates it was because ES's grandfather confronted an Indian agent at the end of the driveway with a shotgun. The grandfather told the Indian agent that if he came back and tried to take his children, he would kill him. It worked for the residential school, but it did not excuse ES or her siblings from attending the Tsartlip day school. ES never talked much about her time at the school, other than to say the nuns who ran the school were mean. ES was left-handed, but was forced to learn to write with her right hand. The nuns walked between the rows of desks during writing practice, and if they caught her attempting to use her left hand, they would rap her knuckles with a ruler. It was cruel but effective, because she had beautiful penmanship and the author never saw her write with her left hand. ES was an avid reader with wide-ranging tastes, and she loved those cheesy westerns written by Louis L'Amour. ES never made it past the fifth grade.

GH had a much harder upbringing. He was born around 1930, and he was one of the last W̱SÁNEĆ people to practice SX̱OLE (reef net fishing) in the old way. The government made SX̱OLE illegal because it did not like that the W̱SÁNEĆ fishermen were catching so many salmon. Later, GH and the others became government-approved commercial fishermen, and this is the work he still does today. At an early age, GH witnessed his parents' death in a boating accident, after which he was raised by a very strict uncle. One day, when he was about 14, some Indian agents showed up on the SŦÁUTW̱ reserve in a car and took him away to residential school. They did not allow him to say goodbye to anyone or pack anything from home. GH refused to speak or allow ES to teach the author or his siblings SENĆOŦEN, the W̱SÁNEĆ language, because in his mind the family was better off learning English. This was a direct result of GH's time in residential school. Both GH and ES were very focused on the author's success when it came to western education.

By the time the author began attending school in the 1970s, Indigenous children had a choice of either attending the on-reserve Tsartlip day school or integrating into the Saanichton district school system. The author was a quick study, learned to read early, and was good at math. What more does one need in the early days of western education? In high school, the author discovered theatre and dance, which would prove to be the start of a 25-year career in the performing arts. The author had a measure of success in the performing arts, worked across Canada, and travelled the world. However, it had always been his intention to return to postsecondary education, and once he retired from theatre at the age of 42, he was finally able to do that.

Postsecondary Education: The Return

The author had a very fortunate beginning to his postsecondary education when he entered the Indigenous Studies diploma program at Camosun College in September 2008. The Camosun program was such a positive and inspiring learning experience because of the design of the program and the people teaching and overseeing it. Most of the staff and instructors were Indigenous, and this was reflected in the overall pedagogy. Indigenous perspectives in research and writing were encouraged and respected. Indigenous guest speakers from local Indigenous nations, organizations, and other institutions were a regular part of the program. Accordingly, the author and his learning cohort were exposed to a variety of Indigenous knowledges.

In the summer of 2010, the author moved on from Camosun College to the University of Victoria. It was a difficult and humbling period because of the much larger class sizes and the gap in ages between the author and the much younger university students. The reading load was higher than it had been at Camosun College, as were the expected levels of reading comprehension and writing skills. The learning curve was steep but not insurmountable, and by the time the author left the University of Victoria in August of 2013, he had mastered the required research and writing skills. Camosun College and the University of Victoria were overwhelmingly positive experiences for the author. The academic framework in both institutions allowed for a freedom of Indigenous expression that the author appreciated. The instructors and professors at both institutions encouraged Indigenous perspectives from their students, and this provided a solid grounding for the author. That grounding was vital to his survival as he moved from the undergraduate level to the more challenging graduate studies level.

York University: September 2013 - August 2014

York University has a population of approximately 50,000 students, which is more than Camosun College and the University of Victoria combined. In September, the campus is besieged by students, and it is quite an overwhelming experience. York University is a city and community unto itself, with a definite institutional and colonial environment. The author lived on campus in one of four high rises dedicated to housing for York University students. Living on campus meant there was no need to travel on the overcrowded city buses, especially during the winter, when the bus service was sporadic. Instead, the author was able to walk to class no matter how bad the weather. Disadvantages included the many undergraduates in the building who were young and not always interested in learning, which meant the building could sometimes get noisy. Additionally, 2013 saw the worst winter in over a decade and included an ice storm that shut down campus for a week. None of this really made a difference, because the program the author was enrolled in had a massive reading component, which meant he was reading from sunrise until sunset, so the weather outside was irrelevant.

As a first-generation university student, the author had some difficulty in adapting to undergraduate learning. When he moved to York University, it became evident that he was not prepared for the change to graduate seminars. In retrospect, there was no way around the sense of panic in those first few weeks. The program cohort for the year-long MA program was about 10 graduate students. The author was much older than most of the others, and was, of course, the only Indigenous graduate student in the program. The members of the cohort had diverse life and educational experiences. A few members had obtained their undergraduate degrees from the theatre department at York University, and they therefore had the advantage of already knowing some of the professors. They also had the advantage of prior knowledge of performance studies theory and an overall understanding of how York University's Department of Theatre and Performance Studies functioned. The author, on the other hand, had to learn a whole new language just to participate in the weekly seminars. The learning curve was steep, and the author had never read so much as during those 12 months at York University.

The author had completed his undergraduate degree at the University of Victoria in three years by taking classes year-round. He had been in classes from the summer of 2010 through to the end of summer 2013, after which he had immediately moved from Victoria to North York, Ontario to start the one-year MA program at York University. The author inevitably began to suffer academic burnout toward the end of the winter 2014 term, as the academic load and the years of unending study caught up to him. He met with the York University MA Theatre and Performance Studies program chair to discuss extending his studies for an extra semester because he felt he was no longer enjoying the experience. He had lost all sense of learning, and it had become about surviving from one written assignment to the next. The author reasoned that cutting back on classes and taking a few over the summer might allow him to rediscover the enjoyment in learning.

The author met with the program director and a couple of professors, and all agreed this was the best course of action. The author then received an email from Trent University with an offer to attend the Indigenous Studies PhD program in the fall of 2014. He contacted Dr. Paula Sherman immediately to request late entrance into the program in January 2015. Unfortunately, they could not hold a spot, and a missed September 2014 intake meant reapplication the next year with no guarantee of acceptance the second time around. In the end, the author ended up writing three final papers within a two-week period and passing all three seminars with very good grades before completing two more seminars and an internship over the summer. He was then eligible to begin the Indigenous Studies PhD program at Trent in the fall of 2014.

The sheer amount of reading in the one-year Theatre and Performance Studies MA program was astounding. The author was introduced to performance studies readings from Erving Goffman, Victor Turner, and Richard Schechner—the founders of performance studies theory. It became evident to him how performance studies theory intersected with W̱SÁNEĆ traditional practices. The author continued to develop assignments that explored the praxis of performance studies theory and traditional W̱SÁNEĆ knowledge.

One of the final seminars the author took was in the Department of Cinema & Media Studies, and the topic was archives. The class focused on archives and archivists, and how they were invaluable research tools and potential gold mines for artistic and academic projects. It was an interesting class, and the readings and lectures were engaging. Taking this seminar led the author to discover *The Archive and the Repertoire* (2003) by Diana Taylor and resulted in a profound shift in his research focus. Each seminar student was required to choose a week in which they were responsible for leading a discussion of the readings. The author chose

The University as a Site for ĆÁȽ

this book because the synopsis mentioned that Diana Taylor was a Latin America scholar—and this book was the only Indigenous option available. This seminar and the related presentation experience marked a pivotal point in the author's academic journey, and it remains one of the best examples of when the author's Indigenous worldviews collided with those of other graduate students, both in this seminar at York University and in academe generally.

The other graduate students were interested in learning the many ways the archives are a treasure trove of material for documentaries, museum exhibits, and academic research. They were interested in the ways the myriad archived materials could benefit any future projects, and they seemed to be seeking best practices for obtaining access to those. There was a great deal of animated discussion when it came to the stories of those items "found" in an archive that had become lost for various reasons. The rediscovery of archival artifacts and the process of making them available to the public was a boon for researchers, and often led to awards and grants. However, the author knew instinctively what Taylor's book meant from an Indigenous perspective because he knew W̱SÁNEĆ knowledge did not have a written or an archival component. Therefore, W̱SÁNEĆ knowledge was held and conveyed in forms that were not archivable in the way that had been studied in this seminar.

Diana Taylor is an American academic, a professor of performance studies and Spanish at New York University and founding director of the Hemispheric Institute of Performance and Politics. In *The Archive and the Repertoire* (2003), Taylor posits the rise in prominence and favouring of the written word in western society over embodied knowledge. Taylor gives a brief explanation for the terms archive and the repertoire as "the archive of supposedly enduring materials (i.e., texts, documents, buildings, bones) and the so-called ephemeral repertoire of embodied practice/knowledge (i.e., spoken language, dance, sports, ritual)" (2003, p. 19). In other words, anything tangible or archivable in western society becomes more legitimate than the non-archivable. The author understood when Taylor made the distinction between the "archive" and the "repertoire" that W̱SÁNEĆ knowledge was 100% the repertoire.

These concepts were new to the author at that time, and he had done no research on them beyond reading Taylor's book. The author could only interpret Taylor's work through his relationship to W̱SÁNEĆ knowledge, and so that interpretation was limited. When it was his turn to lead the seminar discussion and present Taylor's book, the author made the mistake of speaking as if the other students shared the same perspectives and worldviews regarding Indigenous and W̱SÁNEĆ knowledge. The author spoke of the archive and the repertoire as written about by Taylor, of embodied knowledge, and of how W̱SÁNEĆ knowledge was never written. He spoke of how W̱SÁNEĆ knowledge was not archivable, was not individual, but instead was a shared, collective knowledge. Once the author finished speaking and looked up, he saw nothing but blank faces staring back in confusion. Then came a barrage of questions that left the author confused by student reactions. His cohort asked questions like: "If it's not written down, where is it kept?" and "What do you mean, 'embodied'? Like in the arm or leg?" The non-indigenous seminar students could not grasp or accept the idea of a collective knowledge that was not tangible and could not be locked away in a box. The idea of knowledge anywhere outside of a book was incomprehensible to them. It was fascinating and remains one of the most interesting university experiences that the author has taken part in, though the reality of the situation would not become apparent until much later, after he had left York University.

The lack of Indigenous content in the MA Theatre and Performance Studies program at York University played a huge part in the author's decision to move from there to the Indigenous Studies PhD program at Trent University. The author fully expected that attending the Indigenous Studies program at Trent University would mean returning to an environment that respected and encouraged Indigenous Knowledge in research. Trent's vision statement (Trent University, 2014) for the Indigenous Studies PhD program indicated this was the case. Therefore, it seemed that a return to Indigenous Studies would complete the education circle the author had started at Camosun College. In the end, the author finished his remaining summer courses at York University and moved to Peterborough, Ontario to begin the next stage of his education.

Trent University: September 2014 - Present

Prior to arriving at Trent University, the author had been fortunate to study under supportive and nurturing instructors and professors. He had managed to avoid those in the academy who were not open to Indigenous or alternative knowledges. On those occasions when he had found himself in a class or seminar where the professor was ignorant of other pedagogies, it had been a simple matter of producing work those professors would approve of. However, the author expected that in an Indigenous Studies PhD program, scholarship would continue to be developed utilizing Indigenous theory and methodologies. The author anticipated that at the doctoral level, there would be academic freedom to do Indigenous, and specifically W̱SÁNEĆ, research.

It was and is the intention of this W̱SÁNEĆ researcher to produce writing accessible to the W̱SÁNEĆ Peoples—a goal that has created conflict with a few key individuals in the Indigenous Studies PhD program at Trent University and has demonstrated where they get their vision statement twisted. The vision statement as it was written in 2014 promised a respectful environment in an Indigenous program grounded in Indigenous knowledges and community, that focused on both traditional and contemporary Indigenous Knowledges (Trent University, 2014).

The University as a Site for CÁ̵T

Yet the reality was an Indigenous Studies PhD program focused on social science research frameworks taught aggressively by a non-Indigenous professor. Conflict with the white professor was immediate because of disparate worldviews, and the uneven power dynamic allowed them to employ oppressive bullying tactics. The way this was done suggested that these tactics had been used before, and this proved to be the beginning of two and a half years of trauma for the author.

The Indigenous Studies PhD program at Trent University had a large core comprehensive reading list (Trent University, 2014). The 106 books on the list were divided into the following categories:

1. Traditional Knowledge (Canada and Internationally)
2. Indigenous Knowledge/Thought/Orality
3. Language
4. Discipline of Native Studies/IK and the Academy
5. Governance/Self-Government/Sovereignty
6. Lands and Spaces
7. Research Inquiry and Ethics
8. Indigenous Advocacy: Activism, Anti-colonialism, Resistance, and Resurgence
9. Other Critical Perspectives

Core comprehensive reading lists are meant to contain the basic knowledge from any given field that students are expected to demonstrate a mastery of in both written and oral exams. Trent recently narrowed the core comprehensive reading list for the Indigenous Studies PhD program down to 70 titles. The newer list has been revised and updated to include many contemporary Indigenous scholars. The Indigenous Studies PhD program core comprehensive reading list at Trent University circa 2014 attempted to include too many older readings. Some of the older material could have been assigned as seminar readings rather than kept on the core comprehensive reading list. This would have made room for newer, more contemporary works in the developing Indigenous Studies field. But in 2014, this was the content of the program's core comprehension reading list, and regardless of how it had come to be configured, the author set about reading it.

Eventually the author divided the core comprehensive reading list into two categories. The first category were the readings assigned for the seminars, which were also a part of the core list for comprehensive exams. The second category were the readings useful for the author's W̱SÁNEĆ research as well as for the core comprehensive exams. Of particular interest were those works by Indigenous scholars that intersected with embodied Indigenous Knowledge. Embodied Indigenous Knowledge had been written about by Indigenous scholars prior to the genesis of the field of Indigenous Studies. Concepts had been articulated regarding Indigenous

Knowledge as it related to Indigenous songs, stories, ancestors, land, spiritual places, and relationality.

In his book *The People and the Word* (2005), Indigenous literature scholar Robert Warrior has this incredible insight:

Embodied discourse that relies on memory does not always or even primarily rely on language and speech acts. Many actions in Native life are neither primarily oral nor even linguistic, such as ceremonially presenting someone with provisions, taking part in a ritual fast, being part of a societal dance, or cooking a communal meal. All these actions can have complex levels of meaning within the confines of Native tradition, but those meanings are not necessarily best elucidated by textualizing them. (p. xxix)

Diana Taylor and Robert Warrior each define embodied Indigenous knowledge in the most interesting and relevant ways. In *The Archive and the Repertoire* (2003), Taylor lists the non-written aspects of spoken language, dance, sports, and ritual, while Warrior (2005) takes it one step further to include non-spoken acts such as cooking a communal meal or other public and private group activities. Indigenous Knowledges are encoded in these activities and transferred from generation to generation. When interpreted from these perspectives, embodied Indigenous Knowledge yields vibrant and interesting results.

According to Willie Ermine in *Aboriginal Epistemology* (1995), the difference between Indigenous and non-Indigenous research is that the latter strives for objective extraction of knowledge, whereby the researcher is separate and therefore fragmented from the knowledge gathering process. Compartmentalization of Indigenous Knowledge leads to the issue of fragmentation caused when conducting Indigenous research using standard western research methods. Gregory Cajete presents the Indigenous alternative in *Native Science* (2000):

The Native American paradigm is comprised of and includes ideas of constant motion and flux, existence consisting of energy waves, interrelationships, all things being animate, space/place, renewal, and all things being imbued with spirit. (p. x)

The keyword for this author is the interrelationship of knowledge gathering and knowledge transfer found within Indigenous ontologies and epistemologies. The author notes Cajete's (2000) casual use of the phrase "Native American paradigm," as this concept is of particular importance when exploring Indigenous pedagogy in the academy.

Indigenous scholars in the past were required to engage with Indigenous knowledge from the western academic perspective. This meant engaging from that objective and fragmented place. Fragmentation results in compartmentalized scholarship such as that found in Donald Fixico's *Oral Tradition and Traditional Knowledge* (2003). In this piece, Fixico examines the category "story" from an interesting and telling perspective. He compartmentalizes it and then reveals how story relates to the categories of land, spirituality, language, and Ancestors. The result is that Fixico westernizes the concept of story by first isolating it and then relating it to the other categories of embodied Indigenous Knowledge, when in fact all five categories are interrelated in such a way that they blend into one another. It is this fragmented, western, eurocentric academic format that the present author's research seeks to avoid.

One of the most prolific and respected Indigenous scholars is Dr. Marie Battiste. Battiste has been researching the issues of Indigenous peoples and education for decades. One of Battiste's earliest articles was "Enabling the Autumn Seed: Toward a Decolonized Approach to Aboriginal Knowledge, Language, and Education" (1998). In this article, Battiste (1998) criticizes the education process for Indigenous people and quite harshly critiques institutional eurocentrism. Eurocentrism refers to European exceptionalism and worldviews centred on western concepts. Battiste (1998) critiques how:

Eurocentrism is not like a prejudice from which informed peoples can elevate themselves. In schools and universities, traditional academic studies support and reinforce the Eurocentric contexts and consequences, ignoring Indigenous world views, knowledge, and thought, while claiming to have superior grounding in Eurocentric history, literature, and philosophy. (p. 22)

The dominant pedagogy this author experienced illustrated that very point—how western theory and methods are perceived by the academy to be the only legitimate place from which Indigenous knowledge can be researched. Indigenous students are then expected to write from a western positionality, regardless of their personal, political, or Indigenous orientation.

Battiste (1998) next engages with issues of why any critique of eurocentrism[1] can:

raise anguished discourse about knowledge and truth. As questions are raised about alternative ways of knowing and diversity, the discussion quickly slips into paradigm maintenance by supporters for the Eurocentric cannon. Thus, Eurocentrism resists change while it continues to retain a persuasive intellectual power in academic and political realms. (p. 23)

Battiste, highlighting eurocentric resistance through paradigm maintenance, illustrates one major obstacle that has been hindering the progress of Indigenous Knowledge in the academy. In this article, Battiste goes on to discuss how Indigenous scholars and educators need to be cognizant of these issues as they decolonize teaching and learning practices. She advocates for healing and progress by first acknowledging Indigenous worldviews and then using this acknowledgement as the starting point for the future of Indigenous research (Battiste, 1998).

Battiste's entire career has been dedicated to furthering Indigenous educational progress in academe. In 2002, Battiste co-wrote "Decolonizing Education in Canadian Universities: An Interdisciplinary, International, Indigenous Research Project" with Lynne Bell and L.M. Findlay. The article is a detailed examination of the progress toward including Indigenous Knowledge in the academy that had been made up to that point. It offers some interesting and inspiring insights as well as the usual critiques of academic eurocentrism.

For those of us who have been educated in colonial, Eurocentric environments and had our Aboriginal identities revised or our white armor polished, we have needed to unpack Eurocentric processes to reveal the cognitive assimilative regime that has done such damage and what can be done to effectively change it (Battiste et al., 2002, p. 90). The cognitive assimilative regime Battiste references here was in full swing in the one Indigenous research course in the Indigenous Studies PhD program at Trent University. The author experienced the attempted assimilation and understood the damage that has been done in plain sight to the field of Indigenous Studies.

Verna J. Kirkness and Ray Bernhardt wrote "First Nations and Higher Education: The Four R's – Respect, Relevance, Reciprocity, Responsibility" (1991). In this piece, the two writers examine the lack of representation of Indigenous students in colleges and universities in Canada and the United States, and offer suggestions for addressing these issues. The scholars discuss the difficulties Indigenous students encounter when entering the environment of the academy and point out the low retention rates that most institutions achieve. They articulate the problems and failures found at most institutions in creating equal education opportunities and safe environments for Indigenous students. Then they pose the following challenges to academic institutions:

If we are to address this perennial issue in a serious manner, we have to ask ourselves some hard questions:

Why do universities continue to perpetuate policies and practices that historically have produced abysmal results for First Nations students, when we have ample research and documentary evidence to indicate the availability of more appropriate and effective alternatives?

The University as a Site for ĆÁȾ

Why are universities so impervious to the existence of de facto forms of institutionalized discrimination that they are unable to recognize the threat that some of their accustomed practices pose to their own existence?

What are some of the obstacles that must be overcome if universities are to improve the levels of participation and completion of First Nations students? (Kirkness & Bernhardt, 1991, p. 2)

This article was published in 1991, yet in an Indigenous Studies program in 2014—23 years later—these same questions still applied. Not only was the author surprised by the seeming lack of progress that had been made integrating Indigenous Knowledge in the academy, but he was also surprised at the lack of scholarship on this subject written by Indigenous people in the year 2015.

One of the author's favorite articles deconstructs the differences between Indigenous and non-indigenous teaching pedagogies—and does so with razor-sharp insight. Bryan McKinley Jones Brayboy and Emma Maughan wrote "Indigenous Knowledges and the Story of the Bean" (2009), which centres on an Indigenous Teacher Preparation Program (ITPP) at Western University. One of the authors is Indigenous and the other non-indigenous, and the balance of both points of view is evident in their writing. During their writing process, Brayboy and Maughan maintained constant interaction through formal and informal meetings with both faculty and students, in addition to weekly sessions with both. At one of the final meetings, the students were asked what they thought of the program thus far. One Indigenous student referred to the faculty and support staff as Mickey and Minnie Mouse because of their propensity to speak quickly and use academic jargon. This invariably made the students think that the faculty were more interested in impressing themselves than in making actual connections with or educating the Indigenous students. In their piece, the two authors astutely comment on how this "implicates the epistemic clashes inherent in how knowledge is used and how hierarchies of knowledge are produced and reproduced" and how "[t]hese clashes raise critical connections between power and the (re)production and transmission of knowledge" (Brayboy & Maughan 2009, p. 2). Academic jargon and the strict use of western theory and methodologies can be tools for the continued oppression and alienation felt by many Indigenous students.

The most interesting and entertaining portion of the article is the "Story of the Bean" from which the title is taken (Brayboy & Maughan, 2009). One of the requirements for the Indigenous students was to assist in a teaching environment where they were assessed by site teacher educators (STE) based on a rubric provided by the university. In one of those teaching environments, the STE was concerned that their Indigenous teaching assistant was not ready to teach because she felt this

Indigenous teaching assistant did not understand the curriculum. The curriculum of concern was for a Grade 4 class and had as an exercise a classroom of students planting seeds—one in soil and the other in sand. The Grade 4 students were then tasked with measuring different amounts of water for each in addition to keeping track of the plant growth. They measured the plant growth with a ruler and were responsible for keeping track of these results in a journal. The idea was for the Grade 4 students to experience the way scientists conduct an experiment. The learning outcomes for this exercise were math through the measurement of water during watering and in calculating the plant growth. The students also developed writing skills through the act of journaling. It was meant to be a very straightforward exercise typical of most curricula for students of that age (Brayboy & Maughan, 2009).

The STE felt that her Indigenous student teacher was not ready to teach in the classroom environment, and was prepared to fail her. That would have meant the Indigenous student teacher would not have been able to obtain her teaching certificate. At a meeting with faculty, students, and STEs, the Indigenous student teacher was asked what she thought of her teaching curriculum and her experience of working as a teaching assistant. Her response was a perfect example of approaching pedagogy from an Indigenous Knowledge perspective. The Indigenous student teacher replied that the class curriculum as it had been structured was not the way she would have taught the lesson. She then proceeded to lay out how, working from a holistic Indigenous perspective, she would have taught a lesson in plant growth. She started by clarifying that she would never have planted seeds for no reason—meaning she would not have wasted the plants or the labour by planting something knowing it was just for show. She also mentioned that it was a waste of time to plant seeds in the sand because everyone knows that seeds do not grow as well in sand, so that part of the experiment was unnecessary. The Indigenous teaching assistant then proceeded to lay out her vision of an Indigenous lesson plan in plant growth.

The Indigenous teaching assistant said she would first remove the lesson from the classroom and take it outdoors, where plants naturally exist. The lesson plan would begin by teaching the students about the many different plants and their seeds. She envisioned teaching the students how and when the different plant seeds were meant to be planted, and that in the traditional Indigenous practice, this was done when the stars aligned in a specific way. The Indigenous student teacher's lesson would also include the traditional stories, which contained the Indigenous Knowledge about the stars, the plants, and the seasons for planting. The experiment went from an in-classroom exercise with no real purpose to a real-world exercise in planting different seeds, the best time of year to plant them based on the stars, and their uses, along with their traditional stories. Of course, the STE became extremely interested in the proposed Indigenous lesson plan (Brayboy & Maughan, 2009).

Brayboy and Maughan (2009) articulate numerous key insights regarding Indigenous Knowledge in the academy and helped to address reasons for this author's growing discomfort in the Indigenous Studies PhD program at Trent University. The author was inspired by the way ontological and epistemological Indigeneity was allowed to function once the lesson was removed from the usual colonized classroom setting and students were potentially allowed to become engaged through an Indigenous perspective. This process would allow the students and the teacher to engage with the outside world instead of the usual learning typically done stuck inside a classroom. It is important to recognize that at all levels of teaching and learning, from kindergarten through to graduate studies, there are valuable alternatives to usual practices. Indigenous ways of being and knowing have value, and eurocentric western theory and methodologies should never be the only option. The latter should certainly never be forced upon an unwilling student.

The Brayboy and Maughan (2009) article alluded to a way that conducting W̱SÁNEĆ research might look as opposed to what we were studying in the INDG 6601 – Indigenous Research Theory and Methods seminar. An inordinate amount of time was spent studying theory and methodologies grounded in the social sciences paradigms. It would have been far more useful to spend the time on Indigenous-authored books and articles that engaged with issues of Indigenous students and Indigenous Knowledges in the academy. Instead, the author and his cohort were made to spend much of their time on the very reason engaging with Indigenous Knowledge in the academy remains a struggle. That reason is the continued hegemony of western eurocentric research grounded in social sciences paradigms in the academy in general, and its continued dominance in the field of Indigenous Studies in particular.

Dr. Marie Battiste authored a report for the National Working Group on Education and the Minister of Indian Affairs: Indian and Northern Affairs Canada (INAC) titled "Indigenous Knowledge and pedagogy in First Nations Education: A Literature Review with Recommendations" (2002). The report contains some critical statements directed at education institutions in Canada and focuses on the prevailing eurocentric western mindset, while also advocating for the uplifting and acceptance of Indigenous Knowledge and research in the academy. The reference list and the appendix of annotated Indigenous education resource materials alone are invaluable for Indigenous researchers. However, for the purposes of this chapter, Battiste's (2002) writing about literature reviews is most relevant:

[I]n the European (or Eurocentric) knowledge system, the purpose of a literature review is to analyze critically a segment of a published topic. Indigenous knowledge comprises the complex set of technologies developed and sustained by Indigenous civilizations. Often oral and symbolic, it is transmitted through the structure of

Indigenous languages and passed on to the next generation through modeling, practice, and animation, rather than through the written word. In the context of Indigenous knowledge, therefore, a literature review is an oxymoron because Indigenous knowledge is typically embedded in the cumulative experiences and teachings of Indigenous people rather than in a library. (p. 2)

This is an extremely important quote and highlights one of the most persistent obstacles to the acceptance of Indigenous Knowledge in the academy and in graduate research. This idea is that knowledge is only acceptable if it comes in book form. There is complete lack of understanding or acceptance of Indigenous Knowledge because it is collective and embodied, and as Taylor wrote, it is not archivable. Battiste's report is a prime example of critiquing the western academic complex while also advocating for Indigenous Knowledge.

Jeff Corntassel has written a surprisingly funny academic article titled "An Activist Posing as an Academic?" (2003), in which he exposes some of the dangers of working as a junior academic within the university environment. Corntassel tells a personal story about an interview he had for a tenure track position, in which he was accused by the interview committee of lacking objectivity. Corntassel writes that "[b]y refusing to apologize for being a Tsalagi professor, I practiced the academic freedom that these scholars lauded publicly but suppressed privately" (2003, p. 161). This reminded the author of the unease he felt at the thought of an ethics board reviewing any proposed research conducted on the WSÁNEĆ Nation. The idea that this more than likely all non-Indigenous ethics committee would decide whether to grant permission seemed unnecessary and oppressive. The author found an echo of his own feeling in Corntassel's statement that, "[r]ather than adopting a 'walking in two worlds' philosophy, I was Tsalagi first and foremost" (2003, p. 179). Corntassel shares a vital quote from an unnamed Cherokee/Creek professor, who laments, "I thought we already fought these battles. You're fighting the same damn battles that we fought in the 1970s" (2003, p. 166). This is interesting because the articles referenced in this chapter were written in the 1990s, but could still be applied to the academy today. Obviously, there has been a great deal of progress and there is a demonstrable wealth of academic work from which current academic research can be drawn. The point is the dominant narratives so jealously guarded by the academy are still creating eurocentric barriers for Indigenous academics, and professors are effectively strong-arming graduate students into writing in the accepted western formats.

No discussion of this subject would be complete without including the incredible work of Linda Tuhiwai Smith and her husband Graham Smith. The Indigenous researchers from New Zealand are arguably well ahead of North America when it comes to carving out a space for Indigenous Knowledge in the academy. The director of Camosun's Indigenous Studies program, Todd Ormiston, regularly met and corresponded with Professor Smith when the latter served as an advisor/mentor for Ormiston's PhD dissertation. Graham Smith's wife and academic partner Linda Tuhiwai Smith's *Decolonizing Methodologies* (2021) is probably on every reading list for every Indigenous education course in the world, and rightfully so. Linda Tuhiwai Smith published her book in the UK and the US in 1998, at a time when Indigenous voices in the academy were almost unheard of. In it, she advocates for an engagement with dominant theory, but from an Indigenous perspective. In her chapter about Kaupapa Māori research, she engages with concepts like critical theory and positivism while exploring the ways that Māori research engages, relates to, and pushes back against them. More recent research work advocated by Graham Smith and subsequent writing by Linda Tuhiwai Smith indicate a movement away from this type of engagement and toward a more transformative pedagogy.

Professor Graham Hingangaroa Smith gave a keynote address to the Alaskan Federation of Natives Convention in Alaska in 2003, titled "Indigenous Struggle for the Transformation of Education and Schooling." In the talk, Smith advocates for avoiding what he terms the "politics of distraction," so that as Indigenous people, we can experience "the freeing of the indigenous mind from the grip of dominant hegemony" (2003, para. 2). He provides several lists articulating ways to reach this goal under the headings "The Need to Centralize the Issue of Transformation," and "A Call to Theory," and finally "Kaupapa Māori Theory" (Smith, 2003). Smith's keynote focuses on the ways Indigenous communities can transform themselves through the detailed lists. What was most important for this author was Smith's point that "[t]he term 'decolonization' is a reactive notion; it immediately puts the colonizer and the history of colonization back at the 'centre'" (Smith, 2003, para. 3). The author first learned of this concept as an undergraduate, when Dr. Taiaiake Alfred gave a talk in which he advocated for a movement away from colonizing language and toward transformative and/or resurgent ones.

Smith similarly advocates for the continued development of Indigenous-focused research and "to position our own ways of knowing as being relevant and significant in the 'elite' knowledge production and reproduction 'factories'" (Smith, 2003, para. 5). He emphasizes how Indigenous scholars must have an "understanding of the politics surrounding theory, the understanding of the flaws of theory and academic work of the past, and most of all, the proactive development of indigenous theorizing by ourselves" (Smith, 2003, para. 6). Smith (2003) considers the struggle between the academy and Indigenous communities to be only one part of the overall picture. He argues transformative work focused on Indigenous communities must also be done. This is significant because Smith does not advocate for the usual engagement with western theory and methodologies, but instead for the development of our own individual Indigenous theories and methodologies. Smith does not use the word paradigm, but ultimately an Indigenous or more specifically a Kaupapa Māori paradigm would accomplish his goals.

TOL, NEW SEN TTE SOŁ: A Senćoten Phrase Translated As "I Know The Road."

We used to live several families in one longhouse, but the government decided they didn't like that. One day they came onto the reserve and burned down all our longhouses. At the time, our great-grandmother's house was overgrown with blackberry bushes and so they couldn't see it, so they missed it. It became a gathering place for the WSÁNEĆ people. (Lola Garcia, personal communication, December 2015)

Prior to colonization, WSÁNEĆ knowledge transfer involved embodied knowledge and experiential learning. Engaging in WSÁNEĆ ways of being (ontology), ways of knowing (epistemology), and ways of doing (axiology and methodology) was not possible without those embodied and experiential components. Traditional pre-contact WSÁNEĆ living meant several generations of WSÁNEĆ families lived in one longhouse or bighouse, and this was a key component of fostering community and enhancing WSÁNEĆ knowledge transfer. In Saltwater People, Dave Elliot Sr. (1983) states:

Those people were the teachers. From the time of understanding when a child began to think, the teaching had already started. Your mother, father, your uncles, your aunts, your older brothers, sisters, your grandparents were all your teachers. (p. 79)

Residential schools and Indian day schools were effective in disrupting this process, and were key to the destabilization of traditional WSÁNEĆ knowledge transfer. Instead, WSÁNEĆ children were forced to sit in colonized classroom settings and learn to think from the neck up. They experienced disembodied teaching and learning.

The author's experience in the Indigenous Studies PhD program at Trent University has been a contentious one. The author would like to point out that this is not a denouncement of the program, the professors, the staff, or Trent University itself - this is merely one Indigenous student experience of an Indigenous Studies PhD program. Through this traumatic experience, the author has pushed back against a forced indoctrination into social sciences research theories and methodologies and instead chosen to focus on seeking out those Indigenous scholars whose work support Indigenous paradigms. The author's university experience is not unique, and this chapter features Indigenous scholars who share the same struggles.

One issue the author found confusing about the Indigenous Studies PhD program at Trent University was the aggressiveness of the social science rhetoric. Two white professors and an MBA holder each made the point that "we are social sciences, and you are humanities" (personal communication) as if this somehow excused or was an adequate explanation for the backlash the author received after drafting a dissertation proposal from a W̱SÁNEĆ Knowledge perspective. The author obtained a BA in political science from the University of Victoria (social sciences), and then an MA from York University's Theatre and Performance Studies program (humanities). However, he was then in an Indigenous Studies PhD program that he considered neither social sciences nor humanities. There was something angry and oppressive about the unnecessary categorization and subsequent dismissal once it became clear the author consider himself an Indigenous Studies scholar, and more precisely, an Indigenous scholar researching W̱SÁNEĆ Knowledges who knew that social sciences/humanities were in no way a part of that, period.

Alternative Research Perspectives

In Walter D. Mignolo's "Spirit Out of Bounds Returns to the East: The Closing of the Social Sciences and the Opening of Independent Thoughts" (2014), he refers to "The Gulbenkian Report" (Wallerstein, 1996). The 1996 article "Open the Social Sciences" was based on a talk Immanuel Wallerstein gave to the Social Science Research Council in 1995. Wallerstein was the chair of the Gulbenkian Commission when they met three times during the years 1994 and 1995. What stood out when the author read this article was the conceit of the social scientists involved in the Gulbenkian Commission and the absolute certainty that they held the key to the next stage of social science restructuring. The Gulbenkian Commission members demonstrated a complete lack of awareness that perhaps some would prefer not to restructure the social sciences, but would instead prefer to find alternative research theories and methodologies.

At one point in his article, Wallerstein (1996) laments that "the tripartite division itself—humanities, social science, natural science—is coming into question" (p. 6). Wallerstein is wary of the intermingling and blurring of the disciplines, and this wariness is reminiscent of the way the two white professors and the MBA holder categorized the humanities and social sciences in the Indigenous Studies PhD program at Trent University. In an earlier section of the article, Wallerstein (1996) criticizes the proliferation of alternative knowledges such as women's studies and black studies (to which, this author believes, he would add Indigenous Studies). Wallerstein's (1996) main question, then, is how to restructure, or how to "try to rethink new rationales, new ways of divisioning" (p. 6), with the goal of reshaping the social sciences and fixing it so that any alternative paradigms would remain under social sciences control. It is from this perspective that Mignolo's 2014 article commences.

Mignolo (2014) states that "[t]he social sciences expanded around the world. They became the empire companion. Like in any other sphere of imperial expansion, those who are happy with the expansion are those enacting it" and "[t]hose who have to endure the consequences may adapt and surrender, or delink" (p. 585). It goes without saying, then, that the two white professors and the MBA holder in the Indigenous Studies PhD program at Trent University would qualify as both "those who are happy with" and "those enacting" the social sciences' continued cognitive imperialism. Indigenous scholars, intellectuals, and activists have been challenging this cognitive imperialism for decades now. Given the choice, this author too chooses to delink.

Mignolo (2014) further writes that "[p]eople around the world have been and continue to be good thinkers without recourse to the 'social sciences,'" and that "[b]eyond the reasons Western social scientists may have to defend and promote the social sciences, they are not the only options" (pp. 586–587). It is the author's contention that it is imperative for Indigenous students to question the programs, professors, and institutions responsible for knowledge-making - rather than to passively submit to indoctrination. Mignolo (2014) further elaborates:

It would be pretentious and arrogant if Western social scientists appointed themselves to solve the problems that European imperialism created in other latitudes. And it would be pure submission if thinkers from other latitudes identify their problems starting from Western social sciences instead of starting from the consequences of coloniality of knowledge in their own local histories. (p. 590)

WSÁNEC Knowledge can and should be written without having to resort to filtering it through a social sciences framework before it is deemed acceptable within the university system and to those individuals gatekeeping that system. The way to begin is by exploring the very structures that allow systemic racism in the university system to persist.

THE OPPOSITE OF PARADIGM MAINTENANCE: PARADIGM DECONSTRUCTION

Shawn Wilson's *Research is Ceremony* (2008) served as a blueprint for the development and implementation of an Indigenous/W̱SÁNEĆ paradigm. The book grew from Wilson's doctoral research and, along with Leanne Simpson's *Dancing on Our Turtle's Back* (2011), represents what this author considers to be the epitome of good, authentic, Indigenous writing. In Wilson's (2008) book, he states that he will not be comparing Indigenous paradigm components to non-Indigenous counterparts for validation, because this would only centre non-indigenous work. He says the same thing about non-Indigenous theory and methodologies because the goal is to establish an Indigenous paradigm and not to centre non-indigenous scholarship.

Enroute to articulating an Indigenous paradigm, Wilson (2008) first lays out the progression of Indigenous research from contact up to the present. He passes through the now familiar phases of being discovered; being written about; writing like them; writing for Indigenous peoples, nations, and communities; finding an Indigenous voice in academe; and now establishing Indigenous research paradigms. This is an oversimplification of Wilson's (2008) text; however, because that content is not the focus of this chapter, the author will now move on to some of the more interesting and relevant concepts in Wilson's book. The book can be read in a circular way, as it begins and ends with the concept of what makes an Indigenous paradigm. Within the text itself, Wilson (2008) employs various written voices to illustrate aspects of Indigenous pedagogy. For example, he writes to his two sons directly to establish a rapport with the reader. Wilson also introduces his research participants using a traditional Indigenous introductory format, in addition to using personal names to honour their contributions to his research. Finally, Wilson compiles several separate interviews into one single interview to reflect a talking circle format for the reader. These are what Wilson would term strategies of Inquiry, described as "build[ing] upon a methodology to fill in how you will arrive at the research destination" (2008, p. 39). Since for Wilson the research destination is an Indigenous paradigm, these tools are necessary for its articulation.

Before Wilson begins to unpack the particulars of an Indigenous paradigm, he first explains that:

A paradigm is a set of underlying beliefs that guide our actions. So a research paradigm is the beliefs that guide our actions as researchers. These beliefs include the way that we view reality (ontology), how we think about or know this reality (epistemology), our ethics and morals (axiology) and how we go about gaining more knowledge about reality (methodology). (2008, p. 13)

Wilson cites the extensive and thorough work of Yvonna S. Lincoln and Egon G. Guba (1994) when writing about dominant paradigms. Rather than butcher his succinct two-page description of positivism, post-positivism, critical theory, and constructivism, the author instead directs the reader to pages 35–37 of his book. While the author seeks to avoid centring non-Indigenous writing, it is imperative to address three articles: Lincoln and Guba's 1994 article, which is cited in Wilson's book; a response by John Heron and Peter Reason to that article; and a further response from Lincoln and Guba to the response to their 1994 article.

In "Competing Paradigms in Qualitative Research," Guba and Lincoln (1994) define a paradigm "as the basic belief system or worldview that guides the investigator, not only in choices of method but in ontologically and epistemologically fundamental ways" (p. 106). Guba and Lincoln (1994) disclose a preference for constructivism, and this is important to note because of their classification of critical theory. They describe critical theory as "a blanket term denoting a set of several alternative paradigms, including additionally (but not limited to) neo-Marxism, feminism, materialism, and participatory inquiry" (Guba & Lincoln 1994, p. 109). Guba and Lincoln (1994) admit that this is a judgement call, which is in part due to their disinterest in engaging with the many different points of view embedded within the larger critical theory category.

Guba and Lincoln (1994) further articulate how "[a] paradigm may be viewed as a set of basic beliefs (or metaphysics) that deals with ultimates or first principles" and how "[t]he beliefs are basic in the sense that they must be accepted simply on faith (however well argued); there is no way to establish their ultimate truthfulness" (p. 107). These two quotes are interesting and because they are in direct contravention to what the author was told by the two white professors and the MBA holder at Trent University. The three argued that an Indigenous paradigm did not exist and maintained that their paradigms were the only legitimate ones. Not only did they do so, but they tried then to impose those worldviews on this author. Yet of course an Indigenous paradigm exists, and of course it is just as relevant as their proposed paradigms—more so in the author's opinion, considering that he is an Indigenous researcher conducting WSÁNEĆ research. In this case, the author's perspective and worldview take precedence over theirs. Meanwhile, according to Guba and Lincoln (1994), their preferred paradigms are not absolutes but basic beliefs or worldviews the author was expected to accept on good faith.

According to Guba and Lincoln (1994), questions related to ontology, epistemology, axiology, and methodology—in other words, questions related to ways of being, ways of knowing, and ways of doing research—are answered differently by, and can therefore be used to define, individual paradigms. However, Guba and Lincoln (1994) point out "the sets of answers given are in all cases human constructions; that is, they are all inventions of the human mind and hence subject to human error" (p. 108). Guba and Lincoln (1994) continue by saying "[n]o construction is or can be incontrovertibly right; advocates of any particular construction must rely on persuasiveness and utility rather than proof in arguing their position" (p. 108). The struggles this author experienced in the Indigenous Studies PhD program at Trent University were becoming clearer.

Guba and Lincoln (1994) display a self-awareness and humility that this author found lacking in the two white professors and the MBA holder in the Indigenous Studies department at Trent University. Guba and Lincoln (1994) write that "[w] hat is true of paradigms is true of our analyses as well. Everything that we shall say subsequently is also a human construction: ours" (p. 108). This is an indication of their commitment to true and ethical scholarship, and to their ability to admit their ignorance, which in turn allows them to be open to more learning and growth. Guba and Lincoln (1994) go so far as to admit that "[t]he reader cannot be compelled to accept our analyses, or our arguments, on the basis of incontestable logic or indisputable evidence; we can only hope to be persuasive and to demonstrate the utility of our position for, say, the public policy arena" (p. 108). There is a vast difference between acting as an agent of the university system and hoping to be persuasive. Guba and Lincoln are true thinkers and real educators who would not try to impose their worldviews upon others.

The main criticism this author has of Guba and Lincoln's 1994 article relates to their characterization of the category critical theory. The criticism also serves as a wider critique for the social sciences in general. Critical theory, as articulated by Guba and Lincoln (1994), serves as a catch-all descriptor for alternative paradigms that do not fit within the other three categories. This then serves as a point from which those alternative knowledges can be captured and encompassed, furthering the goal of restructuring proposed by the Gulbenkian Commission report. However, this is somewhat addressed when Guba and Lincoln (1994) write "that except for positivism, the paradigms discussed are all still in formative stages; no final agreements have been reached even among their proponents about their definitions, meanings, or implications" (p. 109). That idea inspired this chapter, which is devoted to challenging the hegemony of non-indigenous contemporary paradigms in social science and Indigenous research in the academy.

John Heron and Peter Reason wrote "A Participatory Inquiry Paradigm" (1997) in response to Guba and Lincoln's 1994 article. The Guba and Lincoln article situated participatory inquiry under the blanket term "Critical Theory et al." along with feminism and Marxism. Heron and Reason (1997) sought to articulate a standalone participatory inquiry paradigm alongside positivism, post-positivism, critical theory, and constructivism. In view of the aims of this chapter, the author found Heron and Reason's (1997) article to be too philosophical and oriented toward what Guba and Lincoln would call persuasiveness and utility.

According to Heron and Reason (1997), participatory inquiry is itself a blanket term, and additional forms include action inquiry, participatory action research, and emancipatory action research, among others. In fact, scholars "Fals-Borda and Rahman (1991) reported that some 35 varieties of participative action inquiry have been identified worldwide" (Heron & Reason, 1997, p. 284). It is worth noting that this article, along with several others published by Heron and Reason, discusses their preferred form of participatory inquiry, cooperative inquiry. The timing of these publications aligns quite nicely with the meetings of the Gulbenkian Commission in 1994–1995 and the subsequent publication of the Gulbenkian Report in 1995. At a time when the Social Science Research Council was positing ways to restructure the social sciences, this participatory inquiry paradigm would seem to have been an ideal response and solution. The main critique the author has of this paradigm is the ambiguity of the methodology. It is almost as if the authors cast the net too wide so that they may include as many alternative knowledge systems as possible. There are too many end goals, and not enough explanation of how Heron and Reason arrived at them.

The main issue with Indigenous research is captured in the following Heron and Reason (1997) quote: "Qualitative research about people is a halfway house between exclusive, controlling, quantitative, positivist research on people and fully participatory, cooperative research with people" (p. 285). This is an evergreen issue for Indigenous Nations, groups, and organizations. Outsiders come in and their only objective is the acquisition of data. Therefore:

The great majority of its projects are still unilaterally shaped by the researchers, however emergent that shape may be, however much informed consent is sought, and however much the researchers may be concerned to check their findings with informants' views. (Heron & Reason, 1997, p. 285)

Even if the researchers commit to a more participatory research inquiry in theory, "[i]n practice, it may be reduced to no more than seeking fully informed consent of all informants to the researcher's pre-existent or emerging operational plan" and if that is not sufficient, then "to modifying the plan to obtain such consent" (Heron & Reason, 1997, p. 285). Heron and Reason (1997) put forth cooperative inquiry, their preferred form of participatory inquiry paradigm, as the answer to this monumental and recurring problem with Indigenous research in academia.

The problem with Heron and Reason's (1997) proposition is academe itself. The notion of any research project in which there is complete cooperation from inception to inscription is preposterous and naïve. The author grew up within the W̱SÁNEĆ Nation and could not possibly be more of an insider there, yet he still struggles with issues of accountability to the nation while also attempting to produce scholarly work that meets the demands of academia. Therefore, the idea that an outsider can come in and work with Indigenous people, and that their work is going to be for Indigenous people and not the academy, is frankly laughable. It is far more realistic to have as academic goals to work with rearguard intellectuals (Santos, 2018) and post-abyssal knowledges with the intent of delinking through epistemic disobedience (Mignolo, 2009) than it is to think outsiders are going to come into Indigenous spaces with their extractive research goals and produce something other than more social science interpretations of Indigenous Knowledges.

This is the main critique of Heron and Reason's (1997) participatory inquiry paradigm, and why the author views it with skepticism—particularly considering Wallerstein's (1996) Gulbenkian Report. That said, it cannot ever be a bad thing for any researcher to attempt to work collaboratively with Indigenous groups and peoples with a goal of shared agency and voice throughout the entire research process. However naïve it may be, Heron and Reason's (1997) hope that a participatory paradigm will lead to "enabling a balance between people of hierarchy, cooperation, and autonomy" (p. 287) is laudable. Unfortunately, in the author's experience, the academy is not a very cooperative or accommodating entity.

It is the author's hope that the Indigenous Studies department at Trent University is open to self-correction of its social sciences rhetoric and cognitive imperialism. Heron and Reason (1997) write:

There is an urgent need to revision our view of ourselves as coinhabitants of the planet. As many of us have asserted, with greater or lesser degrees of concern, the current Western worldview has come to the end of its useful life, and, as well as some remarkable achievements in material well-being and human possibility, has left us with a legacy of human alienation and ecological devastation. (p. 291)

It is time to embrace the paradigm shifts currently happening in the academy, Indigenous Studies, and in the social sciences. It is time to acknowledge that there are other worldviews out there—Indigenous worldviews and Indigenous paradigms.

The response to Guba and Lincoln's 1994 article is a close reading of Heron and Reason, as well as an extension of and expansion upon the first article. In Guba and Lincoln's "Paradigmatic Controversies, Contradictions, and Emerging Confluences" (2005), there are pages of tables and many philosophical musings about the shifting paradigm landscape. Guba and Lincoln (2005) address a few of the criticisms put forth by Heron and Reason (1997), and they do expand upon the previous article. However, the humility the author noted in the 1994 article (Guba & Lincoln), which showed their commitment to learning and growth, once again shines through as a ray of hope for the future of Indigenous Studies in academe.

Rather than attempting to assimilate alternative knowledges within the social sciences, Guba and Lincoln (2005) instead acknowledge the changes happening within social science research itself:

For purposes of this discussion, we believe the adoption of the most radical definitions of social science are appropriate, because the paradigmatic controversies are often taking place at the edges of those conversations. Those edges are where the border work is occurring, and, accordingly, they are the places that show the most promise for projecting where qualitative methods will be in the near and far future. (p. 179)

This paragraph shows that not all social sciences researchers have a narrow and limited worldview, and that there are non-indigenous social scientists who can see the benefits of embracing all research. The author's experience at Trent would fall under what Guba and Lincoln (2005) term "a crisis of representation (which serves to silence those whose lives we appropriate for our social sciences, and which may also serve subtly to re-create this world, rather than some other, perhaps more complex, but just one)" (p. 184). However, all that is required to re-create a more just academic world is a shift toward accepting alternate worldviews.

Guba and Lincoln (2005) are inspirational and affirmational in their quest for learning and growth. They are open to new possibilities in ways the author did not encounter at Trent University:

Representation may be arguably the most open-ended of the controversies surrounding phenomenological research today, for no other reasons than that the ideas of what constitutes legitimate inquiry are expanding and, at the same time, the forms of narrative, dramatic, and rhetorical structure are far from being either explored or exploited fully. Because, too, each inquiry, each inquirer, brings a unique perspective to our understanding, the possibilities for variation and exploration are limited only by the number of those engaged in inquiry and the realms of social and intrapersonal life that become interesting to researchers. (Guba & Lincoln, 2005, p. 185)

This author does not wish to add anything to the already perfect words of these preeminent social science scholars, and especially not something negative. However, it is worth noting that researchers are also limited by those in charge of the institutions, programs, and departments. Those currently in charge have the capacity to cause a great deal of damage to the trajectory and progress of researchers who are supposed to be under their guidance. If they act out of ego or petty narcissistic retaliation, they have the power to delay and/or disrupt research.

Guba and Lincoln (2005) as well as Heron and Reason (1997) use tables when deconstructing the paradigms. They compartmentalize ontology, epistemology, axiology, and methodology before deconstructing each individually. Shawn Wilson, in *Research is Ceremony* (2008), instead chooses a more Indigenous approach and uses a circle to articulate ontology, epistemology, axiology, and methodology. Wilson (2008) does this because "the elements of an Indigenous research paradigm are interrelated or interdependent; it is difficult to separate one to write about," and because "there is no distinction between where one element ends and the next begins" (p. 69). The same issue arose when this author considered the compartmentalization inherent in the white professor's concept of a literature review from an Indigenous perspective—that approach simply did not work for Indigenous research because of the inherent relationality of Indigenous research.

Relationality is a vital concept in Indigenous research. In *Research as Ceremony*, Wilson (2008) writes:

Relationality seems to sum up the whole Indigenous research paradigm to me. Just as the components of the paradigm are related, the components themselves all have to do with relationships. The ontology and epistemology are based upon a process of relationships that form a mutual reality. The axiology and methodology are based upon maintaining accountability to these relationships. (pp. 70-71)

Shawn Wilson (2008) puts forth a possible way forward. No longer should we compartmentalize Indigenous ways of being (ontology), ways of knowing (epistemology), and ways of doing (axiology and methodology) by dissecting Indigeneity, lands, and traditions so that they can be fed back to the university in a format deemed acceptable. The holistic relationality of an Indigenous paradigm is in contradiction to, and therefore prevents, research that dissects and compartmentalizes.

Indigenous researchers have always had to contend with systemic and institutional racism and their proponents. Shawn Wilson (2008) writes that:

[a]s proponents of a holistic view of our worlds, Indigenous scholars may recognize the holistic approach to oppression that is evident in all of the ways that Indigenous peoples are held down by research and the dominant view of knowledge and the world is upheld. (p. 17)

It follows, then, that the holistic approach inherent in an Indigenous paradigm is the antidote to the holistic approach of oppression from those who would harass and oppress us. Relationality holds the key, or as Wilson (2008) states, "[f]rom an epistemology and ontology based upon relationships, an indigenous methodology and axiology emerge. An indigenous axiology is built upon a concept of relational accountability" (p. 77). This author is an Indigenous, W̱SÁNEĆ researcher, and if he is truly working from a holistic, Indigenous, W̱SÁNEĆ paradigm, then those relational accountabilities extend far beyond the bounds of standard ethics approval within the university system.

The author has heard Leanne Simpson say on a few occasions that university thinkers think from the neck up. He would add that most often, their heads are firmly placed within the hallowed halls of the ivory tower. Therefore, they fail to grasp the importance of our responsibilities as Indigenous researchers. When these tower-heads go out and do "Indigenous" research, they are visiting Indigenous lands, communities, and peoples for data. Then they take that data back to the hallowed halls of the ivory tower and they work on it there—from the neck up. Wilson (2008) writes:

[i]f the importance of relationships were understood at an inner or core level by dominant system researchers and academics, I wouldn't have witnessed the misunderstandings and resistance to an Indigenous research paradigm in connection with my own work and that of other Indigenous researchers. (p. 79)

The fierce opposition to this author's proposed PhD dissertation research is why he has had to address the issue of an Indigenous paradigm in his doctoral research.

In *Research is Ceremony* (2008), Wilson quotes the three Rs as articulated by Cora Weber-Pillwax. They are respect, reciprocity, and responsibility. Wilson (2008) and Weber-Pillwax are referring to the relationship of the researcher with an Indigenous research community or group. However, these relational concepts also apply to non-indigenous groups and places as well—places such as universities, for example. Wilson (2008) writes:

So the presentation or knowledge transfer is again all about continuing healthy relationships. Having a relationship with an idea also means that you must honour and respect that idea. The environment where the idea is to be discussed or further built upon must be appropriately developed and maintained. A healthy relationship cannot be built or flourish in an unhealthy environment. (p. 125)

If two white professors and an MBA holder gang up on a graduate student and repeatedly question the legitimacy of that student's research, they are not creating a healthy environment.

When the author writes about the W̱SÁNEĆ Nation, he is not writing about W̱SÁNEĆ data. This is not data the author has extracted from his nation and people to think about from the neck up so that he may then produce a boring social science dissertation. The author embodied W̱SÁNEĆ living. He grew up running barefoot on W̱SÁNEĆ lands and swimming naked in W̱SÁNEĆ seas. The author travelled and fished among W̱SÁNEĆ islands and ran up the sacred ŁÁU, WEL̵N̵EW̱ mountain to ceremonially bathe in the running stream, the way his ancestors have done since time immemorial. The author has buried countless relatives in the W̱SÁNEĆ grounds the way his ancestors have done since time immemorial. He wrote this chapter in large part because his research approach was questioned by faculty teaching in his PhD program. The author's PhD dissertation research question is this: How do I, a W̱SÁNEĆ artist and academic, utilize embodied W̱SÁNEĆ knowledge in my artistic and academic work?

SURVIVING THE UNIVERSITY EXPERIENCE

The academic publishing process is interesting, and this author would like to address a few important points raised by one of the reviewers. One reviewer noted that the chapter conveyed a sense of loneliness and that the struggles the author experienced are shared by many others in the Indigenous academic community (personal communication). They also suggested engaging additional contemporary Indigenous scholars such as Taima Moeke-Pickering, Adrienne J. Keene, Autumn Asher BlackDeer, Celeste Pedri-Spade, and Erica Violet Lee. The idea was to engage with additional Indigenous voices, thus ensuring that this author's text was not the only perspective. The author is grateful and open to the insights from the reviewer but asks that the reader consider the following responses:

The author returned to the main body of this chapter to revise and clarify that the research was conducted up to and including his early PhD program years of 2014–2016. The author would like to thank the reviewer for pointing out the sense of loneliness conveyed in the text because that is how the author felt at the time. The author is aware that his struggles were not unique and sadly acknowledges that if there are academic gatekeepers who prefer to maintain the status quo and universities continue to be slow to act, Indigenous students will continue to struggle. The author became aware, through social media, that his contemporaries in Indigenous academia were dealing with the same issues.

This chapter and the author's Indigenous Studies PhD research are in response to the toxic and oppressive social science pedagogy the author experienced while on campus in the Indigenous Studies PhD program at Trent University from 2014 to 2016. The author is aware that recent voices have been published in the years following his initial research but would prefer to preserve this initial research and writing because it represents a highly specific critique of the events that happened at Trent University. The author intends to write a follow-up to this research, during which time he plans to fully and thoroughly engage with the previously mentioned Indigenous voices.

Of the eight manuscripts the author found from the aforementioned Indigenous scholars, one was published in the winter of 2016, one in 2018, and the rest were published from 2020 onwards. The intricacy of the manuscripts written by these Indigenous authors prevents this author from using an addendum to an already completed dissertation and book chapter. For example, "We Deserve to Thrive: Transforming the Social Work Academy to Better Support Black Indigenous, and Person of Color (BIPOC) Doctoral Students" by Autumn Asher BlackDeer and Maria Gandarilla Ocampo was published in the summer of 2022. Were this manuscript available to the author in 2016, it would have given him great hope. It would have countered the voices from the university that were trying to tell him he was overreacting and excessively sensitive and that perhaps he was reading too much into events and that seeking accountability from the white professor was out of line.

This article is apropos of this author's experiences at Trent from 2014 to 2016 and beyond as it addresses an ongoing issue that has yet to reach its conclusion for him. Blackdeer and Ocampo (2022) articulate the micro and macroaggressions experienced by BIPOC doctoral students and state, "there were also exposés in which BIPOC scholars in the academy began to acknowledge the mistreatment and discrimination they experienced and/or were experiencing by [sic] white peers and their institutions" (p. 704). Blackdeer and Ocampo (2022) are references social work here, but this author has direct experience with how it can be "frustrating and painful for BIPOC doctoral students to experience repeated racialized harm from white individuals who tout themselves as and are elevated as 'anti-racists scholars' or 'allies'" (p. 710). According to Blackdeer and Ocampo (2022), once these incidents are reported:

Schools might want to consider, what does a particular incident suggest about the culture of the school and its role in enabling this incident to occur? What were the dynamics at play and how might the school address these to ensure that such incidents do not happen again? Engaging in this reflection allows schools to shift from seeing racism and bias as solely an individual problem to the systemic problem that it is. (p. 714)

Will Trent University consider the reported incident as one individual outlier occurrence or see it for the systemic problem that it is? Time will tell. The author would like to save this article until such a time as he can fully engage with it and layer in his own PhD studies experiences.

The original conclusion of this chapter was inadequate for this author and he credits one of the reviewers for prompting a more satisfying version. The author would like to conclude with one final quote from Taima Moeke-Pickering (2020): "[w]e must keep writing to future Indigenous academics, students, and allies if we want to sustain a decolonial positionality in the academy" (p. 268). Storytelling as pedagogy infuses both the author's PhD dissertation as well as this anthology chapter. The author hopes this chapter will aid current and future Indigenous studies scholars, sparing them from duplicating the research that the author has already done. Indigenous pedagogy dictates that when one reaches the next level, it becomes their responsibility to help those following them.

The author would like to humbly thank the editors Sheila Cote-Meek and Taima Moeke-Pickering for giving him the opportunity to add his voice to this important conversation.

HÍSW̱KE SIÁM

REFERENCES

Battiste, M. (1998). Enabling the autumn seed: Toward a decolonized approach to Aboriginal knowledge, language, and education. *Canadian Journal of Native Education*, 22(1), 16–27.

Battiste, M. (2002). *Indigenous knowledge and pedagogy in First Nations education: A literature review with recommendations*. Indian and Northern Affairs Canada.

Battiste, M., Bell, L., & Findlay, L. M. (2002). Decolonizing education in Canadian universities: An interdisciplinary, international, indigenous research project. *Canadian Journal of Native Education*, 26(2), 82.

Brayboy, B. M. K. J., & Maughn, E. (2009). Indigenous knowledges and the story of the bean. *Harvard Educational Review*, 79(1), 1–21. doi:10.17763/haer.79.1.l0u6435086352229

Cajete, G. (2000). *Native science: Natural laws of interdependence*. Clear Light Publishers.

Corntassel, J. (2003). An activist posing as an academic? *American Indian Quarterly*, 27(1), 160–171. doi:10.1353/aiq.2004.0029

Cote-Meek, S. (2014). *Colonized classrooms: Racism, trauma and resistance in post-secondary education*. Fernwood Publishing.

Elliott, D., Sr. (1990). Salt water people as told by David Elliot Sr. (2nd ed.). Native Education, School District 63 (Saanich).

Ermine, W. (1995). Aboriginal epistemology. In J. Barman, (Ed.), *First Nations education in Canada: The circle unfolds* (pp. 101–112). UBC Press.

Fixico, D. (2003). *The American Indian mind in a linear world: American Indian studies and traditional knowledge*. Routledge.

Guba, E. G., & Lincoln, Y. S. (1994). Competing paradigms in qualitative research. In N. K. Denzin & Y. S. Lincoln (Eds.), *Handbook of qualitative research* (pp. 105–117). Sage.

Guba, E. G., & Lincoln, Y. S. (2005). Paradigmatic controversies, contradictions, and emerging confluences. In N. K. Denzin & Y. S. Lincoln (Eds.), *The Sage handbook of qualitative research* (pp. 191–215). Sage.

Heron, J., & Reason, P. (1997). A participatory inquiry paradigm. *Qualitative Inquiry*, 3(3), 274–294. doi:10.1177/107780049700300302

Kirkness, V.J., & Barnhardt, R. (1991). First Nations and higher education: The Four R's—respect, relevance, reciprocity, responsibility. *Journal of American Indian Education, 30*(3), 1–15.

Mignolo, W. D. (2009). Epistemic disobedience, independent thought and decolonial freedom. *Theory, Culture & Society, 26*(7-8), 159–181. doi:10.1177/0263276409349275

Mignolo, W. D. (2014). Spirit out of bounds returns to the East: The closing of the social sciences and the opening of independent thoughts. *Current Sociology, 62*(4), 584–602. doi:10.1177/0011392114524513

Moeke-Pickering, T. (2020). The Future for Indigenous Education: How Social Media Is Changing Our Relationships in the Academy. In S. Cote-Meek & T. Moeke-Pickering (Eds.), *Decolonizing and indigenizing education in Canada* (pp. 267–277). Canadian Scholars.

Ocampo, M. G. (2022). We Deserve to Thrive: Transforming the Social Work Academy to Better Support Black, Indigenous, and Person of Color (BIPOC) Doctoral Students. *Advances in Social Work, 22*(2), 703–719. doi:10.18060/24987

Santos, B. S. (2018). *The end of the cognitive empire: The coming of age of epistemologies of the South*. Duke University Press. doi:10.1215/9781478002000

Simpson, L. (2011). *Dancing on Our Turtle's Back*. Arbeiter Ring Press.

Smith, G. H. (2003, October). *Indigenous struggle for the transformation of education and schooling* [Keynote speech]. The Alaskan Federation of Natives (AFN) convention, Anchorage, Alaska, US. http://www.ankn.uaf.edu/curriculum/Articles/GrahamSmith/

Smith, L. T. (2021). *Decolonizing Methodologies: Research and Indigenous Peoples*. Zed Books. doi:10.5040/9781350225282

Taylor, D. (2003). *The archive and the repertoire: Performing cultural memory in the Americas*. Duke University Press.

Trent University. (2014). *Trent University: Indigenous Studies Ph.D. Program Student Handbook 2014–2015*. Trent University.

Tuck, E., & Yang, K. W. (2012). Decolonization is not a metaphor. *Decolonization, 1*(1), 1–40.

Universities Canada. (2015). *Universities Canada principles on Indigenous education.* Universities Canada. https://www.univcan.ca/media-room/media-releases/universities-canada-principles-on-indigenous-education/

Wallerstein, I. (1996). Open the social sciences. *Items: Social Science Research Council, 50*(1), 1–6.

Warrior, R. (2005). *The people and the word: Reading Native nonfiction.* University of Minnesota Press.

Wilson, S. (2008). *Research is ceremony.* Fernwood Publishing.

ENDNOTE

[1] Lowercase eurocentrism is used by the author purposely

Chapter 8
An Indigenous Early Childhood Pedagogy

Jeffrey Wood
 https://orcid.org/0000-0003-0228-7482
Laurentian University, Canada

ABSTRACT

This chapter explores the principles necessary to implement an Indigenous early childhood pedagogy and the importance of the land, language, culture, and identity in learning for Indigenous children. This approach sees children in relation; sees them holistically, including the physical, emotional, mental, and spiritual; helps nurture the gift each child has for the community; focuses on the language, traditional teaching, ceremony, and storytelling; and finally decolonizes the curricula and the classroom. To effectively teach indigenous culture we need to teach the language and to teach the language we need to be on the land.

INTRODUCTION

As educators, we make pedagogical decisions with and for the children we work with, either consciously or unconsciously, throughout the day. Our pedagogical beliefs determine everything in our teaching practice and classrooms (Turner & Wilson, 2010) with real consequences and implications for the children we work with. This is even more important to consider when we are working with Indigenous children, given the history of residential schools and a provincial school system based on white middle class cisgender norms. This chapter attempts to articulate the principles we need to consider when developing an Indigenous early childhood pedagogy to guide our work with the youngest children in our schools, and in preschools and daycares. This pedagogy focuses on young children because it is the beginning of their schooling and as such is the foundation of the school years that follow. In focusing on introducing an Indigenous pedagogy in the early years, it is hoped that a spark of curiosity into the language and culture will be ignited that will carry the children throughout their years of schooling.

This work is an attempt to consolidate the learning I have gained from working with Indigenous communities throughout Ontario and from the teachings I have received from Elders and Knowledge Keepers. What follows are principles that can be applied across different communities and should be considered when thinking about implementing restorative Indigenous culture and language teaching (Simard & Blight, 2011). However, as Indigenous language and communities are necessarily local, the way this pedagogy looks and is taken up will be different depending on the community it is used in – and this work is in no way an attempt to suggest a singular approach. It is to be expected that the work you do in your home community, or where you work, will be different than the programs, classrooms and schools I am drawing on for my inspiration.

Situating Myself and This Work

I am from Métis and settler ancestry and live on the traditional lands of the Atikameksheng Anishinaabek under the Robinson-Huron Treaty. I am father, husband, and uncle. I am a professor in the School of Education and the School of Indigenous Relations at Laurentian University and the Early Learning Lead for the Moosonee and Moose Factory District School Area Boards. I am the former Regional Coordinator for the Ontario Provincial Centre of Excellence Early Years and Child Care and a former kindergarten teacher, and I have been researching and working with young children for the past 25+ years. Throughout this time, I have been working to understand how to support the language and cultural learning of young children in Ontario. Through my work with different communities, I have learned from Elders and Knowledge Keepers as well as from teachers and students. Each community is different and had different lessons for me to learn – and I am still learning. As much as I believe that language and culture are local and tied to the land, and that as such the educational pedagogy will necessarily look different in each community, I think that there are principles that can be used to guide educators in the development of their local pedagogies.

ELEMENTS TO CONSIDER FOR AN INDIGENOUS EARLY CHILDHOOD PEDAGOGY

There are seven overarching principles that should guide the development of an Indigenous early childhood pedagogy; the way these principles are enacted will be different in each community and even slightly different in each school and classroom. They are presented here in no particular order; all are important considerations when developing and implementing an Indigenous early childhood pedagogical approach.

The Importance of all my Relations

For Indigenous children, the importance of positive relationships cannot be understated. From an Indigenous perspective, there is no such thing as a sole individual. Children, and for that matter all of us, are always in relation to each other, our human and non-human kin, the earth, water (snow & ice) and sky, our ancestors, the spirit world, etc. We are always learning from each other and with each other. This has profound implications for teaching, learning environments and assessment.

Community Participation

Learning is seen as a collective experience, where everyone has a role to play in sharing knowledge and supporting each other. Elders, Knowledge Keepers, family and community members need to be welcomed in as partners in the education of the children.

Elders and Ancestors

Indigenous early childhood pedagogy recognizes the important role of elders and ancestors in passing on knowledge and wisdom. Elders are the guardians of traditional knowledge, and their wisdom is highly valued in Indigenous communities and needs to be included in the classroom. Elders need to be consulted well before an Indigenous early childhood pedagogy can be enacted.

Land-Based Learning

The land and the environment are essential in shaping Indigenous knowledge and culture. Land-based learning allows learners to connect with the natural world and to understand the interdependence of all living things and who they are as Indigenous people. The language comes from the land, the culture comes from the language and identity comes from the culture (Wood, Daviau & Daviau, 2018). The importance of maintaining a harmonious relationship with the natural world and a connection to the land cannot be understated in the education of young children. This includes understanding the cultural significance of the land and the environment.

Respect

Respect for self, others, and the environment is a fundamental principle of Indigenous early childhood pedagogy. It is a way of teaching individuals to value and appreciate the interconnectedness of all living things.

Children are Seen Holistically

All aspects of life are interconnected, including the physical, emotional, mental, and spiritual. Therefore, learning should address all of these aspects of a person; knowledge cannot be compartmentalized and separated from other aspects of life.

Ceremony

Ceremony is an important part of the learning process. The practice of ceremony helps to create a sense of connection to the community, ancestors, and the spirit and natural worlds.

Storytelling and Oral Traditions

There are many ways of knowing and each community has a unique perspective to share. Oral traditions include the sharing of historical and personal experiences to teach and pass on knowledge. These stories help to convey the knowledge and wisdom of the community and help to build a sense of community identity. As such, each community will value and tell different stories – making the idea of a Pan-Indigenous curriculum just as problematic as colonial curricula.

Learning in Context

Learning needs to happen in context; learning is situated within the cultural, historical, and social contexts of the learners. An Indigenous pedagogy recognizes that learning is not separate from the environment and the community in which it takes place.

Language and Culture

Language and culture are essential aspects of the learning process for Indigenous children. Language connects us to our ancestors, but it is also critical for the preservation of the stories, culture, and identity of Indigenous people. Language shapes how we see and navigate the world. We need to focus on the verb centred and semantic structure of Indigenous languages and learn out on the land where the language is alive.

Experiential Learning

Language learning needs to be hands-on, allowing learners to engage with the world around them. This approach recognizes that people learn best when they are actively involved in the learning process.

Land-Based

We need to get out onto the land so that Indigenous children can learn the language in context of Mother.

Each Child has a Unique Gift for the Community

It is the responsibility for the adults in the child's life to help them recognize their gift and to nurture that gift (sometimes this gift is received in ceremony or seen in a vision by the child or an Elder). Children are also seen as a gift and as a blessing.

Traditional Teachings

Each Indigenous community has its own version of the sacred circle teachings and teachings for living a good way. It is essential that these beliefs and teachings are integrated into an Indigenous early childhood pedagogy.

Decolonization of Curricula and the Classroom

It is not enough to indigenize curricula and classrooms by adding Indigenous history, stories and ideas into them; we need to eliminate colonial structures and return to a learner focused approach – and transform curricula, not just tweak them.

WHY AN INDIGENOUS EARLY CHILDHOOD PEDAGOGY?

Indigenous early childhood pedagogy has its roots in the long history of Indigenous knowledge systems and practices (Battiste, 2013). Indigenous peoples have developed their own systems of education for millennia, based on unique worldviews and cultural practices. These systems have been deeply intertwined with spiritual and ceremonial practices, and with the land itself (Elder B. Sutherland, Moose Cree First Nation, personal communication, August 2018). However, with the colonization of Indigenous lands and peoples, many of these knowledge systems and practices were suppressed and even actively targeted for erasure (Cardinal, 1999). Colonial education systems sought to assimilate Indigenous children into Western cultural norms, and often used brutal and genocidal tactics to suppress Indigenous cultures and languages (Truth and Reconciliation Commission of Canada [TRC], 2015a). This had a devastating impact on Indigenous communities and on the transmission of Indigenous language, knowledge and practices.

In response to the decreasing numbers of fluent Indigenous language speakers, many Indigenous communities have introduced language learning into their schools over the past 20 years. Despite these efforts, however, the number of fluent speakers has not increased but has instead continued to decrease dramatically (Corbiere, 2014; Statistics Canada, 2017). These failures are largely due to teaching approaches that view Indigenous language from a grammatical, structuralist perspective (Elder E.L. Bob, Atikameksheng Anishnawbek First Nation, personal communication, 2021-2023; Corbiere, 2014), without considering the important relationship between language, culture, and the land. Our approach to language needs to change. The ultimate goal of any Indigenous language program is to create fluent language speakers who are in touch with their culture and their own cultural identity. An Indigenous early childhood pedagogical approach works as a restorative practice: to restore local Indigenous language, culture and history.

I have the privilege of carrying out research with Indigenous teachers and children in their classrooms through my work as a university researcher and through my work with schools in Ontario. Out of concern for the failure of a structuralist approach, many of the schools I have worked with (federally funded First Nation schools and provincially funded public schools) have started to use a morphological and semantic place-based approach to First Nation language learning. I have, at times, been part of committees designing language programs and have also conducted research exploring the efficacy of a variety of Indigenous programming. Each school and community is unique, and each has taken a different approach to making their local Indigenous language foundational to their teaching. Their initiatives have shown remarkable results – both for the children and the teachers. This framework for an Indigenous early childhood pedagogy is an attempt to synthesize these efforts and explore the commonality between these successful programs and others.

Things to Consider Before Starting

Before we can even attempt to implement an Indigenous early childhood pedagogy, it is important to consult and meet with the Elders, Knowledge Keepers, Band Council, and the community. By listening to and learning from the stories that are important in the place we are in, we learn about the local history (and in some instances reclaim the history and stories for the community), and we learn about the local land and the language. We need to engage in ceremony for ourselves and for the children we are going to be working with (Elder E.L. Bob, Atikameksheng Anishnawbek First Nation, personal communication, 2021-2023; Elder B. Sutherland, personal communication, August 2018). The number and types of ceremony will be determined by the Elders who are leading the project. Only once this has been done can an Indigenous early childhood pedagogy be introduced, and the different principles outlined here be adopted.

LEARNING IN RELATION

"All my relations" is at first a reminder of who we are and of our relationship with both our family and our relatives. It also reminds us of the extended relationship we share with all human beings. But the relationships that Native people see go further, the web of kinship to animals, to the birds, to the fish, to the plants, to all the animate and inanimate forms that can be seen or imagined. (King, 1990, p. ix)

Indigenous early childhood pedagogy is focused on the child in relation. When we think about relations from an Indigenous perspective, we think about all our relations, including family and extended relatives and community members; the land, water, ice and sky along with our wider human and nonhuman kin; the animals, birds and fish, our ancestors and future generations (Elder E.L. Bob, personal communication, 2021-2023; King, 2003; Elder B. Sutherland, personal communication, August 2018). We are a part of nature, not separate from it; we are all connected. This then means that the land is one of our relations and we are always in relation to the land (whether we recognize this or not). Within this perspective, language comes from the land, culture comes from language and identity comes from culture (Wood, Daviau & Gunner, 2019; Corbiere, 2014). Children need to have a strong sense of identity and pride in who they are in order to be able to learn effectively (Battiste, 2013; Toulouse, 2011).

When we think about the child and their learning, the child is at the centre of complex, overlapping relations that go beyond the children and teachers. From this inclusive perspective of relationship, we move away from centering on the child or the teacher and are far more inclusive about what we mean by being in relation. These relationships are sacred and ethical. Children are seen holistically as spiritual, emotional, physical and mental beings (Neegan, 2005; Toulouse, 2016). So we continue to focus on the children as the Elders have taught us (Elder E.L. Bob, personal communication, 2021-2023; Elder J. Denis, Métis Nation, personal communication, September 2017; Elder B. Mason, Sandy Lake First Nation, May 2022; Elder B. Sutherland, personal communication, August 2018) but we do so with the child in relation. This not only changes our attitude toward the children we are working with, but it changes our classrooms and schools. With relation at the centre of an Indigenous early childhood pedagogy, families and community members become active partners. Educators and children need the involvement of adults from outside the school to effectively help each child reach their potential. This requires active participation from families and the community, including Elders and Knowledge Keepers. Elders, in particular Elders who are gifted with a passion for the language and a heart for children, need to be contacted before adopting an Indigenous early childhood pedagogy and need to be engaged in supporting the project throughout. Elders help with centring the project on the land, culture and history of the specific place where the school, daycare or early childhood centre is located. Elders are needed to guide and support all the work we do with Indigenous children. Elders and Knowledge Keepers are necessary for identifying the land and stories that will be used within an Indigenous early childhood pedagogy, and for helping the educators and children involved understand them. Ideally, the Elders and Knowledge Keepers will be involved in determining the location of the school and outdoor learning spaces.

LAND-BASED LEARNING

[I]f we do not create a generation of people attached to the land and committed to living out our culturally inherent ways of coming to know, we risk losing what it means to be Nishnaabeg within our own thought systems. (Alfred, as cited in Simpson, 2014, p. 13)

Land-based education is essential in the education of young Indigenous children, especially given the legacy of colonialism. The land is one of our relations and becomes a teacher, helping us learn the language and culture through what we hear, see and do in context. Cutting off Indigenous children from the land, therefore, puts those children at risk of disconnection from their identity, culture and language – leading to further colonization. In light of this, time spent on the land should be an essential part of daily teaching practice (Huston & Michano-Drover, 2022).

Land-based pedagogies provide access to Indigenous ways of knowing and being (Ball & Simpkins, 2004). Relations with the land enable children to conceive of themselves in relationship to particular places and environments. Inside a school or daycare, children become separated from the land – in contrast to land-oriented pedagogical choices which enable access to Indigenous languages and local knowledge holders and relations. Early childhood education connected with the land positions children to engage complexly in local worlds, thereby situating children's learning in a particular place, providing meaningful context for furthering intricate understandings and building memories (Toulouse, 2016).

The land brings us into relation with our nonhuman kin. The land demands what is possible and speaks to us (Wood, Daviau & Gunner, 2019). Being on the land enables children to reconnect to their Indigenous culture and identity. It also allows adults to learn alongside the children, transforming our understanding of the children and ourselves. When we are out on the land it allows some of our children to become more fully themselves and lets us as educators see them in a new way (Wood, 2022). Land-based education is not only about going out on the land, but about bringing the land into the classroom. Land-based education does not need to be difficult – it requires being responsive to the children and the land. Spending time on the land is not really optional; the question is, how we will embrace seeing the land as a teacher and incorporate it into our daily teaching practice?

THE CHILD

It's necessary that we believe that the child is very intelligent, that the child is strong and beautiful and has very ambitious desires and requests. This is the image of the child that we need to hold. (Malaguzzi, 1994, p. 56)

The schools I work with take a holistic approach to learning and the learner, seeing children though four dimensions as spiritual, physical, emotional, and mental. The educators emphasize that each student is capable, self-reliant, intelligent, curious, creative, and unique (Project Zero & Reggio Children, 2001; Toulouse, 2016). The educators have made tremendous efforts to show each child in the classroom respect and love. This simple yet effective act of empowerment is capable of transforming students' lives and represents a tangible step towards healing centuries of intentional subjugation. Much of this culturally restorative practice is not radical; rather, it is simply about showing love, being honest, and making a genuine attempt to connect to the real lives of children in relation. Most importantly, however, this approach values and acknowledges the culture and language the students bring to school with them. This approach allows educators to really engage with their students and to get to know them in deep, personal ways. In turn, these personal connections allow teachers to form strong relationships with their students; and it is these relationships that provide the basis for mutual trust and respect. This is critical, as trust is a necessary ingredient to learning for Indigenous children (Simard & Blight, 2011). A positive relationship is the foundation of all learning and needs to be intentional and respectful from the beginning.

The Gift

From an Indigenous early childhood pedagogical perspective, we see each child as unique and as having a contribution or gift to serve the community (Wood, 2022; Malaguzzi, 1994; Toulouse, 2016). Children are also seen as a gift and as a blessing in themselves. We see them as active full community members figuring out their place in the community. How might this change the way we teach?

What is important shifts away from a common curriculum and skills toward an understanding of individual children, their needs, and their interactions across time, space, and materials. The teacher's role shifts to one where they work to help the child identify their gift and then to nurture the gift of each child. This approach forces our gaze onto the child as a unique member of the community, while also decentering the child (Spyrou, 2018) by acknowledging the child as in relation. This means including all places, materials and human and nonhuman kin the child is in relation with holistically (Toulouse, 2016). This approach makes it very difficult to use and follow preplanned programs and curricula, as it is the needs and gifts of each of the children in a classroom or school that should drive pedagogical decisions. This makes the close connection and involvement of Elders, Knowledge Keepers and community members all that more important, as it is not possible for educators to be experts in all areas. Collaboration is essential and needs to be planned for. This leads toward a shift in assessment as well.

Importance of Spirit

The Elders teach us we are spirit and are only in the physical form for a short time and will return to the spirit world (Elder E.L. Bob, personal communication, 2021-2023; Wagamese, 2016). Everything has spirit – not just humans, but our non-human kin too, as well as the land, water, ice, and sky. Slowing down and listening carefully builds an awareness of the spirit world. This is an essential part of an Indigenous early childhood pedagogical approach. The children we work with are spirit and their spirit needs to be nurtured along with their mental, physical and emotional needs (Peltier, 2022; Toulouse, 2016). The current provincial curriculum in Ontario is atheistic and does not have space for the spiritual; but an Indigenous early childhood pedagogy necessarily creates a space for children to be able to talk about spiritual matters and where their spirits are nurtured.

Ceremony

Introducing spiritual practices into our classrooms like sharing circles, drumming circles, dance, feasts, and the telling of legends (at appropriate times of the year) addresses the spiritual needs and curiosity of Indigenous students. Schools can host powwow for the children, hold ceremony on important times of the year (like the solstice and equinox) and have feasts where the culture and language are celebrated as well as the spiritual needs of the children, their families and the community. In addition, they can provide traditional teachings on powwow, and regalia; the clans system; the language; and traditional resources and tools, such as the drum and shaker. These elements, and the importance of tradition and spirituality, can also be integrated respectfully throughout the school's daily lesson plans and school routines.

This work can be seen as a response to the TRC's (2015a) call for the development of culturally restorative practices (Simard & Blight, 2011); responding specifically to calls to action ten and twelve. These ceremonies and practices will be different depending on local traditions, customs and beliefs. Consultation with Elders will help to guide what is and isn't appropriate for a classroom, school, daycare and school board. It is important to have an understanding of community views on ceremony. The inclusion of spiritual awareness is vital for Indigenous children to fully understand who they are.

STORYTELLING AND ORAL TRADITIONS

All of the Indigenous communities I work with have strong oral traditions. Stories are central to who we are as a people and as such they need to be central to any teaching that we do (Elder E.L. Bob, personal communication, 2021-2023; Bruner, 1996). An Indigenous early childhood pedagogy needs to be centered on story and legend.

The truth about stories is that that's all we are. The Okanagan storyteller Jeannette Armstrong tells us that, "Through my language I understand I am being spoken to, I'm not the one speaking. The words are coming from many tongues and mouths of Okanagan people and the land around them. I am a listener to the language's stories, and when my words form I am merely retelling the same stories in different patterns. (King, 2003, p. 2)

Stories and legends are used to share knowledge and the culture and though they are often entertaining they are told with purpose at specific times, in specific places, for specific reasons. The stories and legends tell us who we are. Storytelling is central to most, if not all, Indigenous cultures. Stories teach us about where we live and as such there will be stories that are unique to each community – and some stories may sound familiar but be slightly different from one community to another. Stories are told as we pass certain places; the land becomes a container for the story and the story often teaches us about that land or what an ancestor(s) did on that land. We tell other stories and legends at specific times of the year to remind us how the land changes and/or explain why. Other stories teach us who we are and how to live in a good way with all our relations. All stories and legends have protocols and are to be taught in specific ways and times. Consultation with Elders and Knowledge Keepers are as important as telling stories in our classrooms.

Trickster Stories

In Anishinabek cultures stories of Nanabush or Nanabozho are used as teaching tools. Nanabush was sent by the Great Spirit, Gitchi Manitou, to the Anishinaabe as a teacher. In all his stories he is portrayed as trickster; in Indigenous cultures on the west coast of Canada, Raven is a trickster. These tricksters get into trouble by being selfish, over curious, vain, etc. and are used to teach children (and remind adults) central lessons to the culture in a fun and entertaining way. Humor is a learning tool that is used in many Indigenous communities to share the culture and teachings (Toulouse, 2016). As we laugh at Nanabush we learn who we are as Anishinaabe and how to live in a good way with all our relations. "Nanabush makes mistakes so that the children can learn from them" (Elder E.L. Bob, personal communication, October, 2022). Stories are a vital way to transmit culture, language and identity; they explain how the world works and how we can live in the world and our communities in a good way. We think narratively (Bruner, 1996) and not only are stories useful, they make learning easier and the lessons more memorable.

LANGUAGE AND CULTURE

We're taught that our language comes from the Creator, and that speaking it acknowledges our connection. We're taught that our voice is a sacred gift and that there is a lot of power in our words. When we speak, our words go around the world forever. (Peltier, as cited in Ball, 2007, p. ii)

When working with young Indigenous children, we want to see them develop strong Indigenous identity and fluent language use. This is necessary to preserve Indigenous culture and languages. To save Indigenous languages, we need to move away from the Western colonial emphasis on nouns and grammar that seems to serve English language learners well (Corbiere, 2014). The process of learning the language needs to bring the language to life as organic, engaging, and playful. Language must be treated as something that is real and lived – that is, the different parts of the language are not taught synthetically in a step-by-step, isolated manner, but instead are taught to the children in a way that is immersive, supportive, holistic and on the land (Elder E.L. Bob, personal communication, 2021-2023; Peltier, 2022). The ultimate goal of an Indigenous early childhood pedagogical approach is to create fluent First Nation speakers who are in touch with their culture and their own cultural identity.

Being proud of who we are as a people is a very important aspect that must be conveyed to our younger generations. This will be accomplished by providing opportunities to understand our people more fully through developing resources and learning opportunities regarding our local history, traditions, and our local stories. (Corbiere, 2014, p. 12)

Connection to the land is an essential consideration in any Indigenous language program. There are real differences between the language that is spoken in each Indigenous community, even when communities use the "same" language. Communities' stories are different, as they emphasize what is considered important locally (Wood, 2022). It is for this reason that consultation with Elders is so important. Language is tied to the land, and each community is on different land (Ball & Simpkins, 2004; Peltier, 2022). Among the tragedies of the residential schools and forced relocation is a loss of connection to place. Before language teaching begins and an Indigenous early childhood pedagogical approach is implemented, the school and local band council need to collect the local stories for the children and the community. Language learning is not only about teaching the children; it is about implementing restorative practice in the community.

The language program is a direct response to the needs of our communities and a response to the TRC (2015b) Calls to action 10 and 14 (p. 2) and should intentionally engage teachers, families, and community members in language learning. Because of the loss of language in First Nation communities, it is unreasonable to expect that children's family members will be fluent speakers of their language. Language learning should be made available to family and community members, and there should be support for school staff to learn the language as well. There should be regular communication with families outlining the language the students are learning and the cultural content that is being covered, so that families are engaged and the children's language learning can be supported.

Another essential component of language revitalization programs is regular invitations to the community to participate in school cultural activities, such as traditional feasts that are held every harvest. By incorporating culture, stories, and language into their daily teaching practices, schools create a space where Indigenous children feel accepted, confident in their identity, and able to share their families' cultures.

Traditional Teachings

Each Indigenous community has its own version of the sacred circle teachings (or medicine wheel teachings) and teachings for living a good way. It is essential that these beliefs and teachings are integrated into an Indigenous early childhood pedagogy (Toulouse, 2016). Even though the medicine wheel teachings have become ubiquitous, they are just the surface of a greater truth that holds the teachings of each Indigenous group. The sacred circle teachings inform us about who we are and how the world works; so do the good life teachings, or Grandmother/Grandfather Teachings. Every Indigenous group has teachings about how to live in a good way and who we are as people and this needs to be integrated into our teaching and planning with children. These teachings should be woven throughout an Indigenous early childhood pedagogy approach as they govern how we are to live and interact with others in our specific Indigenous group and should be integrated into everything we do (Ball & Simpkin, 2004; Battiste, 2013).

INDIGENOUS IDENTITY

Stories teach us who we are and represent the culture and worldview of specific Indigenous people and as such are at the heart of Indigenous Identity; not globally but in a very specific way. From an Indigenous early childhood pedagogical perspective, our schools need to focus on the importance of individual and community well-being by focusing on cultural identity and connections to traditional knowledge and spirituality (Ball & Simpkins, 2004; Toulouse, 2016). Some of the traditional Indigenous practices can include the integration of the Seven Grandfather teachings (like that of the community I currently live in), which consist of Nbwaakaawin (Wisdom), Zaagdawin (Love), Mnaadendmowin (Respect), Aakdehewin (Bravery), Gwekwaadziwin (Honesty), Dbaadendiziwin (Humility) and Debwewin (Truth).

In addition, the school should provide traditional teachings and the teaching of the language. These elements need to be integrated throughout the day so that they are not an add-on that is covered on Friday afternoons. The language, culture and identity are central to teaching and to the learning environment. The importance of tradition and spirituality should be demonstrated throughout the school routines and daily lesson plans.

When the communities I work in have taken a culture-oriented approach, there has been an improvement in the children's outlook on school. In addition to the anticipated increase in student identity, it has also led to concrete academic improvements. For example, after one year of cultural and language programming at one school, the students' reading scores showed an improvement that was nothing short of remarkable (Wood, Daviau & Daviau, 2018) and significantly improved how the students viewed their school and their school performance (Wood, Daviau & Daviau, 2018; Wood, Daviau & Gunner, 2019). By incorporating culture, stories, and language into daily teaching practices, schools create a space where Indigenous children feel accepted, confident in their identity, and able to share their families' cultures.

This is largely to the credit of the educators, who have worked hard to listen carefully to the children, know who they are deeply and who have made tremendous efforts to show each child in the classroom respect. An Indigenous early childhood pedagogical approach can act as a response to the Report of the TRC's (2015b) calls for the adoption of restorative educational practices within Indigenous communities as found in the Calls to Action 10, 12 and 14 (p. 2). The importance of being on the land cannot be understated: identity comes from the culture, culture comes from the language, and the language comes from the land.

TEACHING

When we are considering an Indigenous early childhood pedagogical approach it is typically within the context of school and education. So, what are the implications for teaching? The focus of teaching within an Indigenous framework is on relation, respect, culture, language and identity.

What matters to Indigenous peoples in education is that children, youth, adults and Elders have the opportunity to develop their gifts in a respectful space ... It is about fostering identity, facilitating well-being, connecting to land, honouring language, infusing with teachings and recognizing the inherent right to self-determination. (Toulouse, 2016, p. 4)

The success of an Indigenous early childhood pedagogical approach will be largely due to the educators who work with the children; the people doing the work matter more than any program we develop. The educators need to shift from teaching to engaging in pedagogical listening (Rinaldi, 2006), and to creating classrooms of respect and love. In this approach educators listen for meaning and understanding in what the children do, carefully listening to children's theories, thinking and questions to develop plans and curriculum with the children. Pedagogical listening allows educators to really engage with their students and to get to know them in deep, personal ways. In turn, these personal connections allow teachers to form strong positive relationships with the children they work with; and it is these relationships that provide the basis for mutual trust and respect (Toulouse, 2016). Relationship is a foundation of all learning and in an Indigenous early childhood pedagogical approach it needs to be intentional from the beginning.

Indigenous early childhood pedagogy recognizes and respects diversity, including different learning styles, cultural backgrounds, and languages. This approach necessarily promotes inclusivity and fosters an appreciation for the diversity of human experiences (Ball & Simpkins, 2004). Indigenous language is rooted in the land and in doing, and for children to be learning their culture and language they need to be active – they need to be talking and they need to be doing, both when in the classroom and when on the land (Huston & Michano-Drover, 2022; Peltier, 2022). When a teacher is engaged in whole group instruction it makes it very difficult for this to happen; this type of instruction necessitates one person speaking at a time. Children need to be able to talk and learn together so we need pedagogies that promote talk and social learning; and, for young children, play is essential.

Classroom as the Third Teacher

Educators need to treat the environment as a "third teacher" (Edwards et al., 1998; Ontario Ministry of Education, 2016) and create learning environments that are comfortable, safe, and enhance the students' ability to learn. These spaces can be indoors (typically in classrooms) and outdoors (on the land). The educators need to be intentional about using the educational space, materials, and time to teach the children – whether inside or outside – while keeping in mind that the environment is used to teach the children and that being outdoors is essential in teaching the language (Peltier, 2022). Using the classroom as the third teacher allows educators to focus on small groups of children and address the interests of a variety of children – because of the intentionality with which they have set up the environment, the children they are not directly working with are engaged with centres and invitations on their own. The learning spaces need to be created so that the learning is hands-on, allowing learners to engage with the world around them. This approach recognizes that children learn best when they are actively involved in the learning process through play, as is encouraged in Canadian early childhood curricula (e.g. Ontario Ministry of Education, 2016).

The local place will influence the way in which the environment acts as a third teacher. It changes what the children, families, and the community value, what they see as interesting and important to know. Place is an important consideration. The land is a teacher. When students are engaged in real activities that use the language it is more meaningful and easier to remember. At one school I work with, the language teacher took the children outside to use language related to the goose harvest. With the guidance of the language teacher, and from children who had joined their families as a part of the harvest, the children created a blind in the snow and set up decoy geese. The language teacher capitalized on the children's natural interest and excitement about the goose harvest; creating small groups with various roles so that everyone was engaged in learning using the language throughout the activity, teaching the children words and language directly related to the goose harvest. Some of the words used by the language teacher were: niska (goose), pâskisikan (gun), mâwacihcikew (harvest), ašohikan (hunting blind), etc. But, more importantly, the language teacher and the children used the language in a meaningful context, learning the words associated with the activity but also incidentally the conjugation of and structure of the language (e.g. nîmipâskisikanew – to take a gun along). Taking children on the land is a rich opportunity to use the language in context; whether it is like the example above, where the language teacher periodically creates land-based language learning opportunities, or other programs I work with, where the children have land-based learning daily in which the children and a dedicated educator explore and create learning spaces in the bush adjacent to the school.

Assessment as Ascribing Value

From an Indigenous early childhood education perspective, assessment shifts from being an external measure examining the child's performance against outside measures toward observing and documenting the child in order to better understand the child and their gift (Malaguzzi, 1994). We assess what we value (Rinaldi, 2006); we need to rethink assessment and see it as a daily practice that helps the educators decide what direction to take the classroom – after all, provincial curriculum rarely tells educators how and what to teach. We need to use assessment to better understand the children in relation. Relationships add complexity to assessment processes. If we focus only on the individual, if we think of learning as a linear process, and if we think of learning as only curricular-based, we miss the interconnections and relationships that occur in the classroom between members of the group, between learning and knowledge, and between children's dreams and realities. When we assess children in only one context with tools that are reductionist, we often only see deficits. When educators are open to the learning trajectories designed by children, the intelligence of the group emerges (Wood & Speir, 2013). When we ask simple questions, we see children as simple and limited; when we listen, and support the deep questions of children, we see them as intelligent and capable (Wood & Speir, 2013).

Practices such as pedagogical documentation (Rinaldi, 2004; Turner & Wilson, 2010; Wien, Guyevskey & Berdoussis, 2011) become important for collecting data and sharing observations with the educational team members as well as family members, Elders, Knowledge Keepers and community members who are working with the child. They allow us to see children in relation and help educators to better understand the children's theories and understandings.

Learning does not proceed in a linear way, determined and deterministic, by progressive and predictable stages, but rather is constructed through advances, standstills, and "retreats" that take many directions. The construction of knowledge is a group process. Each individual is nurtured by the hypotheses and theories of others, and by conflicts with others, and advances by co-constructing pieces of knowledge with others through a process of contamination and disagreement. Above all, conflict and disturbance force us to constantly revise our interpretive models and theories on reality, and this is true for both children and adults. (Rinaldi, 2006, p.103)

The use of this daily type of assessment does not mean an abandonment of mandated report cards - in many ways the reporting required by the provinces will be made easier for the educators as they will have ample assessment data on each child that will be considerably richer than that required. The question in assessment is: what do we value?

DECOLONIZATION OF CURRICULA

From an early childhood pedagogical approach, the child in relation should be at the centre and all the elements already discussed should be integrated into teaching and educational considerations. The process of decolonizing curricula requires more than a minor adjustment to teaching practice or the inclusion of Indigenous stories or history.

Throughout this chapter I have resisted a Pan-Indigenous approach to pedagogy because Indigenous language and culture are intimately local – but the Indigenous experience of colonialism is the same across groups (though some of the specifics may be slightly different). Residential Schools, the Sixties Scoop, Indigenous Child Welfare, and Missing and Murdered Indigenous Women, Girls, and Two Spirit+

are all colonial legacies and affect all Indigenous communities and people. The people who ran residential schools had a pedagogy they followed: this pedagogy saw Indigenous children as less than human, which led to unspeakable treatment and abuse (TRC, 2015a). What is proposed by an Indigenous early childhood pedagogy is a response to this and a call to be in relation with the children we work with in a good way. We need to acknowledge the colonial past and present and actively eliminate colonial practices from our schools and classrooms (Battiste, 2013). This is not to suggest that we leave Indigenous children without the ability to be successful in the provincial school system, should they want to go on to higher education (for example). By giving children the ability to codeswitch (Wheeler & Swords, 2004) between their Indigenous language, culture and identity as they reach older grades (I do not think this needs to be done before grade three unless the child's gift and/or interest demands it) they will be able to choose the educational path that most interests them and reflects their gift.

CONCLUSION

Language comes from the land, culture comes from language, identity comes from culture, and all learning is done in relation. In order to save our Indigenous languages and culture, they must be made real, organic, and engaging (Corbiere, 2014). Culture and language programs should take up new approaches that truly engage our children and that connect them to the land (Peltier, 2022). And this learning needs to start when children are young: in preschool and Kindergarten. In order to do the work of having fluent First Nations speakers who are in touch with their culture and who can create a vibrant language community, we need to start at the beginning of schooling, with an Indigenous early childhood pedagogy that makes a difference in the lives of our children and our communities – both now and in the future.

The pedagogies we use determine how the children we work with are seen and what is possible for them – and for us as educators. In choosing pedagogies that value the children for who they are as members of a specific community – for who they are now, with respect and love, and in relation – they can learn to be proud of who they are and can be nurtured in the unique gift they each have for our communities. We need to engage with an Indigenous early childhood pedagogy for the children we work with and for the survival of Indigenous cultures, language and identity.

REFERENCES

Ball, J. (2007). *Aboriginal young children's language and literacy development: research evaluating progress, promising practices, and needs.* Canadian Language and Literacy Networked Centre of Excellence. http://www.ecdip.org/docs /pdf/CLLRNet%20Feb%202008.pdf

Ball, J., & Simpkins, M. (2004). The community within the child: Integration of Indigenous knowledge into First Nations childcare process and practice. *American Indian Quarterly, 28*(3/4), 480–498. doi:10.1353/aiq.2004.0091

Battiste, M. (2013). *Decolonizing education: Nourishing the learning spirit.* Purich Publishing.

Bruner, J. (1996). *The culture of education.* Harvard University Press. doi:10.4159/9780674251083

Cardinal, H. (1999). *The unjust society.* Douglas & McIntyre.

Corbiere, A. (2014). *First Nation revival program framework for curriculum development.* Kenjgewin Teg.

Huston, L., & Michano-Drover, S. (2022). Placing the child's hands on the land: Conceptualizing, creating, and implementing land-based teachings in a play space. In S. S. Peterson & N. Friedrich (Eds.), *The role of play and place in young children's language and literacy* (pp. 81–94). University of Toronto Press. doi:10.3138/9781487529239-007

King, T. (Ed.). (1990). *All my relations: An anthology of contemporary Canadian Native prose.* McClelland & Stewart.

King, T. (2003). *The truth about stories: A Native narrative.* House of Anansi Press.

Malaguzzi, L. (1994). Your image of the child: Where teaching begins. *Child Care Information Exchange,* 52–52.

Neegan, E. (2005). Excuse me: Who are the first peoples of Canada? A historical analysis of Aboriginal education in Canada then and now. *International Journal of Inclusive Education, 9*(1), 3–15. doi:10.1080/13603110420000299757

Ontario Ministry of Education. (2016). *The kindergarten program.* Queen's Printer of Ontario.

Peltier, S. (2022). Seven Directions early learning for Indigenous land literacy wisdom. In S. S. Peterson & N. Friedrich (Eds.), *The role of play and place in young children's language and literacy* (pp. 33–51). University of Toronto Press. doi:10.3138/9781487529239-004

Project Zero & Reggio Children. (2001). *Making learning visible: Children as individual and group learners*. Reggio Children.

Rinaldi, C. (2004). The relationship between documentation and assessment. *Innovations in Early Education: The International Reggio Exchange.*, *11*(1), 1–4.

Rinaldi, C. (2006). *In dialogue with Reggio Emilia: Listening, researching and learning*. Routledge.

Simard, E., & Blight, S. (2011). Developing a culturally restorative approach to aboriginal child and youth development: Transitions to adulthood. *First Peoples Child & Family Review*, *6*(1), 28–55. doi:10.7202/1068895ar

Spyrou, S. (2018). *Disclosing childhoods: Research and knowledge production for a critical childhood studies*. Palgrave Macmillan. doi:10.1057/978-1-137-47904-4

Statistics Canada. (2017). *Census in brief: The Aboriginal languages of First Nations people, Métis and Inuit.* Catalogue no. 98-200-X2016022. https://www12 .statcan.gc.ca/census-recensement/2016/as-sa/9 8-200-x/2016022/98-200 -x2016022-eng.pdf

Toulouse, P. (2011). *Achieving Aboriginal student success: A guide for K to 8 classrooms*. Portage & Main Press.

Toulouse, P. (2016). *What matters in Indigenous education: Implementing a vision committed to holism, diversity and engagement*. People for Education.

Truth and Reconciliation Commission of Canada. (2015a). *Honouring the truth, reconciling for the future: Summary of the final report of the Truth and Reconciliation Commission of Canada*. The Commission.

Truth and Reconciliation Commission of Canada. (2015b). *Truth and Reconciliation Commission of Canada: Calls to action*. The Commission.

Turner, T., & Wilson, D. G. (2010). Reflections on documentation: A discussion with thought leaders from Reggio Emilia. *Theory into Practice*, *49*(1), 5–13. doi:10.1080/00405840903435493

Wagamese, R. (2016). *Embers: one Ojibway's meditations*. Douglas & McIntyre.

Wheeler, R., & Swords, R. (2004). Codeswitching transforms the dialectally diverse classroom. *Language Arts*, *81*(6), 470–480.

Wien, C. A., Guyevskey, V., & Berdoussis, N. (2011). Learning to document in Reggio- inspired education. *Early Childhood Research & Practice*, *13*(2), 1–12.

Wood, J. (2022). The importance of the land, language, culture, identity and learning in relation for Indigenous children. In S. S. Peterson & N. Friedrich (Eds.), *The role of play and place in young children's language and literacy* (pp. 109–226). University of Toronto Press. doi:10.3138/9781487529239-009

Wood, J., Daviau, C., & Daviau, N. (2018). *Anishinaabemowin revival program*. Indspire Research Report.

Wood, J., Daviau, C., & Gunner, B. (2019). *Enhancing Cree language with culture*. Indspire Research Report.

Wood, J., & Speir, S. (2013). *Assessment as attributing value: Documentation and assessment in early learning*. Ministry of Education, Assessment and Policy Branch.

KEY TERMS AND DEFINITIONS

All my relations: We are always in relation to each other, our human and non-human kin, the earth, water (snow & ice) and sky, our ancestors, the spirit world, etc. We are always learning from each other and with each other.

Decolonization: We need to acknowledge the colonial past and present and actively eliminate colonial practices from our schools, curricula and pedagogies.

Early Childhood: The age groups covered being discussed are from birth to Grade 2 or eight years old.

Holistic: All aspects of life are interconnected, including the physical, emotional, mental, and spiritual. Therefore, learning should address all of these aspects of a person; knowledge cannot be compartmentalized and separated from other aspects of life.

Indigenous People: This chapter uses Indigenous to refer to Ontario's first peoples generally but it is always used with the understanding that all Indigenous people and groups are unique and specific.

Land-Based Learning: The land and the environment are essential in shaping Indigenous knowledge and culture. The language comes from the land and defines what is important for each indigenous group.

Pedagogy: Pedagogy is the beliefs we have about teaching and learning and governs our actions and practice in the classroom.

Traditional Teachings: Each Indigenous community has its own version of the sacred circle teachings and teachings for living a good way. It is essential that these beliefs and teachings are integrated into an Indigenous early childhood pedagogy.

Chapter 9
Reconciliatory Pedagogies:
Embodying Our Walk as Settler Teachers in Canadian High Schools

Erin Keith
https://orcid.org/0000-0002-6212-6173
St. Francis Xavier University, Canada

Krista LaRue Keeley
Regina Public Schools, Canada

ABSTRACT

Two Canadian settler teachers explore the intention and iterative, enduring process of reconciliation in high school classrooms through storytelling of their own lived experiences. They respectfully 'call-in' other settler teachers who may feel paralyzed for fear of appropriation and the heaviness of this reconciliatory work. Weaving in how the 5Rs have guided the two teachers' journeys toward incorporating Indigenous pedagogies into their praxis and suggesting how these principles could support other settler educators who are beginning their decolonization journey, an Interwoven Living Framework that illuminates their learning 'from' is developed. The framework is grounded in actionizing the 5Rs through the critical work of listening to, learning from, working, and walking with First Peoples. Using narratives, the teachers story their "walk" inspired by the words of an Indigenous student from their class, Poppy. They share a place to begin towards truly understanding how to become an entrusted Indigenous ally-to-be and how to actionize this collective work in high school landscapes.

DOI: 10.4018/978-1-6684-3425-3.ch009

INTRODUCTION

As two educators who acknowledge the many past and present injustices Canada's First Peoples have endured and continue to experience, we commit to enact reconciliation mindfully every day within our praxis as Canadian settler teachers. Through embodying the critical engagement skills of humility, hope, inspiration, listening, and by taking small steps to overcome our fears of appropriation, making mistakes, and being uncomfortable, we journey together to find other settlers committed to the same moral action of learning, unlearning, self-relation, and truth-telling. We must embrace our white ignorance and break free from the "paralysis" (Rice et al., 2020) of discomfort we may experience so as to hold space and humility for other ways of knowing (Simcoe et al., 2018). We are guided by Regan (2010) who coined the term reconciliatory pedagogy which urges non-Indigenous folks to "solve the settler problem" (p. 11) and "mak[e] space for decolonization" (p. 6). Guided by the Truth and Reconciliation Commission's (TRC) (Truth and Reconciliation Commission of Canada [TRC], 2015) Calls to Action, this ethical, pedagogical space aims to "unsettle the settler within" (Regan, 2010, p. 147) and rightfully centers Indigenous Peoples' voices as they reclaim and revitalize their cultures, language, histories, and stories. In a high school context, we attempt to demonstrate and model reconciliatory pedagogy within our classrooms and broader school community in hopes that other settler teachers will journey alongside us, carrying the burden of opening healing pathways for Indigenous students, their families, and communities in responsible, respectful, relational, reciprocal, and relevant (Kirkness & Barnhardt, 2001; Tessaro & Restoule, 2022) ways of knowing, being and doing.

SITUATING OURSELVES: STEPPING TOWARDS RECONCILIATION

Erin: As an emerging scholar at St. Francis Xavier University, Nova Scotia, who recently has been transplanted from Ontario, I aim to explore and critically analyze the colonial education barriers facing Indigenous students and families in Nova Scotia. Using my 20 years of experience as a teacher, learner, and hopeful ally, I acknowledge my privilege as a white, cisgendered woman, living and flourishing as a settler guest on the ancestral and unceded lands of the territory of the Mi'kmaq People. This territory is covered by the "Treaties of Peace and Friendship" which Mi'kmaq and Wolastoqiyik (Maliseet) Peoples first signed with the British Crown in 1725. Employing epistemologies that are intersectional, empathetic, hopeful, and heartening, I pledge to learn, unlearn, unearth, and grow my understanding of how the approaches to reconciliation model (Poitras Pratt & Danyluk, 2019) and reconciliatory pedagogies of decolonization can interrupt hegemonic high school practices and re-center the gifts and strengths that Indigenous families and students bring through their cultural multiplicities and multifaceted identities.

Krista: As an educator of both children and adults within the province of Saskatchewan, I seek to investigate the harms Eurocentric pedagogies do to students, including those from Indigenous communities, and support the journeys of educators in the necessary epistemic shift toward reconciliatory educational practices. I acknowledge the place in which I reside, learn, work, and play is the traditional lands of the Cree, Saulteaux, Dakota, Nakota, Lakota, and in the homeland of the Métis Nation. It is treaty land, referred to as Treaty 4 Territory. I respect and honour the Treaties that were made on all territories, acknowledge the harms and mistakes of the past, and am committed to walk forward with Indigenous nations in the spirit of truth, reconciliation, and collaboration. I acknowledge it was on Treaty 4 Territory where the last residential school closed its doors in 1996 and home to the Muscowequan Indian Residential School where in 2023, over 2000 "anomalies" were found after ground penetrating radar (Otis, 2023). As a white settler educator on this land, it is my responsibility to work together with Indigenous communities to support all children, families, and communities impacted by the seemingly unending horrors of Residential Schools and the ongoing generational trauma of colonization. As a white settler educator and developing scholar, I am committed to listening, learning, and walking the path of decolonization, knowing my journey begins in a place of white privilege and ignorance. I will continue to travel this path, honouring intersectionality, equity, and the process of unlearning with humility, respect, and love.

Acknowledging Our Responsibility

Guided by the words of Mi'kmaq Scholar Dr. Marie Battiste (2015), "[e]very school is either a site of reproduction or a site of change" (p. 175). As two settlers with experience teaching in high schools in both Ontario and Saskatchewan, it is imperative we understand what we are replicating within our classrooms and the broader school landscape, so we do not perpetuate further harm and retraumatization to Indigenous communities. The colonization of Canada stripped Indigenous learners of ancestral culture, language, and knowledge practices, and replaced them with an educational system void of the wholistic and rich learning that was once commonplace in Indigenous nations (National Collaborating Centre for Indigenous Health [NCCIH], 2017). While Indigenous pedagogies are "wholistic, relational, experiential, community-focused, ritual-centered, ceremonial, spiritual, and interdependent" (Papp, 2020, p. 27), conventional Eurocentric pedagogies tend to promote independence, compliance, competition, and discipline (Rios et al., 2020; Serafini, 2002). As educators, we all want the best for the students in our care, however, Canadian statistics illustrate Indigenous students are not finding success in the educational experiences we are offering at the same rate when compared to non-Indigenous students (Statistic Canada, 2019). With Indigenous high school graduation rates approximately 20% lower and incarceration rates more than eight times higher (Perreault, 2022), it is clear the educational experiences we, as settlers, are offering in high schools are only replicating harmful practices. When educators intentionally create schools as sites of change, the results can be dramatic. A study of a Saskatchewan high school demonstrated when large scale decolonization efforts are made, Indigenous students see higher levels of success in credit attainment and graduation rates (Papp, 2020).

The TRC (2015) echoes the urgency of Battiste (2015) through the Calls to Action that advocate, in part, for change in the various education systems around Canada (Wong, 2022). Much of the required change is structural and the concern of leaders at the highest levels of education, however, as educators, it is our responsibility as change-leaders to create learning spaces and experiences that support the success of Indigenous learners by amplifying their rich diversity of histories, values, and practice (Bartlett, 2021). The commitment to reconciliation and the decolonization of education, in sustaining and collective ways, is our ethical duty, as settler educators. Since white, cis gendered, heterosexual, middle class women make up the majority of the Canadian teaching profession (Mueller & Nickel, 2017), we must embrace enduring decolonization practices, practice Indigenous pedagogies guided by Elders and Knowledge Keepers, and mirror Indigenous worldviews in our learning spaces. The journey toward decolonization and reconciliation is not only one for Indigenous communities to travel, but for us, the white settlers who perpetuate ongoing colonization. This can be an intimidating and even polarizing task for many non-Indigenous educators. Too often, we shy away from Indigenizing practice and learning spaces due to our perceptions of relevance, readiness, comfort, knowledge, and fear of offending (Rice et al., 2020; Riley et al., 2019). However, this burden and responsibility is ours to carry as settlers.

JOURNEY TOWARDS RECONCILIATION AS TEACHER SETTLERS

In our various experiences working in high schools, many well-meaning settler teachers often look for a checklist of "Indigenous approved" activities to incorporate into their daily classroom practice. They miss making a personal connection to their reconciliatory work and fail to self-examine the motives behind 'why' the work is imperative. Cote-Meek and Moeke-Pickering (2021) challenge educators to think more deeply about the truth of colonization when attempting to engage in reconciliation. They urge settler educators that reconciliatory changes are not small activities for educators to make themselves feel better but must be "sustained" and "transformative". As settler teachers ourselves, we acknowledge that "it takes a long-standing concerted effort to build trust and build relationships that are truly reconciliatory" (Cote-Meek & Moeke-Pickering, 2021, 15:59) and we are committed every day in our classrooms to "do better" through relational actions.

An Envisioned Framework

Acknowledging that school systems, policies, processes, and pedagogies are still wrapped in "cognitive imperialism" (Battiste, 2015, p. 26), we were intentional in drawing from rich Indigenous research and knowledge in developing a transformative path towards reconciliation that other settler teachers could enter and travel along as a living framework for our reconciliation work. We were also reflexive to heed Chrona's (2022) warning that non-Indigenous peoples, like ourselves, should not "know what is best" (p. 48) for Indigenous Peoples but rather understand that each settler teacher's journey towards reconciliation is personal and unique so multiple entry points are needed along the envisioned path. There is no one size fits all approach to reconciliation, so we wanted to honour this in our framework. In addition, if Indigenous high school students are to leave the education system with "dignity, purpose, and options" (Networks of Inquiry and Indigenous Education (NOIIE), 2022, para. 4), then teachers need to value the enduring work involved with reconciliation by honouring the strengths of Indigenous students, families, communities, and support them to grow by nourishing the gifts they innately have. Being led by these two guiding beliefs, we envisioned a living framework that infuses long-standing Indigenous knowledge(s) of the *4Rs* (Kirkness & Barnhardt, 1991, 2001) as well as a journey model of reconciliation called the *Approaches to Reconciliation Model* (AtRM) (Poitras Pratt & Danyluk, 2019) as our north star.

4Rs Are Now 5Rs

The 4Rs of Indigenous pedagogy, conceptualized by Kirkness and Barnhardt (1991, 2001), was a reaction to how Indigenous students in universities were experiencing "a form of assimilation" (Tessaro & Restoule, 2022, p. 133) through Eurocentric educational pedagogies that forced them to sacrifice their cultural values and ways of knowing while in learning spaces. The 4Rs framework became a transformative paradigm for Indigenous education that has been woven into academic higher education literature and grounds our critical work. The framework is based on four guiding interrelated principles that can also help to decolonize public school education and create a revitalizing space that empowers Indigenous learners. Recognizing that some settler teachers have gone "through their entire educational career without learning about Indigenous Peoples and the history and legacy of residential schooling in Canada" (Milne, 2017, p. 10) themselves, centering the Rs within our living and integrated framework was imperative so that courageous conversations could occur among school colleagues and shifts in understandings always took a learning-unlearning stance vs. one that replicated ignorance.

The 4Rs, *Respect, Relevance, Responsibility, Reciprocity* (Kirkness & Barnhardt, 1991, 2001), have recently been augmented by Restoule to include a fifth R, *Relationship* (Lake & Atkins, 2021; Restoule, 2008; Tessaro & Restoule, 2022). Relationship in Indigenous knowledge(s) has many meanings and understandings such as the spiritual, relational connection to the Earth and all its elements (Alteo & Boron, 2022), the constitutional rights and renewing relationships with government (Department of Justice Canada, 2018), the respectful, growing learning alliances between First Peoples and settlers (Chrona, 2022), and of course the reciprocal connectedness between teachers and Indigenous students, families, and communities. The 5Rs of Indigenous pedagogy are fundamental when grounding and shifting our collective, relational work toward Indigenous allyship. We recognize that allyship is not a title we can bequeath ourselves, but rather an honour that First Peoples give us when the reconciliation work is enacted and noted (Poitras Pratt & Danyluk, 2019). Next, each of the five *Rs* will be further explored.

Respect. Respect involves acknowledging and respecting the feelings, wishes, rights, and traditions of others (Tsosie et al., 2022). It also refers to the recognition of Indigenous Peoples' histories, knowledge, cultures, and languages as valued "human knowledge" (Kirkness & Barnhardt, 2001, p. 102) that colonial institutions, like schools, must respect by decentering Eurocentric knowledge in pedagogical practice. Respect therefore requires acknowledging the diversity of Indigenous Peoples knowledge and the harmful and violent impacts of colonization and systemic oppression. Respect requires teachers to center mindful listening and valuing Indigenous knowledge(s) systems and ways of knowing, and recognizes the role of Elders and community members as Knowledge Keepers.

Relevance. Relevance involves making education meaningful and applicable to the lives of Indigenous learners. This requires creating educational programs and materials that reflect Indigenous worldviews, experiences, and aspirations, and that prioritize local contexts and priorities (Kovach, 2008). Relevance also involves engaging Indigenous learners in meaningful and culturally responsive ways, and creating opportunities for students to connect with their communities and cultures.

Reciprocity. Reciprocity refers to the principle of mutual exchange and collaboration that is continuous and intentional sparked from the vulnerability of learning from one another, often within their place of knowing (Kirkness & Barnhardt, 2001). It is "the belief that as we receive from others, we must also offer to others" (Rice, 2007, p. 7) in order to "jointly build knowledge from the ground up" (Kirkness & Barnhardt, 2001, p. 105). This involves creating partnerships and relationships based on trust and mutual respect, and recognizing that Indigenous communities have valuable knowledge and expertise to share with non-Indigenous partners. Reciprocity also involves recognizing and addressing power imbalances, presence of coloniality, and ensuring that benefits and responsibilities are shared (Tsosie et al., 2022).

Responsibility. Responsibility involves taking action to support the ongoing revitalization of Indigenous languages, cultures, and knowledge systems. According to Wilson (2020), teachers have a relational accountability to recognize and address the ongoing impacts of colonization and systemic oppression within their practice, place, and system, and to actively work to promote social justice and equity for Indigenous students. One impactful way of being accountable is supported by Davidson's (2020) literacy work. Davidson urges settler teachers to remain informed and learn from past mistakes by ensuring that classroom materials, resources, literacies, etc. are inclusive not only of Indigenous content but also authentic experiences and perspectives of Indigenous Peoples. Responsibility also involves creating opportunities for Indigenous learners to become leaders and advocates for their communities, and supporting their ongoing learning and development. It is a respectful, valued and ensuring understanding that Indigenous Peoples are responsible for their own narratives, stories, and histories, both in the present and for future generations (Tsosie et al., 2022).

Relationship. Indigenous Peoples view relationships as fundamental to their ways of being, knowing, and relating to the world around them (Chrona, 2022). The fifth 'R' of relationships underpins Kirkness and Barnhardt's (1991, 2001) 4Rs. Restoule (2017) refers to relationships as the process of cultivating, tending, and making conscious efforts to build, foster, sustain, and learn from one another. Similar to Battiste's (2000) view, relationships underlie all aspects of Indigenous education between teacher and students as well as between community, culture, and school. Unlike a colonial view of relationships, Indigenous Peoples see relationships as an integral to their worldview and guide their interactions with other people, the natural world, and the spiritual realm (Cajete, 2000). Indigenous Peoples believe that all things are interconnected and interdependent, and that the land, water, and other natural resources are seen as sacred and are treated with reverence and respect (Cajete, 2000). It is imperative that settler teachers understand this deeper relational connection and learn from the stories and teachings of their Indigenous students, families, and communities (Archibald, 2008; Brunette-Debassige & Wakeham, 2021).

Another relational understanding settler teachers should be mindful of is that the intergenerational trauma experienced by survivors of residential schools and their families, as well as many other oppressive social inequities and human rights abuses that they have faced, schools are traditionally not safe places (Cowan, 2020). As settler teachers, building trust, acknowledging the impacts of trauma, but not being focused solely on the past rather inviting students to re-story themselves through sharing their strengths, hopes, and aspirations, and continuing to learn about trauma-informed practices blended with cultural teachings (Gaywish & Mordoch, 2018) are all steps along the relational journey educators can consider.

Approaches to Reconciliation Model (AtRM)

Reconciliation efforts in both Ontario and Saskatchewan high schools have focused on implementing updated curriculum that infuse Indigenous perspectives in wholistic ways. Although not all subjects have undergone a refresh, the mandate from local school boards led by the Ministries of Education, is for teachers to embed culturally responsive pedagogies and Indigeneity into all pedagogical decisions across all subjects (Wong, 2023). This could include showcasing Indigenous artists and musicians, novel choices that highlight Indigenous writers, social studies that embed historical narratives but also highlights First Peoples' current achievements, and language revitalization opportunities from community Knowledge Keepers. For many settler teachers though, these mandates, although in alignment with the TRC Calls to Action since 2015, are still compunctious due to fear and a lack of understanding of where to begin. As a result, the reconciliatory journey for some settler teachers is still very much in its early stages. For this reason, a path that guides settler teachers is needed. A path that teachers can enter where they are on their reconciliatory journey and be supported by guiding prompts and iterative ways of knowing.

Interwoven into the 5Rs, the Approaches to Reconciliation Model (AtRM) (Poitras Pratt & Danyluk, 2019) is a model that "posits that the work of reconciliation is accessible to all Canadians if they are open to new perspectives, and if they are willing to listen and learn" (p. 7). It is a cyclical model that invites settler teachers to approach reconciliations from a choice of three reflexive yet action-oriented approaches. The approaches include (Poitras Pratt & Danyluk, 2019, p. 7): a) Listening to and Learning from Indigenous Peoples; b) Walking with and Learning from Indigenous Peoples; and c) Working with and Learning from Indigenous Peoples. Each approach promotes teacher agency, self-reflexivity, and choice with the first approach focused more on private Indigenous knowledge building by reading books, listening to music, and watching films. The second approach asks teachers to take their knowledge into more public settings to attend and learn from public acts of reconciliation such as Indigenous-led events. This could be attending local community Pow Wows or engaging in Indigenous dance, music, food, and art celebrations. The third approach is most complex with teachers supporting Indigenous community projects and being visibly active in disrupting hegemonic and colonial school

Figure 1. Interwoven living framework

Note. This figure is created by Keith and Keeley (2023), and adapted from "Exploring reconciliatory pedagogy and its possibilities through educator-led praxis," by Poitras Pratt, Y. and Danyluk, P.J. (2019) The Canadian Journal for the Scholarship of Teaching and Learning, 10(3).; "First Nations and higher education: The four R's – Respect, relevance, reciprocity, responsibility," by Kirkness, V. J., Barnhardt, R. (2001). In R. Hayoe & J. Pan (Eds.), Knowledge across cultures: A contribution to dialogue among civilizations (pp.1-21). Comparative Education Research Centre, University of Hong Kong. https://www.uaf.edu/ankn/publications/collective-works-of-ray-b/Four-Rs-2nd-Ed.pdf; The five r's of Indigenous research: Relationship, respect, relevance, responsibility, and reciprocity [Workshop], by Restoule, J.P. (2008, Nov. 26). Wise Practices II: Canadian Aboriginal AIDS Network Research and Capacity Building Conference, Toronto, Ontario, Canada.; "Indigenous pedagogies and online learning environments: a massive open online course case study," by Tessaro, D., & Restoule, J.P. (2022). AlterNative : an International Journal of Indigenous Peoples, 18(1), 182–191. https://doi.org/10.1177/11771801221089685

practices, such as teacher centric pedagogies, binary assessment practices, lack of culturally responsive and relevant learning resources, prioritizing Indigenous content without considering the representation of Indigenous perspective and voice, etc. to ensure Indigenous students feel valued, welcomed, and that they belong. Poitras Pratt and Danyluk (2019) caution that the AtRM model is not a checklist, but a process that welcomes all educators, regardless of where they are in their reconciliation path. It asks teachers to acknowledge and reflexive of their cultural and intellectual humility, to be mindful, active listeners of Indigenous Peoples, and to foster trusting relationships with Indigenous students, their families, communities, and colleagues.

Combining the AtRM (Poitras Pratt & Danyluk, 2019) and the 5Rs of Indigenous pedagogy (Kirkness & Barnhardt, 1991, 2001; Restoule, 2017; Tessaro & Restoule, 2022) offers an interwoven living framework that unites and guides non-Indigenous teachers on their walk and commitment towards reconciliation. By centering the 5Rs in each of the three AtRM approaches, small acts of reconciliation begin to bud and over time, grow. Flourishing under the gusty clouds which signify both spirit and dynamic change, teachers gain greater confidence and agency through their reconciliation ways of knowing. Along the path of learning 'from', leaves blossom into a sustaining living practice of Indigenous pedagogy (see Figure 1).

INTERWOVEN LIVING FRAMEWORK IN ACTION

Listening to, and Learning From

This AtRM approach centers mindful listening at its essence as well as critical self-reflection. Poitras Pratt and Danyluk (2019) remind settlers that Indigenous Peoples are members of unique and varied communities with vast representations of language, culture, traditions, knowledge(s). Singular stories of indigeneity are to be disrupted. Mindful, active listening by settlers should prompt the question, "what action can I take to reconcile?" (Poitras Pratt & Danyluk, 2019, p. 8). By listening and learning from Elders, Knowledge Keepers, Indigenous music, literature, artists, or other mediums, settler teachers can foster a space of reconciliatory practice that affirms Indigenous Peoples living truths and validates for Indigenous students that they belong.

Responsibility and Reciprocity

Krista: I have spent a lot of my academic life researching and writing about the 21st century classroom. Through this work and my own reconciliation journey, I have begun to understand and recognize much of what students are in need of is supported through the return of Indigenous pedagogies. I wanted to engage in reconciliatory practices in the classroom, but I first had a responsibility to engage in my own personal learning journey through reading and listening to Indigenous educational scholars, Elders, and Knowledge Keepers. Through this work, I have learned to plan educational opportunities with specific instructional methods in mind. Indigenous pedagogies call for the decentering of the teacher in the classroom and the centering of the student. Through this decentering, the teacher is no longer the one who makes all the decisions and the plans, but instead practices reciprocity. Centering the student allows for them to learn through inquiry and wholistic learning opportunities co-created by students and teacher.

Additionally, I have had the immense honour to work with educators who have taken the responsibility of this work beyond personal learning. For example, Smith (2014) and Aspen-Baxter (2022), both settler educators, dedicated their post-secondary theses to intense critical reflection on their own practice and sought to 'do better' in the lives of Indigenous students in their care. Aspen-Baxter (2022) wrote how deeply uncomfortable and painful this phase can be. She always strived to be a "good teacher" who was loving and accepting of all, but learned she unwittingly participated in harmful practices, as many settler educators do. It took putting her ego aside and understanding it was her responsibility to begin this journey through listening and learning, even when shame and discomfort arose. Smith (2014), who focused on Treaty Education in Saskatchewan, highlighted the importance of listening to Indigenous leaders and Elders as "some of the most powerful learning experiences in [her] journey" (p. 83) and she has taken their teachings to heart and allows those words to guide her current practice. Both of these educators have helped me on my own path, supporting my learning through listening meaningfully, learning deeply, questioning assumptions, and accepting discomfort when engaging in this reflective work.

Walking With, and Learning From Indigenous Peoples

The second AtRM approach is a more public and physical act than the previous one. Settlers are walking with First Peoples and learning to understand while immersing themselves in Indigenous culture, celebrations, and events. Counter-stories of First Peoples are made visible because settlers have already listened and witnessed in the previous stage using a critical and reflective lens. They demonstrate their wish to become allies through their presence and when possible, are able to speak to what they have learned to other settlers without fear of misstep. From a teaching perspective, settler teachers have a foundational knowledge and understanding to draw upon when making intentional reconciliatory pedagogical choices in their classrooms.

Reciprocity and Responsibility

Krista: Democratic practices in the classroom are an example of how I attempt allyship. As a high school educator, due dates and deadlines are decisions that are made daily. In the past, I would decide when assignments were due without consultation with students. I believed I knew how long my students needed to complete specific tasks and assumed when I assigned homework, it would get done. I would feel like a pushover if the students asked for more time and I "gave in." If it was not a sufficient amount of time, the student would take their work home to ensure the deadline was met. I found this practice solidified my power in the classroom and students' personal responsibilities were not meaningfully considered. In the spirit of decentering myself in the classroom, I began to adopt a democratic approach to not only what we did in the classroom, but also their deadlines. I will always go through the project or assignment and negotiate the deadline based on how long students feel they will need to complete the assignment to the best of their ability and through conversation, we always find a common date that works for everyone. I have found this practice supports students' internalization of deadlines and are more likely to complete their work on time— without having to send it home for homework. This is where responsibility comes into play. As an educator, I am responsible for respecting the out-of-school responsibilities many Indigenous students have, be it family engagements, cultural gatherings, and the need for emotional, physical, mental, and spiritual rest. This practice can support the wholistic wellbeing of Indigenous students by supporting their voice and learning in the classroom and honouring their responsibilities outside of school. In my journey, I am always working toward reconciliation and to address Reciprocity in a meaningful way would be to add to this classroom experience by inviting Knowledge Keepers, Elders, and others in the Indigenous community to support myself and my students' learning. Inviting stories from the Indigenous community into the classroom allows me as an educator to truly understand the reality of the students in my learning space and give me a deep context to this important work.

Erin: First Peoples voices and narratives must be centered in high school learning. However, in some educational systems, there is a lack of authentic resources available for settler teachers that have distinct representations of community and knowledge(s) across First Nations, Métis, and Inuit Peoples. First Peoples do not unilaterally share the same knowledge and perspectives as learned in the previous AtRM stage, so using a critical eye when selecting resources for students is vital (Chrona, 2022; Davidson, 2020). Davidson (2020) suggests that settler teachers develop their own judgment related to Indigenous resources and has suggested several questions and considerations to be reflexive of. Some of these include:

1. Who developed the resource?
2. How are Indigenous Peoples represented in the resource?
3. Does the resource contain traditional Indigenous stories? Also, does the resource indicate that permission has been given to use the story in a public context and/ or for educational purposes? And, does the resource indicate what protocols and/or guidelines (if any) should be followed when using this story for educational purposes?
4. Does the resource contain Indigenous art? Is the artwork credited to an author?
5. Does the resource honour the diversity of Indigenous Peoples?

Davidson (2020) also suggests several additional teacher resources to aid in resource evaluation such as Strong Nations, Indigenous Storybooks, and BCTF Indigenous Education. Another partnership resource for Grade 10–12 teachers in British Columbia was curated by the First Nations Education Steering Committee (FNESC) is entitled, *English First Peoples Grade 10–12 Teacher Resource Guide* (FNESC, 2018). The guide outlines evaluation criteria for Grade 10–12 settler teachers to assist them in responsibly selecting resources to use in their reconciliatory pedagogies. The guide also offers many learning activities and resources that could align to several high school subjects including English, Civics, Social Studies, History, Law, etc. with several First Peoples contributors collaborating on this guide.

Relevance

Krista: Creating meaningful and relevant connections to the community is important to Indigenous Pedagogy, regardless of subject area. Teaching poetic structure in English Language Arts has significant potential to perpetuate colonial practices, as often the poets being studied are old white men and the work done in class is for the teacher's eyes only. When planning, I wanted this unit to have relevance to the Indigenous students in our learning space and was intentional when choosing poets and authors who are Indigenous, while providing the opportunity for an authentic audience for their writing. After studying Indigenous poetry and a lengthy discussion about the purpose and goals of learning poetry, the students decided they wanted to write a co-written poetic children's book about the environment. The students worked together, wrote, revised, and edited their children's book with meticulous attention to detail, as many eyes will see their work. The class decided this was a story for the community and wanted to have a book launch party where we invited the community for a reading and collaborative celebration. As a teacher, I also embraced reciprocity in learning as I took the role of facilitator and supporter, and the students led their own learning.

Relationships and Reciprocity

Krista: While it will take lifelong unlearning to parse through the colonial assumptions and thinking patterns engraved in my mind, striving toward honouring the 5Rs of Indigenous pedagogy and my own reconciliation walk through the AtRM are paramount to my personal and professional growth, for students, my colleagues, and my community. In order to make a public statement of my commitment to reconciliation, I chose to focus on the creation of meaningful relationships, the 5th R in the 5Rs of Indigenous pedagogy. Since intentionally creating space for reciprocal relationships, the learning processes have become more equitable as students experience greater feelings of belonging and agency. The co-constructed relationships with Indigenous students continue to be life-changing and open my eyes to a world made invisible to me by my own privilege and propelled my sense of urgency to transform my own practice through critical reflection on how I contribute to a harmful system and how my practice could change to better serve the Indigenous students in my care.

Prioritizing reciprocal relationships with students has led to changes in the way I handle interruptions, conflict, and distractions within the school day. In my earlier teaching years, I would get frustrated and even offended when students were disruptive or even worse, late for my class. The practice of co-constructing relationships, along with the other Rs, have begun to help me better understand the students I teach and my role within their lives— to provide love, support, and a safe welcoming space to learn and grow. Now, I often leave my classroom door open and welcome latecomers with phrases like, "I am so happy you are here" or "It is great to see you." This practice has fostered a strong sense of community within the school, leading to enhanced feelings of safety and belonging among all students.

Working With, and Learning From Indigenous Peoples

Building upon the previous stage of walking with, settler teachers in this AtRM approach are firmly grounded in ensuring "that the lessons of reconciliation are accessible to all [students] who are willing to listen and learn" (Poitras Pratt & Danyluk, 2019, p. 10). It is iterative and sustaining work that requires continued learning from Indigenous community members and culturally responsive resources. Students are provided with opportunities for service-learning and community-building within all subjects. Learning resources are carefully selected to honour diverse Indigenous cultures as well as other cultures from around the globe. Non-Indigenous students begin to reshape their own personal truths and understandings related to reconciliation to make transformative commitments of their own which hopefully will carry forward beyond their years in high school. Equally important,

Indigenous students now see themselves reflected in their learning which empowers them to showcase more of who they as trust has been nurtured.

Relevance

Krista: Poitras Pratt and Danyluk (2019) describe the third phase of the AtRM is *Working with and Learning from* as taking action. When I consider this phase, I think about how I am, as an educator, explicitly forwarding reconciliation and supporting students through their own journey. One way I have attempted this work was to introduce the AtRM to a Sexual and Gender Diversity (GSD) class. We took the model, dissected and discussed what each phase means when traveling on their own Truth and Reconciliation journey. Since this course discussed the GSD community, after we investigated the model as created, we applied it to GSD allyship. Through the introduction of this model and space to investigate their place in reconciliation, and later GSD allyship, students not only co-created relevant ways to engage in reconciliation practices in their own lives, but a framework to support this work in their future. This project allowed the students to gain the framework and vocabulary to support their work as young activists. Throughout the semester, this allowed us to take an intersectional look at reconciliation, allyship, and our responsibility as Canadians to support Decolonization efforts.

Reciprocal and Relationships

Erin: In recent years, some First Peoples' Elders and Knowledge Keepers have become overly taxed by school districts' increased focus on Indigenous education (Chrona, 2022). Even though settler teachers may wish to work with and learn from local First Peoples' community members, their capacity to share may not be possible, nor realistic. Also, since relationships should be reciprocal, settler teachers need to consider 'what' they will return by respectfully asking Elders for their insights. Another relational consideration for settler teachers is that when working alongside Elders and Knowledge Keepers, ask them what knowledge *they* would like to share (FPCC, n.d.). Also be mindful that knowledge may not wish to be shared for a variety of reasons including past traumas, fear of losing intellectual property rights, and even cultural appropriation or exploitation (Chrona, 2022; Tuck & Yang, 2014). These wishes must be respected as honouring First Peoples' knowledge(s) means understanding that sharing is not always possible. Settler teachers should inquire with administration and Indigenous district colleagues to understand how to connect with local Indigenous communities prior to attempting connections on their own. First Peoples knowledge systems are complex. Their rights are also protected by a United Nations declaration (United Nations. *United Nations declaration on the rights of Indigenous People*, 2008) signed by Canada in 2011 that serves as the most comprehensive international instrument on the rights of Indigenous Peoples. Settler teachers should read the declaration as part of AtRM first stage prior to initiating respectful and collaborative relationships in honouring their rights.

On Making Mistakes

Krista: As a settler teacher, I have gotten a lot of things wrong when doing this work. This is the fear of so many educators and this fear will often get in the way of pursuing reconciliation in their own lives and classrooms. What I have learned every time I have been corrected or, while well-meaning, realized I have engaged in harmful practices is reconciliation is not based on one action, but a continued and sustained lifelong practice; facing these mistakes with humility, openness to learn, and a commitment to do better. It is acceptable for me to listen, learn, and incorporate the 5Rs of Indigenous pedagogy and make mistakes or be corrected by research, students, parents, other educators, and Indigenous communities. Mistakes are expected; they are how we learn. Do not let mistakes stop you. What is not acceptable, is not even trying. This work is hard but completely and utterly necessary, for the success and dignity of Indigenous students.

Erin: For reconciliation pedagogy to be sustaining, I must continue to "call out" racism within my classroom and broader school community (Paris & Alim, 2017). Racism exists. When it exists, reconciliation pedagogy does not thrive (Muhammad, 2023). My Indigenous students deserve settler educators who can learn and grow their praxis as anti-racist leaders and who will engage in challenging conversations. We are not to be misconstrued as saviours, or that we are good intentioned (Chrona, 2022) in our actions. Rather we are relational learners and allies-to-be for First Peoples who recognize the impact of our work. I need to be humble foremost, and to regularly check my own privilege and unconscious biases to ensure that I am not perpetuating racism or whiteness in my teaching. Centering the Interwoven Living Framework into my praxis will help guide my journey so that Indigenous students, families, communities, and colleagues have a reconciliatory space to continue to thrive.

Discussion or Recommendations

The anecdotes and stories of our journeys are small demonstrations of how settler educators can engage in reconciliation within the classroom, regardless of where they are in their own journey. The Interwoven Living Framework offered in this chapter will help settler educators with all levels of experience, in any high school context, a place to start and reconciliatory access points for those who are uncertain of how to do this enduring work meaningfully. Simple actions and abiding to a checklist are not examples of this work. It is, as the framework suggests, the lifelong interweaving of reconciliatory practices that are rooted in internal reflection, personal learning and listening, and sustained action.

Although this work is never complete, it is important to begin: begin with curiosity, with a spirit of inquiry and interest; begin with intention, understanding that every decision you make in the classroom can support this work; begin with humility, knowing you will make mistakes and have to learn from them; and begin with a commitment to this work and the Indigenous students in your learning spaces. There are countless ways to manage a classroom, deliver content, and evaluate learning and some of these methods have the potential to harm, replicating colonial and conventional learning; and some have the potential to heal and change our system. Change can look like the small intentional adjustments made to prioritize relationships with Indigenous students, to adopting reciprocal instructional methods, to the upheaval of colonial practice in exchange for fully immersive Indigenous Pedagogies and worldviews. Sorting our own experiences within the Interwoven Living Framework was a transformative exercise which allowed for the deep reflection of intention, practice, and impact on Indigenous students. The Interwoven Living Framework not only provides educators a place to begin, but a path forward. We see this chapter and framework as a resource for future and current educators to support their first or 100th step in bringing reconciliatory and decolonized practices into Canada's high schools in meaningful and sustained ways.

CONCLUSION AND POPPY'S FINAL WORDS

As educators, we commit our lives to the children who live, play, and learn in our collective communities. According to Battiste (2015), "every school is a site of reproduction or a site of change" (p. 175). If we do not commit to creating change in our learning spaces, we are knowingly and intentionally harming the success and well-being of Indigenous students in our care. There is urgency in this work, and it is no longer acceptable to opt out due to fear or a lack of understanding. Indigenous students notice our efforts, or lack of efforts. From the insightful words of Poppy Pinay (personal communication), a grade 11 Indigenous student at a Saskatchewan high school, we leave you with her final contemplative thoughts about reconciliatory pedagogies and why they are crucial.

As an Indigenous student, reconciliation is crucial for me in the classroom. When a teacher attempts to indigenize the classroom setting, it feels liberating. Because we feel embraced in the class, we can be our real selves. Since we are not frightened of being criticized, we can learn more deeply. My advice to white teachers is to evaluate themselves to see whether they have any bias against Indigenous Peoples. Consider your actions and ideas regarding our People, and whether there is a reason for your thinking. Learn about our People, culture, and traumas so you can better understand your Indigenous students. Teachers do not have to be experts, even knowing that teachers actually care about Indigenous Peoples and issues and are working toward learning makes me feel as though we belong.

REFERENCES

Archibald, J. (2008). *Indigenous storywork: Educating the heart, mind, body, and spirit*. UBC Press.

Aspen-Baxter, L. (2022). *Confronting the Ugly Truth: The (Un)Making of a 'Good' White Teacher on the Canadian Prairies.* [Master of Education thesis, University of Saskatchewan]. University of Saskatchewan Harvest. https://hdl.handle.net/10388/13874

Atleo, C., & Boron, J. (2022). Land Is Life: Indigenous relationships to territory and navigating settler colonial property regimes in Canada. *Land (Basel)*, *11*(5), 1–12. doi:10.3390/land11050609

Battiste, M. (2000). Maintaining Aboriginal identity, language, and culture in modern society. In M. Battiste (Ed.), *Reclaiming Indigenous voice and vision* (pp. 192–208). UBC Press.

Battiste, M. (2015). *Decolonizing Education: Nourishing the learning spirit*. Purich Publishing Limited.

Brunette-Debassige, C., & Wakeham, P. (2021). Translating the four Rs of Indigenous education for literary studies: Learning from and with Indigenous stories. *Studies in American Indian Literatures*, *32*(3-4), 13–41. doi:10.1353/ail.2020.0016

Cajete, G. (2000). *Native science: Natural laws of interdependence*. Clear Light Publishers.

Chrona, J. (2022). *Wayi Wah!: Indigenous pedagogies: An act for reconciliation and anti-racist education*. Portage & Main Press.

Cote-Meek, S., & Moeke-Pickering, T. (2021, April 8). *Decolonizing and Indigenizing education in Canada*. [Video]. Youtube. https://www.youtube.com/watch?v=t8XIN46vHHI

Cowan, K. (2020). How residential schools led to intergenerational trauma in the Canadian Indigenous population to influence parenting styles and family structures over generations. [http://ejournals,library,ualberta.ca/index/php/cjfy]. *Canadian Journal of Family and Youth, 12*(2), 26–35. doi:10.29173/cjfy29511

Davidson, S. F. (2020). Evaluating Indigenous education resources for classroom use. *Teacher Magazine, May/June.* BC Teachers' Federation. https://issuu.com/teachernewsmag/docs/teacher_magazine_may_2020

Department of Justice Canada. (2018). *Principles: Respecting the Government of Canada's relationship with Indigenous Peoples.* Government of Canada. https://www.justice.gc.ca/eng/csj-sjc/principles.pdf

First Nations Education Steering Committee. (2018). *English First Peoples grade 10– 12 teacher resource guide.* FNESC. https://www.fnesc.ca/wp/wp-content/uploads/2018/08/PUBLICATION-LFP-EFP-10-12-FINAL-2018-08-13.pdf

First Peoples' Cultural Council. (n.d.). *Working with Elders.* FPCC. https://fpcc.ca/wp-content/uploads/2021/05/FPCC-Working-with-Elders_FINAL.pdf

Gaywsh, R., & Mordoch, E. (2018). Situating intergenerational trauma in the educational journey. *in education, 24*(2), 3-23. https://www.researchgate.net/publication/351147643_Situating_Intergenerational_Trauma_in_the_Educational_Journey

Kirkness, V. J., & Barnhardt, R. (1991). First Nations and higher education: The four R's – Respect, relevance, reciprocity, responsibility. *Journal of American Indian Education, 30*(3), 1–15.

Kirkness, V. J., & Barnhardt, R. (2001). First Nations and higher education: The four R's – Respect, relevance, reciprocity, responsibility. In R. Hayhoe & J. Pan (Eds.), *Knowledge across cultures: A contribution to dialogue among civilizations* (pp. 1–21). Comparative Education Research Centre, University of Hong Kong. https://www.uaf.edu/ankn/publications/collective-works-of-ray-b/Four-Rs-2nd-Ed.pdf

Kovach, M. (2008). *Indigenous methodologies: Characteristics, conversations, and contexts.* University of Toronto Press.

Lake, J., & Atkins, H. (2021). *Facilitating Online Learning with the 5R's: Embedding Indigenous Pedagogy into the Online Space* [Master of Education project, University of Victoria]. UVicSpace. http://hdl.handle.net/1828/12915

Mueller, J. 7 Nickel, J. (Eds.) (2017). *Globalization and Diversity: What Does It Mean for Teacher Education in Canada?* Canadian Association for Teacher Education. https://cate-acfe.ca/wp-content/uploads/2019/11/Final-Working-Conference-Book-Halifax-2017.pdf

Muhammad, G. (2023). *Unearthing joy: A guide to culturally and historically responsive curriculum and instruction.* Scholastic Books.

National Collaborating Centre for Indigenous Health. (2017). *Education as a social determinant of First Nations, Inuit, and Metis Health.* NCCIH. https://www.nccih.ca/495/Education_as_a_social_determinant_of_First_Nations,_Inuit_and_M%C3%A9tis_health.nccih?id=226

Networks of Inquiry and Indigenous Education. (2022). *Homepage: The Networks.* NOIIE. https://noiie.ca/about-us/

Otis, D. (2023, January 17). In the search for unmarked graves at Residential School sites, what do Radar 'anomalies' mean? *CTVNews.* https://www.ctvnews.ca/canada/in-the-search-for-unmarked-graves-at-residential-school-sites-what-do-radar-anomalies-mean-1.6233149

Papp, T. A. (2020). A Canadian study of coming full circle to traditional Aboriginal pedagogy: A pedagogy for the 21st Century. *Diaspora, Indigenous, and Minority Education, 14*(1), 25–42. doi:10.1080/15595692.2019.1652587

Paris, D., & Alim, H. S. (2017). Culturally sustaining pedagogies: Teaching and learning for justice in a changing world. *The Journal of Teaching and Learning, 11*(1), 35–37. doi:10.22329/jtl.v11i1.4987

Perreault, S. (2022, July 19). *Victimization of First Nations people, Métis and Inuit in Canada. (Catalogue no. 85-002-X).* Statistics Canada. https://www150.statcan.gc.ca/n1/pub/85-002-x/2022001/article/00012-eng.htm

Poitras Pratt, Y., & Danyluk, P. J.Poitras Pratt. (2019). Exploring reconciliatory pedagogy and its possibilities through educator-led praxis. *The Canadian Journal for the Scholarship of Teaching and Learning, 10*(3), 1–16. doi:10.5206/cjsotl-rcacea.2019.3.9479

Regan, P. (2010). *Unsettling the settler within: Indian residential schools, truth telling, and reconciliation in Canada.* ubc Press.

Restoule, J. P. (2017). Where Indigenous knowledge lives: Bringing Indigenous perspectives to online learning environments. In E. A. McKinley & L. T. Smith (Eds.), *Handbook of Indigenous education.* Springer.

Rice, C., Dion, S. D., Fowlie, H., & Breen, A. (2020). Identifying and working through settler ignorance. *Critical Studies in Education*, *63*(1), 15–30. doi:10.1080/17508487.2020.1830818

Rice, J. (2007). Icelandic charity donations: Reciprocity reconsidered. *Ethnology*, *46*(1), 1–7. https://www.proquest.com/docview/205148513?pq-origsite=gscholar&fromopenview=true

Riley, T., Monk, S., & VanIssum, H. (2019). Barriers and breakthroughs: Engaging in socially just ways towards issues of indigeneity, identity, and whiteness in teacher education. *Whiteness and Education*, *4*(1), 88–107. doi:10.1080/23793406.2019.1625283

Rios, J. A., Ling, G., Pugh, R., Becker, D., & Bacall, A. (2020). Identifying critical 21st-century skills for workplace success: A content analysis of job advertisements. *Educational Researcher*, *49*(2), 80–89. doi:10.3102/0013189X19890600

Serafini, F. W. (2002). Dismantling the factory model of assessment. *Reading & Writing Quarterly*, *18*(1), 67–85. doi:10.1080/105735602753386342

Simcoe, J., Allan, B., Perreault, A., Chenoweth, J., Biin, D., Hobenshield, S., Ormiston, T., Hardman, S. A., Lacerte, L., Wright, L., & Wilson, J. (2018, September 5). *Holding space and humility for other ways of knowing and being*. Pulling Together A Guide for Teachers and Instructors. https://opentextbc.ca/indigenizationinstructors/chapter/holding-space-and-humility-for-other-ways-of-knowing-and-being/

Smith, T. (2014). *An Unsettling Journey: White Settler Women Teaching Treaty in Saskatchewan* [Master of Education thesis, University of Regina]. Indigenous Studies Portal. https://ourspace.uregina.ca/bitstream/handle/10294/5830/Smith_Tamara_200231376_MED_C&I_Spring2014.pdf

Statistics Canada. (2019, July 19). *High school completion rate by sex and selected demographic characteristics, inactive*. [Data set] https://www150.statcan.gc.ca/t1/tbl1/en/tv.action?pid=3710014701&pickMembers%5B0%5D=1.1

Tessaro, D., & Restoule, J. P. (2022). Indigenous pedagogies and online learning environments: A massive open online course case study. *Alternative*, *18*(1), 182–191. doi:10.1177/11771801221089685

Truth and Reconciliation Commission of Canada. (2015). *Calls to action*. TRCC. https://www2.gov.bc.ca/assets/gov/british-columbians-our-governments/indigenous-people/aboriginal-peoples-documents/calls_to_action_english2.pdf

Tsosie, R. L., Grant, A. D., Harrington, J., Wu, K., Thomas, A., Chase, S., Barnett, D., Beaumont Hill, S., Belcourt, A., Brown, B., & Plenty Sweetgrass, R. (2022, Summer). The six Rs of Indigenous research. *Journal of American Indian Higher Education*, *33*(4). https://tribalcollegejournal.org/the-six-rs-of-indigenous-research/

Tuck, E., & Yang, K. W. (2014). R-words: Refusing research. In D. Paris & M.T. Winn (Eds). Humanizing Research: Decolonizing Qualitative Inquiry with Youth and Communities (pp. 213–237). Sage.

United Nations. (2008). *United Nations declaration on the rights of Indigenous People (UNDRIP)*. UN. https://www.un.org/esa/socdev/unpfii/documents/DRIPS_en.pdf

Wilson, S. (2020). *Research is ceremony: Indigenous research methods*. Fernwood publishing.

Wong, D. (2022, September 27). Truth and Reconciliation Commission Calls to Action for Education. *People for Education*. https://peopleforeducation.ca/calls-to-action-for-education/

Wong, J. (2023, February 11). As more high schools add Indigenous-focused compulsory courses, some warn against a siloed approach. *CBC News*. https://www.cbc.ca/news/canada/edu-indigenous-compulsory-learning-1.6738509

Chapter 10
Indigenous Pedagogies and the Implications of EdTech, Data, and AI in the Classroom

Robyn K. Rowe
 https://orcid.org/0000-0003-0591-6213
Queen's University, Canada

Amy Shawanda
 https://orcid.org/0000-0002-0343-9946
University of Toronto, Canada

ABSTRACT

The increased integration of educational technologies (EdTech) in recent history, combined with modern wireless connectivity and cloud potential, has led to a surge in data being extraction from the educators and learners who use them. Consequently, scientific innovations in artificial intelligence (AI) systems trained by large volumes of data are changing the educational landscape. Naturally, pedagogical approaches to education are evolving in line with philosophical, ideological, and theoretical understandings of technology, its uses, and its applications. This chapter explores the complex and evolving role of EdTech, its design, development, and deployment through Indigenous Pedagogies. In it, the authors weave through discussions that embrace Indigenous epistemologies, worldviews, cultures, and traditions. At the same time, they consider the transformative potential of embedding Indigenous Pedagogies into the ways we think about technology, beyond present understandings of EdTech. In doing so, the authors generate a discussion that aims to empower, educate, and lead to meaningful EdTech action.

DOI: 10.4018/978-1-6684-3425-3.ch010

INTRODUCTION

The rapid emergence of modern technologies (tech) designed to enhance learning, have transformed the teaching methods and practices used in educational spaces in Canada and around the world. Individual and institutionally imposed theoretical and philosophical positions and conventions that underscore how educators teach – namely, their pedagogy – have been influenced by and because of the integration of innovative education technologies (EdTech) (Swanson, 2016). King and Schielmann (2004) define educational pedagogies as being "embedded in culture and guided by the specific educational priorities and goals of a given society. They are reflected in models of generating and transmitting knowledge and skills, in teaching methods and learning styles" (p. 33). Not unlike the past, colonial ideologies entrenched in societal, economic, and political contexts continue to perpetuate narratives of power, oppression, extraction, and control. Unseen in the past however is the ongoing rise in seemingly limitless wireless and cloud connectivity that is enabling data extraction, analysis, and interpretations of data collected through EdTech. Concerns over how "digital educational platforms are collecting data from and around the classroom" have raised "questions about the implications of such platforms for children's human rights" (Yu & Couldy, 2022, p. 127). At the same time, Artificial Intelligence (AI) systems trained by large volumes of data are propelling datafication efforts, further increasing the use of EdTech in the classroom. EdTech innovations include "computer-based learning, computerized tools and applications which provide multimedia options, animations, virtual environments, games and simulations, mobile learning, digital portfolios, wikis, blogs and more" (Swanson, 2016, p. 25).

The uses of EdTech as teaching and learning tools, has been superseded by its role in data collection and subsequent AI development. As explained by the United Nations Human Rights Council's Report on *Artificial intelligence and privacy, and children's privacy*, understanding the potential harms and benefits of AI "requires clear, comprehensive explanation to users and data providers, as well as executives, managers and others involved in decisions about AI solutions and their operations" (General Assembly special rapporteur 46/37, p. 10). AI can (and does) perpetuate existing social bias and discrimination (Crawford, 2021; Raso et al., 2018). Combating the perpetuation of biases in educational settings specifically, necessitates clear and comprehensive understandings of EdTech and its applications (namely data and AI) by boards of education, institutions, educators, Learners, and their families. Importantly, those understandings must consider the role of ongoing colonial agendas and be embedded within decolonial Knowledges, because, for Indigenous Peoples "we can no longer pretend that it is in our best interest to get on board with the project of modernity and economic development as a pathway to self-determination" (Waziyatawin and Yellow Bird, 2012, p.5).

Big Data collection within educational settings is fuelling the EdTech and AI industries, with little regard for the real-life implications that could further harm Indigenous Peoples, who also hold a sacred and collective responsibility as stewards of the lands, waters, and all of Creation. Research and data-driven narratives are too-often explained through the lenses of disparity, deprivation, disadvantage, dysfunction, and difference (Walter, 2016). Decolonizing both our opinion of and action towards the uses of EdTech, data, and AI requires a genuine understanding of the systemically racist and colonial ideologies that are embedded within the ways that all data are defined, collected, used, stored, and reported. Furthering a unified understanding that data are not immaterial or lifeless, and that they require appropriate care and consent is necessary to ensure that the digital traces of all life do not create or (further) perpetuate harm. Throughout this chapter we encourage readers to keep in mind what Crawford (2021) describes as the "colonizing impulse" to extract:

The field of AI is explicitly attempting to capture the planet in computationally legible form. This is not a metaphor so much as the industry's direct ambition. The AI industry is making and normalizing its own proprietary maps, as centralized God's-eye view of human movement, communication, and labor...This colonizing impulse centralizes power in the AI field: it determines how the world is measured and defined while simultaneously denying that this is an inherently political activity. (p.11)

Throughout this chapter, we focus on EdTech as one component of the AI-industry's multi-layered system of power (Crawford, 2021). Where, "some AI scientists have stated their desire to capture the world and to supersede other forms of knowing" (Crawford, 2021, p.11).

Unsurprisingly, existing education, training, theory, and knowledge driving the ambitious goals of EdTech, data capture, and AI, have actively excluded *meaningful* contributions from diverse Indigenous voices in EdTech's design, development, and deployment. Perhaps Indigenous worldviews are excluded from this space because of the lesser-spoken sacrifice that all of Creation makes in the name of 'innovation' and 'progress'. That is, the great ecological and environmental costs resulting from declining Earth minerals and natural resources that are used to create and fuel modern technologies, accelerating the rates of global climate change beyond repair (Crawford, 2021). Effectively obstructing the sacred roles of Indigenous Peoples as stewards and inherent rights holders.

During COVID-19, settler governments around the world supported an increase in EdTech-generated data collection. Due to mandated stay-at-home orders which included a move to virtual education for educators and Learners, there was a rapid increase in the amount of people using both publicly and privately owned EdTech platforms. As Human Rights Watch explains, governments have been found to have "put at risk or violated children's rights directly" (Han, 2022, p.3). Data collected through EdTech includes (but is not limited to) demographic, behavioural, and geographic information (Han, 2022). EdTech acts as a Learner surveillance tool violating user privacy and human rights "for purposes unrelated to their education" (Han, 2022, p.1).

Theorizing and drawing connections between modern settler colonialism and long-standing Indigenous perspectives in data-driven spaces has been taking shape in countries around the world. Globally, Indigenous Data Sovereignty (IDSov) movements are advocating for Indigenous Peoples' collective rights over Indigenous-defined data (e.g., see GIDA-global.org) (Hudson et al., 2023). As such, activating Indigenous Peoples' self-determination through IDSov extends to the misuse of Indigenous Peoples' data generated and gathered through EdTech and used in AI. Although the work of Indigenous Peoples, organizations, scholars, and advocates around the world have made incredible progress within the fields of IDSov and Indigenous Data Governance (IDGov) (Kukutai & Taylor, 2016), we must continue to expand our thinking, generate theories, and deepen discussions that respect our diverse and collective Sacred Knowledges and keeps planetary life at the centre of our understandings, realities, and work (Waziyatawin and Yellow Bird, 2012).

Purpose of this Chapter

Despite a lack of diverse user engagement and participation in EdTech discussions, in this chapter we question what educators know, do, and believe about EdTech applications in classroom settings (Lovelace, 2010). Notably, we recognize that educators are already overburdened by the demands of teaching, service, and life, so while we may question what educators know, do, and believe in relation to EdTech, this chapter offers readers (both Indigenous and non-Indigenous) alternative ways of thinking about their uses. At the same time, we recognize the power dynamics that exist within educational settings. In other words, even educators with keen awareness of EdTech's harms and limitations may feel powerless to create the necessary change. We align the positioning of our thinking in this space with the work of Waziyatawin and Yellow Bird (2012) in *For Indigenous Minds Only: A Decolonization Handbook,* whose decolonial work affirms that "Indigenous Peoples have the power, strength, and intelligence to develop culturally specific decolonization strategies to pursue our own strategies of liberation" (p.1).

Ongoing learning and unlearning can ensure that Indigenous ways of seeing and living within the world are embedded into EdTech's design, development, and deployment. Because "decolonizing actions must begin in the mind, and that creative, consistent, decolonized thinking shapes and empowers the brain, which in turn provides a major prime for positive change" (Waziyatawin and Yellow Bird, 2012, p.2). As Windchief and San Pedro (2019) explain, "we do not think alone… for Indigenous [K]nowledges, the valuing of many truths cannot be divorced from collective knowledge" (p.25). As such, throughout this chapter, we draw on collective Indigenous philosophies, theories, and pedagogies to ensure that non-colonial ways of thinking are included in the advancements of EdTech and AI. At the same time, we critically reflect on some mainstream theories and explore the many complexities concerning the uses and intentions of EdTech and its advancements – including data and AI-technologies – in the classroom, for both Learners and educators.

This chapter is divided into five sections: 1) Introduction, 2) Braiding our Remembering, 3) (Re)Envisioning Indigenous Knowledges, 4) Articulating an EdTech Pedagogy, and 5) Conclusions. We began above by introducing the work and continue by situating ourselves below in line with Indigenous protocols. In section two, we provide a general outline of the role of historical colonialism that informs our ideological position for our expanded discussion on EdTech as a component of contemporary data/digital colonialism. We explore the role of AI-applications within EdTech, its lack of regulation and privacy protection, and its relationship to colonialism and ongoing power dynamics, while discussing the impacts of EdTech applications on human/children's rights. In section three, we dive into pedagogy in the classroom, weaving through a comparative discussion around modern educational pedagogies and Indigenous ways of knowing and doing. We apply an Indigenous critical methodology to reflect on and support the development of our thinking by weaving our understandings through Indigenous Knowledges, developing our thinking through a Nanaboozhoo/Trickster metaphor. In our efforts to further weave our discussion through a pedagogical approach we are more familiar and comfortable with, section four embodies the Anishinaabe Seven Grandfather Teachings. In this section, we further illustrate our approach to understanding EdTech's implications, while offering readers suggestions on how to apply similar thinking in their own learning journeys. The goal here is not to provide a 'how-to' guide for employing Indigenous Pedagogical approaches when using EdTech, rather, it is simply a piece of our own learning/unlearning process. Our hope is that this way of thinking will encourage readers to see the potential for thinking differently (albeit critically, ethically, and equitably) about EdTech's uses and applications. Additionally, in section four, we pose critical questions on the uses of EdTech, data, and AI, and offer readers alternative ways of approaching their pedagogical thinking in classroom applications. Finally, the conclusion draws on discussions shared throughout the chapter and leaves readers with an expanded understanding of the complexities facing Indigenous Learners now and in the future.

How We Come to Know, Together

It was motherhood that originally connected us. We united in our shared experiences as university students and Anishinaabe-kwewag (First Nations' women), carrying the added responsibility of raising children and pursuing higher education in an institution that was not designed for our realities. Amidst our busy schedules of school, kid's activities, and participating in ceremonies and our own extracurriculars, we bonded over our desire to make a better life for ourselves and our children. More than that, we shared in our desire to ensure that our children's educational paths be grounded in Anishinaabe culture, traditions, and language.

We each spent more than a decade in post-secondary and share in the joy of finally achieving the thing we set out to do, completing our Masters in Indigenous Relations at the same time in 2017 and pursuing PhDs at separate institutions, both completing them in 2022. Long before the opportunity to share in this writing was put before us, we kept in touch through text and virtual video calls, giving us the chance to connect, even though we now live hours apart. In our own ways, we have taken advantage of the technologies available to us to sustain our friendship/relationship, and at the same time, began critically and reflexively discussing our individual hardships and experiences as parents facing the many technological advances in the classrooms of today. In our roles as mothers, we shared in the anxious anticipation of what our children are facing in an ever-changing technological and artificial world. We come to this heart-work guided by our combined, ancestral, and ever-expanding Knowledges on Indigenous methodologies, pedagogies, and IDSov. In writing this chapter, we were driven by our shared efforts to advance decolonial, anti-colonial, and anti-racist pedagogical discussions on EdTech and its applications. Through Indigenous and critical approaches that draw on the many cultural, systemic, historical, socio-political, economic, and ecological realities of Indigenous Peoples, we assert Indigenous Peoples' right to self-determination in spaces where Indigenous Peoples' education data are being captured. In keeping with our intentions as mothers and academics, we explore the centralizing and disruptive power of technology, data, and AI in the classroom for present and future generations.

BRAIDING OUR REMEMBERING

Theory, Colonialism, and Educational Belonging

In Paulo Freire's (2018) book entitled *Pedagogy of the Oppressed,* he proposed that the process of humanization, in other words, the process of civilization or "domesticating" (p.51), requires power, control, and dominance by oppressors against the oppressed.

Likewise, Smith (2021) speaks of the homogenization of Indigenous Peoples' distinct ways of being, doing, and living through acts of colonialism. Freire's (2018) pedagogy points to "oppression and its causes [as] objects of reflection by the oppressed, and from that reflection... [comes] their necessary engagement in the struggle for their liberation" (p.48). Praxis, Freire (2018) posits, requires both "reflection and action upon the world in order to transform it" (p.51). In Jacqueline Quinless' (2022) book entitled *Decolonizing Data: Unsettling Conversations about Social Research Methods,* speaking on the importance of teaching students (who later apply those teachings as educators), she notes the need to reflect on past colonial harms, despite feelings of discomfort, and embeds "respect and relational accountability as pathways that open space for Indigenization" (Quinless, 2022, p.xiii). For Indigenous Peoples, the critical role of cultural teachings and remembering the impacts of historic and ongoing colonization is one way of pushing back on long-standing oppressive and colonial practices. This process is central to ensuring that systems of education meaningfully enact decolonization in alignment with Indigenous-led priorities, which centre Earth's ongoing protection.

Though a fulsome retelling of colonialism is beyond the scope of this chapter, Rowe et al. (2021) offer a comprehensive summary:

For many thousands of years, prior to settler arrival, Indigenous Peoples were rich in culture, traditions and languages and lived on the lands that are now called Canada (Truth and Reconciliation Commission of Canada [TRC], 2015). With European arrival and settler expansion, policies were created that stripped First Nations, Inuit and Métis of this diversity while treaties were designed to cede and surrender Indigenous land to the Crown (TRC, 2015). In what has been described as cultural genocide, settler policies were aimed at assimilation and Indigenous elimination (TRC, 2015). These policies were designed to disempower Indigenous governments, undermine inherent Indigenous rights and lead to the surrendering of Indigenous traditional territory. (p.82)

In elaborating on five-centuries of Indigenous Peoples' awareness of the devastation occurring across Turtle Island, Waziyatawin and Yellow Bird (2012) explain that "for that length of time, our ancestors have continued to sound the alarm to the ongoing, un-restrained feeding frenzy of non-renewable resources by the corporate-led, capitalist engines of colonial society" (p.4). All the while, colonization has actively sought Indigenous Peoples' assimilation and annihilation (Battiste & Youngblood, 2000). Speaking to the active process of Eurocentric narratives of erasure, Montavlo (2021) explains colonial processes work to:

Rearticulate Indigenous peoples and ways of knowing as backwards, unmodern and otherwise primitive. These colonial tropes serve to erase Indigenous technologies and peoples and extend racialized binaries of civilization vis-á-vis savagery. In this colonial imaginary, Indigenous [P]eople themselves are seen as obstacles to modernity's forward march, when modernity itself has been predicated on the exploitation and oppression of Indigenous peoples, lands, rights, knowledge, lifeways, and resources. (para. 5)

The exploitation, salvation, and homogenization of Indigenous Peoples, communities, and Nations has shaped the educational landscapes and centralized power in Canada and countries around the world in alignment with colonial vision and intent (Battiste & Youngblood, 2000; Smith, 2021). Colonialism is deeply woven throughout every component of mainstream education systems and throughout all technology. Addressing one without the other would be ineffective in achieving the desired decolonial result. That is, if we are to assume that the desired decolonial result should still include western technologies as a component in Learning environments. Markedly, colonization and its processes' inadequate inclusion of Indigenous Pedagogical approaches in the classroom, and colonial violence in educational settings, have been noted as contributors to the ongoing and substandard state of Indigenous educational attainment in Canada (TRC, 2015; see also Cote-Meek, 2014; Dussault & Erasmus, 1996; O'Connor, 2013).

Quinless (2022) writes, "state-centric colonial structures exert a form of structural violence on Indigenous peoples because they exercise colonial power over them by legitimizing western ways of thinking" (p. xiii). A person who is culturally-illegitimized in the classroom may feel a lack of belonging and is be more unlikely to succeed in school settings to the same degree as someone who feels that their place in educational settings is respected in its embodiment of their beliefs and values. Linda King and Sabine Schielmann (2004) share:

Traditional [I]ndigenous education and its structures should be respected and supported. Our knowledge has not been written down by us – on the contrary: we dance it, we draw it, we narrate it, we sing it, we practise it. There is a need for a deeper understanding of what knowledge and learning are and the many paths that lead to them. (p.7)

Indigenous wellbeing is intrinsically connected to traditional and Ancestral Knowledges. Therefore, meaningful inclusion of Indigenous Knowledges is an essential component of supporting Indigenous empowerment and wellbeing. However, Indigenous empowerment must align with Indigenous Peoples' rights to self-determination and self-governance and can include mechanisms advocated for

Indigenous Pedagogies and the Implications of EdTech, Data, and AI

through IDSov and IDGov initiatives around the world. In theorizing Indigenous-defined EdTech and AI pedagogies, we ask ourselves (and encourage you to do the same), in what ways does EdTech empower or limit Indigenous ways of knowing and doing in classroom settings? And, if Indigenous Peoples' songs, languages, and dances become readily accessible in EdTech, what are the long-term implications? In other words, in what ways does embedding Indigenous Knowledges into EdTech change the ways that Indigenous Peoples currently perceive the transmission of Sacred Knowledge?

Technology in the Classroom

The ever-evolving rate at which novel technologies are being used in the classroom has led to a significant body of research from tech-industry experts and educators, debating the benefits and potential harms of their inclusion in educational settings (Purnava, 2022; Reid, 2003; Watkins, 2020). Relating EdTech's implications in AI to ongoing colonialism, Dr. Hēmi Whaanga (2020), a linguist and te reo Māori specialist, warns that there is "potential for AI and related technologies to be used against Indigenous [P]eoples as an extension of colonial practices of exploitation, extraction and control, particularly those that displace a peoples' understanding of themselves with a worldview that favors the colonizer" (p.34). Inevitably, scholars have sought to understand the influence of tech-centric teaching and learning for both educators and Learners (Goos et al., 2000; Purnava, 2022; Reid, 2003; Watkins, 2020).

Although we bear ongoing witness to the rapid advancements in technology in recent years, classroom inclusion of EdTech is not a new concept. Its import into educational settings is evidenced throughout history, including the use of overhead projectors in the classroom beginning around the 1930s and scientific calculators in the 1940s, to personal computer integration in the 1980s (Purdue Online, n.d.). In recent years, most mainstream classrooms have been equipped with interactive white boards, called smartboards, all but replacing the long-established use of chalkboards. A common expression from our own childhoods that justified why we must learn how to complete mathematical equations on paper argued that it would be impractical to carry a calculator around in your pocket. Today, nullifying this expression, it is more common than not to own a smartphone, with a calculator at our fingertips. Touted as learning support tools, mobile technologies such as smartphones, tablets, and other devices are being increasingly integrated into both in-person and virtual learning and teaching environments (Nikolopoulou et al., 2022). Notably, efforts to meet the diverse needs and abilities of all Learners are outlined in the United Nations Convention on the Rights of Persons with Disabilities (General Assembly resolution 61/106) leading to an increase in the use and efficiency of several assistive technologies including e-readers, audiobooks, text-to-speech software, and more.

What *is* new is the ability to connect EdTech tools wirelessly and extrapolate data from their usage which are then used to advance AI. Cordes (2020) explains:

AI is largely framed in consumer industries as tools or products to make life's wide range of tasks easier, quicker, and often what is perceived as better. Since AI is trained with data to do things such as reason, predict, and represent, data become the archives of profound significance and vulnerability. (p. 60)

Not without its limitations, data extrapolated for AI advancement has the potential to improve Indigenous communities' well-being, if, according to Cordes (2020), it receives an appropriate "data diet":

A healthy AI data diet often includes the most current data needed to stay relevant in decision making. When a proper data diet is digested and analyzed, it is done with care so as to not solely serve the status quo. For Indigenous communities, this means that it will not disproportionately serve settler states but instead lead to Indigenous communities' well-being and restitution where it is appropriate. And while data seems sterile, placeless, quantifiable, and scientific, it is entwined with place-based knowledge, whether it is cultivated on land or in territories of cyberspace. (p. 67)

Despite efforts to make EdTech more accessible, it is still something that is not afforded to all people equally. For instance, many Indigenous communities in northern and remote areas of Canada, continue to face limitations in their wireless connectivity and/or affordability of such services (Collier, 2018). Further, educators and Learners of every age may be limited by their technological know-how and may struggle to navigate EdTech platforms. From experience, inviting a guest to speak during a virtual lesson can prove to be a challenging situation. Not everyone is familiar with tech or EdTech and in Indigenous classrooms where Elders and Traditional Peoples are always welcome, a lack of accessibility can be discouraging. At the same time, there is a level of discomfort associated with sharing Traditional Knowledges in a virtual environment, making the lesson not as fulsome as it would have been if it were in-person.

Rise in EdTech During COVID-19

The benefits and limitations of EdTech was made more apparent during the shift from in-person learning to exclusive online education in countries around the world resulting from the March 2020 declaration of a global COVID-19 pandemic (Watkins, 2020). As Raso et al. (2018) explained years before the COVID-19 pandemic:

Privacy is the single right that is most impacted by current implementations of AI. Other rights that are also significantly impacted by current AI implementations include the rights to equality, free expression, association, assembly, and work. Regrettably, the impact of AI on these rights has been more negative than positive to date. (p.4)

Covid-19 protocols dramatically accelerated an already booming digital economy (Han, 2022). Human Rights Watch released a report on a technical analysis of products implemented for use by "children whose families were able to afford access to the internet and connected devices, or who made hard sacrifices in order to do so" (Han, 2022, p.2). As mothers, we shared in our desire to ensure our children continued to learn and amidst a global crisis, we provided consent on behalf of our children, without an awareness as to what we were agreeing to. Han (2022) found that children "were exposed to the privacy practices of the EdTech products they were told or required to use during Covid-19 school closures" (p. 2).

The rise in users accessing Learning Management Systems/LMS software such as BrightSpace, Moodle, and Google Classroom, which provide educators and Learners with streamlined access and sharing of assignments, resources, lessons, and more (Dreamson et al., 2018), further amplified the privacy risks to those using said services during the pandemic. Human Rights Watch also reported that:

Google Classroom, Google's teacher-student communication platform, reported that the pandemic had almost quadrupled its users to more than 150 million, up from 40 million in 2019; similarly, G Suite for Education, Google's classroom software, reported doubling its users to more than 170 million students and educators...The explosive demand also generated record revenues and profits. As the global economy plummeted, venture capital financing for EdTech startups surged to a record setting US$16.1 billion in 2020, more than doubling the $7 billion raised in 2019. (as cited in Han, 2022, p. 17)

At the same time, "technology companies that [provide] free services to schools also benefited, gaining significant market share as millions of students became familiar with their product" (Han, 2022, p.18). For instance, the Zoom Video Communications platform:

provided free services to more than 125,000 schools in 25 countries, as well as limited free services for the general public, [and] reported its sales skyrocketing

326 percent to $2.7 billion and its profits propelled from $21.7 million in 2019 to $671.5 million in 2020. (Han, 2022, p. 18)

While corporations saw record-high revenues and profits resulting from educator and Learner data acquisition (amidst the global crisis), Indigenous Peoples continued to experience the "adverse effects of contemporary colonial practices" and "grapple with systemic health and social inequities that have been magnified because of the Pandemic" (Rowe et al., 2020, p.90). EdTech's transformation from a tool intended to streamline and automate the educator and Learner experience has eagerly taken the shape of mass surveillance and data capture. Human Rights Watch noted that:

Most government- built EdTech platforms did not allow their users to decline to be tracked; most of this surveillance happened secretly, without the child's knowledge or consent. In such cases, it was impossible for children to opt out of such surveillance and data exploitation without opting out of school and giving up on formal learning altogether during the pandemic. (as cited in Han, 2022, p. 98)

While EdTech has a demonstrable record of improving Learner outcomes (Watkins, 2020), their uses fail in meeting the diverse needs of Indigenous diasporic Peoples and communities (Adam et al., 2022).

(RE)ENVISIONING INDIGENOUS KNOWLEDGES

Theory, Pedagogy, and EdTech

Mainstream orientations driving the use of EdTech, data, and AI in the classroom include educational theories of behaviour, cognitivism, constructivism, humanism, and emerging because of the digital age, connectivism. In other words, theories that influence the pedagogical approaches of mainstream educators on how and when to use AI-advancing EdTech are concerned with how effectively Learners can: demonstrate an observable change in learning outputs (behaviour); the ability to memorise and retrieve information (cognitivism); the ability to develop new understandings based on what is learned (constructivism); the capacity to progress towards self-actualization (humanism); or the ability and knowledge to know how to find information (connectivism) (Lockey et al., 2021). Unlike mainstream orientations approaches to pedagogy rooted in Indigenous Ways of Knowing and doing have the potential to deepen shared and decolonial understandings of EdTech uses and its applications in the classroom.

Mashford-Pringle and Shawanda (2023) make clear that "Indigenous [P]eoples think and interpret the world and its realities in different ways from non-Indigenous Peoples because of their experiences, histories, cultures, and values" (p. 2). Indigenous Knowledges around the world are as diverse as the Knowledge Holders who carry these gifts (also Sometimes called Knowledge Keepers). Indigenous Peoples pass on Knowledges in a variety of ways including story, song, and dance (to name a few). In other instances, prophecies, visions, dreams, and more can become a source for Indigenous Knowledges that were once lost to time and colonialism. The ways that Indigenous Knowledges are deployed in educational settings will depend greatly on the Indigenous Persons (Knowledge Holders, Elders, and/or Traditional People) and communities who are involved in the work. With this in mind, we can expand on more common educational pedagogies by envisioning a future where Indigenous Knowledges are woven more profoundly throughout them. In this way, we can embrace Indigenous Pedagogical approaches into the ways we create, think about, and use EdTech and its applications.

Weaving relevant Indigenous Pedagogies through the ways educators teach and think about teaching, has the potential to promote long-standing Indigenous practices as usable technologies that could enrich the classroom learning experience beyond present understandings of EdTech. For example, highlighting the use of the Medicine Wheel as an Indigenous epistemology that can be woven through Indigenous worldviews, cultures, and traditions, Mashford-Pringle and Shawanda (2023) explain:

For the survival of the Nations, Indigenous people have studied the movements of celestial bodies, the migration of animals and fish, the patterns of the weather, the cycle of the seasons, the circle of life, etc. Therefore, Indigenous Peoples have studied their surroundings for centuries, passing down information such as what to hunt and gather, as well as how to store and use food for later use. The moon, sun, and stars were used to analyze information about climate, agriculture, navigation, and even quantum physics. Cultural traditions, languages, rituals, and symbols inform the thesis statement, research questions, purpose, methodology, methods, analysis, discussion, and future directions. For example, Indigenous Peoples developed technologies like canoes, snowshoes, and fishing weirs through the use of hypotheses, experimentation, and the discarding of failed hypotheses and methods in favour of newer, more relevant ones. (p. 2)

More than ever, critical praxis rooted in Indigenous theories are necessary to counteract the technological takeover that has become a hyperfocus for educators and Learners in and outside of educational settings.

Indigenous theories are rooted in Indigenous epistemologies, worldviews, cultures, traditions, and the interwovenness of relationships connecting Indigenous Peoples to all things in Creation. As Shawn Wilson (2005) explains in his book entitled *Research is Ceremony: Indigenous research methods*, "Indigenous epistemology is all about ideas developing through the formation of relations. An idea cannot be taken out of this relational context and still maintain its shape" (p. 8). The same thinking can be applied to the ways that data are captured and mined from EdTech and ultimately detached from the contexts with which they were created, propelling AI. Wemigwans (2018) suggests using a "Digital Bundle" where we use Indigenous Knowledges within the realm of digital technology to protect, promote, and resurge our presence, histories, and pedagogies online. Wemigwans (2018) shares that:

In continuing to create digital bundles and to come together to decide on the future of an Indigenous presence on the Internet, Indigenous communities will control information and thus shape the minds of their people in ways that support healing and regeneration. (p. 227).

Thinking through a Digital Bundle therefore requires respect and recognition of traditional Indigenous protocols and practices, and a collective exploration on the benefits and harms of sharing information in a digital world, now and in the future.

An 'EdTech Trickster' Metaphor

Indigenous Nations colonized by settlers have become dependent on the same colonial structures that were built on greed, cruelty, overproduction, and over-consumption. EdTech's simplicity and convenience distracts from all the aspects of it that are inconvenient and uncomfortable. As Lombrozo (2017) explains, "these technological tools aren't just teachers in the business of sharing information and rational persuasion; they're tricksters in the business of manipulating us — albeit at our bidding" (para. 9). In seeking a metaphor to illustrate the duality of EdTech's potential benefits and harms, Nanaboozhoo, an Anishinaabe spirit characterizable as both a teacher and a trickster, came to mind. As Penak (2018) shares, "Trickster can be as much a "doing" as a "being", and can be understood as a process we interact with, as much as a person" (p. 262).

Recognizing that stories of Nanaboozhoo are commonly shared orally (and wanting to respect the teachings shared by Wemigwans) we sought a simplified retelling of the tale available sources online. Though Trickster stories vary across Indigenous groups, the Canadian Encyclopedia explains "[Nanaboozhoo] plays a dual role in Indigenous oral traditions. On the one hand, he protects and even creates life. On the other, he is associated with mischief and breaking the rules.

His adventures and misadventures are meant to teach right from wrong and how to live a good life" (Gadacz, 2020, para. 4). On the one hand, the 'EdTech Trickster' is accessible, user-friendly, and convenient. The EdTech Trickster is fun and keeps its users engaged and learning, while collecting, combining, and de-identifying pieces of its users' information, all while getting to know them better. The EdTech Trickster then takes those pieces of user data and through AI-automated processes, it can generate personalized learning and tutoring opportunities, simplify grading, individualize marketing strategies, keep users interested in line with its user's real-life aspirations, and more.

On the other hand, The EdTech Trickster lacks effective policies, regulation, and oversight. In fact, "computers can correctly re-identify virtually any person from an anonymized dataset, using just a few random pieces of anonymous information" (Han, 2022, p.23), making the risk of re-identification a typical component of the EdTech Trickster. The EdTech Trickster is disconnected from community and culture. As Penak (2018) enforces, "Trickster gets into trouble when *disconnected* from traditional teachings, family, community, nation, culture, and land" (p. 262). The EdTech Trickster overlooks the complex relationship between Indigenous Peoples, the land, cultures, and technology. The EdTech Trickster inadequately engages or builds relationships with its users and fails to uphold genuine Indigenous Knowledges and Pedagogies. The EdTech Trickster roots itself in capitalism and sells its user's data for a price. The EdTech Trickster is biased in its views, tricking users into believing only the realities that it wants users to believe, while ignoring ongoing systemic and colonial truths. In its gathering and automating of user data, the EdTech Trickster increases a user's risks to privacy violations and of becoming targets of data and AI generated marketing, misinformation, algorithmic profiling, and more. The harms of which inequitably impact structurally marginalized groups more than others.

The EdTech Trickster keeps important facts away from its users and instead encourages its users to avoid thinking too hard about any potential repercussions. At the same time, the EdTech Trickster knows that the available tools and software create a space where cheating is not only possible but simplified. At the same time, the EdTech Trickster creates a space where conceptions of our current realities are altered and propagated through automation. Adding a new layer of social and political complexity to our current worldviews, the EdTech Trickster centralizes power into technological spaces. At the same time, the creation of the EdTech Trickster is incompatible with Indigenous values that embody the sustainability of Earth and all of Creation.

ARTICULATING AN EDTECH PEDAGOGY

The Seven Grandfather Teachings

The Seven Grandfather Teachings are guiding principles the Anishinaabek use on their journey to Mino-Bimaadiziwin [towards living a good life]. Benton-Banai (2010) explains, "Ojibway tradition tells us that there were Seven Grandfathers who were given the responsibility by the Creator to watch over the Earth's people" (p. 60). In this story, a young boy is tasked to help the Anishinaabek. With the help from Ngig, he received Seven Gifts from the Grandfathers. The young boy and Ngig rested seven times on their journey back to the Anishinaabek. At each stop, a Grandfather shared a teaching, to take back to the People and these teachings are:

(1) To cherish knowledge is to know **WISDOM**.
(2) To know **LOVE** is to know peace.
(3) To honour all of the Creation is to have **RESPECT**.
(4) **BRAVERY** is to face the foe with integrity.
(5) **HONESTY** in facing a situation is to be brave.
(6) **HUMILITY** is to know yourself as a sacred part of the Creation.
(7) **TRUTH** is to know all of these things (Benton-Banai, 2010, p. 64).

The Seven Teachings gifted to the young boy and Ngig by the Seven Grandfathers are Wisdom, Love, Respect, Bravery, Honesty, Humility, and Truth. The Grandfathers shared a caution with the young boy about the gifts and explained "for each gift, there was an opposite, as evil is the opposite of good. He would have to be careful to instruct his people in the right way to use each gift" (Benton-Banai, 2010, p. 64). In the natural laws, we understand that everything has a duality in Creation. As demonstrated through the metaphor of the EdTech Trickster, in this section, we embrace and critically reflect on the duality, underscoring the advantages and disadvantages of EdTech and its applications through the Seven Grandfathers. As with all things, the wellbeing of the Earth is central to each of the Seven Grandfather Teachings. Below, we offer an alternative way of embracing the Seven Grandfathers, by weaving our thoughts through our understandings of the Teachings. Each Teaching discussion generates critical and decolonial questions to consider when navigating classroom usage of EdTech, data, and AI. We are hopeful that these questions will generate thoughtful discussions to support alternative pedagogical thinking on EdTech and its applications.

Wisdom

To cherish knowledge is to know Wisdom. Indigenous Peoples around the world have always had their technologies. To reiterate the work of Mashford-Pringle and Shawanda (2023) shared above, examples of Indigenous technologies include canoes, snowshoes, and fishing weirs. Traditional Indigenous Knowledges have maintained the Earth since time immemorial. Today, advances in both Indigenous and Western sciences continue to benefit from Indigenous Wisdom in several ways. For example, long-standing Indigenous Knowledges provide "insight into environmental change, wildlife population monitoring, sustainable harvesting practices, behavioural ecology, ecological relationships and so much more" (Popp, 2018, para.12). Indigenous Peoples' instinctive creativity and imagination driving Indigenous innovation have been adapted through time and are a big part of Indigenous resurgence and reclamation today. Smith (2021) highlights the significant progress Indigenous Peoples have made in reclaiming Traditional Knowledges, which requires a process of "remembering" (p. 167), "envisioning" (p. 174), and "protecting" (p.180). The process of remembering requires that we reflect on our physical, mental, emotional, and spiritual trauma (Wesley-Esquimaux & Smolewski, 2004). As Smith (2021) explains, "[t]his form of remembering is painful because it involves remembering not just what colonization was about but what being de-humanized meant for our cultural practices" (p.167). Historically, there have been technological advances that were used against Indigenous Peoples. As such, it is critical that Indigenous Peoples engage in the innovation and deployment of technology, so that Indigenous Peoples and communities derive benefit from them (Lewis, 2020).

Approaching Wisdom Teachings

As part of "remembering" it is critical for educators to learn about past and present colonial harms. Through this ongoing learning and unlearning, educators and Indigenous Peoples can work together to re-imagine a future that connects everyone globally. When educators move into this mindset, they are assisting Indigenous Peoples in setting meaningful EdTech agendas, on Indigenous Peoples' own terms. There is wisdom in knowing that Indigenous Peoples have the capacity and knowledge to develop and activate EdTech protocols and permissions in line with Indigenous worldviews. Educators must "envision" a future in which EdTech and its uses do not further subjugate Indigenous cultures, Knowledges, or Nations. At the same time, Wisdom encourages that we recognize the complexity of power and control from a variety of perspectives. Arista (2020) explains,

Technological literacy, and the capacity to create and transpose our literatures, stories, songs and chants into digital mediums, may unfortunately leave the power of creation in the hands of those developers who have been trained to code, but not trained to know, circumventing communal and ancestral rules for who has the authority to pass on and keep knowledge in numerous communities. (p. 104)

By applying Indigenous Pedagogies to understand EdTech and its applications, educators can actively counter colonialism by "protecting" Indigenous ways of knowing and doing. As Smith (2021) explains, decolonizing educational spaces includes "protecting peoples, communities, languages, customs and beliefs, art and ideas, natural resources and things Indigenous [P]eoples produce... it can be as real as land as abstract as a belief about the spiritual essence of the land" (p. 180).

Love

To know love is to know peace. The teaching of Love focuses on self, family, community, Creation, and Ancestors. This teaching is about connectedness that "positions individuals in sets of relationships with other people and the environment" (Smith, 2021, p. 170). Indigenous kinship Protocols (Lewis, 2020) are what sets the tone of relationships with one another that are built upon trust, connection, and Love for one another. From an educational perspective, there must be a Love for teaching. The educator is an integral part of ensuring that relationships are built, through friendship and learning in the classroom. The Ontario College of Teachers (2016) states "at the heart of a strong and effective teaching profession is a commitment to students and their learning" (p. 15). The reciprocity protocol is both Respectful and Loving. Lewis (2020) adds,

Indigenous kinship protocols can point us towards potential approaches to developing rich, robust and expansive approach to our relationships with AI systems and serve as guidelines for AI system developers. Such protocols would reinforce the notion that, while the developers might assume they are building a product or tool, they are actually building a relationship to which they should attend. (p. 8)

As technology becomes more prevalent in our lives, we should foster those children who show interest in Science, Technology, Engineering, and Mathematics (STEM) fields so they are ready to enter the world of AI and be employable in the future (Watkins, 2020). Waktins (2020) also adds "in the wake of the Fourth Industrial Revolution—where the lines between digital, physical and biological spaces are blurred—the "skills economy" is at the forefront of the conversation" (p. 2). Considering current EdTech advances, Learners (and by extension, their data) have already become part of the digital ecosystem. For instance, mandated Learner integration into EdTech, virtual reality, and EdTech gaming is happening in countries around the world, where EdTech users often have the ability to connect and communicate to one another (Han, 2022; Watkins, 2020).

One might posit that AI is here to stay, however, Earth's non-renewable resources may have other ideas. Critically, reflecting on the concept of Love within EdTech and its applications may require that we weigh how much we Love the Earth's gifts of fresh air, clean water, and healthy foods, over our Love of innovation and progress for the sake of progress. Many educators have adapted well to using EdTech, and may even argue they Love it, however, for the Love of their students and their roles teaching, we pose the following:

- What is my relationship to EdTech?
- Am I comfortable with using devices that collect personal student data and information without consent or privacy protections?
- Do I have a clear understanding of how EdTech will use data to advance AI?
- Am I comfortable with the possibility of technology perpetuating colonial harms?
- What is my relationship to AI when disseminating knowledge in the classroom?
- How can I embrace Indigenous Pedagogies in my thinking about EdTech and its applications?
- How can I ensure that I am leading a learning environment that is safe from harms associated with the digital world?

Smith (2021) asserts that "the ability to create and be creative… [is] about the spirit of creating that Indigenous communities have exercised for thousands of years" (p. 180). For the Love of our future generations, Indigenous Peoples and communities must be more actively engaged in EdTech conversations to ensure that pedagogies developed from those conversations align with Indigenous rights to self-determination as asserted by the UNDRIP, IDSov, and governance.

Approaching Love Teachings

Instinctively, embedding Indigenous ways of knowing into EdTech may feel like the necessary pathway. For instance, for the Love of our people and in line with Indigenous-led cultural preservation and rejuvenation, engaging in AI development that "[has] our world view[s] embedded in them" (Kesserwan, 2018, para. 13), may feel like the logical next step. Kesserwan (2018) notes that "[i]ntegrating Indigenous perspectives would allow us to build a different kind of AI" (para. 13), however, if

Indigenous Peoples are not part of AI development from its inception, is it enough? We question what the cost is/could be of adapting once more to fit within the box that colonial design has once again put before us.

Although the potential for using EdTech and AI as tools to preserve and share Indigenous languages and cultures is possible, it is not without its limitations. For instance, Child explains that "most voice-to-text technologies are developed for English. While English is noun-based, many Indigenous languages like Kwak'wala are verb-centred, forcing researchers to develop their own recognition systems from scratch" (as cited in Marlow, 2022, para. 12). Kesserwan (2018) questions whether AI can fully grasp Indigenous languages and integrate the complexity of our languages "the Inuit...have over 50 words for the concept of snow, but what perspective can their traditional language possibly offer about modern technology?" (para. 2). There are many Indigenous Elders and Language Carriers that are walking through the Western Doorway taking Traditional Knowledges and languages with them when they pass on. Indigenous communities are in a critical state to capture the language that is left. However, the counter argument is that Indigenous Peoples should be out on the land to learn their languages with Language Carriers. We must question how we can ensure Indigenous language retention in a world facing global catastrophe. If we become dependent on technologies such as EdTech to learn and teach our Knowledges to future generations, how do we recapture Traditional Knowledges if, for instance, the technology becomes corrupted or virus-filled, or, if the Earth's resources that create and power these devices runs out. At the same time, in our efforts to reclaim Indigenous ways of knowing and doing today, Arista (2020) explains "if we want to think like our ancestors, if we want to think *with* our ancestors through the words they left us orally and textually, if we want to re-ignite relations again, how might this be achieved" (p. 104) in a world where Indigenous Peoples further rely on non-Indigenous technologies? As Indigenous Peoples, our Love for the Earth and one another must supersede our Love for innovation and technology. Indigenous cultural and language preservation should not rely on technologies such as EdTech and AI and we should instead find ways to develop technologies that align with Indigenous worldviews to ensure the sustainability of all of Creation.

Respect

To honor all of the Creation is to have respect. Respect requires a deep understanding that we are all connected. Not just humanity, but Creation as a whole. Indigenous Peoples have been prophesizing global devastation for generations and as we work to counter the ecological crisis and the increasing loss in biodiversity in a world where wealth is not distributed equally and social harms such as racism, sexism, genocide, and ethnocide persist (Nelson, 2008; TRC, 2015), we must return to this Teaching and actively honour our relationship with the Earth. As Chief Oren Lyons explains:

What happens to you and what happens to the Earth happens to us as well, so we have... common interests. We have to somehow try to convince people who are in power to change the direction that they've been taking. We need to take a more responsible direction and begin dealing with the realities of the future to ensure that there is a future for the children, for the Nation... It is our advantage as well as yours to be doing that. (as cited in Nelson, 2008, p.22)

Strengthening and rekindling relations with one another and the Earth, acknowledging the realities (present and future) that have resulted from colonialism and western technological innovations is necessary if we are to counter the disrespect we have been demonstrating up until now.

Approaching Respect Teachings

Respect for others in real-life and online is important, but, again, we must centre that Respect around the Earth and all Creation. As societies advance EdTech, data extraction efforts, and AI, our connections to Mother Earth should not be compromised. To be Respectful begins with yourself. Do you honour yourself, your relationships, and Mother Earth? Beginning with our Respect for nature, Kite (2020) explains, "[b]uilding (in a Good Way) a physical computing device to house an AI would first require study and consultation with a committee of Knowledge Keepers with expertise in computation, ethics, and mining" (p. 77). With this in mind, we encourage reflection that questions how technologies such as EdTech are developed. We must all put in Respectful efforts to think through questions that link EdTech, data, and AI to the bigger picture of Creation. Consider the following when technologies such as EdTech and its applications are created:

- What materials are needed?
- Where are the materials located?
- How are they extracted or removed from their locations?
- What are the social, ecological, and economic impacts of this extraction?
- How are nearby communities, towns, and Peoples impacted?
- How will the technologies be constructed and where?
- What natural resources are required and used to power these innovative technologies?

Applying an Indigenous pedagogical lens to the creation of EdTech would therefore weave meaningful understandings through Respect and connection to the Earth. Western innovations have failed to hold the environment to the high standard that Indigenous Peoples have for a millennium. For more than five-hundred years settler dominance and power has been exercised through acts of colonization, including land, territory, and resource theft and extraction, environmental degradation, the spread of disease, forced assimilation, and oppression (Smith, 2021; TRC, 2015). In speaking to an Indigenous Elder, they shared their reluctance to get on the Internet because they were aware of the number of components that use different manmade materials such as rubbers, plastics, and glass. Another Elder shared, "we cannot control what other people do, we can only control what we do, so we must continue to walk this world with our ancestral and traditional Knowledges intact". Though this is an inexact quote and teaching gained through personal communication, we interpret the meaning to be that although we cannot change how the whole world functions, if all of humanity returned to traditional Indigenous ways, controlling their own actions, then a unified collective Respect for the Earth would naturally ensue.

We must also Respect each other. When students arrive to the classroom there should be an exchange of Respect between educators and students. Educators have a lot to learn from their students and students have a lot to learn from their educators. Watkins (2020) explains "technology is a tool that needs to be supported by teacher training and informed by pedagogy to yield its benefits" (p. 3). When the answers for the questions posed above have been unravelled, we can begin to ask new questions that would enable a deeper more radical Respect for the Earth. Consider what you can do to Respect the land and counterbalance the environmental damages resulting from technological innovation. For instance, Respect for the land requires that we are out and on it. We cannot genuinely Respect nature in all its beauty and life if we are detached from it.

At the same time, advances in technologies have enabled Learners the ability to browse the virtual world for answers to any question. Whether through website where past Learners have uploaded their course work to share with future Learners, or through AIs such as ChatGPT that operates with 'human-like' performance to do the thinking on a Learner's behalf. The ability to find answers to questions that would typically require memorization, the application of critical thinking, and more, makes the possibility of cheating (or letting the EdTech Trickster in), easier. The future of education is at a crossroads, as Respect for ourselves, one another, and Creation is strained through these innovations. More than that, the future of our minds and reality as we know it is in question as AI centralizes power with its ability to respond to autonomous inquiry. As Bourgeois-Doyle (2019) explains, "[i]t is likely that members of the next generation will know nothing other than a world in which technology also collects data, learns, and seemingly thinks for them" (p.

9). Learners who choose to apply AI programs to do their thinking for them are failing to gain the necessary skills to function effectively in the work and careers they have chosen to pursue. While we do not feel that Learners should be cut off from technology, rather we argue that Learners and educators must be willing to think more critically about the roles of technology; as a tool for writing, learning, accessing resources, while remaining vigilant to ensure that the ability to function without said tools is still possible. Learners must therefore become responsible digital citizens (Watkins, 2020).

However, recognizing the difficulty that exists in pushing back on progress, there needs to be institutional recognition that when educators detect cheating, it takes a lot of unnecessary time to prove. While Indigenous educators are focused on ensuring that their students are learning the course content, more efforts should be made to embed Respectful Indigenous pedagogy into the policies and practices developed within institutions to ensure that the use of EdTech does not create further burden for educators. Mechanisms to ensure accountability is in place within institutions on behalf of educators, Learners, and Indigenous communities who engage within academic spaces, are necessary to ensure Respect in the digital age is rooted in ethics and morality. Without which, we could concede of a world where formal education is no longer relevant.

Bravery

Bravery is to face the foe with integrity. Bravery in the context of EdTech and Indigenous pedagogical thinking requires that we reframe our understandings within a changing world. Smith (2021) explains that "[r]eframing is about taking much greater control over the ways in which Indigenous issues and social problems are discussed and handled" (p. 175). Perhaps, as Wemigwans (2018) suggests, Bravery is also "being Indigenous on the Internet" (p. 56) and "taking Indigenous Knowledge online" (p. 208). The Internet is a tool that is available and accessible to many Indigenous Peoples, and in line with Indigenous connection, it is an effective way of keeping in touch with family and friends around the world. Connected EdTech platforms enables Indigenous Peoples the ability to access education from a variety of locations, without requiring the need to move to major urban centres. However, Bravery is also standing up when something is not right. So, while the Internet and some EdTech has the potential to advance Indigenous Knowledges and propel our ambitions, mechanisms to protect ourselves from misappropriation, misinformation, and other potential harms, is lacking. Being Brave is about more than settling for the status quo, it is also about more than the application of pedagogy or conceiving of a better world. Bravery is about imagining something better, and as Freire (2018) puts it, creating transformative action.

Approaching Bravery Teachings

When critically considering the applications of EdTech including data extraction and AI's potential, we question the ways in which information is collected, linked, shared, and used. Be Brave enough to question the applications of these technologies:

- Whose data is collected and in what ways?
- Are Indigenous data disaggregated and capable of being pulled out of datasets on their own?
- Where are data stored, by whom, and for how long?
- Who has access to them?
- How and when are data/Knowledge/information deleted/removed?

The same questions can be applied when thinking about how Indigenous Knowledges, woven through Indigenous Pedagogies, and enveloped within mainstream curriculum are suddenly accessible through EdTech platforms online. At the same time, we question how Indigenous Knowledges that are woven through course syllabi are held, stored, and maintained by the users who download them onto their personal or institutionally loaned computers and laptops. Asking questions is part of being Brave and understanding the teaching of Bravery. Learners, educators, institutions, administrators, and policy developers must apply Indigenous Pedagogies to question the applications and intentions of EdTech and its uses. Until we take the necessary actions to ensure that the answers to our questions align with Indigenous Pedagogies, we must be mindful about what Indigenous content is uploaded, shared, distributed, and accessible through EdTech and its applications. Until then, we must encourage the training and advancement of Indigenous technologists, computer scientists, engineers, programmers, and software developers who can work in relationship with Indigenous Peoples to effectively develop measures that protect our unique and collective Knowledges now and into the future.

Honesty

Honesty in facing a situation is to be brave. Up until this point in the paper we have woven our understandings of the strengths and opportunities of EdTech throughout. Advancements to reconcile with Indigenous Peoples (TRC, 2015), requires an underpinned understanding of what it means to be both Truthful and Honest. Acting upon the embodiment of the meaning of Bravery, as shared above, requires doing the right thing. This is Honesty. We place Smith's (2021) Intervening Project here because "intervening takes action research to mean literally the process of being proactive and of becoming involved as an interested worker for change" (p. 168). Bourgeois-Doyle (2019) explains that AI is here and it,

will permeate our lives whether we take action to exploit it for public good benefits or not. We all need to learn more, but the greatest challenges and opportunities for ensuring that AI evolves to human benefit rest in the engagement of youth. (p. 8)

Therefore, engaging with youth Learners and embedding Indigenous Pedagogies into the ways that youth think about technologies, including EdTech, guided by the Seven Grandfathers and understandings of Indigenous sovereignty (including IDSov), will empower a future where EdTech and its applications align more clearly with Indigenous intent.

Approaching Honesty Teachings

If we consider what it means to be Brave and extend it to what it means to be Honest, Indigenous-defined approaches to EdTech and its applications has the potential to radically alter EdTech's current limitations. Indigenous educators strive to ensure that their classroom teachings and materials balance the realities of the western world with the realities of Indigenous Peoples. For instance, we expel an extensive amount of mental energy, time, and care into our syllabi, lesson plans, activities, discussions, and more to ensure a healthy and sustainable future for our Learners. At the same time, Indigenous educators often prioritize relationship building in the classroom and through engagement with the land.

To activate Honesty, institutions, educators, and Learners must remain true to the values and morals learned through questioning everything. We must all remain accountable to ourselves and the Earth, encouraging unique, ethical, and critical thoughts, opinions, and experiences. Being Brave enough to be Honest requires institutions and policy makers to ensure that educators, Learners, and their families have been meaningfully informed of the risks and benefits to using EdTech. That also means ensuring that the ability to decline to consent to have data collected is Respected. Again, this necessitates Indigenous pedagogical approaches to create effective policies and other mechanisms that ensure that Indigenous Learners are protected within classrooms that use virtual technologies.

Humility

Humility is to know yourself as a sacred part of the Creation. Humility is knowing Indigenous Knowledges are sacred and beneficial to those who apply them ethically, while centring the Earth and all of Creation. Balancing the application of Indigenous Pedagogies when thinking about EdTech and its uses must therefore be done selflessly. We can apply Smith's (2021) Discovering Project to understand the beauty of Indigenous Knowledges as being about discovering the gentle balance between Indigenous and western pedagogies, and Indigenous and non-Indigenous technologies, "and making [Indigenous] [K]nowledge systems work for Indigenous development" (p. 182). Recognizing both the complexity and persistent resilience of Indigenous Knowledges and the endurance of EdTech and its applications, Indigenous Pedagogies must be proactively engaged within the conception, creation, shaping, and delivery of modern technologies.

Approaching Humility Teachings

The futility of resisting technological advancement necessitates a deep illumination and elimination of selfish colonial and capital driven technologies through Indigenous ways of knowing and doing. When creating, sharing, and accessing Indigenous Knowledges through EdTech, we encourage institutional, educator, and Learner accountability and responsibility to understanding and applying Indigenous Pedagogies that align to Indigenous cultural protocols (Wemigwans, 2018). Putting pride and ego aside by embracing Indigenous Knowledges will support the future sustainability and security of all life on earth. Although many people embrace technologies and use them as part of their day-to-day, Indigenous Knowledges woven through relationships with Elders, Knowledge Holders, and other traditional persons, could lead to what Wemigwans (2018) calls a digital bundle.

Truth

Truth is to know all of these things. Embracing the Teachings of the Seven Grandfathers can heighten our understandings of EdTech's potential strengths and harms. Narratives of the Truth of EdTech that are uncovered and preserved through Indigenous Pedagogies can lead to a future where Indigenous Peoples have addressed the concerns outlined throughout this chapter and beyond and may "[light] new fires for the internet" (Wemigwans, 2018, p. 207). As Smith (2021) shares,

For Indigenous [Peoples] stories are ways of passing down the beliefs and values of a culture in the hope that the new generations will treasure them and pass the story down further. The story and story teller both serve to connect the past with the future, one generation with the other, the land with the people and the people with the story. (p. 166)

Indigenous stories and pedagogies have sustained Indigenous Peoples for thousands of years. In Truth, we must continue to generate critical conversations about EdTech's uses, including how the online world can generate falsehoods.

Approaching Truth Teachings

The Seven Grandfather Teachings offered here provide a new way of thinking about and embracing Indigenous-led Truths by critically reflecting on, and connecting with EdTech, data, and AI in new ways. Like the EdTech Trickster metaphor, we have multiple understandings, lessons, and uses in how we engage with EdTech and AI. The potential for EdTech to exceed our current understandings of its applications are worth exploring. Considerations for EdTech present and future must ensure that Indigenous Pedagogies align with the Knowledges of Indigenous Elders, Knowledge Holders, and traditional persons, while ensuring the connection to the Earth remains intact. Take moments to sit with the Land, reflect on these Teachings and your own, read up on these topics, speak to people, and never stop learning.

CONCLUSION

EdTech's role in sharing knowledge, and AI's role in shaping it, leaves much to be desired. As Indigenous mothers, stewards, and scholars, we recognize that transformative action is necessary to strengthen and safeguard the present and future realities of our world for our children and all of Creation. As we reflect upon this chapter, we want to reiterate that the goal of this work was never to offer readers one Indigenous Pedagogical approach for thinking through the uses of tech, EdTech, and AI. Rather, our intention has been to uplift the voice of many pedagogical thinkers, to support our efforts in unravelling the complexities of this discussion. Throughout, we have advocated for the use of Indigenous Pedagogical approaches in the ways that people think about EdTech, while reflecting on the systemic, historical, socio-political, economic, and ecological power dynamics that propel its advancements. By bringing traditional Indigenous Knowledges, Sacred Teachings, and the Seven Grandfather Teachings into a 21st century discussion on EdTech, we have engaged with an Indigenous Pedagogy that has offered readers new ways of thinking critically about the issues surrounding EdTech, AI, and its uses.

While we have only scratched the surface here, a key takeaway is that current educational pedagogies are insufficient to meet the priorities of Indigenous Peoples in a technologically and colonially driven world. It is essential to protect the intimate and private information of Learners and educators while extending that protection to Indigenous Nations, in line with Indigenous Peoples' inherent and sovereign rights (underscored by UNDRIP and IDSov movements). Without protections, Indigenous data generated from EdTech enhances the ability for data users to generate a bird's eye view of Indigenous community ongoings. Those who stand to benefit from EdTech data collection are unlikely to be the Indigenous Peoples whose data have been collected, rather, it will increase profits for the corporations who collect and sell the data.

To create genuine and actionable change in these spaces, transparent, multidisciplinary education and further critical reflections, are needed. To develop effective Indigenous Pedagogies to apply in EdTech situations, work must begin at the beginning. That is, at the EdTech tools themselves. Considerations that engage with Indigenous Peoples to understand Indigenous alignment with EdTech, their uses, and their applications, are desperately needed to genuinely transform not only how educators and users think about this matter, but to ensure that Indigenous Pedagogies are built into the technologies themselves. Embracing Indigenous Pedagogies in all its domains; mental, emotional, physical, and spiritual, would necessitate adapting and deploying Indigenous ways of seeing, knowing, being, and doing. In one way, the application of Indigenous theory and practice could lead to transformative changes to EdTech itself, to the ways it functions, to the purposes for its uses, and even to the physical spaces in the world where EdTech is created and used.

Critically, the modern evolution of EdTech and its processes embody the same aspirations of known colonial processes: economic exploitation, resource extraction, market creation and expansion, and homogenization (or what Freire calls humanization). From an Indigenous perspective, it is increasingly apparent that colonial ideologies are perpetuating narratives that support data, technology, and its advancements. At the same time, there is little discussion around the ways that Indigenous Pedagogy can inform ethical and moral understandings of technological, and AI uses in the classroom. It requires deep and meaningful exploration from an Indigenous lens, as we have offered in this chapter using the EdTech Trickster metaphor and the Seven Grandfather Teachings. Leveraging Freire's (2018) pedagogy, the process of studying and theorizing the order of the world requires transformative action. As such, meaningful commitments and actionable changes are needed, now more than ever, if we are to reclaim, reflect, and Respect Indigenous Peoples ways of knowing and doing within education. Arguably, disentangling modern understandings of technology from those rooted in ancestral Indigenous Knowledges is necessary to encourage advancements in Indigenous technologies and Indigenous Pedagogies, in line with decolonization and anti-colonialism.

Nahow, Miigwetch.

REFERENCES

Adam, T., Sarwar, M. B., & Moustafa, N. (2022). Decolonising EdTech: A resource list for tackling coloniality and digital neocolonialism in EdTech. *EdTech Hub*. https://edtechhub.org/2022/02/25/decolonising-edtech-a-resource-list-for-tackling-coloniality-and-digital-neocolonialism-in-edtech/

Battiste, M., & Youngblood, J. (2000). *Protecting Indigenous knowledge and heritage: A global challenge*. UBC Press.

Benton-Banai, E. (2010). *The Mishomis Book: The Voice of the Ojibway*. University of Minnesota Press.

Bourgeois-Doyle, D. (2019, March). *Two-Eyed AI: A Reflection on Artificial Intelligence*. The Canadian Commission for UNESCOs Idea Lab. https://spectrum.library.concordia.ca/id/eprint/986506/7/Indigenous_Protocol_and_AI_2020.pdf

Collier, B. (2023). *Broadband internet in indigenous communities*. HillNotes. https://hillnotes.ca/2021/12/08/broadband-internet-in-indigenous-communities/

Cordes, A. (2020). Gifts of Dentalium and fire: Entwining trust and care with AI. In *Indigenous Protocol and Artificial Intelligence Position Paper* (pp. 58-68). https://spectrum.library.concordia.ca/id/eprint/986506/7/Indigenous_Protocol_and_AI_2020.pdf

Cote-Meek, S. (2014). *Colonized classrooms: Racism, trauma and resistance in post-secondary education*. Fernwood Publishing.

Crawford, K. (2021). *The atlas of AI: Power, politics, and the planetary costs of artificial intelligence*. Yale University Press.

Dreamson, N., Thomas, G., Lee Hong, A., & Kim, S. (2018). The perceptual gaps in using a learning management system: Indigenous cultural perspectives. *Technology, Pedagogy and Education*, 27(4), 431–444. doi:10.1080/1475939X.2018.1490665

Dussault, R., & Erasmus, G. (1996). *Report of the royal commission on aboriginal peoples*. Queen's University Library. https://qspace.library.queensu.ca/handle/1974/6874

Freire, P. (2018). Pedagogy of the oppressed. (50th Anniversary Edition). Bloomsbury Publishing Inc.

Gadacz, R. R. (2020). Nanabozo. *The Canadian Encyclopedia*. https://www.thecanadianencyclopedia.ca/en/article/nanabozo

General Assembly resolution 61/106, *Convention on the rights of persons with disabilities,* A/RES/61/106 (13 December 2006). https://undocs.org/en/A/RES/61/106

General Assembly special rapporteurs 46/37, *Artificial intelligence and privacy, and children's privacy,* A/HRC/46/37 (25 January 2021). https://undocs.org/en/A/HRC/46/37

Goos, M., Galbraith, P., Renshaw, P., & Geiger, V. (2000). Reshaping teacher and student roles in technology-enriched classrooms. *Mathematics Education Research Journal, 12*(3), 303–320. doi:10.1007/BF03217091

Han, H. J. (2022). *"How dare they peep into my private life?" Children's rights violations by governments that endorsed online learning during the Covid-19 pandemic.* Human Rights Watch. https://www.hrw.org/report/2022/05/25/how-dare-they-peep-my-private-life/childrens-rights-violations-governments

Hudson, M., Carroll, S. R., Anderson, J., Blackwater, D., Cordova-Marks, F. M., Cummins, J., David-Chavez, D., Fernandez, A., Garba, I., Hiraldo, D., Jäger, M. B., Jennings, L. L., Martinez, A., Sterling, R., Walker, J. D., & Rowe, R. K. (2023). Indigenous Peoples' Rights in Data: A contribution toward Indigenous Research Sovereignty. *Frontiers in Research Metrics and Analytics, 8,* 1173805. doi:10.3389/frma.2023.1173805 PMID:37215248

Kesserwan, K. (2018). *How can Indigenous knowledge shape our view of AI?* Policy Options. https://policyoptions.irpp.org/magazines/february-2018/how-can-indigenous-knowledge-shape-our-view-of-ai/

King, L., & Schielmann, S. (2004). *The challenge of indigenous education: Practice and perspectives.* Paris: UNESCO. https://unesdoc.unesco.org/ark:/48223/pf0000134773

Kite, S. (2020). How to build anything ethically. In *Indigenous Protocol and Artificial Intelligence Position Paper* (pp. 75-84.). Spectrum. https://spectrum.library.concordia.ca/id/eprint/986506/7/Indigenous_Protocol_and_AI_2020.pdf

Lewis, J. E. (2020). *Indigenous Protocol and Artificial Intelligence.* Indigenous Protocol and Artificial Intelligence Position Paper. https://spectrum.library.concordia.ca/id/eprint/986506/7/Indigenous_Protocol_and_AI_2020.pdf

Lockey, A., Conaghan, P., Bland, A., & Astin, F. (2021). Educational theory and its application to advanced life support courses: A narrative review. *Resuscitation Plus, 5,* 100053. doi:10.1016/j.resplu.2020.100053 PMID:34223327

Lombrozo, T. (2017). *Technology can be a tool, a teacher, a trickster*. NPR Cosmos and Culture. https://www.npr.org/sections/13.7/2017/07/17/537667988/technology-can-be-a-tool-a-teacher-a-trickster

Loveless, A. (2011). Technology, pedagogy and education: Reflections on the accomplishment of what teachers know, do and believe in a digital age. *Technology, Pedagogy and Education, 20*(3), 301–316. doi:10.1080/1475939X.2011.610931

Marlow, K. (2022). *How AI and immersive technology are being used to revitalize Indigenous languages*. CBC News. https://www.cbc.ca/news/canada/british-columbia/bc-indigenous-language-preservation-ai-1.6332285

Mashford-Pringle, A., & Shawanda, A. (2023). Using the Medicine Wheel as theory, conceptual framework, analysis, and evaluation tool in health research. *Elsevier. SSM. Qualitative Research in Health, 3*, 100251. doi:10.1016/j.ssmqr.2023.100251

McMaster, G. (2020). *Creating ethical AI from Indigenous perspectives*. University of Alberta. https://www.ualberta.ca/folio/2020/10/creating-ethical-ai-from-indigenous-perspectives.html

Montalvo, M. G. (2021). *Indigenous Technologies at the Berkeley Center for New Media*. Berkeley Center for New Media. http://bcnm.berkeley.edu/resources/3997/indigenous-technologies

Nelson, M. K. (Ed.). (2008). *Original instructions: Indigenous teachings for a sustainable future*. Bear & Company.

Nikolopoulou, K., Gialamas, V., & Lavidas, K. (2022). Mobile learning-technology barriers in school education: Teachers' views. *Technology, Pedagogy and Education*, 1–16. doi:10.1080/1475939X.2022.2121314

O'Connor, K. (2013). *The use of ICTs and e-learning in Indigenous education*. Canadian eLearning Network. https://k12sotn.ca/papers/the-use-of-icts-and-e-learning-in-indigenous-education/

Ontario College of Teachers. (2016). *Exploring the ethical standards for the teaching profession through Anishinaabe art* [booklet]. OCT. https://www.oct.ca/-/media/PDF/Exploring%20Ethical%20Standards%20through%20Anishinaabe%20Art/2015%20Ethical%20Stndrds%20and%20Anishinaabe%20Art_en%20web_accssble.pdf

Penak, N. (2018). A story pathway: Restoring wholeness in the research process. In McGregor, D., Restoule, J-P., & Johnston, R. (Eds.), Indigenous research: Theories, practices, and relationships (pp. 257-270). Canadian Scholars.

Popp, J. (2018). How Indigenous knowledge advances modern science and technology. *The Conversation.* https://theconversation.com/how-indigenous-knowledge-advances-modern-science-and-technology-89351

Purdue Online. (n.d.). *The evolution of technology in the classroom.* Purdue University. https://online.purdue.edu/blog/education/evolution-technology-classroom

Purnava, J. (2020, August 5). The role of technology in Canadian classrooms. *INKspire.* https://inkspire.org/post/the-role-of-technology-in-canadian-classrooms/-MCe6KZyeU-4tTnYheH9

Quinless, J. M. (2022). *Decolonizing data: Unsettling conversations about social research methods.* University of Toronto Press. doi:10.3138/9781487530099

Raso, F. A., Hilligoss, H., Krishnamurthy, V., Bavitz, C., & Kim, L. (2018). Artificial intelligence & human rights: Opportunities & risks. *Berkman Klein Center Research Publication,* (2018-6). http://dx.doi.org/ doi:10.2139/ssrn.3259344

Reid, C. (2003). Studying cultural diversity using information and communication technologies in teacher education: Pedagogy, power and literacy. *Technology, Pedagogy and Education, 12*(3), 345–360. doi:10.1080/14759390300200163

Rowe, R. K., Bull, J. R., & Walker, J. D. (2020). Indigenous self-determination and data governance in the Canadian policy context. In M. Walter, T. Kukutai, S. R. Carroll, & D. Rodriguez-Lonebear (Eds.), *Indigenous data sovereignty and policy* (pp. 81–98). Routledge Publishing. doi:10.4324/9780429273957-6

Rowe, R. K., Rowat, J., & Walker, J. D. (2020). First Nations' survivance and sovereignty in Canada during a time of COVID-19. *American Indian Culture and Research Journal, 44*(2), 89–99. doi:10.17953/aicrj.44.2.rowe_rowat_walker

Running Wolf V. Arista N. (2020). Indigenous Protocols in Action. *Indigenous Protocol and Artificial Intelligence Position Paper* (pp. 93-101). doi:10.11573/spectrum.library.concordia.ca.00986506

Smith, L. T. (2021). *Decolonizing Methodologies Research and Indigenous Peoples.* Bloomsbury Publishing. doi:10.5040/9781350225282

Swanson, J. A. (2016). *The Impact of Technology Integration upon Collegiate Pedagogy from the Lens of Multiple Disciplines.* International Association for Development of the Information Society.

Truth and Reconciliation Commission of Canada. (2015, July 23). Final report of the truth and reconciliation commission of Canada: Honouring the truth, reconciling for the future. *Truth and Reconciliation Commission of Canada*. James Lorimer & Company.

Walter, M. (2016). Data politics and Indigenous representation in Australian statistics. In T. Kukutai & J. Taylor (Eds.), *Indigenous data sovereignty: Toward an agenda* (pp. 79–98). Australian National University Press. doi:10.22459/CAEPR38.11.2016.05

Watkins, E. K. (2020). *Technology in Schools – A Tool and a Strategy*. People for Education. https://peopleforeducation.ca/wp-content/uploads/2020/05/Technology-In-Schools-Final-May-5.pdf

Wemigwans, J. (2018). *A digital bundle: Protecting and promoting Indigenous Knowledge*. University of Regina Press.

Wesley-Esquimaux, C. C., & Smolewski, M. (2004). Historic trauma and Aboriginal healing. *Ottawa: Aboriginal Healing Foundation, 3*, 1-99. https://epub.sub.uni-hamburg.de/epub/volltexte/2009/2903/pdf/historic_trauma.pdf

Whaanga, H. (2020). AI: a new (r)evolution or the new colonizer for Indigenous peoples? *Indigenous AI*, 34-38. https://hdl.handle.net/10289/15164

Wilson, S. (2008). *Research is ceremony: Indigenous research methods*. Fernwood Publishing.

Windchief, S., & San Pedro, T. (2019). *Applying Indigenous research methods*. Routledge. doi:10.4324/9781315169811

Yu, J., & Couldry, N. (2022). Education as a domain of natural data extraction: Analysing corporate discourse about educational tracking. *Information Communication and Society, 25*(1), 127–144. doi:10.1080/1369118X.2020.1764604

Compilation of References

Absolon, K., & Herbert, E. (1997). Community action as practice of freedom: A first Nations perspective. In B. Wharf & M. Clague (Eds.), *Community organising: Canadian experiences* (pp. 205–227). Oxford University Press.

Adam, T., Sarwar, M. B., & Moustafa, N. (2022). Decolonising EdTech: A resource list for tackling coloniality and digital neocolonialism in EdTech. *EdTech Hub*. https://edtechhub.org/2022/02/25/decolonising-edtech-a-resource-list-for-tackling-coloniality-and-digital-neocolonialism-in-edtech/

Andrews, D. J. C., Brown, T., Castillo, B. M., Jackson, D., & Vellanki, V. (2019). Beyond damage-centered teacher education: Humanizing pedagogy for teacher educators and preservice teachers. *Teachers College Record*, *121*(6), 1–28. doi:10.1177/016146811912100605

Archibald, J. (2008). *Indigenous storywork: Educating the heart, mind, body, and spirit*. UBC Press.

Archibald, J. A. (2019). Raven's Story About Indigenous Teacher Education. In E. McKinley & L. Smith (Eds.), *Handbook of Indigenous Education*. Springer. doi:10.1007/978-981-10-1839-8_1-2

Aspen-Baxter, L. (2022). *Confronting the Ugly Truth: The (Un)Making of a 'Good' White Teacher on the Canadian Prairies*. [Master of Education thesis, University of Saskatchewan]. University of Saskatchewan Harvest. https://hdl.handle.net/10388/13874

Assembly of First Nations. (2012). *Honouring air*. https://www.afn.ca/honoring-air/

Atleo, C., & Boron, J. (2022). Land Is Life: Indigenous relationships to territory and navigating settler colonial property regimes in Canada. *Land (Basel)*, *11*(5), 1–12. doi:10.3390/land11050609

Ball, J. (2007). *Aboriginal young children's language and literacy development: research evaluating progress, promising practices, and needs*. Canadian Language and Literacy Networked Centre of Excellence. http://www.ecdip.org/docs/pdf/CLLRNet%20Feb%202008.pdf

Ball, J., & Simpkins, M. (2004). The community within the child: Integration of Indigenous knowledge into First Nations childcare process and practice. *American Indian Quarterly*, *28*(3/4), 480–498. doi:10.1353/aiq.2004.0091

Compilation of References

Battiste, M. (2002). Indigenous knowledge and pedagogy in First Nations education: A literature review with recommendations. Report prepared for the National Working Group on Education, Indian and Northern Affairs Canada, Ottawa, ON.

Battiste, M. (2013b). You can't be the doctor if you're the disease: Eurocentrism and Indigenous renaissance. *CAUT Distinguished Academic Lecture*, 1-19.

Battiste. (2013). *Decolonizing education : nourishing the learning spirit*. Purich Publishing Limited.

Battiste, M. (1998). Enabling the autumn seed: Toward a decolonized approach to Aboriginal knowledge, language, and education. *Canadian Journal of Native Education*, 22(1), 16–27.

Battiste, M. (2000). Maintaining Aboriginal identity, language, and culture in modern society. In M. Battiste (Ed.), *Reclaiming Indigenous voice and vision* (pp. 192–208). UBC Press.

Battiste, M. (2002). *Indigenous knowledge and pedagogy in First Nations education: A literature review with recommendations*. Indian and Northern Affairs Canada.

Battiste, M. (2013). *Decolonizing Education – Nourishing the Learning Spirit*. Purich.

Battiste, M. (2013). *Decolonizing education: Nourishing the learning spirit*. Purich Publishing.

Battiste, M. (2013). *Decolonizing Education: Nourishing the Learning Spirit*. UBC Press.

Battiste, M. (2013a). *Decolonizing education: nourishing the learning spirit*. Purich Publishing.

Battiste, M. (2015). *Decolonizing Education: Nourishing the learning spirit*. Purich Publishing Limited.

Battiste, M., Bell, L., & Findlay, L. M. (2002). Decolonizing education in Canadian universities: An interdisciplinary, international, indigenous research project. *Canadian Journal of Native Education*, 26(2), 82.

Battiste, M., & Youngblood, J. (2000). *Protecting Indigenous knowledge and heritage: A global challenge*. UBC Press.

Bedard, R. (2014, July 8). *Beading 101 Technique Series, Beading Needle Style #2* [Video]. Youtube. www.youtube.com/watch?v=q9lhLRBs3Xw

Bell, N. (2013). Just do it: Anishinaabe culture-based education. *Canadian Journal of Native Education*, 36(1).

Benton-Banai, E. (2010). *The Mishomis Book the Voice of the Ojibway*. University of Minnesota Press Beaulieu, K. (2018, August 24). The seven lessons of the medicine wheel. *SAY Magazine*. https://saymag.com/the-seven-lessons-of-the-medicine-wheel/#:~:text=The%20circle%20 acknowledges%20the%20connectedness,the%20daily%20sunrise%20and%20sunset

Benton-Banai, E. (2010). *The Mishomis Book: The Voice of the Ojibway*. University of Minnesota Press.

Bopp, J., Bopp, M., & Lane, P. (2012). *The sacred tree: Reflections on Native American spirituality.* Four Worlds Development Institute.

Borrows, J. (2017). Outsider Education: Indigenous Law and Land-Based Learning. *Windsor Yearbook of Access to Justice, 33*(1), 1–27. doi:10.22329/wyaj.v33i1.4807

Bourdieu, P. (1978). Sport and social class. *Social Sciences Information. Information Sur les Sciences Sociales, 17*(6), 819–840. doi:10.1177/053901847801700603

Bourgeois-Doyle, D. (2019, March). *Two-Eyed AI: A Reflection on Artificial Intelligence.* The Canadian Commission for UNESCOs Idea Lab. https://spectrum.library.concordia.ca/id/eprint/986506/7/Indigenous_Protocol_and_AI_2020.pdf

Bouvier, V. (2022). *Kaa-waakohtoochik (The ones who are related to each other): An inquiry of Métis understandings with/in/through the city* [Doctoral thesis, University of Calgary]. University of Calgary. https://prism.ucalgary.ca

Bouvier, V., & MacDonald, J. (2019). Spiritual Exchange: A Methodology for a Living Inquiry With All Our Relations. *International Journal of Qualitative Methods, 18.* doi:10.1177/1609406919851636

Bouvier, V. (2018). Truthing: An ontology of living an ethic of shakihi (love) and ikkimmapiipitsin (santified kindness). *Canadian Social Studies, 50*(2), 39–44. doi:10.29173/css17

Bracken, S., & Novak, K. (Eds.). (2019). *Transforming Higher Education Through Universal Design for Learning: An International Perspective.* Routledge. doi:10.4324/9781351132077

Brayboy, B. M. J. (2005). Toward a Tribal Critical Race Theory in Education. *The Urban Review, 37*(5), 425–446. doi:10.100711256-005-0018-y

Brayboy, B. M. J., & Maughan, E. (2009). Indigenous Knowledges and the Story of the Bean. *Harvard Educational Review, 79*(1), 1–21. doi:10.17763/haer.79.1.l0u6435086352229

Brokenleg, M. (2008). Culture and Helping. Presented in Winnipeg, Canada.

Brown, M. A., & Di Lallo, S. (2020). Talking Circles: A Culturally Responsive Evaluation Practice. *The American Journal of Evaluation, 41*(3), 367–383. doi:10.1177/1098214019899164

Bruner, J. (1996). *The culture of education.* Harvard University Press. doi:10.4159/9780674251083

Brunette-Debassige, C., & Wakeham, P. (2021). Translating the four Rs of Indigenous education for literary studies: Learning from and with Indigenous stories. *Studies in American Indian Literatures, 32*(3-4), 13–41. doi:10.1353/ail.2020.0016

Buchanan, R., & Hewitt, J. G. (2017). Encountering Settler Colonialism Through Legal Objects: A Painted Drum and Handwritten Treaty from Manitoulin Island. *The Northern Ireland Legal Quarterly, 68*(3), 291–304. doi:10.53386/nilq.v68i3.41

Buchanan-Rivera, E. (2022). *Identity affirming classrooms: spaces that center humanity.* Routledge, Taylor & Francis Group.

Compilation of References

Cajete, G. (2000). *Native science: Natural laws of interdependence*. Clear Light Publishers.

Cajete, G. (2017). Children, myth and storytelling: An Indigenous perspective. *Global Studies of Childhood*, *7*(2), 113–130. doi:10.1177/2043610617703832

Campbell, K. (2020, May 8). Why don't Canadian universities hire more racialized and Indigenous senior administrators? *University Affairs*. https://www.universityaffairs.ca/opinion/in-my-opinion/why-dont-canadian-universities-hire-more-racialized-and-indigenous-senior-administrators/

Campbell, C. (2021). Educational equity in Canada: The case of Ontario's strategies and actions to advance excellence and equity for students. *School Leadership & Management*, *41*(4-5), 409–428. doi:10.1080/13632434.2019.1709165

Cardinal, H. (1999). *The unjust society*. Douglas & McIntyre.

Carlson, K. T. (Ed.). (1997). You are asked to witness: the Stó:lō in Canada's Pacific Coast history. Stó:lō Heritage Trust.

Carlson-Manathara, E. (2021). *Living in Indigenous Sovereignty*. Fernwood Publishing.

Caxaj, C. S. (2015). Indigenous storytelling and participatory action research: Allies toward decolonization? Reflections from the Peoples' International Health Tribunal. *Global Qualitative Nursing Research*, *2*, 1–12. doi:10.1177/2333393615580764 PMID:28462305

Cheechoo, K. (2020). Reframing Reconciliation: Turning Our Back or Turning Back? In S. Cote-Meek & T. Moeke-Pickering (Eds.), *Decolonizing and Indigenizing Education in Canada* (pp. 247–266). Canadian Scholars.

Chrona, J. (2022). *Wayi Wah!: Indigenous pedagogies: An act for reconciliation and anti-racist education*. Portage & Main Press.

Clarke, K., & Yellow Bird, M. (2021). *Decolonizing Pathways Towards Integrative Healing in Social Work*. Routledge.

Coholic, D., Cote-Meek, S., & Recollet, D. (2012). Exploring the acceptability and perceived benefits of arts-based group methods for Aboriginal women living in an urban community within northeastern Ontario. *Canadian Social Work Review*, *29*(2), 149–168.

Collier, B. (2023). *Broadband internet in indigenous communities*. HillNotes. https://hillnotes.ca/2021/12/08/broadband-internet-in-indigenous-communities/

Constitution Act. (1982). s 35, being Schedule B to the Canada Act 1982 (UK), c 11.

Corbiere, A. (2014). *First Nation revival program framework for curriculum development*. Kenjgewin Teg.

Cordes, A. (2020). Gifts of Dentalium and fire: Entwining trust and care with AI. In *Indigenous Protocol and Artificial Intelligence Position Paper* (pp. 58-68). https://spectrum.library.concordia.ca/id/eprint/986506/7/Indigenous_Protocol_and_AI_2020.pdf

Corntassel, J. (2003). An activist posing as an academic? *American Indian Quarterly*, *27*(1), 160–171. doi:10.1353/aiq.2004.0029

Cote-Meek, S., & Moeke-Pickering, T. (2021, April 8). *Decolonizing and Indigenizing education in Canada*. [Video]. Youtube. https://www.youtube.com/watch?v=t8XIN46vHHI

Cote-Meek, S. (2014). *Colonized Classrooms–Racism, Trauma and Resistance in Post-Secondary Education*. Fernwood Press.

Cote-Meek, S. (2014). *Colonized classrooms: racism, trauma and resistance in post-secondary education*. Fernwood Publishing.

Cote-Meek, S. (2014). *Colonized classrooms: Racism, trauma and resistance in post-secondary education*. Fernwood Publishing.

Cote-Meek, S. (2014). *Colonized Classrooms: Racism, Trauma and Resistance in Post-Secondary Education*. Fernwood Publishing.

Cote-Meek, S. (2020). From colonized classrooms to Transformative change in the Academy: We can and must do better! In S. Cote-Meek & T. Moeke-Pickering (Eds.), *Decolonizing and Indigenizing education in Canada* (pp. xi–xxiii). Canadian Scholars.

Cote-Meek, S., & Moeke-Pickering, T. (2011). Indigenous pedagogies and transformational practices. In G. Williams (Ed.), *Talking back, talking forward: Journeys in transforming Indigenous educational practice* (pp. 27–32). Charles Darwin University Press.

Cote-Meek, S., & Moeke-Pickering, T. (Eds.). (2022). *Decolonizing and Indigenizing education in Canada*. Canadian Scholars.

Cowan, K. (2020). How residential schools led to intergenerational trauma in the Canadian Indigenous population to influence parenting styles and family structures over generations. [http://ejournals,library,ualberta.ca/index/php/cjfy]. *Canadian Journal of Family and Youth*, *12*(2), 26–35. doi:10.29173/cjfy29511

Crawford, K. (2021). *The atlas of AI: Power, politics, and the planetary costs of artificial intelligence*. Yale University Press.

Davidson, S. F. (2020). Evaluating Indigenous education resources for classroom use. *Teacher Magazine, May/June*. BC Teachers' Federation. https://issuu.com/teachernewsmag/docs/teacher_magazine_may_2020

Dei, G. J. S. (1993). The challenges of anti-racist education in Canada. *Canadian Ethnic Studies*, *25*(2), 36.

Deloria, V., Deloria, B., Foehner, K., & Scinta, S. (1998). *Spirit & reason the Vine Deloria Jr., reader*. Fulcrum.

Department of Justice Canada. (2018). *Principles: Respecting the Government of Canada's relationship with Indigenous Peoples*. Government of Canada. https://www.justice.gc.ca/eng/csj-sjc/principles.pdf

Dion, S. (2022). *Braided learning: illuminating Indigenous presence through art and story*. Purich Books.

Donald, D. (2016). Homo economicus and forgetful curriculum: Remembering other ways to be a human being. In J. Seidel, & D. W. Jardine (Eds.), Indigenous Education: New Direction in Theory and Practice (pp. 10-17). New Your: Peter Lang.

Donald, D. (2019). Homo economicus and forgetful curriculum. In J. Seidel, & D. W. Jardine (Eds.), Indigenous education: New directions in theory and practice (pp.103-125). New Your: Peter Lang.

Donald, D. (2009). Forts, curriculum, and Indigenous Métissage: Imagining decolonization of Aboriginal-Canadian relations in educational contexts. *First Nations Perspectives*, 2(1), 1–24.

Dreamson, N., Thomas, G., Lee Hong, A., & Kim, S. (2018). The perceptual gaps in using a learning management system: Indigenous cultural perspectives. *Technology, Pedagogy and Education*, 27(4), 431–444. doi:10.1080/1475939X.2018.1490665

Duffy, F., & Raigeluth, C. (2008). The school system transformation (SST) protocol. *Educational Technology*, 48(4), 41–49.

Durie, M. (1994). *Whaiora: Maori health development*. Oxford University Press.

Dussault, R., & Erasmus, G. (1996). *Report of the royal commission on aboriginal peoples*. Queen's University Library. https://qspace.library.queensu.ca/handle/1974/6874

Eck, D. L. (2005). Circumambulation. In L. Jones (Ed.), Encyclopedia of Religion (2nd ed., Vol. 3, pp. 1795–1798). World Catalogue.

Eckel, P., & Kezar, A. (2003). Key strategies for making new institutional sense: Indgredients to higher education transformation. *Higher Education Policy*, 16(1), 39–53. doi:10.1057/palgrave.hep.8300001

Edge, L. E. (2011). *My Grandmother's Moccasins: Indigenous Women, Ways of Knowing and Indigenous Aesthetic of Beadwork*. [Doctoral Dissertation, University of Alberta]. ProQuest Dissertation and Theses Database. https://www.collectionscanada.gc.ca/obj/thesescanada/vol2/002/NR80952.PDF,

Elliott, D., Sr. (1990). Salt water people as told by David Elliot Sr. (2nd ed.). Native Education, School District 63 (Saanich).

Ermine, W. (1995). Aboriginal epistemology. In J. Barman, (Ed.), *First Nations education in Canada: The circle unfolds* (pp. 101–112). UBC Press.

Ermine, W. (2007). Ethical space of engagement. *Indigenous Law Journal at the University of Toronto Faculty of Law*, *6*(1), 193–203.

Fakoyede, S. J., & Otulaja, F. S. (2020). Beads and Beadwork as Cultural Artifacts Used in Mediating Learners' Agentic Constructs in Science Classrooms: A Case for Place-Based Learning. *Cultural Studies of Science Education*, *15*(2), 197–207.

Farrell Racette, S. (2004). *Sewing Ourselves Together: Clothing, Decorative Arts and the Expression of Metis and Half-Breed Identity*. [Doctoral Dissertation, University of Manitoba]. University of Manitoba. https://mspace.lib.umanitoba.ca/handle/1993/3304

First Nations Education Steering Committee. (2018). *English First Peoples grade 10– 12 teacher resource guide*. FNESC. https://www.fnesc.ca/wp/wp-content/uploads/2018/08/PUBLICATION-LFP-EFP-10-12-FINAL-2018-08-13.pdf

First Peoples' Cultural Council. (n.d.). *Working with Elders*. FPCC. https://fpcc.ca/wp-content/uploads/2021/05/FPCC-Working-with-Elders_FINAL.pdf

Fixico, D. (2003). *The American Indian mind in a linear world: American Indian studies and traditional knowledge*. Routledge.

Freire, P. (2018). Pedagogy of the oppressed. (50th Anniversary Edition). Bloomsbury Publishing Inc.

Freire, P. (1970). *Pedagogy of the oppressed*. Penguin Books.

Freire, P. (1970). *Pedagogy of the Oppressed*. Seabury Press.

Freire, P. (1992). *Pedagogy of Hope: Reliving Pedagogy of the Oppressed*. Bloomsbury Academic.

Friedland, H., Napoleon, V., Fraser, H., & Laurent, L. (2016). An Inside Job: Engaging with Indigenous Legal Traditions Through Stories. *McGill Law Journal. Revue de Droit de McGill*, *61*(4), 725–754. doi:10.7202/1038487ar

Gadacz, R. R. (2020). Nanabozo. *The Canadian Encyclopedia*. https://www.thecanadianencyclopedia.ca/en/article/nanabozo

Gass, R. (2011). *What is transformation? And how it advances social change*. ST Project. http://stproject.org/wp-content/uploads/2012/03/What_is_Transformation.pdf

Gaudry, A., & Lorenz, D. (2018). Indigenization as Inclusion, Reconciliation, and Decolonization: Navigating the Different Visions for Indigenizing the Canadian Academy, *AlterNative: an international journal of indigenous peoples*, *14*(3), 218–227.

Gaywsh, R., & Mordoch, E. (2018). Situating intergenerational trauma in the educational journey. *in education*, *24*(2), 3-23. https://www.researchgate.net/publication/351147643_Situating_Intergenerational_Trauma_in_the_Educational_Journey

General Assembly resolution 61/106, *Convention on the rights of persons with disabilities*, A/RES/61/106 (13 December 2006). https://undocs.org/en/A/RES/61/106

Compilation of References

General Assembly special rapporteurs 46/37, *Artificial intelligence and privacy, and children's privacy,* A/HRC/46/37 (25 January 2021). https://undocs.org/en/A/HRC/46/37

Goos, M., Galbraith, P., Renshaw, P., & Geiger, V. (2000). Reshaping teacher and student roles in technology-enriched classrooms. *Mathematics Education Research Journal, 12*(3), 303–320. doi:10.1007/BF03217091

Gordon, D., Meyer, A., & Rose, D. (2016). *Universal Design for Learning.* CAST Professional Publishing.

Gough, N. (2002). *Voicing curriculum visions* (Vol. 151). Counterpoints.

Government of Canada. (2019). *Causes of climate change.* Government of Canada. https://www.canada.ca/en/environment-climate-change/services/climate-change/causes.html

Government of Ontario, Ministry of Education. (2023). *Indigenous Education in Ontario.* MoE. https://www.ontario.ca/page/indigenous-education-ontario

Grande, S. (2000). American Indian Identity and Intellectualism: The Quest for a New Red Pedagogy. *International Journal of Qualitative Studies in Education : QSE, 13*(4), 343–359. doi:10.1080/095183900413296

Grande, S. (2010). *Red Pedagogy: Native American Social and Political Thought.* Rowman & Littlefield Publishers.

Graveline, F. J. (1998). *Circle works: transforming Eurocentric consciousness.* Fernwood Publishing.

Gray, M. (2017). *Beads: Symbols of Indigenous Cultural Resilience and Value* [Master's Thesis, University of Toronto]. TSpace. https://tspace.library.utoronto.ca/handle/1807/82564

Guba, E. G., & Lincoln, Y. S. (1994). Competing paradigms in qualitative research. In N. K. Denzin & Y. S. Lincoln (Eds.), *Handbook of qualitative research* (pp. 105–117). Sage.

Guba, E. G., & Lincoln, Y. S. (2005). Paradigmatic controversies, contradictions, and emerging confluences. In N. K. Denzin & Y. S. Lincoln (Eds.), *The Sage handbook of qualitative research* (pp. 191–215). Sage.

Hammond, C., Gifford, W., Thomas, R., Rabaa, S., Thomas, O., & Domecq, M. C. (2018). Arts-based research methods with indigenous peoples: An international scoping review. *Alternative, 14*(3), 260–276. doi:10.1177/1177180118796870

Han, H. J. (2022). *"How dare they peep into my private life?" Children's rights violations by governments that endorsed online learning during the Covid-19 pandemic.* Human Rights Watch. https://www.hrw.org/report/2022/05/25/how-dare-they-peep-my-private-life/childrens-rights-violations-governments

Hart, M. (2004). *Seeking mino-pimatisiwin: An Aboriginal Approach to Helping.* Fernwood Publishing Company.

Hart, M. A. (2002). *Seeking mino-pimatisiwin: An Aboriginal approach to healing*. Fernwood Publishing.

Heffernan, T. (2022). Forty years of social justice research in Australasia: Examining equity in inequitable settings. *Higher Education Research & Development*, *41*(1), 48–61. doi:10.1080/07294360.2021.2011152

Henderson, J. Y. (2000). Ayukpachi: empowering Aboriginal thought. In M. Battiste (Ed.), *Reclaiming Indigenous voice and vision* (pp. 248–278). University of British Columbia Press.

Heron, J., & Reason, P. (1997). A participatory inquiry paradigm. *Qualitative Inquiry*, *3*(3), 274–294. doi:10.1177/107780049700300302

Hooks, b. (2003). *Teaching Community: A Pedagogy of Hope*. Routledge.

Hudson, M., Carroll, S. R., Anderson, J., Blackwater, D., Cordova-Marks, F. M., Cummins, J., David-Chavez, D., Fernandez, A., Garba, I., Hiraldo, D., Jäger, M. B., Jennings, L. L., Martinez, A., Sterling, R., Walker, J. D., & Rowe, R. K. (2023). Indigenous Peoples' Rights in Data: A contribution toward Indigenous Research Sovereignty. *Frontiers in Research Metrics and Analytics*, *8*, 1173805. doi:10.3389/frma.2023.1173805 PMID:37215248

Huguenin, M. (2020). *Integrating Indigenous Pedagogy in Remote Courses*. Trent University. https://www.trentu.ca/teaching/integrating-indigenous-pedagogy-remote-courses

Huston, L., & Michano-Drover, S. (2022). Placing the child's hands on the land: Conceptualizing, creating, and implementing land-based teachings in a play space. In S. S. Peterson & N. Friedrich (Eds.), *The role of play and place in young children's language and literacy* (pp. 81–94). University of Toronto Press. doi:10.3138/9781487529239-007

Johnston-Goodstar, K., & VeLure Roholt, R. (2017). "Our Kids Aren't Dropping Out; They're Being Pushed Out": Native American Students and Racial Microaggressions in Schools. *Journal of Ethnic & Cultural Diversity in Social Work*, *26*(1-2), 30–47. doi:10.1080/15313204.2016.1263818

Justice, D. H. (2018). *Why Indigenous Literatures Matter*. Wilfrid Laurier University Press.

Kaleimamoowahinekapu Galla, C. (Kanaka Hawai'i) & Holmes, A. (Kanien'keha:ka). (2020). Indigenous Thinkers: Decolonizing and Transforming the Academy Through Indigenous Relationality. In S. Cote-Meek & T. Moeke-Pickering, (Eds.), Decolonizing and Indigenizing Education in Canada (pp. 51-72). Canadian Scholars.

Kanu, Y. (2011). *Integrating Aboriginal perspectives into the school curriculum: Purposes, possibilities, and challenges*. University of Toronto Press.

Kennedy, D. (2017). *Legal Education and the Reproduction of Hierarchy: A Critical Edition*. New York University Press.

Kesserwan, K. (2018). *How can Indigenous knowledge shape our view of AI?* Policy Options. https://policyoptions.irpp.org/magazines/february-2018/how-can-indigenous-knowledge-shape-our-view-of-ai/

Compilation of References

Kimmerer, R. W. (2013). *Braiding sweetgrass: Indigenous wisdom, scientific knowledge and the teachings of plants*. Milkweed Editions.

King, L., & Schielmann, S. (2004). *The challenge of indigenous education: Practice and perspectives*. Paris: UNESCO. https://unesdoc.unesco.org/ark:/48223/pf0000134773

King, T. (2003). *The truth about stories: A Native narrative*. House of Anansi Press.

King, T. (Ed.). (1990). *All my relations: An anthology of contemporary Canadian Native prose*. McClelland & Stewart.

Kirkness, V.J., & Barnhardt, R. (1991). First Nations and higher education: The Four R's—respect, relevance, reciprocity, responsibility. *Journal of American Indian Education, 30*(3), 1–15.

Kirkness, V.J., & Barnhardt, R. (1991). First Nations and higher education: The four R's – Respect, relevance, reciprocity, responsibility. *Journal of American Indian Education, 30*(3), 1–15.

Kirkness, V. J., & Barnhardt, R. (2001). First Nations and higher education: The four R's – Respect, relevance, reciprocity, responsibility. In R. Hayhoe & J. Pan (Eds.), *Knowledge across cultures: A contribution to dialogue among civilizations* (pp. 1–21). Comparative Education Research Centre, University of Hong Kong. https://www.uaf.edu/ankn/publications/collective-works-of-ray-b/Four-Rs-2nd-Ed.pdf

Kite, S. (2020). How to build anything ethically. In *Indigenous Protocol and Artificial Intelligence Position Paper* (pp. 75-84.). Spectrum. https://spectrum.library.concordia.ca/id/eprint/986506/7/Indigenous_Protocol_and_AI_2020.pdf

Knott, H. (2018). Violence and extraction stories from the oil fields. In K. Anderson, M. Campbell, & C. Belcourt (Eds.), Keetsahnak: Our missing and murdered Indigenous sisters (pp. 147-159). University of Alberta Press.

Kovach, M. (2021). *Indigenous methodologies: characteristics, conversations and contexts* (2nd ed.). University of Toronto Press.

Kovach, M. (2021). *Indigenous methodologies: Characteristics, conversations, and contexts*. University of Toronto Press.

Ladson-Billings, G. (1995). But That's Just Good Teaching! The Case for Culturally Relevant Pedagogy. *Theory into Practice, 34*(3), 159–165. doi:10.1080/00405849509543675

Lake, J., & Atkins, H. (2021). *Facilitating Online Learning with the 5R's: Embedding Indigenous Pedagogy into the Online Space* [Master of Education project, University of Victoria]. UVicSpace. http://hdl.handle.net/1828/12915

Lavallee, L. (2009). Practical application of an Indigenous research framework and two qualitative Indigenous research methods: Sharing circles and Anishnaabe symbol-based reflection. *International Journal of Qualitative Methods, 8*(1), 21–40. https://journals.sagepub.com/doi/10.1177/160940690900800103. doi:10.1177/160940690900800103

Lavallee, L. (2022). Is Decolonization possible in the Academy. In S. Cote-Meek & T. Moeke-Pickering (Eds.), *Decolonizing and Indigenizing education in Canada* (pp. 117–134). Canadian Scholars.

Lewis, J. E. (2020). *Indigenous Protocol and Artificial Intelligence.* Indigenous Protocol and Artificial Intelligence Position Paper. https://spectrum.library.concordia.ca/id/eprint/986506/7/Indigenous_Protocol_and_AI_2020.pdf

Lindberg, D. (2018). Miyo Nêhiyâwiwin (Beautiful Creeness): Ceremonial Aesthetics and Nêhiyaw Legal Pedagogy. *Indigenous Law Journal at the University of Toronto Faculty of Law*, *16*(1), 51–65.

Lindberg, T. (1997). What Do You Call an Indian Woman with a Law Degree? Nine Aboriginal Women at the University of Saskatchewan College of Law Speak Out. *Canadian Journal of Women and the Law*, *9*(2), 301–355.

Little Bear, L. (2009). Jagged worlds colliding. In M. Battiste (Ed.), *Reclaiming Indigenous voice and vision* (pp. 77–85). UBC Press.

Lockey, A., Conaghan, P., Bland, A., & Astin, F. (2021). Educational theory and its application to advanced life support courses: A narrative review. *Resuscitation Plus*, *5*, 100053. doi:10.1016/j.resplu.2020.100053 PMID:34223327

Lomawaima, K. T. (2000). Tribal sovereigns. *Harvard Educational Review*, *70*(1), 1–21. doi:10.17763/haer.70.1.b133t0976714n73r

Lombrozo, T. (2017). *Technology can be a tool, a teacher, a trickster.* NPR Cosmos and Culture. https://www.npr.org/sections/13.7/2017/07/17/537667988/technology-can-be-a-tool-a-teacher-a-trickster

Loveless, A. (2011). Technology, pedagogy and education: Reflections on the accomplishment of what teachers know, do and believe in a digital age. *Technology, Pedagogy and Education*, *20*(3), 301–316. doi:10.1080/1475939X.2011.610931

Lussier, D. (2021). *Law with Heart and Beadwork: Decolonizing Legal Education, Developing Indigenous Legal Pedagogy, and Hearing Community* [Unpublished Doctoral Dissertation]. University of Ottawa.

Lussier, D. (2021). A Legal Love Letter to My Children: If These Beads Could Talk. *Indigenous Law Journal at the University of Toronto Faculty of Law*, *18*(1), 1–26.

Macdougall, B. (2010). *One of the family: Metis culture in nineteenth- century northwestern Saskatchewan.* UBC Press.

Malaguzzi, L. (1994). Your image of the child: Where teaching begins. *Child Care Information Exchange*, 52–52.

Compilation of References

Manitoba Trauma Information and Education Centre. (2013). *The Trauma-Informed Toolkit*. Manitoba Trauma Information and Education Centre. https://trauma-informed.ca/wp-content/uploads/2023/04/trauma-informed_toolkit_v07-1.pdf

Manitowabi, S. (2018). *Historical and contemporary realities: Movement towards reconciliation*. Pressbooks. https://ecampusontario.pressbooks.pub/movementtowardsreconciliation

Maracle, L. (2015). *Memory serves oratories*. NeWest.

Marlow, K. (2022). *How AI and immersive technology are being used to revitalize Indigenous languages*. CBC News. https://www.cbc.ca/news/canada/british-columbia/bc-indigenous-language-preservation-ai-1.6332285

Mashford-Pringle, A., & Shawanda, A. (2023). Using the Medicine Wheel as theory, conceptual framework, analysis, and evaluation tool in health research. *Elsevier. SSM. Qualitative Research in Health*, *3*, 100251. doi:10.1016/j.ssmqr.2023.100251

McGuire, P. (2022). Gii Aanikoobijigan Mindimooyehn: Decolonizing views of Anishinaabekwe. In S. Cote-Meek & T. Moeke-Pickering (Eds.), *Decolonizing and Indigenizing education in Canada* (pp. 19–30). Canadian Scholars.

McMaster, G. (2020). *Creating ethical AI from Indigenous perspectives*. University of Alberta. https://www.ualberta.ca/folio/2020/10/creating-ethical-ai-from-indigenous-perspectives.html

McMillan, T. (2023). Anishinaabe Values and Servant Leadership: A Two-Eyed Seeing Approach. *The Journal of Values Based Leadership*, *16*(1), 11. https://scholar.valpo.edu/cgi/viewcontent.cgi?article=1428&context=jvbl

Meyer, M. A. (2013). Holographic epistemology: Native common sense. *China Media Research*, *9*(2), 94–101.

Mignolo, W. D. (2009). Epistemic disobedience, independent thought and decolonial freedom. *Theory, Culture & Society*, *26*(7-8), 159–181. doi:10.1177/0263276409349275

Mignolo, W. D. (2014). Spirit out of bounds returns to the East: The closing of the social sciences and the opening of independent thoughts. *Current Sociology*, *62*(4), 584–602. doi:10.1177/0011392114524513

Moeke-Pickering, T. M. (2010). *Decolonisation as a social change framework and its impact on the development of Indigenous-based curricula for Helping Professionals in mainstream Tertiary Education Organisations* [Doctoral thesis, The University of Waikato]. The University of Waikato Research Comms. https://hdl.handle.net/10289/4148

Moeke-Pickering, T. (2020). The Future for Indigenous Education: How Social Media Is Changing Our Relationships in the Academy. In S. Cote-Meek & T. Moeke-Pickering (Eds.), *Decolonizing and indigenizing education in Canada* (pp. 267–277). Canadian Scholars.

Mona, C. (2017, September 19). *1 needle & 2 needle flat stitch beading techniques*. [Video]. Youtube. https://www.youtube.com/watch?v=smrfuN-fBT4

Montalvo, M. G. (2021). *Indigenous Technologies at the Berkeley Center for New Media*. Berkeley Center for New Media. http://bcnm.berkeley.edu/resources/3997/indigenous-technologies

Monteiro, L. (2020, Sept 1). Structural inequity runs de ep in Canadian institutions, panel says. *The Record*. https://www.therecord.com/news/waterloo-region/2020/09/01/structural-inequity-runs-deep-in-canadian-institutions-panel-says.html

Moore, S. (2017). *Trickster Chases the Tale of Education*. McGill-Queen's University Press.

Mueller, J. 7 Nickel, J. (Eds.) (2017). *Globalization and Diversity: What Does It Mean for Teacher Education in Canada?* Canadian Association for Teacher Education. https://cate-acfe.ca/wp-content/uploads/2019/11/Final-Working-Conference-Book-Halifax-2017.pdf

Muhammad, G. (2023). *Unearthing joy: A guide to culturally and historically responsive curriculum and instruction*. Scholastic Books.

Nabigon, H. (2006). *The hollow tree: Fighting addiction with traditional Native healing*. McGill-Queens University Press. doi:10.1515/9780773576254

Napier, K. (2013, November 28). *Reg Crowshoe - Venue, Action, Language and Song* [Video]. Youtube. https://www.youtube.com/watch?v=HDOrB6RvdlU

National Collaborating Centre for Indigenous Health. (2017). *Education as a social determinant of First Nations, Inuit, and Metis Health*. NCCIH. https://www.nccih.ca/495/Education_as_a_social_determinant_of_First_Nations,_Inuit_and_M%C3%A9tis_health.nccih?id=226

National Disability Authority. (2017). *History of UD*. Centre for Excellence in Universal Design. https://universaldesign.ie/what-is-universal-design/history-of-ud/

Neegan, E. (2005). Excuse me: Who are the first peoples of Canada? A historical analysis of Aboriginal education in Canada then and now. *International Journal of Inclusive Education*, 9(1), 3–15. doi:10.1080/1360311042000299757

Nelson, M. K. (Ed.). (2008). *Original instructions: Indigenous teachings for a sustainable future*. Bear & Company.

Networks of Inquiry and Indigenous Education. (2022). *Homepage: The Networks*. NOIIE. https://noiie.ca/about-us/

Nikolopoulou, K., Gialamas, V., & Lavidas, K. (2022). Mobile learning-technology barriers in school education: Teachers' views. *Technology, Pedagogy and Education*, 1–16. doi:10.1080/1475939X.2022.2121314

Noddings, N. (2012). The caring relation in teaching. *Oxford Review of Education*, 38(6), 771–781. doi:10.1080/03054985.2012.745047

O'Connor, K. (2013). *The use of ICTs and e-learning in Indigenous education*. Canadian eLearning Network. https://k12sotn.ca/papers/the-use-of-icts-and-e-learning-in-indigenous-education/

Compilation of References

Ocampo, M. G. (2022). We Deserve to Thrive: Transforming the Social Work Academy to Better Support Black, Indigenous, and Person of Color (BIPOC) Doctoral Students. *Advances in Social Work*, *22*(2), 703–719. doi:10.18060/24987

Ontario College of Teachers. (2016). *Exploring the ethical standards for the teaching profession through Anishinaabe art* [booklet]. OCT. https://www.oct.ca/-/media/PDF/Exploring%20Ethical%20Standards%20through%20Anishinaabe%20Art/2015%20Ethical%20Stndrds%20and%20Anishinaabe%20Art_en%20web_accssble.pdf

Ontario Ministry of Education. (2016). *The kindergarten program*. Queen's Printer of Ontario.

Otis, D. (2023, January 17). In the search for unmarked graves at Residential School sites, what do Radar 'anomalies' mean? *CTVNews*. https://www.ctvnews.ca/canada/in-the-search-for-unmarked-graves-at-residential-school-sites-what-do-radar-anomalies-mean-1.6233149

Papp, T. A. (2020). A Canadian study of coming full circle to traditional Aboriginal pedagogy: A pedagogy for the 21st Century. *Diaspora, Indigenous, and Minority Education*, *14*(1), 25–42. doi:10.1080/15595692.2019.1652587

Paris, D., & Alim, H. S. (2017). Culturally sustaining pedagogies: Teaching and learning for justice in a changing world. *The Journal of Teaching and Learning*, *11*(1), 35–37. doi:10.22329/jtl.v11i1.4987

Pedagogy. (2020). Merriam-Webster. https://www.merriam-webster.com/dictionary/pedagogy

Peltier, S. (2014). Assessing Anishinaabe children's narratives: An ethnographic exploration of Elders' perspectives. *Canadian Journal of Speech-language Pathology and Audiology : CJSLPA = Revue Canadienne d'Orthophonie et d'Audiologie : RCOA*, *38*(2), 174–193.

Peltier, S. (2022). Seven Directions early learning for Indigenous land literacy wisdom. In S. S. Peterson & N. Friedrich (Eds.), *The role of play and place in young children's language and literacy* (pp. 33–51). University of Toronto Press. doi:10.3138/9781487529239-004

Penak, N. (2018). A story pathway: Restoring wholeness in the research process. In McGregor, D., Restoule, J-P., & Johnston, R. (Eds.), Indigenous research: Theories, practices, and relationships (pp. 257-270). Canadian Scholars.

Perreault, S. (2022, July 19). *Victimization of First Nations people, Métis and Inuit in Canada. (Catalogue no. 85-002-X)*. Statistics Canada. https://www150.statcan.gc.ca/n1/pub/85-002-x/2022001/article/00012-eng.htm

Pete, S. (2017, October 15). *Think Indigenous*. [Audio podcast]. Podtail. https://podtail.com/en/podcast/think-indigenous/think-indigenous-shauneen-pete/

Poitras Pratt, Y., & Danyluk, P. J.Poitras Pratt. (2019). Exploring reconciliatory pedagogy and its possibilities through educator-led praxis. *The Canadian Journal for the Scholarship of Teaching and Learning*, *10*(3), 1–16. doi:10.5206/cjsotl-rcacea.2019.3.9479

Popp, J. (2018). How Indigenous knowledge advances modern science and technology. *The Conversation.* https://theconversation.com/how-indigenous-knowledge-advances-modern-science-and-technology-89351

Prete, T. (2019). Beadworking as an Indigenous Research Paradigm. *Art/Research International 4*(1), 28-57.

Project Zero & Reggio Children. (2001). *Making learning visible: Children as individual and group learners.* Reggio Children.

Purdue Online. (n.d.). *The evolution of technology in the classroom.* Purdue University. https://online.purdue.edu/blog/education/evolution-technology-classroom

Purnava, J. (2020, August 5). The role of technology in Canadian classrooms. *INKspire.* https://inkspire.org/post/the-role-of-technology-in-canadian-classrooms/-MCe6KZyeU-4tTnYheH9

Purton, F., Styres, S., & Kempf, A. (2020). Speaking Back to the Institution: Teacher Education Programs as Sites of Possibility. In S. Cote-Meek & T. Moeke-Pickering (Eds.), *Decolonizing and Indigenizing Education in Canada* (pp. 175–192). Canadian Scholars.

Quinless, J. M. (2022). *Decolonizing data: Unsettling conversations about social research methods.* University of Toronto Press. doi:10.3138/9781487530099

R v. Sparrow, 1 Canadian Supreme Court Ruling 1075, 70 DLR (4th) 385 (1990).

Raso, F. A., Hilligoss, H., Krishnamurthy, V., Bavitz, C., & Kim, L. (2018). Artificial intelligence & human rights: Opportunities & risks. *Berkman Klein Center Research Publication,* (2018-6). http://dx.doi.org/ doi:10.2139/ssrn.3259344

Ray, L. (2015). *Mshkikenh Ikwe Niin (I am Turtle Woman): The Transformative Role of Anishinaabe Women's Knowledge in Graduate Research* [Doctoral Dissertation, Trent University]. Trent University Library and Archives. https://digitalcollections.trentu.ca/objects/etd-513

Ray, L., & Cormier, P. (2012). Killing the Weendigo with Maple Syrup: Anishinaabe Pedagogy and Post-Secondary Research. *Canadian Journal of Native Education, 35*(1), 163–176.

Regan, P. (2010). *Unsettling the settler within: Indian residential schools, truth telling, and reconciliation in Canada.* ubc Press.

Reid, C. (2003). Studying cultural diversity using information and communication technologies in teacher education: Pedagogy, power and literacy. *Technology, Pedagogy and Education, 12*(3), 345–360. doi:10.1080/14759390300200163

Restoule, J.P., & Chaw-win-is. (2017). *Old ways are the new way forward: How Indigenous pedagogy can benefit everyone.* The Canadian Commission for UNESCO's IdeaLab. http://lss.yukonschools.ca/uploads/4/5/5/0/45508033/20171026_old_ways_are_the_new_way_forward_how_indigenous_pedagogy_can_benefit_everyone_final.pdf

Compilation of References

Restoule, J. P. (2017). Where Indigenous knowledge lives: Bringing Indigenous perspectives to online learning environments. In E. A. McKinley & L. T. Smith (Eds.), *Handbook of Indigenous education*. Springer.

Restoule, J. P. (2018). Where Indigenous Knowledge Lives: Bringing Indigenous Perspectives to Online Learning Environments. In E. McKinley & L. Smith (Eds.), *Handbook of Indigenous Education*. Springer., doi:10.1007/978-981-10-1839-8_62-1

Rice, C., Dion, S. D., Fowlie, H., & Breen, A. (2020). Identifying and working through settler ignorance. *Critical Studies in Education*, *63*(1), 15–30. doi:10.1080/17508487.2020.1830818

Rice, J. (2007). Icelandic charity donations: Reciprocity reconsidered. *Ethnology*, *46*(1), 1–7. https://www.proquest.com/docview/205148513?pq-origsite=gscholar&fromopenview=true

Riley, T., Monk, S., & VanIssum, H. (2019). Barriers and breakthroughs: Engaging in socially just ways towards issues of indigeneity, identity, and whiteness in teacher education. *Whiteness and Education*, *4*(1), 88–107. doi:10.1080/23793406.2019.1625283

Rinaldi, C. (2004). The relationship between documentation and assessment. *Innovations in Early Education: The International Reggio Exchange.*, *11*(1), 1–4.

Rinaldi, C. (2006). *In dialogue with Reggio Emilia: Listening, researching and learning*. Routledge.

Rios, J. A., Ling, G., Pugh, R., Becker, D., & Bacall, A. (2020). Identifying critical 21st-century skills for workplace success: A content analysis of job advertisements. *Educational Researcher*, *49*(2), 80–89. doi:10.3102/0013189X19890600

Robertson, K., & Navarro, J. (2020). *Beading as Medicine (Volume 1)*. Kimberley Dawn Robertson. https://www.kimberlydawnrobertson.com/product-page/beading-as-medicine-vol-1-zine

Robertson, K., & Navarro, J. (2020). *Beading as Medicine (Volume 2)*. Kimberley Dawn Robertson. https://www.kimberlydawnrobertson.com/product-page/beading-as-medicine-vol-2-zine

Rosborough, T., Rorick, C. L., & Urbanczyk, S. (2017). Beautiful words: Enriching and Indigenizing Kwak'wala revitalization through understandings of linguistic structure. *Canadian Modern Language Review*, *73*(4), 425–437. doi:10.3138/cmlr.4059

Rose, D. (2001). Universal Design for Learning. *Journal of Special Education Technology*, *16*(2), 66–67. doi:10.1177/016264340101600208

Rowe, R. K., Bull, J. R., & Walker, J. D. (2020). Indigenous self-determination and data governance in the Canadian policy context. In M. Walter, T. Kukutai, S. R. Carroll, & D. Rodriguez-Lonebear (Eds.), *Indigenous data sovereignty and policy* (pp. 81–98). Routledge Publishing. doi:10.4324/9780429273957-6

Rowe, R. K., Rowat, J., & Walker, J. D. (2020). First Nations' survivance and sovereignty in Canada during a time of COVID-19. *American Indian Culture and Research Journal*, *44*(2), 89–99. doi:10.17953/aicrj.44.2.rowe_rowat_walker

Royal Commission on Aboriginal Peoples. (1993). *Ethical Guidelines for Research*. The Commission.

Running Wolf V. Arista N. (2020). Indigenous Protocols in Action. *Indigenous Protocol and Artificial Intelligence Position Paper* (pp. 93-101). doi:10.11573/spectrum.library.concordia.ca.00986506

San Pedro, T. J. (2015). Silence as Shields: Agency and Resistances among Native American Students in the Urban Southwest. *Research in the Teaching of English, 50*(2), 132–153.

Santos, B. S. (2018). *The end of the cognitive empire: The coming of age of epistemologies of the South*. Duke University Press. doi:10.1215/9781478002000

Saysewahum (McAdam S.). (2015). *Nationhood Interrupted: Revitalizing Nêhiyaw Legal Systems*. Purich Publishing.

Scofield, G. A., Briley, A., & Farrell Racette, S. (2011). *Wapikwaniy: A Beginner's Guide to Metis Floral Beadwork*. Gabriel Dumont Institute.

Scott, B. R. (2020). Reconciliation Through Métissage. In S. Cote-Meek & T. Moeke-Pickering (Eds.), *Decolonizing and Indigenizing Education in Canada* (pp. 31–50). Canadian Scholars.

Serafini, F. W. (2002). Dismantling the factory model of assessment. *Reading & Writing Quarterly, 18*(1), 67–85. doi:10.1080/105735602753386342

Shawanda, A. (2020). Baawaajige: Exploring dreams as academic references. *Turtle Island Journal of Indigenous Health, 1*(1), 37–47. doi:10.33137/tijih.v1i1.34020

Shepherd, L. (2016, May 25). The Flower Beadwork People. *Parks Canada*. [Video]. Youtube. www.youtube.com/watch?v= 54ipBLZJ6L4

Simard, E., & Blight, S. (2011). Developing a culturally restorative approach to aboriginal child and youth development: Transitions to adulthood. *First Peoples Child & Family Review, 6*(1), 28–55. doi:10.7202/1068895ar

Simcoe, J., Allan, B., Perreault, A., Chenoweth, J., Biin, D., Hobenshield, S., Ormiston, T., Hardman, S. A., Lacerte, L., Wright, L., & Wilson, J. (2018, September 5). *Holding space and humility for other ways of knowing and being*. Pulling Together A Guide for Teachers and Instructors. https://opentextbc.ca/indigenizationinstructors/chapter/holding-space-and-humility-for-other-ways-of-knowing-and-being/

Simpson, L. (2013). *The Gift is in The Making Anishinaabeg Stories*. High Water Press. https://www.portageandmainpress.com/content/download/17792/220444/version/1/file/9781553793762_TheGiftisintheMaking_excerpt.pdf

Simpson, L. (2011). *Dancing on Our Turtle's Back*. Arbeiter Ring Press.

Simpson, L. B. (2014). Land as pedagogy: Nishnaabeg intelligence and rebellious transformation. *Decolonization, 3*(4), 1–25. https://doi.org/http://whereareyouquetzalcoatl.com/mesofigurineproject/EthnicAndIndigenousStudiesArticles/Simpson2014.pdf

Compilation of References

Simpson, L. B. (2017). *As we have always done: Indigenous freedom through radical resistance.* University of Minnesota Press. doi:10.5749/j.ctt1pwt77c

Smith, G. H. (2003, October). *Indigenous struggle for the transformation of education and schooling* [Keynote speech]. The Alaskan Federation of Natives (AFN) convention, Anchorage, Alaska, US. http://www.ankn.uaf.edu/curriculum/Articles/GrahamSmith/

Smith, T. (2014). *An Unsettling Journey: White Settler Women Teaching Treaty in Saskatchewan* [Master of Education thesis, University of Regina]. Indigenous Studies Portal. https://ourspace.uregina.ca/bitstream/handle/10294/5830/Smith_Tamara_200231376_MED_C&I_Spring2014.pdf

Smith, L. T. (2019). Expanding the Indignous Education Agenda: A Forward. In H. Tomlins-Jahnke, S. Styres, S. Lilley, & D. Zinga (Eds.), *Indigenous Education: New Directions in Theory and Practice* (pp. ix–xi). University of Alberta Press.

Smith, L. T. (2021). *Decolonizing methodologies: Research and Indigenous peoples* (3rd ed.). Zed Books. doi:10.5040/9781350225282

Spyrou, S. (2018). *Disclosing childhoods: Research and knowledge production for a critical childhood studies.* Palgrave Macmillan. doi:10.1057/978-1-137-47904-4

Statistics Canada. (2017). *Census in brief: The Aboriginal languages of First Nations people, Métis and Inuit.* Catalogue no. 98-200-X2016022. https://www12.statcan.gc.ca/census-recensement/2016/as-sa/98-200-x/2016022/98-200-x2016022-eng.pdf

Statistics Canada. (2019, July 19). *High school completion rate by sex and selected demographic characteristics, inactive.* [Data set] https://www150.statcan.gc.ca/t1/tbl1/en/tv.action?pid=3710014701&pickMembers%5B0%5D=1.1

Stefani, G. (2021). *Indigenous Leaders at the Frontlines of Environmental Injustice and Solutions.* NRDC. https://www.nrdc.org/experts/giulia-cs-good-stefani/indigenous-leaders-frontlines-environmental-injustice-and-solutions

Steinhauer, E., Cardinal, T., Higgins, M., Steinhauer, N., Steinhauer, P., Underwood, M., Wolfe, A., & Cardinal, B. (2020). Thinking with Kihkipiw: Exploring an Indigenous Theory of Assessment and Evaluation for Teacher Education. In S. Cote-Meek & T. Moeke-Pickering (Eds.), *Decolonizing and Indigenizing Education in Canada* (pp. 73–90). Canadian Scholars.

Styres, S. (2017). *Pathways for remembering and recognizing Indigenous thought in education: philosophies of Iethi'nihsténha Ohwentsia'kékha (land).* University of Toronto Press.

Swanson, J. A. (2016). *The Impact of Technology Integration upon Collegiate Pedagogy from the Lens of Multiple Disciplines.* International Association for Development of the Information Society.

Tanaka, M. T. D. (2016). *Learning and Teaching Together: Weaving Indigenous Ways of Knowing into Education.* UBC Press.

Taylor, D. (2003). *The archive and the repertoire: Performing cultural memory in the Americas.* Duke University Press.

Tessaro, D., & Restoule, J. P. (2022). Indigenous pedagogies and online learning environments: A massive open online course case study. *Alternative, 18*(1), 182–191. doi:10.1177/11771801221089685

Toulouse, P. (2011). *Achieving Aboriginal student success: A guide for K to 8 classrooms.* Portage & Main Press.

Toulouse, P. (2016). *What matters in Indigenous education: Implementing a vision committed to holism, diversity and engagement.* People for Education.

Trent University. (2014). *Trent University: Indigenous Studies Ph.D. Program Student Handbook 2014–2015.* Trent University.

Truth and Reconciliation Commission of Canada. (2012). *An interim report.* Library and Archives Canada.

Truth and Reconciliation Commission of Canada. (2015). *Calls to action.* Government of Canada. https://www2.gov.bc.ca/assets/gov/british-columbians-our-governments/indigenous-people/aboriginal-peoples-documents/calls_to_action_english2.pdf

Truth and Reconciliation Commission of Canada. (2015). *Calls to action.* TRCC. https://www2.gov.bc.ca/assets/gov/british-columbians-our-governments/indigenous-people/aboriginal-peoples-documents/calls_to_action_english2.pdf

Truth and Reconciliation Commission of Canada. (2015). *Canada's Residential Schools: The Final Report of the Truth and Reconciliation Commission of Canada* (Vol. 1). McGill-Queen's Press-MQUP.

Truth and Reconciliation Commission of Canada. (2015, July 23). Final report of the truth and reconciliation commission of Canada: Honouring the truth, reconciling for the future. *Truth and Reconciliation Commission of Canada.* James Lorimer & Company.

Truth and Reconciliation Commission of Canada. (2015a). *Honouring the truth, reconciling for the future: Summary of the final report of the Truth and Reconciliation Commission of Canada.* The Commission.

Truth and Reconciliation Commission of Canada. (2015b). *Truth and Reconciliation Commission of Canada: Calls to action.* The Commission.

Truth and Reconciliation Commission. (2015). *Honouring the Truth, Reconciling for the Future: Summary of the Final Report of the Truth and Reconciliation Commission of Canada.* UBC. https://irsi.ubc.ca/sites/default/files/inline-files/Executive_Summary_English_Web.pdf

Compilation of References

Tsosie, R. L., Grant, A. D., Harrington, J., Wu, K., Thomas, A., Chase, S., Barnett, D., Beaumont Hill, S., Belcourt, A., Brown, B., & Plenty Sweetgrass, R. (2022, Summer). The six Rs of Indigenous research. *Journal of American Indian Higher Education*, *33*(4). https://tribalcollegejournal.org/the-six-rs-of-indigenous-research/

Tuck, E., & Yang, K. W. (2014). R-words: Refusing research. In D. Paris & M.T. Winn (Eds). Humanizing Research: Decolonizing Qualitative Inquiry with Youth and Communities (pp. 213–237). Sage.

Tuck, E., McCoy, K., & McKenzie, M. (2014). Land education: Indigenous, post-colonial, and decolonizing perspectives on place and environmental education research. *Environmental Education Research*, *20*(1), 1–23. doi:10.1080/13504622.2013.877708

Tuck, E., & Yang, W. (2012). Decolonization is not a metaphor. *Decolonization*, *1*(1), 1–40.

Turner, A. (2013). *Honouring Earth*. Assembly of First Nations. https://www.afn.ca/honoring-earth/

Turner, T., & Wilson, D. G. (2010). Reflections on documentation: A discussion with thought leaders from Reggio Emilia. *Theory into Practice*, *49*(1), 5–13. doi:10.1080/00405840903435493

Two Row Wampum– Guswenta. (2020 June 14). *Onondaga Nation: People of the Hills*. Onondaga Nation. https://www.onondaganation.org/culture

United Nations Convention on the Rights of Persons with Disabilities. (2006). *Convention on the Rights of Persons with Disabilities.* UN. https://www.un.org/development/desa/disabilities/convention-on-the-rights-of-persons-with-disabilities.html

United Nations. (2008). *United Nations declaration on the rights of Indigenous People (UNDRIP)*. UN. https://www.un.org/esa/socdev/unpfii/documents/DRIPS_en.pdf

United Nations. (2022). *When Mother Earth sends us a message*. UN. https://www.un.org/en/observances/earth-day

United Nations. (n.d.). *Climate Change*. Department of Economic and Social Affairs. https://www.un.org/development/desa/indigenouspeoples/climate-change.html

Universities Canada. (2015). *Universities Canada principles on Indigenous education*. Universities Canada. https://www.univcan.ca/media-room/media-releases/universities-canada-principles-on-indigenous-education/

Vizenor, G. (1999). *Manifest manners: Narratives on postindian survivance*. University of Nebraska Press.

Vowel, C. (2015). *Indigenous Writes: A Guide to First Nations, Métis & Inuit Issues in Canada*. Portage & Main Press.

Wabie, J., London, T., & Pegahmagabow, J. (2021). Land-based learning journey. *Journal of Indigenous Social Development*, *10*(1), 50–80. https://journalhosting.ucalgary.ca/index.php/jisd/issue/view/5258

Wagamese, R. (2016). *Embers: one Ojibway's meditations*. Douglas & McIntyre.

Walkem, A. (2004). *Indigenous Peoples Water Rights: Challenges and Opportunities in an Era of Increased North American Integration*. University of Victoria. https://www.uvic.ca/research/centres/globalstudies/assets/docs/publications/IndigenousPeoplesWaterRights.pdf

Wallerstein, I. (1996). Open the social sciences. *Items: Social Science Research Council, 50*(1), 1–6.

Walter, M. (2016). Data politics and Indigenous representation in Australian statistics. In T. Kukutai & J. Taylor (Eds.), *Indigenous data sovereignty: Toward an agenda* (pp. 79–98). Australian National University Press. doi:10.22459/CAEPR38.11.2016.05

Warrior, R. (2005). *The people and the word: Reading Native nonfiction*. University of Minnesota Press.

Water Policy and Governance Group. (2010). *Water Challenges and Solutions in First Nations Communities*. Social Sciences and Humanities Research Council of Canada. https://uwaterloo.ca/water-policy-and-governance-group/sites/ca.water-policy-

Watkins, E. K. (2020). *Technology in Schools – A Tool and a Strategy*. People for Education. https://peopleforeducation.ca/wp-content/uploads/2020/05/Technology-In-Schools-Final-May-5.pdf

Weenie, A. (2020). Askiy Kiskinwahama-ke-wina: Reclaiming Land-Based Pedagogies in the Academy. In S. Cote-Meek & T. Moeke-Pickering (Eds.), *Decolonizing and Indigenizing Education in Canada* (pp. 3–18). Canadian Scholars.

Weenie, A. (2022). Askiy Kiskinwahamakewina: Reclaiming land-based pedagogies in the Academy. In S. Cote-Meek & T. Moeke-Pickering (Eds.), *Decolonizing and Indigenizing education in Canada* (pp. 3–18). Canadian Scholars.

Wemigwans, J. (2018). *A digital bundle: Protecting and promoting Indigenous Knowledge*. University of Regina Press.

Wesley-Esquimaux, C. C., & Smolewski, M. (2004). Historic trauma and Aboriginal healing. *Ottawa: Aboriginal Healing Foundation, 3*, 1-99. https://epub.sub.uni-hamburg.de/epub/volltexte/2009/2903/pdf/historic_trauma.pdf

Whaanga, H. (2020). AI: a new (r)evolution or the new colonizer for Indigenous peoples? *Indigenous AI*, 34-38. https://hdl.handle.net/10289/15164

Wheeler, R., & Swords, R. (2004). Codeswitching transforms the dialectally diverse classroom. *Language Arts, 81*(6), 470–480.

Wien, C. A., Guyevskey, V., & Berdoussis, N. (2011). Learning to document in Reggio-inspired education. *Early Childhood Research & Practice, 13*(2), 1–12.

Wildcat, M., McDonald, M., Irlbacher-Fox, S., & Coulthard, G. (2014). Learning from the land: Indigenous land based pedagogy and decolonization. *Decolonization, 3*(3), i–xv.

Wilson, S. (2008). *Research is ceremony*. Fernwood Publishing.

Compilation of References

Wilson, S. (2008). *Research is Ceremony: Indigenous Research Methods*. Fernwood Publishing.

Wilson, S. (2020). *Research is ceremony: Indigenous research methods*. Fernwood publishing.

Windchief, S., & San Pedro, T. (2019). *Applying Indigenous research methods*. Routledge. doi:10.4324/9781315169811

Wong, D. (2022, September 27). Truth and Reconciliation Commission Calls to Action for Education. *People for Education*. https://peopleforeducation.ca/calls-to-action-for-education/

Wong, J. (2023, February 11). As more high schools add Indigenous-focused compulsory courses, some warn against a siloed approach. *CBC News*. https://www.cbc.ca/news/canada/edu-indigenous-compulsory-learning-1.6738509

Wood, J., Daviau, C., & Daviau, N. (2018). *Anishinaabemowin revival program*. Indspire Research Report.

Wood, J., Daviau, C., & Gunner, B. (2019). *Enhancing Cree language with culture*. Indspire Research Report.

Wood, J. (2022). The importance of the land, language, culture, identity and learning in relation for Indigenous children. In S. S. Peterson & N. Friedrich (Eds.), *The role of play and place in young children's language and literacy* (pp. 109–226). University of Toronto Press. doi:10.3138/9781487529239-009

Wood, J., & Speir, S. (2013). *Assessment as attributing value: Documentation and assessment in early learning*. Ministry of Education, Assessment and Policy Branch.

Woodward, S. (2017). *Universal Design 101*. Rick Hansen Foundation. https://www.rickhansen.com/news-stories/blog/universal-design-101

Yellow Bird, M. J. (1995). Spirituality in First Nations story telling: A Sahnish-Hidatsa approach to narrative. *Reflections: Narratives of Professional Helping*, *1*(4), 65–72.

Yu, J., & Couldry, N. (2022). Education as a domain of natural data extraction: Analysing corporate discourse about educational tracking. *Information Communication and Society*, *25*(1), 127–144. doi:10.1080/1369118X.2020.1764604

About the Contributors

Sheila Cote-Meek is Anishinaabe from the Teme-Augama Anishnabai. She is currently the Director, Indigenous Educational Studies Programs at Brock University and the former Vice-President, Equity, People and Culture at York University where she headed a new division that includes the Centre for Human Rights, Equity and Inclusion, Human Resources and Labour Relations. Prior to this she was Associate Vice-President, Academic and Indigenous Programs at Laurentian University where she led university-wide Indigenous initiatives. She played a lead role in several Indigenous initiatives including for example, increasing the number of Indigenous scholars, the creation of the Indigenous Sharing and Learning Centre, the Master of Indigenous Relations program and the Maamwizing Indigenous Research Institute. She also worked extensively on the faculty relations portfolio in collaboration with Human Resources and the Provost Office. Dr. Cote-Meek holds a PhD in Sociology and Equity Studies from the University of Toronto and is author of Colonized Classrooms – Racism, Trauma and Resistance in Post-Secondary Education (2014), lead editor of Decolonizing and Indigenizing Education in Canada (2020) and co-editor of Critical Reflections and Politics on Advancing Women in the Academy (2020). She is an active researcher and has extensive experience working on equity and inclusion in higher education including substantive experience working with Indigenous communities nationally on social justice and education issues. Dr. Cote-Meek has a strong history of building relationships that provide synergistic opportunities to advance institutions, and she is committed to working toward accessible higher education for all.

Taima Moeke-Pickering is a Maori of the Ngati Pukeko and Tuhoe tribes. She is a full professor in the School of Indigenous Relations at Laurentian University where she teaches courses on Indigenous research methodologies, international Indigenous issues, and United Nations and Indigenous social work. She has extensive experience working with international Indigenous communities, evaluative research, big data analysis, #MMIW and photovoice methodologies. She is co-editor of the book Decolonizing & Indigenizing Education in Canada (2020) and lead editor for the book Critical Reflections and Politics for Advancing Women in the Academy (2020).

***

About the Contributors

Marnie Anderson, BPHE, CSEP-CPT, is a proud Anishinabek, and mixed European woman and academic scholar. She is currently enrolled part-time in the Interdisciplinary Health graduate program at the School of Rural and Northern Health, Laurentian University. Academic background consists of Bachelor of Physical and Health Education at Laurentian and advanced diploma in Physical and Leisure Management from Cambrian Collage. Her academic interests lie in understanding environmental dispossession, First Nation marginalization and policy impacts on Indigenous holistic health in Northern Ontario First Nation communities. Following her Masters Marnie hopes to continue promoting wholisitc health and continue to advocate for the health of the environment.

Anastacia Chartrand is a Science Communications master's student and Graduate Student Association's Vice President of Advocacy for 2022-2023. She spends a lot of time at the Living With Lakes Centre as a student and as chair of the Environmental Sustainability Committee. Anastacia is dedicated to learning how we all can contribute to restoration efforts and climate change adaptation and mitigation, specifically learning about the interconnection of land and Indigeneity. She enjoys advocating for the environment and social equity.

Keri Cheechoo (she/her) is an Iskwew from Long Lake #58 First Nation. She is a mom, a Kookum, and scholar who resists and subverts systemic, structural and institutional racisms. A Cree scholar, she uses poetic pedagogy in a way that connects her spiritual aptitude for writing with educational research.

Sheila Cote-Meek is Anishinaabe from the Teme-Augama Anishnabai. She is currently the Director, Indigenous Educational Studies Programs at Brock University and the former Vice-President, Equity, People and Culture at York University where led a new division that includes the Centre for Human Rights, Equity and Inclusion, Human Resources and Labour Relations. Prior to this she was Associate Vice-President, Academic and Indigenous Programs at Laurentian University where she led university-wide Indigenous initiatives. She played a lead role in several Indigenous initiatives including for example, increasing the number of Indigenous scholars, the creation of the Indigenous Sharing and Learning Centre, the Master of Indigenous Relations program and the Maamwizing Indigenous Research Institute. She also worked extensively on the faculty relations portfolio in collaboration with Human Resources and the Provost Office. Dr. Cote-Meek holds a PhD in Sociology and Equity Studies from the University of Toronto and is author of Colonized Classrooms – Racism, Trauma and Resistance in Post-Secondary Education (2014), lead editor of Decolonizing and Indigenizing Education in Canada (2020) and co-editor of Critical Reflections and Politics on Advancing Women in the Academy

(2020). She is an active researcher and has extensive experience working on equity and inclusion in higher education including substantive experience working with Indigenous communities nationally on social justice and education issues. Dr. Cote-Meek has a strong history of building relationships that provide synergistic opportunities to advance institutions, and she is committed to working toward accessible higher education for all.

Arijana Haramincic is a graduate of the Indigenous BSW program at Laurentian University and has worked in a child welfare field for the past twenty years, in rural and urban settings throughout Ontario. In 2019 she moved to Iqaluit, Nunavut to work with the Department of Family Services. Her graduate research is focusing on Inuitizing and decolonizing child welfare system, the role of a non-Indigenous social worker in creation of ethical spaces through ethical relationships.

Jack Horne is from the W̱SÁNEĆ Nation at the southern tip of Vancouver Island. After a lengthy career in the performing arts, Jack returned to post-secondary education. He has earned a BA from the University of Victoria, and MA from York University, and is currently completing a PhD in Indigenous Studies from Trent University. Throughout his education journey Jack has strived to conduct his research and writing from a distinctly W̱SÁNEĆ/Indigenous perspective. Jack grew up on reserve and is deeply connected to W̱SÁNEĆ culture and traditions. HÍSW̱KE SIAM

Krista Keeley is an educator and professional learning facilitator at Regina Public Schools and the Saskatchewan Teachers' Federation with 12 years of experience teaching everything from Grade 4 English Language Arts to Grade 12 Visual Arts. Specializing in 21st century education and educational leadership, Krista uses that experience to bring transformative change into the classroom and beyond, hoping to support both learners and educators in transforming schools into positive learning spaces for all. Krista completed her Doctorate of Education in Educational Leadership at Western University where she solidified her passion for educational change. Within her 12 years of teaching experience she has recently garnered some recognition through the acceptance of the Saskatchewan Teachers' Federation Arbos award for significant contributions to education and the teaching profession in Saskatchewan. When she is not teaching, Krista is a writer, illustrator and publisher of children's books, a professional artist, and loves traveling and spending time with her cats.

Erin Keith is an Assistant Professor at St. Francis Xavier University (StFX). Her teaching and research focuses on inclusion, EDIAD literacy related to special education and mental health, culturally responsive and relevant pedagogies including engaging families and caregivers as partners, and supporting students through a strength-based lens using Nova Scotia's multi-tiered system of supports (MTSS) model. Erin uses a decolonizing praxis in her research methodologies inspired and guided by many Indigenous, Black, and racialized scholars. She obtained her Doctor of Education from Western University, her Master of Education from the State University of New York at Buffalo, and her Bachelor of Arts from Queen's University. As an Ontario Certified teacher, Erin has worked for over 16 years in public education primarily focused on Special Education roles such as ASD Itinerant, Special Needs Itinerant, Behaviour Support Itinerant, and in-school Special Education teacher. Erin's recent co-authored book entitled, Reframing Mental Health in Schools: Using Case Stories to Promote Global Dialogue shares stories of students from across the globe and how mental health is advocated within their country. She has also contributed and written book chapters on topics such as leadership in Early Childhood education, embracing math inquiry, 'whiteness' in principal leadership, among several others in development. Erin is a member of the Ontario Association of Mental Health Professionals. She has also written for EdCan Network, NAEYC, and been featured on TVOLearn. In addition to her scholarship, Erin partners and learns alongside teacher leaders from across the country including educators and administrators within various Regional Centres for Education in Nova Scotia. (Twitter: @DrErinKeith)

Simon Leslie is a settler who was born and raised in Hamilton, Ontario. Mr. Leslie is currently pursuing a Master's of Indigenous Relations degree at Laurentian University after a decade of teaching and administrating in First Nations communities across Quebec and Labrador. Mr. Leslie's current research is focused on the professional and personal experiences of non-Indigenous teachers employed in First Nations, Métis, and Inuit communities in Canada with the hope that the resultant findings can help inform how professional development is delivered to teachers nationally.

Danielle Lussier, Red River Métis and citizen of the Manitoba Métis Federation, was born and raised in the homeland of the Métis Nation on Treaty 1 Territory. She is a beadworker and mum to three young people who are growing up as visitors on the shores of Lake Ontario. An award-winning change leader, educator, and administrator, she is a passionate advocate and community builder who believes there is room for love and humanity in post-secondary education. As an educator, Dr. Lussier systemically integrates beadwork into her teaching practice, incorporating embodied pedagogies into every space where she leads learning.

About the Contributors

Carolyn Roberts uses her voice to support Indigenous resurgence through education. She is a Coast Salish woman belonging to the Baker family from Squamish Nation and the Kelly Family from the Tzeachten Nation. Carolyn is an Indigenous academic working in the Faculty of Education at Simon Fraser University as a Faculty lecturer and Indigenous Pedagogies Teaching Fellow. She has been an educator and administrator for over 20 years in the K-12 system. Carolyn's work is grounded in educating about Indigenous people and the decolonization of the education system. She works with pre-service teachers to help build their understandings in Indigenous history, education, and ancestral ways of knowing, to create a brighter future for all Indigenous people and the seven generations yet to come.

Robyn Rowe is an Anishinaabe-kwe (First Nations woman) with mixed settler ancestry, a member of Matachewan First Nation, and hereditary member of Teme-Augama Anishnabai in Northeastern, Ontario, Canada. She is a mother of four and holds a PhD in Rural and Northern Health. Dr. Rowe's dissertation explored five-centuries of capital and consumption-led economies that drove assimilation, land and territory dispossession, resource extraction, dependency, and oppression for Indigenous Peoples in Canada. Focusing within the intersections of Indigeneity, equity, and justice, her PhD investigated the historical events that led to modern day forms of data extraction. This work led her to advanced discussions on the projected trajectory of data uses in the fields of AI and genomics. As a Postdoctoral Fellow in Indigenous Digital Rights, Decolonization, and data in AI at Queen's University, she has further woven her knowledge of Indigenous Data Sovereignty and Indigenous Data Governance into the contexts of AI. Notably, Dr. Rowe is an Executive Member of the Global Indigenous Data Alliance (Gida-global.org) and was involved in the co-development of the 'CARE Principles for Indigenous Data Governance' with Indigenous partners from around the world through the Research Data Alliance's International Indigenous Data Sovereignty Interest Group.

Amy Shawanda is an Odawa kwe from Wiikwemkoong, Manitoulin Island. She is a mother, auntie, student, and life-long learner of Anishinaabe cultural ways and Anishinaabemowin. Dr. Shawanda is an Indigenous health researcher, and a Provost Post-Doctoral Fellow at the Dalla Lana School of Public Health at the University of Toronto, Canada. Her research interests primarily lie within the Anishinaabe thinking, being, doing, and connecting with the land. She has specific focus on bringing Indigenous health knowledge into Western health care. Dr. Shawanda's work focuses on strengthening Indigenous ways of being, doing, knowing, and reclaiming through her diverse research interests, including Indigenous pedagogies, research methods and methodologies, star knowledge, Dream Knowledges, history, and storytelling.

About the Contributors

Joey-Lynn Wabie is an Algonquin Anicinabe ikwe from Wolf Lake First Nation in Quebec. She is an assistant professor in Indigenous Social Work at Laurentian University located on Atikameksheng Anishnawbek territory (Sudbury, Ontario). Joey-Lynn works in communities at the grassroots level focusing on wellness, culture, and bringing people together. Her research interests are spiritual wellness/healing, and land-based teaching/learning. Joey-Lynn takes the role of sister, auntie, cousin seriously and is dedicated to ensuring her culture and traditions are passed on through storytelling, ceremony, and the occasional latte.

Taylor Watkins was born and raised in Sudbury, Ontario, and is currently a Canadian Institute of Health Research (CIHR) funded graduate student in the Master of Arts in Interdisciplinary Health Program at Laurentian University. Taylor graduated with a Bachelor of Science (Honours) in Psychology in 2021, before pursuing a master's degree. Taylor's research focuses on exploring the stigmatization of existing Fetal Alcohol Spectrum Disorder (FASD) prevention campaigns to inform effective and non-stigmatizing prevention initiatives in Northeastern Ontario. After completing her master's degree, Taylor aspires to continue her research on FASD in northern Ontario and educational pursuits.

Jeffrey Wood is from Métis and settler ancestry and lives on the traditional lands of the Atikameksheng Anishnawbck under the Robinson-Huron Treaty. He is a professor in the School of Education and the School of Indigenous Relations at Laurentian University and is the Early Learning Lead for the Moosonee and Moose Factory District School Area Boards. Jeffrey has been researching and working with young children for the past 25+ years. His research interests include: early childhood education, early literacies, inquiry learning and Indigenous education.

Index

5Rs 193, 197-198, 200, 202, 206, 208

A

Aachimooshtowihk 18, 27, 37
AI-technologies 219
All my relations 35, 60, 172, 176, 189, 191
All Our Relations 36, 56, 60, 85, 129, 176, 181
Ally-To-Be 193
Anishinaabe 6, 15, 20, 37, 60-61, 66-67, 70, 80, 85-87, 104, 122-123, 134, 181, 219-220, 228, 245
Anti-Racism 40-41, 47, 49, 53
Artificial Intelligence 215-216, 243-244, 246
Arts Based 56
Assessment 6, 16, 18, 20, 30-31, 33, 71, 74, 124, 172, 179, 186-187, 190-191, 202, 213

B

Beadwork 95-97, 106-109, 111, 113-121, 123-126
Berry Fast 79, 85
Best Practices 127-130, 133-134, 143

C

Camosun College 137, 140-141, 144
Circle Work 40-48, 50-53, 112
Circumambulation 16, 18, 27-30, 36-37
Colonialism 1, 67, 95, 99-100, 102, 106, 121, 129, 131, 177, 187, 215, 218-223, 227, 232, 235
Community 4, 6, 13, 25, 40-44, 46-53, 57, 59, 61, 64-66, 75, 79, 81-82, 85, 89-90, 96, 98-99, 101-103, 105-107, 109, 111-112, 114, 116-118, 120, 122-123, 125-127, 129-130, 141, 144, 154, 164-165, 170-177, 179-183, 186-189, 192, 194, 198-200, 204-208, 229, 232, 242
Culture 4-5, 9, 12, 36, 43, 57, 59, 61-62, 68, 71-73, 85, 99, 119, 124, 126, 133-134, 166, 168, 170-172, 174-185, 187-189, 191, 195, 199, 202-203, 210, 216, 220-221, 229, 240, 245-246

D

Data 19, 131, 160, 163-164, 187, 213, 216-221, 224, 226, 228-230, 233, 235-236, 238-239, 241-242, 244, 246-247
Decolonization 7-9, 12, 14-16, 35, 41, 45, 47, 81, 83-84, 98-99, 102, 118, 122, 134, 138, 153, 168, 174, 187, 191, 193-196, 207, 218, 221, 242
Decolonizing 1, 4-9, 13-15, 35, 45-46, 53-54, 64, 67, 77, 81, 83, 98, 102, 113, 120-125, 148, 153, 167-168, 187, 189, 210, 214, 217-218, 221, 232, 246

E

Early Childhood 17, 170, 172-174, 176-180, 182-188, 191-192
EdTech 215-220, 223-243
EdTech Trickster 228-230, 236, 241-242
Educational Technologies 215

Ethical Relationality 25, 116, 127-128, 132

H

High School 95-96, 140, 193-197, 204-206, 208-209, 213
Holistic 17, 56, 59-60, 79-81, 85, 100-102, 104-107, 113-114, 116, 119, 126, 150, 163, 178, 182, 191

I

Identity 47, 54, 121-122, 129, 131, 170, 172-176, 178, 181-184, 188, 191, 210, 213
Ikkimmapiiyipitsiin 25, 27, 37
Indigenization 18, 35, 95, 103, 122, 221
Indigenizing 1, 4, 6-7, 13-15, 55, 67, 77, 121-125, 168, 196, 210
Indigenous 1-22, 26, 28-30, 35-37, 41-44, 46, 48, 50-51, 53-55, 57-59, 61-63, 66-68, 70-72, 74-75, 77-87, 94, 96-131, 134-135, 137-148, 150, 152 205, 207-224, 226-229, 231-232, 234, 236-238, 240-247
Indigenous Education 2-5, 9-14, 36, 42, 54-55, 100, 118, 127-129, 135, 137, 151, 153, 168-169, 190, 197, 199, 205, 207, 210-212, 244-245
Indigenous Knowledge 4-5, 8, 16, 18-19, 21-22, 26, 28-30, 35, 37, 42, 55, 99-101, 103-105, 112-113, 115, 119, 134, 136, 138-139, 144-152, 167, 172, 175, 189, 191, 197-198, 200, 212, 237, 243-244, 246-247
Indigenous Legal Pedagogy 95-96, 103-104, 106, 109, 113-114, 118-120, 123
Indigenous Pedagogy 5-6, 79, 82-83, 102, 125, 146, 157, 166, 171, 173, 193, 197-198, 202, 205-206, 208, 211, 237, 241-242
Indigenous People 5, 40, 46, 57, 62, 66, 72, 74, 77-78, 98, 102, 106, 119, 137-138, 147, 149, 152-153, 160, 172, 174, 183, 191, 208, 214, 227
Indigenous Studies 17, 137, 140, 142, 144-145, 148-149, 151, 153-156, 158, 161, 165-166, 168, 213

Indigenous/WSÁNEĆ paradigm 156
Interconnectedness 23, 40, 53, 60, 62-63, 75, 85, 119, 173

K

Kin 44, 52-53, 129, 172, 176, 178-179, 191
Kinship 43, 113, 127-129, 131-132, 176, 232
Knowledge Keepers 16, 19, 22, 35, 76, 103, 107, 111-112, 171-172, 176-177, 179, 181, 187, 196, 198, 200, 202-204, 207, 227, 235

L

Land 1-2, 4, 12-13, 23, 30-31, 35, 37, 41-42, 56, 58-62, 67-70, 73-76, 78, 80-81, 83-85, 103, 129, 146-147, 171-182, 184-186, 188-191, 195, 199, 210, 221, 224, 229, 232, 234, 236, 239-241
Land Based 56, 84-85
Land-Based Learning 59, 62, 80, 83, 103, 108, 121, 172, 177, 186, 191
Language 2, 4, 21-23, 31-32, 34-35, 37, 40, 55, 57, 67, 85, 104, 113, 120, 136-137, 140-141, 143, 145-147, 153, 167, 171-172, 174-191, 194-195, 200, 202, 205, 210, 220, 234
Learning 2, 4, 9, 13, 16-18, 20, 24-27, 29-31, 35, 40-42, 44-46, 49-55, 57, 59-60, 62-64, 66-68, 70-71, 74, 76-77, 79-80, 83-85, 89, 95-122, 124-126, 132, 134, 137, 140-143, 148, 150-151, 154, 159, 161-162, 170-179, 181-191, 193-207, 209-213, 216, 218-219, 222-227, 229, 231-233, 237, 241, 243-244
Learning From 45-46, 59, 76, 84, 109, 172, 176, 191, 193, 198, 200, 202-203, 206-207, 210
Legal Education 97, 101, 103, 105-106, 108, 113, 119, 122-123

M

Medicine Wheel 5, 56-57, 59, 61-62, 72, 75, 78, 80-81, 85-86, 183, 227, 245
Michif 17, 27, 31-32, 35, 37

Index

Mino-Pimatisiwin 82, 127-128, 131-134
Moontime 79, 85

N

Natural Resources 57, 59, 61, 66, 75, 85-87, 199, 217, 232, 235

O

Oral Knowledge System 16-20, 22, 26-27, 30-31, 33, 35, 37

P

Pedagogy 4-6, 8-10, 12-14, 16, 18, 30, 54, 58, 67, 70, 73, 79-80, 82-84, 95-100, 102-111, 113-115, 117-123, 125, 128-130, 134, 136-137, 140, 146-147, 150-151, 153, 157, 165-167, 170-177, 180, 183, 185, 187-188, 191-192, 194, 197-198, 201-202, 205-206, 208, 211-212, 216, 219-221, 226, 230, 236-237, 241-243, 245-246
Persuasive Legal Aesthetics 107, 116, 120, 125
Poetic Inquiry 128
Post-Secondary Education 1, 3, 13, 54, 98, 116, 118, 121, 167, 243

R

Reciprocity 60-62, 66, 69, 72, 75, 80, 85, 90, 98, 105, 112, 116, 128, 148, 164, 168, 198-199, 201-206, 211, 213, 232
Reconciliation 8, 10-11, 15, 35, 42, 55, 82, 94, 120-122, 124, 135, 175, 190, 193-195, 197-198, 200, 202, 204, 206-210, 212-214, 221, 247
Reflective Expressions 63, 67, 71, 85, 89
Relationality 25, 40-41, 43-44, 52-53, 104, 108, 116, 122, 127-129, 131-132, 146, 162-163
Rites of Passage 61, 63, 79, 85

S

Self-Exploration 62

Settler Teachers 130, 193-194, 196-200, 202-208
Seven Grandfather Teachings 6, 72-73, 183, 219, 230, 241-242
Spheres of Learning 109, 111, 114, 120, 125
Storying Up 28-29, 37
Storytelling 18, 20, 32, 36, 56, 59, 64, 66, 70-72, 74, 79-81, 88, 127-129, 136-139, 166, 170, 173, 180-181, 193

T

Teaching 1, 4, 6, 8, 12, 17, 19, 24, 30-31, 40-41, 43-46, 55-59, 66, 69, 71, 73-74, 79-82, 86, 95-96, 98-100, 102-103, 105, 107, 110, 113, 115, 118, 122, 124-125, 129-130, 137, 140, 148-151, 154, 164, 170-173, 175, 178, 180-187, 189, 191, 195-196, 201, 203, 205-206, 208, 212-213, 216, 218, 221, 223, 227, 230, 232-233, 235-236, 238, 245
Third Perspective 16, 30-34, 37
Traditional Teachings 4-6, 12, 174, 180, 183-184, 192, 229
Transforming Pedagogies 9, 12
Trent University 82, 123, 136-137, 142, 144-145, 148, 151, 154-156, 158, 161-162, 165-166, 168

U

University of Victoria 83, 85, 94, 105, 137, 140-142, 155, 211

V

Validation 18-20, 27, 97, 157

W

Whole-Learner Teaching 125
W̱SÁNEĆ 136-140, 142-145, 151-152, 154-156, 158, 160, 163-164

Y

York University 122, 137, 141-144, 155

Recommended Reference Books

IGI Global's reference books are available in three unique pricing formats:
Print Only, E-Book Only, or Print + E-Book.
Order direct through IGI Global's Online Bookstore at **www.igi-global.com** or through your preferred provider.

Online Distance Learning Course Design and Multimedia in E-Learning

ISBN: 9781799897064
EISBN: 9781799897088
© 2022, 302 pp.
List Price: US$ 215

Global and Transformative Approaches Toward Linguistic Diversity

ISBN: 9781799889854
EISBN: 9781799889878
© 2022; 383 pp.
List Price: US$ 215

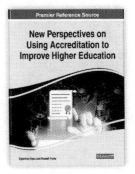

New Perspectives on Using Accreditation to Improve Higher Education

ISBN: 9781668451953
EISBN: 9781668451960
© 2022; 300 pp.
List Price: US$ 215

Impact of School Shootings on Classroom Culture, Curriculum, and Learning

ISBN: 9781799852001
EISBN: 9781799852018
© 2022; 355 pp.
List Price: US$ 215

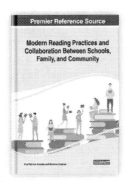

Modern Reading Practices and Collaboration Between Schools, Family, and Community

ISBN: 9781799897507
EISBN: 9781799897521
© 2022; 304 pp.
List Price: US$ 215

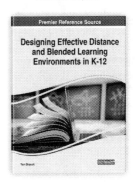

Designing Effective Distance and Blended Learning Environments in K-12

ISBN: 9781799868293
EISBN: 9781799868316
© 2022; 389 pp.
List Price: US$ 215

Do you want to stay current on the latest research trends, product announcements, news, and special offers?
Join IGI Global's mailing list to receive customized recommendations, exclusive discounts, and more.
Sign up at: **www.igi-global.com/newsletters**.

Publisher of Timely, Peer-Reviewed Inclusive Research Since 1988

IGI Global
PUBLISHER of TIMELY KNOWLEDGE

www.igi-global.com   Sign up at www.igi-global.com/newsletters   facebook.com/igiglobal   twitter.com/igiglobal

Ensure Quality Research is Introduced to the Academic Community

Become an Evaluator for IGI Global Authored Book Projects

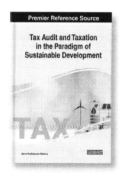   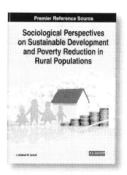

The overall success of an authored book project is dependent on quality and timely manuscript evaluations.

Applications and Inquiries may be sent to:
development@igi-global.com

Applicants must have a doctorate (or equivalent degree) as well as publishing, research, and reviewing experience. Authored Book Evaluators are appointed for one-year terms and are expected to complete at least three evaluations per term. Upon successful completion of this term, evaluators can be considered for an additional term.

If you have a colleague that may be interested in this opportunity, we encourage you to share this information with them.

Easily Identify, Acquire, and Utilize Published
Peer-Reviewed Findings in Support of Your Current Research

IGI Global OnDemand

Purchase Individual IGI Global OnDemand Book Chapters and Journal Articles

For More Information:
www.igi-global.com/e-resources/ondemand/

Browse through 150,000+ Articles and Chapters!

Find specific research related to your current studies and projects that have been contributed by international researchers from prestigious institutions, including:

- Accurate and Advanced Search
- Affordably Acquire Research
- Instantly Access Your Content
- Benefit from the InfoSci Platform Features

It really provides an excellent entry into the research literature of the field. It presents a manageable number of highly relevant sources on topics of interest to a wide range of researchers. The sources are scholarly, but also accessible to 'practitioners'.

\- Ms. Lisa Stimatz, MLS, University of North Carolina at Chapel Hill, USA

Interested in Additional Savings?

Subscribe to
IGI Global OnDemand *Plus*

Learn More

Acquire content from over 128,000+ research-focused book chapters and 33,000+ scholarly journal articles for as low as US$ 5 per article/chapter (original retail price for an article/chapter: US$ 37.50).

7,300+ E-BOOKS.
ADVANCED RESEARCH.
INCLUSIVE & AFFORDABLE.

IGI Global e-Book Collection

- Flexible Purchasing Options (Perpetual, Subscription, EBA, etc.)
- Multi-Year Agreements with No Price Increases Guaranteed
- No Additional Charge for Multi-User Licensing
- No Maintenance, Hosting, or Archiving Fees
- Continually Enhanced & Innovated Accessibility Compliance Features (WCAG)

Handbook of Research on Digital Transformation, Industry Use Cases, and the Impact of Disruptive Technologies
ISBN: 9781799877127
EISBN: 9781799877141

Handbook of Research on New Investigations in Artificial Life, AI, and Machine Learning
ISBN: 9781799886860
EISBN: 9781799886877

Handbook of Research on Future of Work and Education
ISBN: 9781799882756
EISBN: 9781799882770

Research Anthology on Physical and Intellectual Disabilities in an Inclusive Society (4 Vols.)
ISBN: 9781668435427
EISBN: 9781668435434

Innovative Economic, Social, and Environmental Practices for Progressing Future Sustainability
ISBN: 9781799895909
EISBN: 9781799895923

Applied Guide for Event Study Research in Supply Chain Management
ISBN: 9781799889694
EISBN: 9781799889717

Mental Health and Wellness in Healthcare Workers
ISBN: 9781799888130
EISBN: 9781799888147

Clean Technologies and Sustainable Development in Civil Engineering
ISBN: 9781799898108
EISBN: 9781799898122

Request More Information, or Recommend the IGI Global e-Book Collection to Your Institution's Librarian

For More Information or to Request a Free Trial, Contact IGI Global's e-Collections Team: eresources@igi-global.com | 1-866-342-6657 ext. 100 | 717-533-8845 ext. 100

Are You Ready to Publish Your Research?

IGI Global
PUBLISHER of TIMELY KNOWLEDGE

IGI Global offers book authorship and editorship opportunities across 11 subject areas, including business, computer science, education, science and engineering, social sciences, and more!

Benefits of Publishing with IGI Global:

- Free one-on-one editorial and promotional support.
- Expedited publishing timelines that can take your book from start to finish in less than one (1) year.
- Choose from a variety of formats, including Edited and Authored References, Handbooks of Research, Encyclopedias, and Research Insights.
- Utilize IGI Global's eEditorial Discovery® submission system in support of conducting the submission and double-blind peer review process.
- IGI Global maintains a strict adherence to ethical practices due in part to our full membership with the Committee on Publication Ethics (COPE).
- Indexing potential in prestigious indices such as Scopus®, Web of Science™, PsycINFO®, and ERIC – Education Resources Information Center.
- Ability to connect your ORCID iD to your IGI Global publications.
- Earn honorariums and royalties on your full book publications as well as complimentary content and exclusive discounts.

Join Your Colleagues from Prestigious Institutions, Including:

Australian National University

Massachusetts Institute of Technology

JOHNS HOPKINS UNIVERSITY

HARVARD UNIVERSITY

COLUMBIA UNIVERSITY IN THE CITY OF NEW YORK

Learn More at: www.igi-global.com/publish
or by Contacting the Acquisitions Department at: acquisition@igi-global.com

Individual Article & Chapter Downloads
US$ 29.50/each

 Easily Identify, Acquire, and Utilize Published Peer-Reviewed Findings in Support of Your Current Research

- Browse Over **170,000+ Articles & Chapters**
- **Accurate & Advanced** Search
- Affordably Acquire **International Research**
- **Instantly Access** Your Content
- Benefit from the **InfoSci® Platform Features**

THE UNIVERSITY of NORTH CAROLINA at CHAPEL HILL

"*It really provides an excellent entry into the research literature of the field. It presents a manageable number of highly relevant sources on topics of interest to a wide range of researchers. The sources are scholarly, but also accessible to 'practitioners'.*"

- Ms. Lisa Stimatz, MLS, University of North Carolina at Chapel Hill, USA

Interested in Additional Savings?

Subscribe to
IGI Global OnDemand Plus

Learn More

Acquire content from over 128,000+ research-focused book chapters and 33,000+ scholarly journal articles for as low as US$ 5 per article/chapter (original retail price for an article/chapter: US$ 37.50).